REAL WORLD
MACRO

TWENTY-FIFTH EDITION

edited by

Daniel Fireside, John Miller, Bryan Snyder
and the *Dollars & Sense* Collective

REAL WORLD MACRO
TWENTY-FIFTH EDITION

ISBN: 978-1-878585-70-7

Published by:
Economic Affairs Bureau, Inc.
Dollars and Sense
29 Winter Street
Boston, MA 02108
tel: 617-447-2177
dollars@dollarsandsense.org
www.dollarsandsense.org

Real World Macro is edited by the *Dollars & Sense* collective, publishers of *Dollars & Sense* magazine and *Real World Micro*, *Real World Globalization*, *Current Economic Issues*, *Real World Banking*, *The Environment in Crisis*, *Grassroots Journalism*, *Introduction to Political Economy*, *Striking a Balance*, *Unlevel Playing Fields*, and *The Wealth Inequality Reader*.

The 2008 Collective: Faisal Chaudhry, Amee Chew, Daniel Fireside, Ellen Frank, Amy Gluckman, Tyler Hauck, Mary Jirmanus, Toussaint Losier, James McBride, John Miller, Laura Orlando, Larry Peterson, Smriti Rao, Alejandro Reuss, Bryan Snyder, Chris Sturr, Ramaa Vasudevan, Jeanne Winner, and James Woolman.

Production: Noel Cunningham

Manufactured by Vision Lithographics
Printed in U.S.A.

CONTENTS

CHAPTER 8: INTERNATIONAL TRADE AND FINANCE

INTRODUCTION

THE TWO ECONOMIES

It sometimes seems that the United States has not one, but two economies. The first economy exists in economics textbooks and in the minds of many elected officials. It is an economy in which no one goes for long without work, families are rewarded with an ever-improving standard of living, and anyone who works hard can live the American Dream. In this economy, people are free and roughly equal, and each individual carefully looks after him- or herself, making uncoerced choices to advance their own economic interests. Government has some limited roles in this world, but it is increasingly marginal, since the macroeconomy is a self-regulating system of wealth generation.

The second economy is described in the writings of progressives, environmentalists, union supporters, and consumer advocates—as well as honest business writers who recognize that the real world does not always conform to textbook models. This second economy features vast disparities of income, wealth, and power. It is an economy where economic instability and downward mobility are facts of life. Jobs disappear, workers suffer long spells of unemployment, and new jobs seldom afford the same standard of living as those lost. As for the government, it sometimes adopts policies that ameliorate the abuses of capitalism, and other times does just the opposite, but it is always an active and essential participant in economic life.

If you are reading this introduction, you are probably a student in an introductory college course in macroeconomics. Your textbook will introduce you to the first economy, the harmonious world of self-regulating stability. *Real World Macro* will introduce you to the second.

WHY "REAL WORLD" MACRO?

A standard economics textbook is full of powerful concepts. It is also, by its nature, a limited window on the economy. What is taught in most introductory macroeconomics courses today is a relatively narrow set of concepts. Inspired by classical economic theory, most textbooks depict an inherently stable economy in little need of government intervention. But fifty years ago, textbooks were very different. Keynesian economic theory, which holds that government action can and must stabilize modern monetized economies, occupied a central place in introductory textbooks. Even Marxist economics, with its piercing analysis of class structure and instability in capitalism, appeared regularly on the pages of those textbooks. The contraction of economics education has turned some introductory courses into little more than celebrations of today's economy as "the best of all possible worlds."

Real World Macro, designed as a supplement to a standard macroeconomics textbook, is dedicated to widening the scope of economic inquiry. Its articles rub mainstream theory up against reality by providing vivid, real-world illustrations of economic concepts. And where most texts uncritically present the key assumptions and propositions of traditional macroeconomic theory, *Real World Macro* asks provocative questions: What are alternative propositions about how the economy operates and who it serves? What difference do such propositions make? What might actually constitute the best of all possible macroeconomic worlds?

For instance, *Real World Macro* questions the conventional wisdom that economic growth lifts all boats or benefits all of us. While mainstream stream textbooks readily allow that economic growth has not benefited us all to the same degree, we ask just who does benefit from economic growth and by how much. We also ask who has been left behind by the economic growth of the last two decades. The answers are quite disturbing. Today, economic growth benefits far fewer of us than just a few decades ago, and has done more to boost profits and less to lift wages than any economic upswing since World War II. The truth is that spreading the benefits of economic growth more widely, through public policy intended to improve the lot of most people in the work-a-day world, would not only make our economy more equitable—but more productive as well.

Similarly, when the Fed prioritizes price stability over employment, monetary policy does not serve us all, as most textbooks suggest, but puts the interests of owners and bondholders ahead of the interests of workers and job-seekers. Those policies come at a considerable human cost. Researchers have found that with every one percentage point increase in the U.S. unemployment rate, 920 more people commit suicide, 650 commit homicide, 20,000 suffer heart attacks, 500 die from heart and kidney disease and cirrhosis of the liver, 4,000 are admitted to state mental hospitals, and 3,300 are sent to state prisons.

William Vickery, the Nobel-prize winning economist, used his 1993 presidential address to the American Economics Association to advocate macroeconomic policies that would lower the unemployment rate to roughly 2%. Genuine full employment, Vickery argued, would bring about "a major reduction in the incidence of poverty, homelessness, sickness, and crime." We think that policies like this, and the alternative propositions that lie behind them, are worth debating—and that requires hearing a range of views.

WHAT'S IN THIS BOOK

Real World Macro is organized to follow the outline of a standard economics text. We have specifically keyed our table of contents to David Colander's *Economics* (7th edition) and its *Macroeconomics* "split," but since the topics covered by all major texts are similar, this reader is a good fit with other textbooks as well. Each chapter leads off with a brief introduction, including study questions for the entire chapter, and then provides several short articles from *Dollars & Sense* magazine that illustrate the chapter's key concepts—60 articles in all. In many cases, the articles have been updated or otherwise edited to heighten their relevance.

Here is a quick walk through the chapters.

Chapter 1, Measuring Economic Performance, starts off the volume by taking a critical look at the standard measures of economic activity. What do those measures actually tell us about the quality of life in today's economy, and what crucial aspects of economic life do they leave uncounted? This chapter also examines the current economic recovery and asks why it has created so few jobs and made so few people better off.

Chapter 2, Wealth, Inequality, and Poverty examines these two end products of today's economic growth. *Dollars & Sense* authors show who is accumulating wealth and who isn't, and argue that inequality is not a prerequisite to economic growth.

Chapter 3, Savings and Investment, peers inside the pump house of economic growth and comes up with some provocative questions. How are stock prices determined? Who owns them and who doesn't? What caused the mortgage crisis and what can be done about it? In addition, we ask what public policies have proven track records of promoting investment, and what role can pension funds play in promoting investment?

Chapter 4, Fiscal Policy, Deficits, and Debt, assesses current government spending and taxing policies. The chapter's authors argue that tax cuts for the rich, the new military buildup, a failed health care policy, and previous proposals to privatize Social Security won't stimulate economic growth, but have already squandered budget surpluses that could have provided for social needs.

Chapter 5, Monetary Policy and Financial Markets, explains how the Fed conducts monetary policy. It asks whose interests the Fed serves: those who hold financial assets, or the rest of us, and how it can be transformed to better serve our needs.

Chapter 6, Unemployment and Inflation, reveals how macroeconomic policy that prioritizes price stability over employment puts the interests of owners and bondholders ahead of the interests of workers. The chapter begins with a critique of the "natural rate" of unemployment. It also looks at the effects of unemployment, inflation, and productivity growth on workers' bargaining power and living standards. In addition, it discusses how stock market fundamentals stand in the way of most workers getting ahead, what is happening to black unemployment rates, and the spread of offshore outsourcing.

Chapter 7, Perspectives on Macroeconomic Policy, introduces alternatives to classical-inspired macroeconomic theory. It begins with a critical analysis of the New Classical economics claim that the macroeconomy is inherently stable and moves on to discuss Keynesian, Marxist, and feminist perspectives on macroeconomic theory and policy, and neoliberal economic policymaking.

Chapter 8, International Trade and Finance, critically assesses the prevailing neoliberal policy prescriptions for the global economy. The articles criticize globalization based on "free trade" and financial liberalization. They also look at the role of China in today's global economy and oil in the war in Iraq. Finally, the articles assess proposals to reform international financial institutions, eliminate sweatshop conditions, and bring about fair trade between developed countries and the developing world. Finally, the chapter considers the impact that the decline of the dollar will have on the global economy.

KEY TO COLANDER

In each chapter introduction, we provide a key that links our text to David Colander's *Economics*, 7th edition, and its macroeconomics "split," *Macroeconomics*, 7th edition. Professors and students using other textbooks should, of course, feel free to ignore these keys. Here is the summary key for the entire table of contents.

Here and in the individual chapter keys, *Economics* Chapter 1 is abbreviated "E1," and *Macroeconomics* Chapter 1 is abbreviated "M1."

Chapter 1—Colander chapters E2, E22, E23; or M2, M6, M7.

Chapter 2—Colander chapters E22-E26; or M6-M10.

Chapter 3—Colander chapters E24-E26, E33; or M8-M10, M18.

Chapter 4—Colander chapters E25-E26, E30-E31, E33; or M9-M10, M14-M15, M18.

Chapter 5—Colander chapters E27-E28, E33; or M11-M12, M18.

Chapter 6—Colander chapter E29; or M13.

Chapter 7—Colander chapters E22, E25-E26; or M6, M9-M10.

Chapter 8—Colander chapters E21 and E32-E33; or M16-M19.

Real World Macro is now keyed to other popular textbooks!

Visit dollarsandsense.org/bookstore/infomacro.html to see the keys.

CHAPTER 1

MEASURING ECONOMIC PERFORMANCE

INTRODUCTION

Most macroeconomics textbooks begin with a snapshot of today's economy as seen through the lens of the standard measures of economic performance. This chapter provides a different view of today's economy, one far more critical of current economic policy and performance that asks what the standard measures of economic performance really tell us.

In "Bumpy Landing: Rough Ride Continues as the Economy Slows," John Miller looks closely at the current economic expansion that began in November 2001 but that is currently unravelling. Despite its length and record corporate profits, this expansion has created fewer jobs and done less to lift wages than any economic expansion since World War II. Miller argues that the looming housing crisis and an ever-widening trade deficit make unlikely that Fed Chair Ben Bernanke will be able to pull off a soft landing of the economy that avoids a recession. But even if he should, the economic rough-ride of the last five years will continue for most working people as the economy slows (Article 1.1).

This decade's economic expansion took nearly four years to replace the jobs lost in the preceding recession, something every other U.S. economic recovery accomplished within two and a half years from the onset of the recession. Of course, that is counting jobs by the payroll survey favored by most economists. The Bush administration and the editors of the *Wall Street Journal* favor using the household survey, which shows the recovery creating more new jobs. But, as John Miller points out, when used appropriately, both surveys tell the same sad story of a recovery that has performed poorly by historical standards (Article 1.2).

Real GDP, or Gross Domestic Product adjusted for inflation, is the economist's measure of the value of economic output. Increases in real GDP define economic growth, and for economists, rising real GDP per capita shows that a nation is enjoying an improving standard of living. Our authors are not convinced. Jonathan Rowe argues that GDP actually counts environmental destruction, worsening health, and ruinous overconsumption as contributions to economic growth and national well-being (Article 1.3). While Rowe worries that GDP includes the wrong things, Lena Graber and John Miller discuss what it excludes: work in the home that is essential to economic well-being. They report that counting home-based work—from cleaning to child care—would add 33% to 112% to the GDP of industrialized economies and even more to the GDP of developing economies (Graber and Miller, Article 1.4).

Of course, macroeconomics textbooks examine not only the ups and downs of the business cycle, but also trade-offs in economies whose resources are fully employed. Many present the famed trade-off between "guns" and "butter." Economists use a production possibilities curve to demonstrate the opportunity cost of devoting economic resources to certain kinds of production. For example, the opportunity cost of producing arms ("guns") is the set of social goods ("butter") that society must forego. That trade-off is being made today in the United States, and Monique Morrissey presents a vivid depiction of its staggering social cost (Article 1.5). Michele Sheehan wraps up the chapter by weighing the opportunity cost of the Bush Administration's tax cuts for the rich in terms of public programs that might have been enacted instead (Article 1.6).

DISCUSSION QUESTIONS

1. (Article 1.1) How has this decade's economic expansion of the U.S. economy done when it comes to economic growth, creating jobs, and lifting wages?
2. (Article 1.1) In what ways have the post-bubble U.S. economy and policy responses been similar to or different from those in Japan after that country's economic boom ended? Have U.S. policymakers been effective in counteracting the threat of economic stagnation and in improving the economic prospects of most people?
3. (Article 1.2) What are the chief differences in the Payroll and Household surveys of employment? How different is the picture of the current recovery painted by each survey. Which survey do you regard as more accurate and why?

KEY TO COLANDER

E = *Economics*   M = *Macroeconomics*

This chapter is designed to be used with chapters E2 and E22-E23, or M2 and M6-M7.

  Chapter E22 or M6 contains sections on dating business cycles and economic performance (the topic of Article 1.1) and measuring unemployment rates (the topic of Article 1.2).

  Article 1.3 and 1.4 complement the section "Some Limitations of National Income Accounting" in chapter E23 or M7. Both Rowe and Colander discuss the Genuine Progress Indicator.

  Article 1.5 and 1.6 go with the discussion of production possibilities curves in E2 and M2.

4. (Article 1.3) How is GDP measured, and what does it represent? What are Rowe's criticisms of GDP? Do you find them convincing?

5. (Article 1.3) Rowe discusses the Genuine Progress Indicator (GPI) as an alternative measure of economic progress. What are the differences between GDP per capita and the GPI? Which do you think provides a better measure of economic progress, and why?

6. (Article 1.4) Wages for housework might sound outlandish, but what are the economic justifications for valuing work in the home? Do you find them persuasive?

7. (Article 1.4) Suppose we decided that home-based work should be included in macroeconomic measures. That still leaves some practical questions. How should it be counted? And should work in the home be paid? If so, by whom?

8. (Article 1.5) After reviewing Morrisey's article describe the opportunity cost of today's military buildup. Then identify where the U.S. economy is today in a production possibilities diagram.

9. (Article 1.6) Review the list of 2001-2003 tax cuts Sheehan presents in her article and their costs in social programs. Assess in each case if the benefits of the tax cut matched its opportunity cost.

BUMPY LANDING:

ROUGH RIDE CONTINUES AS ECONOMY SLOWS

BY JOHN MILLER

Landing a plane is tricky business. A pilot must contend with a host of variables—weather, visibility, runway conditions, and air traffic—to make a safe landing.

The same holds for landing an economy, according to the conventional analysis. The pilot of the U.S. macroeconomy, the chair of the Federal Reserve Board, must check inflationary expectations, corral labor costs, and shrink debt burdens to slow the economy while not pushing it off the runway of moderate economic growth into a recession or a full-blown crash.

If all goes according to plan, the economy will taxi in at a 2% to 3% growth rate, land softly, and refuel with lower costs and higher profit margins for the next economic takeoff.

Much of the economics profession seems to think that Fed chair Ben Bernanke will be able to pull off just such a soft landing. The consensus forecast of business economists sees the economy growing "just enough to keep investors happy and inflation at bay" in 2007. *The Wall Street Journal's* survey of 60 business economists predicts 2.5% GDP growth for the year, the slowest growth rate in five years but fast enough to avoid a recession. Even Lakshman Achuthan, managing director at the Economic Cycle Research Institute, who—unlike 95% of U.S. economists—accurately predicted the 2001 recession, expects an uptick in the vast U.S. service sector in 2007, keeping the economy out of recession.

But others, including former Fed chair Alan Greenspan, won't rule out a hard landing that drives the economy into recession. Speaking via satellite to investors in Singapore, Hong Kong, and Australia, Greenspan labeled the current expansion, now in its sixth year, "long in the tooth" and put the probability of the U.S. economy slipping into a recession by the end of 2007 at one-third.

Some see recession as the most likely scenario for 2007. Nouriel Roubini, director of the RGE Monitor and economist at the Stern School of Business at NYU, says, "The [U.S.] economy will experience a hard landing, at best in the form of a growth recession (growth in 0%-1% range) for most of 2007, or more likely, an actual recession." For Dean Baker and Mark Weisbrot, chief economists at the Center for Economic and Policy Research, the enormity of the housing bubble makes a "housing crash recession" a near certainty in 2007.

Recession or no, this much is clear. The economy will slow in 2007, and the landing, no matter how soft it may feel to the passengers in first class, will be a bumpy one for those in the economy seats. After all, the last five years of economic expansion have been a rough ride for most everyone one in the back of the economic plane. Working people never saw their real wages take off, and the usual ration of new jobs never materialized. This February, Fed chair Bernanke took the unusual step of calling upon policymakers to put in place "some limits on the downside risks to individuals" to protect the dynamism essential for economic progress, although his monetary policy will likely do just the opposite.

NOT A PRETTY PICTURE

The current economic expansion began in November 2001, following an eight-month economic slowdown brought on by the bursting of the stock market bubble and the collapse of the Internet-driven investment boom of the late 1990s.

The 2001 recession had been neither long nor deep. Nonetheless, the economic recovery that followed was far from robust. The economic plane seemed to do little more than taxi down the runway despite the efforts of the Fed to get the economy airborne through record low interest rates and the Bush administration's repeated pro-rich tax cuts. During the first two and half years of the expansion, economic growth was sluggish, never reaching 3.0%; real personal income (income of households adjusted for inflation) grew much more slowly than in past recoveries; and the economy continued to lose jobs.

The economy finally took off in the third quarter of 2003 when GDP growth rates spiked to 7.5% following the invasion of Iraq in March of that year, which produced the biggest quarterly increase in military spending since the Korean War. After that, consumer spending fueled by the housing bubble and investment spending bolstered by ever-rising corporate profits kept the economy airborne. The expansion logged growth rates between 3% and 4% until slowing to just over a 2% growth rate in the second half of 2006, and to 0.6% in the first quarter of 2007, the slowest quarterly growth rate since fourth quarter 2002.

All told, annual GDP growth in this expansion has averaged just 2.9%, well below the 4.2% average in earlier postwar business cycles of similar length. Employment growth

---

*Dates denote when the article appeared in *Dollars & Sense* magazine.

TABLE 1
AVERAGE ANNUAL GROWTH RATES IN THE FIVE YEARS FOLLOWING THE END OF A RECESSION

Recession Ending in	1949	1954	1958	1961	1970	1975	1980	1982	1991	2001	Average for Post-World War II Recoveries (not including current recovery)
Wages and Salaries	5.8%	3.5%	4.4%	5.4%	1.9%	3.8%	2.3%	4.4%	2.4%	1.9%	3.8%
Corporate Profits	7.2%	7.4%	10.0%	12.1%	6.6%	6.6%	6.6%	10.1%	8.4%	12.8%	8.3%

Source: CBPP calculations based on Commerce Department data.

continues to be the weakest of any postwar economic recovery, just 0.9% a year as opposed to an average of 2.4%—and just one-half the rate posted by the "jobless recovery" of the 1990s. In addition, wages and salaries improved just 1% a year on average in the current expansion, far below the 2.6% average of postwar expansions, with most of those gains coming only in the past year.

But in two areas this expansion has been exceptional. First, at 64 months, it already has steamed past the usual 51-month length of postwar expansions. Second, it has racked up a record level of corporate profits.

The two are closely related. What typically brings a capitalist expansion to a close is increasing business costs, usually rising wages, which cut into profit margins and bring investment to a halt. Long-running economic expansions tighten labor markets. With jobs plentiful, the balance of class power tilts toward workers, allowing them to push for higher wages which, in turn, eat into corporate profits.

While the expansion might be getting old, the usual signs of aging have not been apparent. Corporate cost cutting, including the outsourcing of manufacturing and white-collar jobs, has kept workers' bargaining power in check, performing a kind of liposuction on any unsightly bulges in wages and salaries. And because labor is the largest expense for business overall, preventing wage gains is the equivalent of a botox injection for corporate profits.

This pro-corporate cosmetic surgery has not been pretty. The current economic recovery has done more to improve profits and far less to raise wages than any other expansion since World War II. A recent study conducted by the Washington, D.C.-based Center on Budget and Policy Priorities, reports the alarming details. From 2001 to 2006, corporate profits rose 12.8% a year after adjusting for inflation, compared to the 8.3% average growth rate in other postwar recoveries of equal duration. By contrast, over the same period inflation-adjusted wages and salaries grew just 1.9% a year, well below the 3.8% average annual rate posted by earlier postwar expansions. For three years of the expansion, real wages actually declined. And even total labor compensation (the sum of all paychecks *plus* employee benefits, including rapidly rising health insurance premiums) grew at

just a 2.5% annual rate in this expansion, well below the 4.1% average rate for earlier postwar expansions. (See Table 1.)

For the first time on record, a larger share of the income growth from an economic expansion went into corporate profits, some 46% of it, than to wages and salaries. As a result, by the end of 2006 wages and salaries had fallen to just a 51.6% share of national income, the lowest level on record, with data going back to 1929. At the same time, corporate profits as a share of national income reached 13.8%, the highest level on record.

And what there was for income gains was unevenly distributed. From the beginning of the expansion in 2001 until 2005, the average income of the richest 5% of households rose 3.1% after adjusting for inflation, while the average income of the middle fifth of the population rose just 0.9%, and the poorest fifth just 0.7%. This expansion was the first in 40 years to fail to reduce the poverty rate, which rose from 11.7% in 2001 to 12.6% in 2005. And 5.4 million more people were without health insurance in 2005 than when the expansion began in 2001.

GOOD JOBS AT GOOD WAGES: DON'T HOLD YOUR BREATH

Joshua Feinman, chief economist at Deutsche Asset Management, attempts to put the best face on the situation in a 2006 article with the surprisingly honest title "Is Capital Eating Labor's Lunch?" That proposition, admits Feinman, has "the ring of plausibility." After all, real wages for the median American worker have stagnated, while a cumulative 14% increase in labor productivity added to corporate profits from third quarter 2001 through the end of 2005.

Still Feinman is not convinced for two reasons. First, he finds that the share of national income going to corporate profits has reached record levels in large part because interest costs have fallen, with record low interest rates as emerging Asian nations have parked money in "safe investments" in the United States. Second, returns to labor usually lag in periods with slack labor markets and strong productivity gains. He likens the current period to the first five years of the long 1990s expansion, which saw compensation begin to catch up only at the end of the expansion.

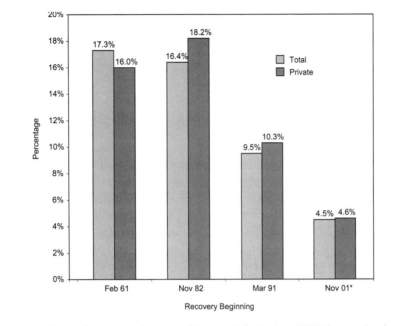

PAYROLL GROWTH AT FIVE TOTAL (PRIVATE + GOVERNMENT) AND PRIVATE PAYROLL GROWTH
FIVE YEARS INTO RECOVERY (FOR POSTWAR RECOVERIES LASTING AT LEAST FIVE YEARS)

Source: Jared Bernstein, "Jobs recovery at five reveals uniquely weak expansion," Economic Policy Institute, 12/13/06 <www.epi.org/content.cfm/webfeatures_snapshots_20061213>; from BLS Establishment data.

*Current recovery figures include benchmark revision.

In other words, the current tilt of the benefits of growth away from labor is perhaps not unprecedented, and corporate profits have benefited from an abundance of capital flowing into the United States from the developing world. Both of these assessments might strike most workers as cold comfort.

But for the editors of the *Wall Street Journal*, it is enough to convince them that better wages are on their way. The editors point out that that as the economy moves from recovery to sustained expansion, productivity grows first, which boosts profits, then employment picks up, and finally wages rise as labor markets tighten. Like Feinman, they cite the first five years of the 1990s expansion, when unemployment remained high and wages stagnated.

No one should hold her breath waiting for this expansion to produce higher wages and better jobs. The editor's catch-up argument is predicated on sustained job creation tightening labor markets and tilting the balance of class power in labor's favor.

But the great American jobs machine seems to be out of order. The current expansion has created fewer jobs and added fewer work hours than any other expansion since World War II. Economist Jared Bernstein of the labor-funded Economic Policy Institute documents just how dismal job creation has been over five years of this economic expansion. From November 2001 through November 2006, the payrolls of private employers and the government grew just 4.5%—much more slowly than the other three postwar expansions five years in length

for which we have data. (See "Payroll Growth at Five.")

The current expansion has a long way to go even to match the performance of the jobless recovery of the early 1990s. At this point, the 1990s expansion had seen payrolls grow 9.5% and had replaced the jobs *lost* in the previous recession in 31 months, as opposed to the 45 months this expansion took to accomplish that feat. Had the current business cycle added jobs at the same rate as the 1990s cycle, it would have created 12 million jobs by now, not 5 million. That shortfall should be enough to dash any optimism about improving labor market conditions.

During this expansion the U.S. economy has lost 2.9 million manufacturing jobs. Job growth has been concentrated in the service sector. Even information technology, the great promise of the 1990s, lost more than 1.1 million jobs in the last five years.

Given those numbers, it seems reasonable to ask "What's Really Propping Up the Economy?" as did a September 2006 cover story in *Business Week*. Their answer was a health care industry that added 1.7 million jobs over the last five years. The rest of the private sector added none: the jobs created by the housing boom were more than outweighed by the losses from the info tech bust. The remaining job growth this decade came from the public sector.

Paul Craig Roberts, supply-side economist and fierce critic of the Bush administration, goes yet further. The U.S. economy is experiencing "a job-depression," in his view. For Roberts, the Bureau of Labor Statistics list of ten fastest growing occupations from 2004 to 2014 only confirms the

TABLE 2
FASTEST-GROWING OCCUPATIONS, 2004 TO 2014

Rank	Occupation	Projected Employment Growth 2004-2013	Income	Education Required
1	Home health aide	56%	up to $20,184	Short-term on-the-job training
2	Network systems and data communications analyst	54.6%	$43,605 and up	Bachelor's degree
3	Medical assistant	52.1%	$20,185 to $28,589	Moderate on-the-job training
4	Physician assistant	49.6%	$43,605 and up	Bachelor's degree
5	Computer software engineer, applications	48.4%	$43,605 and up	Bachelor's degree
6	Physical therapy assistant	44.2%	$20,185 to $28,589	Associate's degree
7	Dental hygienist	43.3%	$43,605 and up	Associate's degree
8	Computer software engineer, systems software	43%	$43,605 and up	Bachelor's degree
9	Dental assistant	42.7%	$20,185 to $28,589	Moderate on-the-job training
10	Personal and home care aide	41%	up to $20,184	Short-term on-the-job training

Source: Bureau of Labor Statistics, "Occupational employment projections to 2014," *Monthly Labor Review* Nov. 2005, Table 2 <www.bls.gov/emp/emptab21.htm>; found at Forbes.com <www.forbes.com/2007/03/09/jobs-boomers-labor-lead-careers_cx_hc_0309jobs_slide_8.html?thisSpeed=15000>

sorry state of the U.S. labor market. Seven of those jobs are in health care, and the other three are in information services. (See Table 2.) Home health aide, a job paying up to $20,184 a year, tops the list. So much for good wages. And in a fit of xenophobia, Roberts rails that most of the better computer jobs on the list are likely to go to foreigners holding work visas.

Offshore outsourcing and offshore production, which have battered service-sector as well as manufacturing workers, have surely contributed to U.S. labor market woes. Even dyed-in-the-wool free-trader Alan Blinder, former Clinton administration economic advisor and vice-chair of the Fed, now argues that outsourcing is sapping the U.S economy's ability to create good jobs at good wages. Blinder estimates that as many as 40 million American jobs are now at risk of being shipped out of the country in the next decade or two, including computer programmers, actuaries, bookkeepers, film and video editors, and even economists. That is more than double the total number of workers employed in manufacturing today. With that wide swath of the U.S workforce in tradable jobs exposed to competition from abroad, it could be long time before any economic expansion enhances

workers' bargaining power enough to push up wages.

That is true even though the official unemployment rate remains historically low at about 4.5%. The continuous decline in the ratio of employment to population explains why the unemployment rates are no higher despite the weak labor market. Many people have stopped actively looking for jobs and dropped out of the unemployment statistics. The labor force participation rate—the fraction of the population either working or actively looking for work—has fallen sharply since George Bush took office; if it had stayed at its January 2001 level, the official unemployment rate would be above 7%.

BUMPY LANDING

And those were good times. Today the economy is beset with a constellation of seemingly intractable problems: a slumping housing market, an ever widening trade deficit, slowing business spending, and consumers up to their eyeballs in debt with few prospects for better jobs or higher wages.

But it is the bursting of the housing bubble that has spooked even the most optimistic. Everyone acknowledges that the turmoil in the subprime mortgage market has created serious financial problems for the least well-off homeowners. Subprime loans—loans to borrowers with poor credit records—made up a record 13% of a $10.2 trillion mortgage market in 2006 and financed about one-half of the jump in homeownership rates from 65% to 69% over the last decade.

But these loans came with inordinate risks that left these new homeowners vulnerable to foreclosure. Some 80% had adjustable rate mortgages, or ARMs, with interest payments that increase as interest rates rise in the economy. And 47% of mortgages issued last year to subprime customers contained "creative features"—such as interest-only payments or low initial "teaser" interest rates—that make the burden of these loans rise precipitously over time. On top of that, borrowers have taken on ever more debt relative to their assets: the value of their loans reached 86.5% of the value of their property in 2006, up from 78% in 2000.

When interest rates were low and home prices rising, these loans remained viable. But since the Fed hiked short-term interest rates by four percentage points beginning in 2004 and the rise in housing prices slowed in 2005, subprime borrowers could no longer keep up with their payments. Foreclosures on subprime mortgage markets soared, more than doubling last year from 2005. At least 20 subprime mortgage lenders have gone out of business.

The biggest worry is that the subprime meltdown will spread to the broader housing market and the economy. But even if the subprime mortgage crisis is contained, that is hardly good news for working people and the poor. *Business Week* reporter Peter Coy argues that the Fed rate hikes have turned into "a regressive tax on weak borrowers." Families with ARMs will see their monthly payments skyrocket as short-term interest rates rise. In contrast, better mortgage holders may benefit as lenders flee the subprime market and rush into the safer traditional mortgage market, lowering those mortgage rates.

But that assumes the crumbling housing market will not spread across the economy, driving it into recession. There is real reason to think otherwise.

First, the housing recession seems to be getting worse, not better. After a run-up in housing prices led to a near doubling of sales of new and existing homes since the mid-1990s, inflation-adjusted home prices are now dropping—down between 4% and 5% in real terms nationwide from their levels at the same point in 2005, and down much more sharply in overvalued areas such as parts of Florida and California. Homes for sale averaged 6.9 months of supply in the six months ending in October 2006, the largest average supply since 1991.

Second, the subprime mortgage crisis does seem to be spreading. The same risky loans—teaser rates, interest-only, and ARMs—are now found in near-prime and some prime mortgages, making up as much as one-half of new loans in those markets. And default and foreclosure rates rose sharply for those mortgage loans as well last year.

Third, the sheer size of the housing bubble puts the economy at risk. The Federal Reserve Bank of Dallas estimates that after the run-up in housing prices from 2001 to 2005 and the bursting of the stock market bubble, real estate and stock wealth represent about equal shares of total household net wealth. Historically, a $100 rise in housing wealth has produced about a $6 rise in long-run consumption, while the same increase in stock wealth has generated only a $4 gain. And this expansion has been especially dependent on consumption, which rose as a share of GDP from about 67% in the late nineties to 70% over the last five years. In other words, a hit to home prices has a greater effect on the macroeconomy than a drop-off in stock prices—cause for concern since the deflation of the housing bubble is still underway.

All this leads economists Baker and Weisbrot from the Center for Economic and Policy Research to predict that the bursting of the housing bubble will do just as much to depress the economy as the bursting of the stock market bubble that brought on the 2001 recession, especially since recession-like conditions have already taken hold in the automobile industry and manufacturing generally.

Many economists still believe that Ben Bernanke will be able to engineer a soft landing of the economy even under these precarious conditions. As they see it, if the economy is heading toward a hard landing, the Fed will aggressively cut interest rates to perk up spending and prevent a recession. The Fed tried just such a strategy in 2001, rapidly cutting interest rates, but it did not prevent a recession then. And with today's glut of tech goods, housing, and autos and other consumer durables, it seems unlikely the Fed would be able to rescue the economy this time either.

On top of that, an ever-widening trade deficit will further hamstring Fed interest rate policy. Last year, the U.S. current account deficit, the broadest measure of the balance of trade in goods and services, expanded to a record $763.6 billion, a full percentage point over the 5%-of-GDP level financial analysts have traditionally used as a marker of financial distress in developing countries.

That large a deficit makes cutting interest rates risky business. Lower interest rates make U.S. bonds less attractive to investors. To finance last year's record trade deficit, the United States needed to borrow on average more than $70 billion a month in foreign funds. If the Fed lowered interest rates, it would have a hard time keeping foreigners buying the bonds that pay for the trade deficit. And should some large foreign creditors dump their dollar holdings, the value of the dollar would plummet, causing interest rates to spike and the U.S. stock and bond markets to tumble. That would be a hard landing indeed.

BETTER ECONOMIC POLICY

Despite the constrained flight pattern of a capitalist economy, better public policy could surely reduce the turbulence in today's economy.

First off, if Ben Bernanke were sincerely interested in placing "limits on the downside risks in today's economy," he would not burst the housing bubble by hammering those already saddled with deceptive and predatory mortgages. Teaser rates, ARMs with no limits or controls, and other risky and predatory mortgage practices should never have been allowed in the first place. But the Fed chair was in a position to institute the proper regulatory oversight that might have pricked the housing market bubble without the worst-off having to endure a painful credit crunch.

Similarly, if the editors of the *Wall Street Journal* were truly interested in heralding in an era of higher wages, they would surely endorse increasing the minimum wage, one of the key ingredients that allowed working people to make some nice wage gains in the second half of the 1990s.

Finally public investment, which has fallen to about *one-half* its levels during the 1960s and 1970s relative to the size of the economy, must be restored to maintain the nation's economic competitiveness and reduce the trade deficit. That means increased public investments in education, job training, and child care as well as in basic infrastructure, the environment, energy, and research and development.

The Campaign for America's Future, the pro-labor policy group, has outlined just such an industrial policy, dubbed the Apollo Project for Good Jobs and Energy Independence. Their program would develop energy efficiency technologies while it creates good jobs by making our economy more competitive. It would dramatically reduce imports of foreign oil and help U.S companies take the lead in emerging markets for efficient appliances and alternative fuels.

Policies that would provide immediate relief from the harmful effects of outsourcing and offshore production are also needed. The list should include wage insurance, education opportunities, job placement help for displaced workers, and national health care, financed by rolling back President Bush's upper-income tax cuts which have stood in the way of an economic growth that spreads its benefits widely.

Those policies would make for a smoother economic ride for most of us.

Resources: Aviva Aron-Dine and Isaac Shapiro, "Share of National Income Going to Wages and Salaries at record low in 2006," Center on Budget and Policy Priorities, 3/29/07; Jared Bernstein, "Jobs recovery at five reveals uniquely weak expansion," Economic Policy Institute, 12/13/06; Eduardo Porter and Jeremy Peter, "This Expansion Looks Familiar," *New York Times*, 4/6/07; Nouriel Roubini, "Who is to Blame for the Mortgage Carnage and Coming Financial Disaster?" RGE Monitor 3/19/07; Nouriel Roubini, "The Housing and Global Bust," *RGE Monitor* 3/18/07; Christian Weller, "The U.S Economy in Review: 2006" Center for American Progress, 12/21/06; Christian Weller, "The End of the Great American Housing Boom," Center for American Progress, 12/06; Mark Weisbrot, "Economy Looks Bad for 2007," Center for Economic and Policy Research, 1/07; Dean Baker, "Recession Looms for the U.S. Economy in 2007," Center for Economic and Policy Research, 11/06; Nick Timiraos, "The Subprime Market's Rough Road," *Wall Street Journal*, 2/17/07; Peter Coy, "Under the Fed's Hammer," *Business Week*, 3/19/07; "What's Really Propping Up the Economy," *Business Week* 9/25/06; David Wessel and Bob Davis, "Pain From Free Trade Spurs Second Thoughts," *Wall Street Journal* 3/28/07; Paul Craig Roberts, "Nuking the Economy," *Counterpunch* 2/11/06; Paul Craig Roberts, "Data Shows America's Job Growth Benefits Immigrants, Outsourcers," Counterpunch, 3/3/06; "The Coming of Wage," *Wall Street Journal*, 10/2/06; "Good Jobs at Good Wages," *Wall Street Journal* 7/11/06; "The Current Depression" *Wall Street Journal*, 2/3/07; Joshua Feinman, "Is Capital Eating Labor's Lunch?" Deutsche Asset Management, 10/06; John V. Duca, "Making Sense of the U.S. Housing Slowdown," *Economic Letter*, Federal Reserve Bank of Dallas, 11/06.

MISSING JOBS STILL LOST

BY JOHN MILLER

"MISSING JOBS FOUND"

... It turns out that this economic expansion is different from those in the past, but not in the way that many thought. New jobs are being created as usual, but they are different kinds of jobs. The U.S. economy is undergoing a structural change as more people become self-employed or form partnerships, rather than working for large corporations.

This transformation confounds the government's employment surveyors because they rely on the payroll data of about 400,000 existing companies ...

These [new] jobs show up in the "household survey." The government collects this data from workers rather than companies, and while it is more volatile month-to-month due to the smaller sample size (60,000 households), over the past three years it consistently told us that something unusual is happening. If you believe the payroll figures, the U.S. still has to create 700,000 more new jobs before it will return to the peak pre-recession level of 2001. But according to what individual Americans are saying, we've already surpassed that level by two million jobs.

In short, these are good times for most American workers ...

—The Wall Street Journal, *October 11, 2004*

The Bush administration may have struck out trying to find weapons of mass destruction in Iraq, but the *Wall Street Journal* editors say they have found the jobs that have gone missing during this jobless economic recovery.

Using the household survey of employment as their Geiger counter, the Journal's editors claim to have unearthed hundreds of thousands of new jobs overlooked by the traditional payroll survey of employment favored by the Bureau of Labor Statistics, the Congressional Budget Office, and most economists. With those extra jobs, the household survey has the Bush administration adding jobs to the economy, not losing them, and the recovery, as of September, creating 1,628,000 jobs on top of replacing the jobs lost since the last recession began, in March 2001. That picture is far more to the liking of the Journal's editors than the one painted by the payroll survey, which depicts the Bush administration as losing jobs and the recovery still down 940,000 jobs since the onset of the recession some three and a half years ago. Replacing the jobs lost to the recession is something the average postwar recovery managed to accomplish within two years.

But the truth is that, when used appropriately, the payroll and household employment surveys tell "the same (sad) story," in the words of Cleveland Federal Reserve Bank economists Mark Schweitzer and Guhan Venkatu. "Both surveys," they note, "show that employment has performed poorly in this recovery relative to the usual post-World War II experience." By historical standards, over four million jobs remain missing in today's economy.

WHY THE PAYROLL SURVEY IS MORE ACCURATE THAN THE HOUSEHOLD SURVEY

Federal Reserve Board Chair Alan Greenspan feels the Journal editors' pain. Still, he can't bring himself to endorse using the household survey to measure monthly employment growth. Earlier this year, Greenspan told Congress, "Having looked at both sets of data ... it's our judgment that as much as we would like the household data to be the more accurate, regrettably that turns out not to be the case."

Why do Alan Greenspan, the Bureau of Labor Statistics (BLS) that conducts both surveys, and the nonpartisan Congressional Budget Office regard the payroll survey to be "the more accurate," to provide "more reliable information," and to "better reflect the state of the labor market" than the household survey?

The first reason is statistical reliability. The payroll or establishment survey, which the BLS calls the Employment Statistics Survey, asks employers at about 400,000 worksites how many people they employ. The payroll sample includes every firm with 1,000 employees or more and covers about one-third of the total number of workers. The household survey—its formal name is the Current Population Survey—asks people in 60,000 households about their employment status. That is a small fraction of the total number of workers; the sample size of the payroll survey is 600 times larger. As a result, the household survey is subject to a large sampling error, about three times that of the payroll survey on a monthly basis.

Second, the payroll survey is better anchored in a comprehensive count of employment than the household survey. The household survey checks its result against a direct count of employment only once a decade when the decennial census is completed. On the other hand, every year the BLS adjusts the payroll survey's estimate of employment to correspond to the unemployment insurance tax records that nearly all employers are required to file. The preliminary revision based on the March 2004 benchmark added 236,000 workers, or a two-tenths of one percent increase in employment. The *Journal* suggests the revision shows the payroll numbers to be faulty; on the contrary, it should be taken as sign of their reliability, especially since the household survey is "benchmarked" but once a decade.

Beyond statistical reliability, the two surveys differ conceptually as well. Some of those differences narrow the gap between the job count of the two surveys, while others widen that gap. For instance, the two surveys treat multiple jobholders differently. The payroll survey counts each job reported by employers, even if the same worker holds two jobs. The household survey, on the other hand, counts multiple jobholders as employed only once. Also, while the household survey sample is quite limited, it does equally well counting jobs at new firms and long-established firms. The more thorough payroll survey only slowly integrates new firms into its sample, which can present problems in periods of rapid job growth. Finally, the household survey counts the self-employed, while the payroll survey of business establishments does not.

It is this third point that the Journal editors have seized on to explain why the payroll survey has undercounted the growth of jobs in the current recovery. They put it this way: "[W]hen a higher ratio of people make their livelihood as independent consultants to their old company, or as power sellers on eBay, they don't show up in the establishment survey."

Perhaps—if it were true that a higher ratio of people are self-employed. But even Harvard economist Robert Barro, a senior fellow at the conservative Hoover Institute, isn't buying it. In his March *Wall Street Journal* op-ed piece, Barro called "the large expansion of self-employment" explanation "a non-starter." Self-employment in the household survey just hasn't risen that much. As a ratio of household employment, self-employment rose somewhat after 2002, but even now that ratio is barely above its level at the onset of the recession in 2001, and it remains well below its level throughout most of the 1990s. What's more, an increase in self-employment is common in a weak labor market and typically disappears as labor market conditions improve and many of the self-employed find wage and salary employment. Finally, Barro estimates that "self-employment and other measurable differences between the two surveys explain only 200,000 to 400,000 of the extra three million jobs in the household survey."

THE SAME SAD STORY

Even the household survey indicates this recovery has done far less to create jobs than other postwar recoveries. According to the household survey, the current recovery had added just 1.5% to total employment by January 2004, some 26 months after the recession officially ended in November 2001. Other postwar recoveries added an average of 5.5% to the number of jobs over the same period. The payroll survey paints an even more dismal picture: it shows the U.S. economy losing 0.5% off its job base during 26 months of recovery, while prior recoveries since 1949 added an average of 6.9% to employment in that amount of time.

Economists Schweitzer and Venkatu agree that it is more sensible to compare each employment survey to its own results during other postwar business cycles rather than to the other survey. They compare the ratio of employment (measured by the household survey) to total population in this recovery with the average pattern over postwar business cycles. In a recession, the employment-population ratio typically declines for about a year and a half and then returns to its previous level within about three years. But in this recovery, the employment-population ratio has declined nearly continuously. As a result, after three years of economic recovery, that ratio now stands at 62.3% (in September 2004), a full two percentage points below its 2001 pre-recession level of 64.3%.

By that standard, the U.S. economy is still missing 4,252,000 jobs—the number required to simply return to the employment-population ratio in 2001, and to equal the performance of the average postwar recovery. Schweitzer and Venkatu conclude that "both measures [the payroll survey and the household survey] show a surprisingly similar picture of the weak labor market performance that has prevailed during this recovery relative to previous business cycle periods."

The continuous decline in the ratio of employment to population makes clear why the unemployment rate is not higher, given the weak labor market. It is not because new jobs have gone uncounted; after all, unemployment rates are derived from the household survey. Rather, it is because many people have stopped looking for jobs and thus have dropped out of the unemployment statistics. The labor force participation rate—the fraction of the population either working or looking for work—has fallen sharply since George Bush took office; if it had stayed at its January 2001 level, the official unemployment rate would be 7.4%.

STILL MISSING

By any measure—the payroll survey, the household survey, or even the unemployment rate—the *Wall Street Journal* has not managed to locate the missing jobs in the U.S. economy. An honest inspection of the data reveals what most working people already know: when it comes to creating jobs, this recovery is the weakest since the Great Depression. That truth will continue to go missing on the editorial pages of the *Wall Street Journal*.

Resources: "Missing Jobs Found," *Wall Street Journal* 10/11/04; Mark Schweitzer and Guhan Venkatu, "Employment Surveys Are Telling the Same (Sad) Story," Economic Commentary (Federal Reserve Bank of Cleveland, 5/15/04); Robert Barro, "Go Figure," *Wall Street Journal*, 3/9/04; Bureau of Labor Statistics, "Employment from the BLS household and payroll surveys: summary of recent trends," 10/8/04; Elise Gould, "Measuring Employment Since the Recovery: A comparison of the household and payroll surveys," (Economic Policy Institute, December 2003); Steven Hipple, "Self-employment in the United States: an update," *Monthly Labor Review*, July 2004.

THE GROWTH CONSENSUS UNRAVELS

BY JONATHAN ROWE

Economics has been called the dismal science, but beneath its gray exterior is a system of belief worthy of Pollyanna.

Yes, economists manage to see a dark cloud in every silver lining. Downturn follows uptick, and inflation rears its ugly head. But there's a story within that story—a gauzy romance, a lyric ode to Stuff. It's built into the language. A thing produced is called a "good," for example, no questions asked. The word is more than just a term of art. It suggests the automatic benediction which economics bestows upon commodities of any kind.

By the same token, an activity for sale is called a "service." In conventional economics there are no "dis-services," no actions that might be better left undone. The bank that gouges you with ATM fees, the lawyer who runs up the bill—such things are "services" so long as someone pays. If a friend or neighbor fixes your plumbing for free, it's not a "service" and so it doesn't count.

The sum total of these products and activities is called the Gross Domestic Product, or GDP. If the GDP is greater this year than last, then the result is called "growth." There is no bad GDP and no bad growth; economics does not even have a word for such a thing. It does have a word for less growth. In such a case, economists say growth is "sluggish" and the economy is in "recession." No matter what is growing—more payments to doctors because of worsening health, more toxic cleanup—so long as there is more of it, then the economic mind declares it "good."

This purports to be "objective science." In reality it is a rhetorical construct with the value judgments built in, and this rhetoric has been the basis of economic debate in the United States for the last half century at least. True, people have disagreed over how best to promote a rising GDP. Liberals generally wanted to use government more, conservatives less. But regarding the beneficence of a rising GDP, there has been little debate at all.

If anything, the Left traditionally has believed in growth with even greater fervor than the Right. It was John Maynard Keynes, after all, who devised the growth-boosting mechanisms of macroeconomic policy to combat the Depression of the 1930s; it was Keynesians who embraced these strategies after the War and turned the GDP into a totem. There's no point in seeking a bigger pie to redistribute to the poor, if you don't believe the expanding pie is desirable in the first place.

Today, however, the growth consensus is starting to unravel across the political spectrum and in ways that are both obvious and subtle. The issue is no longer just the impact of growth upon the environment—the toxic impacts of industry and the like. It now goes deeper, to what growth actually consists of and what it means in people's lives. The things economists call "goods" and "services" increasingly don't strike people as such. There is a growing disconnect between the way people experience growth and the way the policy establishment talks about it, and this gap is becoming an unspoken subtext to much of American political life.

The group most commonly associated with an antigrowth stance is environmentalists, of course. To be sure, one faction, the environmental economists, is trying to put green new wine into the old bottles of economic thought. If we would just make people pay the "true" cost of, say, the gasoline they burn, through the tax system for example, then the market would do the rest. We'd have benign, less-polluting growth, they say, perhaps even more than now. But the core of the environmental movement remains deeply suspicious of the growth ethos, and probably would be even if the environmental impacts somehow could be lessened.

In the middle are suburbanites who applaud growth in the abstract, but oppose the particular manifestations they see around them—the traffic, sprawl and crowded schools. On the Right, meanwhile, an anti-growth politics is arising practically unnoticed. When social conservatives denounce gambling, pornography, or sex and violence in the media, they are talking about specific instances of the growth that their political leaders rhapsodize on other days.

Environmentalists have been like social conservatives in one key respect. They have been moralistic regarding growth, often scolding people for enjoying themselves at the expense of future generations and the earth. Their concern is valid, up to a point—the consumer culture does promote the time horizon of a five year old. But politically it is not the most promising line of attack, and conceptually it concedes too much ground. To moralize about consumption as they do is to accept the conventional premise that it really is something chosen—an enjoyable form of self-indulgence that has unfortunate consequences for the earth.

That's "consumption" in the common parlance—the sport utility vehicle loading up at Wal-Mart, the stuff piling up in the basement and garage. But increasingly that's not what people actually experience, nor is it what the term really means. In economics, consumption means everything people spend money on, pleasurable or not. Wal-Mart is just one dimension of a much larger and increasingly unpleasant whole. The lawyers' fees for the house settlement or divorce; the repair work on the car after it was rear-ended; the cancer treatments for the uncle who was a three-pack-a-day smoker; the stress medications and weight loss regimens—all these and more are "consumption." They all go into the GDP.

Cancer treatments and lawyer's fees are not what come to mind when environmentalists lament the nation's excess consumption, or for that matter when economists applaud America's "consumers" for keeping the world economy afloat. Yet increasingly such things are what consumption actually consists of in the economy today. More and more, it consists not of pleasurable things that people choose, but rather of things that most people would gladly do without.

Much consumption today is addictive, for example. Millions of Americans are engaged in a grim daily struggle with themselves to do less of it. They want to eat less, drink less, smoke less, gamble less, talk less on the telephone—do less buying, period. Yet economic reasoning declares as growth and progress, that which people themselves regard as a tyrannical affliction.

Economists resist this reality of a divided self, because it would complicate their models beyond repair. They cling instead to an 18th century model of human psychology—the "rational" and self-interested man—which assumes those complexities away. As David McClelland, the Harvard psychologist, once put it, economists "haven't even discovered Freud, let alone Abraham Maslow." (They also haven't discovered the Apostle Paul, who lamented that "the good that I would I do not, but the evil that I would not, that I do.")

Then too there's the mounting expenditure that sellers foist upon people through machination and deceit. People don't choose to pay for the corrupt campaign finance system or for bloated executive pay packages. The cost of these is hidden in the prices that we pay at the store. As I write this, the *Washington Post* is reporting that Microsoft has hired Ralph Reed, former head of the Christian Coalition, and Grover Norquist, a right-wing polemicist, as lobbyists in Washington. When I bought this computer with Windows 95, Bill Gates never asked me whether I wanted to help support a bunch of Beltway operators like these.

This is compulsory consumption, not choice, and the economy is rife with it today. People don't choose to pay some $40 billion a year in telemarketing fraud. They don't choose to pay 32% more for prescription drugs than do people in Canada. ("Free trade" means that corporations are free to buy their labor and materials in other countries, but ordinary Americans aren't equally free to do their shopping there.) For that matter, people don't choose to spend $25 and up for inkjet printer cartridges. The manufacturers design the printers to make money on the cartridges because, as the *Wall Street Journal* put it, that's "where the big profit margins are."

Yet another category of consumption that most people would gladly do without arises from the need to deal with the offshoots and implications of growth. Bottled water has become a multibillion dollar business in the United States because people don't trust what comes from the tap. There's a growing market for sound insulation and double-pane windows because the economy produces so much noise. A wide array of physical and social stresses arise from the activities that get lumped into the euphemistic term "growth."

The economy in such cases doesn't solve problems so much as create new problems that require more expenditure to solve. Food is supposed to sustain people, for example. But today the dis-economies of eating sustain the GDP instead. The food industry spends some $21 billion a year on advertising to entice people to eat food they don't need. Not coincidentally there's now a $32 billion diet and weight loss industry to help people take off the pounds that inevitably result. When that doesn't work, which is often, there is always the vacuum pump or knife. There were some 110,000 liposuctions in the United States last year; at five pounds each that's some 275 tons of flab up the tube.

It is a grueling cycle of indulgence and repentance, binge and purge. Yet each stage of this miserable experience, viewed through the pollyanic lens of economics, becomes growth and therefore good. The problem here goes far beyond the old critique of how the consumer culture cultivates feelings of inadequacy, lack and need so people will buy and buy again. Now this culture actually makes life worse, in order to sell solutions that purport to make it better.

Traffic shows this syndrome in a finely developed form. First we build sprawling suburbs so people need a car to go almost anywhere. The resulting long commutes are daily torture but help build up the GDP. Americans spend some $5 billion a year in gasoline alone while they sit in traffic and go nowhere. As the price of gas increases this growth sector will expand.

Commerce deplores a vacuum, and the exasperating hours in the car have spawned a booming subeconomy of relaxation tapes, cell phones, even special bibs. Billboards have 1-800 numbers so commuters can shop while they stew. Talk radio thrives on traffic-bound commuters, which accounts for some of the contentious, get-out-of-my-face tone. The traffic also helps sustain a $130 billion a year car wreck industry; and if Gates succeeds in getting computers into cars, that sector should get a major boost.

The health implications also are good for growth. Los Angeles, which has the worst traffic in the nation, also leads—if that's the word—in hospital admissions due to respiratory ailments. The resulting medical bills go into the GDP. And while Americans sit in traffic they aren't walking or getting exercise. More likely they are entertaining themselves orally with a glazed donut or a Big Mac, which helps explain why the portion of middle-aged Americans who are clinically obese has doubled since the 1960s.

C. Everett Koop, the former Surgeon General, estimates that some 70% of the nation's medical expenses are lifestyle induced. Yet the same lifestyle that promotes disease also produces a rising GDP. (Keynes observed that traditional virtues like thrift are bad for growth; now it appears that health is bad for growth too.) We literally are growing ourselves sick, and this puts a grim new twist on the economic doctrine of "complementary goods," which describes the way new products tend to spawn a host of others. The automobile gave rise to car wash franchises, drive-in restaurants, fuzz busters, tire dumps, and so forth. Television produced an antenna industry, VCRs, soap magazines, ad infinitum. The texts present this phenomenon as the wondrous perpetual motion machine of the market—goods beget more goods. But now the machine is producing complementary ills and collateral damages instead.

Suggestive of this new dynamic is a pesticide plant in Richmond, California, which is owned by a transnational corporation that also makes the breast cancer drug tamoxifen. Many researchers believe that pesticides, and the toxins created in the production of them, play a role in breast cancer. "It's a pretty good deal," a local physician told the *East Bay Express*, a Bay Area weekly. "First you cause the cancer, then you profit from curing it." Both the alleged cause and cure make the GDP go up, and this syndrome has become a central dynamic of growth in the U.S. today.

Mainstream economists would argue that this is all beside the point. If people didn't have to spend money on such things as commuting or medical costs, they'd simply spend it on something else, they say. Growth would be the same or even greater, so the actual content of growth should be of little concern to those who promote it. That view holds sway in the nation's policy councils; as a result we try continually to grow our way out of problems, when increasingly we are growing our way in.

To the extent conventional economics has raised an eyebrow at growth, it has done so mainly through the concept of "externalities". These are negative side effects suffered by those not party to a transaction between a buyer and a seller. Man buys car, car pollutes air, others suffer that "externality." As the language implies, anything outside the original transaction is deemed secondary, a subordinate reality, and therefore easily overlooked. More, the effects upon buyer and seller—the "internalities" one might say—are assumed to be good.

Today, however, that mental schema is collapsing. Externalities are starting to overwhelm internalities. A single jet ski can cause more misery for the people who reside by a lake, than it gives pleasure to the person riding it.

More importantly, and as just discussed, internalities themselves are coming into question, and with them the assumption of choice, which is the moral linchpin of market thought.

MEASURING PROGRESS

Far from being a true measure of economic (and human) progress, the GDP thrives on bad news. The GDP soars when the government spends millions to clean up a toxic waste site or to treat those suffering from cancer who lived nearby. And the GDP can drop from some very good news. For instance, it is good news for a family if a parent can afford to cut back on work and devote more hours at home. But because she is working less, spending less money on day care, and earning less, the GDP measures it as a drop in economic activity.

In the mid-1990s, the San Francisco group Redefining Progress created an alternative GDP that measures the costs as well as the benefits of economic growth. The "Genuine Progress Indicator," or GPI, accounts for how production and consumption create social ills like inequality, and creates environmental problems that threaten future generations, such as global warming and the depletion of natural resources. It adjusts the GDP downward to account for each of these aspects of economic activity, along with underemployment and the loss of leisure time. It would adjust the GDP upward if there had been more leisure time and social progress.

The result: while the GPI rose somewhat between 1950 and the early 1970s, it has been falling ever since. By 1994 the GPI was 26% lower than in 1973. During the same period, the GDP was growing.

If people choose what they buy, as market theory posits, then—externalities aside—the sum total of all their buying must be the greatest good of all. That's the ideology behind the GDP. But if people don't always choose, then the model starts to fall apart, which is what is happening today. The practical implications are obvious. If growth consists increasingly of problems rather than solutions, then scolding people for consuming too much is barking up the wrong tree. It is possible to talk instead about ridding our lives of what we don't want as well as forsaking what we do want—or think we want.

Politically this is a more promising path. But to where? The economy may be turning into a kind of round robin of difficulty and affliction, but we are all tied to the game. The sickness industry employs a lot of people, as do ad agencies and trash haulers. The fastest-growing occupations in the country include debt collectors and prison guards. What would we do without our problems and dysfunctions?

The problem is especially acute for those at the bottom of the income scale who have not shared much in the apparent prosperity. For them, a bigger piece of a bad pie might be better than none.

This is the economic conundrum of our age. No one has more than pieces of an answer, but it helps to see that much growth today is really an optical illusion created by accounting tricks. The official tally ignores totally the cost side of the growth ledger—the toll of traffic upon our time and health for example. In fact, it actually counts such costs as growth and gain. By the same token, the official tally ignores the economic contributions of the natural environment and the social structure; so that the more the economy destroys these, and puts commoditized substitutes in their places, the more the experts say the economy has "grown." Pollute the lakes and oceans so that people have to join private swim clubs and the economy grows. Erode the social infrastructure of community so people have to buy services from the market instead of getting help from their neighbors, and it grows some more. The real economy—the one that sustains us—has diminished. All that has grown is the need to buy commoditized substitutes for things we used to have for free.

So one might rephrase the question thus: how do we achieve real growth, as opposed to the statistical illusion that passes for growth today? Four decades ago, John Kenneth Galbraith argued in *The Affluent Society* that conventional economic reasoning is rapidly becoming obsolete. An economics based upon scarcity simply doesn't work in an economy of hyper-abundance, he said. If it takes a $200 billion (today) advertising industry to maintain what economists quaintly call "demand," then perhaps that demand isn't as urgent as conventional theory posits. Perhaps it's not even demand in any sane meaning of the word.

Galbraith argued that genuine economy called for shifting some resources from consumption that needs to be prodded, to needs which are indisputably great: schools, parks, older people, the inner cities and the like. For this he was skewered as a proto-socialist. Yet today the case is even stronger, as advertisers worm into virtually every waking moment in a desperate effort to keep the growth machine on track.

Galbraith was arguing for a larger public sector. But that brings dysfunctions of its own, such as bureaucracy; and it depends upon an enlarging private sector as a fiscal base to begin with. Today we need to go further, and establish new ground rules for the economy, so that it produces more genuine growth on its own. We also need to find ways to revive the nonmarket economy of informal community exchange, so that people do not need money to meet every single life need.

In the first category, environmental fiscal policy can help. While the corporate world has flogged workers to be more productive, resources such as petroleum have been in effect loafing on the job. If we used these more efficiently the result could be jobs and growth, even in conventional terms, with less environmental pollution. If we used land more efficiently—that is, reduced urban sprawl—the social and environmental gains would be great.

Another ground rule is the corporate charter laws. We need to restore these to their original purpose: to keep large business organizations within the compass of the common good. But such shifts can do only so much. More efficient cars might simply encourage more traffic, for example. Cheap renewable power for electronic devices could encourage more noise. In other words, the answer won't just be a more efficient version of what we do now. Sooner or later we'll need different ways of thinking about work and growth and how we allocate the means of life.

This is where the social economy comes in, the informal exchange between neighbors and friends. There are some promising trends. One is the return to the traditional village model in housing. Structure does affect content. When houses are close together, and people can walk to stores and work, it encourages the spontaneous social interaction that nurtures real community. New local currencies, such as Time Dollars, provide a kind of lattice work upon which informal nonmarket exchange can take root and grow.

Changes like these are off the grid of economics as conventionally defined. It took centuries for the market to emerge from the stagnation of feudalism. The next organizing principle, whatever it is, most likely will emerge slowly as well. This much we can say with certainty. As the market hurdles towards multiple implosions, social and environmental as well as financial, it is just possible that the economics profession is going to have to do what it constantly lectures the rest of us to do: adjust to new realities and show a willingness to change.

WAGES FOR HOUSEWORK
THE MOVEMENT AND THE NUMBERS

BY LENA GRABER AND JOHN MILLER

The International Wages for Housework Campaign (WFH), a network of women in Third World and industrialized countries, began organizing in the early 1970s. WFH's demands are ambitious—"for the unwaged work that women do to be recognized as work in official government statistics, and for this work to be paid."

Housewives paid wages? By the government? That may seem outlandish to some, but consider the staggering amount of unpaid work carried out by women. In 1990, the International Labor Organization (ILO) estimated that women do two-thirds of the world's work for 5% of the income. In 1995, the UN Development Programme's (UNDP) Human Development Report announced that women's unpaid and underpaid labor was worth $11 trillion worldwide, and $1.4 trillion in the United States alone. Paying women the wages they "are owed" for unwaged work, as WFN puts it, would go a long way toward undoing these inequities and reducing women's economic dependence on men.

Publicizing information like this, WFH—whose International Women Count Network now includes more than 2,000 non-governmental organizations (NGOs) from the North and South—and other groups have been remarkably successful in persuading governments to count unwaged work. In 1995, the UN Fourth World Conference on Women, held in Beijing, developed a Platform for Action that called on governments to calculate the value of women's unpaid work and include it in conventional measures of national output, such as Gross Domestic Product (GDP).

So far, only Trinidad & Tobago and Spain have passed legislation mandating the new accounting, but other countries—including numerous European countries, Australia, Canada, Japan, and New Zealand in the industrialized world, and Bangladesh, the Dominican Republic, India, Nepal, Tanzania, and Venezuela in the developing world— have undertaken extensive surveys to determine how much time is spent on unpaid household work.

THE VALUE OF HOUSEWORK

Producing credible numbers for the value of women's work in the home is no easy task. Calculating how many hours women spend performing housework—from cleaning to childcare to cooking to shopping—is just the first step. The hours are considerable in both developing and industrialized economies. (See Table 1.)

What value to place on that work, and what would constitute fair remuneration—or wages for housework—is even more difficult to assess. Feminist economists dedicated to making the value of housework visible have taken different approaches to answering the question. One approach, favored by the UN's International Research and Training Institute for the Advancement of Women (INSTRAW), bases the market value of work done at home on the price of market goods and services that are similar to those produced in the home (such as meals served in restaurants or cleaning done by professional firms). These output-based evaluations estimate that counting unpaid household production would add 30-60% to the GDP of industrialized countries, and far more for developing countries. (See Table 2.)

A second approach evaluates the inputs of household production—principally the labor that goes into cooking, cleaning, childcare, and other services performed in the home, overwhelmingly by women. Advocates of this approach use one of three methods. Some base their calculations on what economists call opportunity cost—the wages women might have earned if they had worked a similar number of hours in the market economy. Others ask what it would cost to hire

	Childcare Time	Cleaning Time	Food Prep Time	Shopping Time	Water/Fuel Collection	Total Country Time[a]
Australia (1997[b])	2:27	1:17	1:29	0:58	n.a.	3:39
Japan (1999)	0:24	2:37	n.a.	0:33	n.a.	3:34
Norway (2000)	0:42	1:16	0:49	0:26	0:01	3:56
U.K. (2000)	1:26	1:35	1:08	0:33	n.a.	4:55
Nepal (1996)	1:28	2:00	5:30	0:13	1:10	11:58

TABLE 1
WOMEN'S TIME SPENT PER DAY PERFORMING HOUSEHOLD
LABOR, BY ACTIVITY, IN HOURS:MINUTES

Note: Some activities, especially childcare, may overlap with other tasks.
[a] Totals may include activities other than those listed.
[b] Only some percentage of the population recorded doing these activities. Averages are for that portion of the population. Generally, figures represent a greater number of women than men involved. *Sources:* Australia: <www.abs.gov.au/ausstats>; Japan: <www.unescap.org/stat>; Norway: <www.ssb.no/tidsbruk_en>; United Kingdom: <www.statistics.gov.uk/themes/social_finances/TimeUseSurvey>; Nepal: INSTRAW, *Valuation of Household Production and the Satellite Accounts* (Santo Domingo: 1996), 34-35; <www.cbs.nl/isi/iass>.

someone to do the work—either a general laborer such as a domestic servant (the generalist-replacement method) or a specialist such as a chef (the specialist-replacement method)—and then assign those wages to household labor. Ann Chadeau, a researcher with the Organization for Economic Cooperation and Development, has found the specialist-replacement method to be "the most plausible and at the same time feasible approach" for valuing unpaid household labor.

These techniques produce quite different results, all of which are substantial in relation to GDP. With that in mind, let's look at how some countries calculated the monetary value of unpaid work.

UNPAID WORK IN CANADA, GREAT BRITAIN, AND JAPAN

In Canada, a government survey documented the time men and women spent on unpaid work in 1992. Canadian women performed 65% of all unpaid work, shouldering an especially large share of household labor devoted to preparing meals, maintaining clothing, and caring for children. (Men's unpaid hours exceeded women's only for outdoor cleaning.)

The value of unpaid labor varied substantially, depending on the method used to estimate its appropriate wage. (See Table 3.) The opportunity-cost method, which uses the average market wage (weighted for the greater proportion of unpaid work done by women), assigned the highest value to unpaid labor, 54.2% of Canadian GDP. The two replacement methods produced lower estimates, because the wages they assigned fell below those of other jobs. The specialist-replacement method, which paired unpaid activities with the average wages of corresponding occupations—such as cooking with junior chefs, and childcare with kindergarten teachers—put the value of Canadian unpaid labor at 43% of GDP. The generalist-replacement method, by assigning the wages of household servants to unpaid labor, produced the lowest estimate of the value of unpaid work: 34% of Canadian GDP. INSTRAW's output-based measure, which matched hours of unpaid labor to a household's average expenditures on the same activities, calculated the value of Canada's unpaid work as 47.4% of GDP.

In Great Britain, where unpaid labor hours are high for an industrialized country (see Table 1), the value of unpaid labor was far greater relative to GDP. The British Office for National Statistics found that, when valued using the opportunity cost method, unpaid work was 112% of Britain's GDP in 1995! With the specialist-replacement method, British unpaid labor was still 56% of GDP—greater than the output of the United Kingdom's entire manufacturing sector for the year.

In Japan—where unpaid labor hours are more limited (see Table 1), paid workers put in longer hours, and women perform over 80% of unpaid work—the value of unpaid labor is significantly smaller relative to GDP. The Japanese Economic Planning Agency calculated that counting unpaid work in 1996 would add between 15.2% (generalist-replacement method) and 23% (opportunity-cost method) to GDP. Even at those levels, the value of unpaid labor still equaled at least half of Japanese women's market wages.

HOUSEWORK NOT BOMBS

While estimates vary by country and evaluation method, all of these calculations make clear that recognizing the value of unpaid household labor profoundly alters our perception of economic activity and women's contributions to production. "Had household production been included in the system of macro-economic accounts," notes Ann Chadeau, "governments may well have implemented quite different economic and social policies."

For example, according to the UNDP, "The inescapable implication [of recognizing women's unpaid labor] is that the fruits of society's total labor should be shared more equally." For the UNDP, this would mean radically altering property and inheritance rights; access to credit; entitlement to social security benefits, tax incentives, and child care; and terms of divorce settlements.

For WFH advocates, the implications are inescapable as well: women's unpaid labor should be paid—and "the money," WFH insists, "must come first of all from military spending."

Here in the United States, an unneeded and dangerous military buildup begun last year has already pushed up military spending from 3% to 4% of GDP. Devoting just the additional 1% of GDP gobbled up by the military budget to wages for housework—far from being outlandish—

TABLE 2 VALUE OF UNPAID HOUSEHOLD LABOR AS % OF GDP, USING OUTPUT-BASED EVALUATION METHOD	
Country	*% of GDP*
Canada (1992)	47.4%
Finland (1990)	49.1%
Nepal (1991)	170.7%

Source: INSTRAW, *Valuation of Household Production and the Satellite Accounts* (Santo Domingo, 1996), 62, 229.

TABLE 3 VALUE OF UNPAID HOUSEHOLD LABOR IN CANADA AS % OF GDP, 1992	
Evaluation Method	*% of GDP*
Opportunity Cost (before taxes)	54.2 %
Specialist-Replacement	43.0%
Generalist-Replacement	34.0%
Output-Based	47.4%

Source: INSTRAW, *Valuation of Household Production and the Satellite Accounts* (Santo Domingo: 1996), 229.

would be an important first step toward fairly remunerating women who perform much-needed and life-sustaining household work.

Resources: Ann Chadeau, "What is Households' Non-Market Production Worth?" *OECD Economic Studies* No. 18 (Spring 1992); Economic Planning Unit, Department of National Accounts, Japan, "Monetary Valuation of Unpaid Work in 1996" <unstats.un.org/unsd/methods/timeuse/tusresource_papers/japanunpaid.htm>; INSTRAW, *Measurement and Valuation of Unpaid Contribution: Accounting Through*

Time and Output (Santo Domingo: 1995); INSTRAW, *Valuation of Household Production and the Satellite Accounts* (Santo Domingo: 1996); Office of National Statistics, United Kingdom, "A Household Satellite Account for the UK," by Linda Murgatroyd and Henry Neuberger, *Economic Trends* (October 1997) <www.statistics.gov.uk/hhsa/hhsa/Index.html>; Hilkka Pietilä, "The Triangle of the Human Ecology: Household-Cultivation-Industrial Production," *Ecological Economics Journal* 20 (1997); UN Development Programme, Human Development Report (New York: Oxford University Press, 1995); Wages For Housework <ourworld.compuserve.com/homepages/crossroadswomenscentre/WFH.html>

November/December 2007

WAR SPENDING PLACED ABOVE DOMESTIC PRIORITIES

BY MONIQUE MORRISSEY

Claiming the mantle of fiscal discipline, President Bush has threatened to veto domestic spending bills for fiscal year 2008 that exceed his budget request. His threat cannot be justified by a claim that Congress is being unusually profligate: Congress's non-defense appropriations bills approximately keep pace with economic growth, and earmarks are down sharply.

Meanwhile, the administration has asked for significant increases in both war appropriations and regular defense appropriations for FY08: $524 billion for defense, military construction, and veterans' affairs, and $193 billion (so far) for war funding. If Congress agrees to these requests, defense spending, which rose from 3.0% of GDP when Bush came into office in 2001 to 4.0% in 2005, 2006, and 2007, will resume its upward climb to between 4.3% and 5.0% of GDP in 2008. (The 4.3% estimate assumes that the ratio of actual outlays to appropriations, as measured by the Congressional Budget Office, is the same in FY08 as in FY07. The 5.0% estimate assumes that all moneys appropriated are actually spent.)

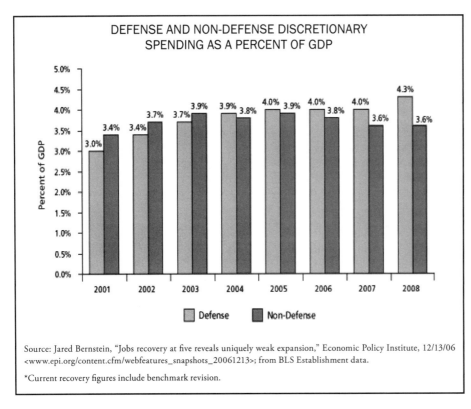

DEFENSE AND NON-DEFENSE DISCRETIONARY SPENDING AS A PERCENT OF GDP

Source: Jared Bernstein, "Jobs recovery at five reveals uniquely weak expansion," Economic Policy Institute, 12/13/06 <www.epi.org/content.cfm/webfeatures_snapshots_20061213>; from BLS Establishment data.

*Current recovery figures include benchmark revision.

Note: Where they differ, Senate and House appropriations bills are averaged. The chart assumes that the ratio of outlays to appropriations is the same in FY07 and FY08. In the case of defense spending, the difference between outlays and appropriations reflects the fact that war funds are not necessarily spent within a fiscal year, and appropriations bills are not cleanly split along functional lines. In the case of non-defense spending, the discrepancy is due to spending from the Highway Trust Fund and the Airport and Airway Trust Fund, which is not included in appropriations bills.

The chart below illustrates what happens if the president gets his way on military spending. It shows that even if Congress gets its way on domestic spending, the entire increase in discretionary spending as a share of GDP since 2002 (the first year President Bush had any input on the budget) will be due to growth in defense spending rather than domestic initiatives. ("Discretionary spending" refers to budget items appropriated by Congress each year, as opposed to mandatory spending, authorized by permanent laws, on programs such as Medicare and Social Security.) The chart actually understates the full cost of the "war on terror," because Homeland Security, State Department, and Foreign Operations funding is counted under non-defense spending. Plus, the figures shown do not include significant long-term war costs, for veterans' health care, for example.

The proposed $70 billion increase in defense appropriations for FY08 would be more than enough to fund the $35 billion expansion of the State Children's Health Insurance Program that the president just vetoed. In addition, it would make up the $21 billion difference between the president and Congress on the domestic appropriations bills that the president has threatened to veto. Polls show that voters are concerned that defense spending—especially on the Iraq war—is placed above government spending on health care, education, and other domestic priorities. The voters are right.

Resources: Author's calculations, based on Congressional Budget Office (CBO), www.cbo.gov/budget/historical.shtml; CBO, *The Budget and Economic Outlook: An Update,* August 2007; *CongressDaily,* "Dems Lay Groundwork for Challenging Bush over Vetoes," September 28, 2007; Center on Budget and Policy Priorities, *The Fight over Appropriations: Myths and Reality,* June 21, 2007.

ARTICLE 1.6

TAX CUTS FOR THE RICH
OR PUBLIC PROGRAMS FOR EVERYONE?

BY MICHELLE SHEEHAN

Who is benefiting from the massive 2001 and 2003 tax cuts? Not the working families President Bush talked about when he pushed the cuts, but the wealthy. The 2001 tax cut was the largest income tax rollback in two decades; it lowered tax rates on the top four income brackets and gave small advance refunds to those less well-off. The 2003 tax cut—the third largest in U.S. history—slashed dividend and capital gains taxes, and accelerated the 2001 rate cut for the top income brackets. Finally, the 2001 estate tax cut reduced the top tax rate each year, meaning that the top 2% of taxpayers will pay progressively fewer taxes on wealth that they leave to heirs.

The figures on the next page represent just a sliver of what the rich will get from the 2001–2003 cuts. The largest tax breaks, and those most geared toward the wealthy, were designed to kick in later. According to Citizens for Tax Justice, the cumulative costs of the 2001–2003 tax cuts will be $824.1 billion in 2010. If the cuts are made permanent beyond 2010, as Bush's 2005 budget proposes, they will cost $5.9 trillion over the next 75 years, and could force massive cuts to already strapped social welfare programs. The right-hand column of the table shows some of the things that the 2001–2003 tax cuts could have paid for in 2004.

TAX CUTS VS. SOCIAL PROGRAMS

2001–2003 Tax Cuts	*Cost of Tax Cuts in 2004*	*Cost in Social Programs**
Estate tax break for top 1%	$7 billion	Provide Section 8 housing subsidies for 1 million families
Dividends and capital gains tax cut for top 1%	$15 billion	Insure 11 million children under Medicaid (2000)
Benefits to top 1% from cuts in corporate taxes	$25 billion	Fund 2 million Americorps members
Personal income tax cut for top 1%	$32 billion	Bridge "No Child Left Behind" budget gap (excluding dividends and capital gains)
Total tax cuts for top 1%	$79 billion	Bridge the Head Start funding gap 18 times over
Dividends and capital gains tax cut for top 5%	$20 billion	Clean up 143 Superfund "megasites"
Benefits to top 5% from cuts in corporate taxes	$36 billion	Fund Amtrak 20 times over (FY 2005)
Total dividends and capital gains tax cut	$28 billion	Provide WIC nutrition subsidies to 47 million parents and children
Total corporate tax cut	$61 billion	Build 871,000 new units of affordable housing
Total tax cut on personal income (excluding dividends and capital gains)	$169 billion	Pay salary and benefits for 3.1 million elementary school teachers (2001)
TOTAL TAX CUTS IN 2004	$266 billion	Pay four years' tuition at public universities for 13 million students *or* more than half of all Social Security benefits

* Numbers for 2003 unless otherwise noted.
Sources: Tax cuts: Citizens for Tax Justice <www.ctj.org>. *Social spending figures:* Center for Budget and Policy Priorities <www.cbpp.org>; Center for Medicare and Medicaid Services <www.cms.hhs.gov>; Americorps <www.americorps.org>; National Education Association <www.nea.org/esea>; U.S. Department of Health and Human Services, Administration for Children and Families <www.acf.hhs.gov> and United Way <national.unitedway.org>; *Environmental Health Perspectives,* March 2003 <ehp.niehs.nih.gov>; Amtrak <www.amtrak.com>; USDA Food and Nutrition Service <www.fns.usda.gov>; National Priorities Project <www.nationalpriorities.org>; Bureau of Labor Statistics, Occupational Employment Statistics <www.bls.gov/oes>; Social Security 2004 Trustees Report <www.ssa.gov>; College Board <www.collegeboard.com>.

CHAPTER 2

WEALTH, INEQUALITY, AND POVERTY

INTRODUCTION

Wealth and inequality are both end products of today's economic growth. But while all macroeconomics textbooks investigate wealth *accumulation*, most give less attention to wealth *disparities*. The authors in this chapter fill in the gap by looking at who makes out, and who doesn't, with the accumulation of wealth.

"Slicing up the Long Barbeque" (Article 2.1) starts the discussion by providing hard numbers on today's income and wealth gaps. Economist Jim Cypher documents the alarming rise in U.S. inequality, which has reached levels not seen since the Great Depression. That is true for income (how much you or your family makes in a year) and wealth (the assets you or your family own minus your debts). Today, the top 1% of households own nearly two-fifths of the nation's wealth; the richest 20% get nearly three-fifths of our national income. Median household income (after adjusting for inflation) is declining. For Cypher, these numbers define who gorged, who served, and who got roasted during the last thirty years.

All told, greater wealth hasn't made for greater equality or social mobility. As Paul Krugman reports, it is not just left critics who say so, but the business press as well. The number of people who go from rags to riches—while always so few as to be near-mythical—has become even smaller since 1980 (Article 2.7). In addition, low-wage workers are five times less likely to have sick days at their job than workers at the top of the wage scale (Article 2.5). On top of that, the limited access to education for people in prison, disproportionately blacks and Latinos, has only added further to their economic exclusion (Article 2.6). Finally, poverty rates,

which, according to most experts, badly underestimate the extent of poverty in the U.S. economy, continue to rise in the current economic recovery (Article 2.4)

Rising inequality and declining social mobility have led to more people seeking employment at Wal-Mart—where wages are lower, benefits poorer, and working conditions worse than at other big-box retailers, such as Costco, as Esther Cervantes and John Miller document in the second and third articles of this chapter. Wal-Mart's low prices seem to come at the cost of an ill-paid workforce that can afford to shop nowhere else. Many are stuck in what economist Howard Karger describes as "the fringe economy of the United States," where poorly paid and heavily indebted consumers are subjected to predatory financial practices, such as excessive interest rates, super-high fees, and exorbitant prices (Article 2.8).

It didn't have to be this way. Chris Tilly debunks the myth that inequality is necessary for economic growth, showing that among both developing and industrial economies and across regions within countries, there is no correlation between higher inequality and faster economic growth. He argues that greater equality actually supports economic growth by bolstering spending, promoting agricultural and industrial productivity, and lessening social conflict (Article 2.9). William Greider provides a blueprint for how the engines of inequality of today's economy can be transformed through workplace democracy, strategic investment of public and union-managed pension funds, and shareholder activism (Article 2.10).

What has happened to world income inequality is a matter of sharp dispute. Many analysts claim that world incomes have converged, leading to a sharp reduction in world inequality in the second half of the twentieth century. Many others report that the gaps between the poorest and the richest people and between countries have continued to widen over the last two decades. Economist Bob Sutcliffe has taken a close look at these studies. In his *Dollars & Sense* interview, Sutcliffe reports that "the wide range of different results of respected studies of world inequality in the last two decades casts doubt on the idea that world inequality has sharply and unambiguously declined or increased during the epoch of neoliberalism" (Article 2.11).

DISCUSSION QUESTIONS

1. (General) The authors in this chapter believe that the distribution of wealth is as important as wealth itself, and consider greater economic equality an important macroeconomic goal. What are some arguments for and against this position? Where do you come down in the debate?

KEY TO COLANDER

E = *Economics*   M = *Macroeconomics*

This chapter fits with chapters E22-E23 or M6-M7; and informs chapters E24-E26 or M8-M10. Inequality and wealth accumulation are also important topics in chapters on monetary policy (E27-E28; M11-M12), inflation, unemployment, and growth (E29; M13), and the section "Policy Issues In Depth" (E30-E31; M14-M15).

Articles 2.1, 2.2, 2.3, 2.5, 2.6, 2.7, 2.8 and 2.10 fit with chapter E22 or M6, and the discussion of who benefits from the "New Economy" in chapter E29 or M13.

Article 2.9 fits with any discussion of the requisites for growth, such as chapter E24 or M8.

Article 2.11 goes with the discussion of the convergence debate in E24 or M8.

---

2. (Articles 2.1, 2.5, 2.6) Who benefited from the wealth accumulation of the 1990s? How did stockholders fare versus wage earners? How did the concentration of wealth-holding by income group and by race change during the decade?

3. (Articles 2.1, 2.4, 2.5, 2.6) "A rising tide lifts all boats," proclaimed John F. Kennedy as he lobbied for pro-business tax cuts in the early 1960s. Did the 1990s boom and the current economic recovery lift all boats? What do the changes in income, wealth, and poverty suggest?

4. (Article 2.4) What are the shortcomings of the federal poverty threshold? How should the United States change the way it calculates the poverty threshold to get a more accurate measure of the incidence of poverty?

5. (Article 2.7) The "New Economy" fed the myth that anyone can get rich quick in this country, but Paul Krugman says it just ain't so. What evidence does he present to argue that social mobility is declining? Do you find his evidence persuasive?

6. (Articles 2.2, 2.3) Wal-Mart is now the largest employer in the United States and the trendsetter for U.S. labor relations. What has been the effect of the Wal-Mart, low-prices, low-cost, low-wage strategy on the U.S. economy? Has it been for the better or the worse? For retail workers? Other workers in the United States and around the globe? U.S. consumers? Corporate America?

7. (Article 2.8) How does Karger define the fringe economy? How big is it? How important is the fringe economy for today's new economy, which we usually think of as a high-productivity, high-consumption economy?

8. (Article 2.9) Why do conservatives argue that inequality is good for economic growth? What counterarguments does Tilly use to challenge this traditional view of the tradeoff between inequality and growth? What evidence convinces Tilly that equality is good for economic growth? Does that evidence convince you?

9. (Article 2.10) Why, in Greider's opinion, is transforming the workplace the key to making the U.S. economy more egalitarian and democratic?

10. (Article 2.11) If Sutcliffe is right that world inequality has neither sharply declined or increased during the epoch of neoliberalism, what does his reading of the world inequality data suggest about the convergence hypothesis—the hypothesis that per capita income in countries with similar institutional structures will converge to the higher level?

ARTICLE 2.1

January/February 2007

SLICING UP AT THE LONG BARBEQUE:
WHO GORGES, WHO SERVES, AND WHO GETS ROASTED?

BY JAMES M. CYPHER

Economic inequality has been on the rise in the United States for 30-odd years. Not since the Gilded Age of the late 19th century—during what Mark Twain referred to as "the Great Barbeque"—has the country witnessed such a rapid shift in the distribution of economic resources.

Still, most mainstream economists do not pay too much attention to the distribution of income and wealth—that is, how the value of current production (income) and past accumulated assets (wealth) is divided up among U.S. households. Some economists focus their attention on theory for theory's sake and do not work much with empirical data of any kind. Others who are interested in these on-the-ground data simply assume that each individual or group gets what it deserves from a capitalist economy. In their view, if the share of income going to wage earners goes up, that must mean that wage earners are more productive and thus deserve a larger slice of the nation's total income—and vice versa if that share goes down.

Heterodox economists, however, frequently look upon the distribution of income and wealth as among the most important shorthand guides to the overall state of a society and its economy. Some are interested in economic justice; others may or may not be, but nonetheless are convinced that changes in income distribution signal underlying societal trends and perhaps important points of political tension. And the general public appears to be paying increasing attention to income and wealth inequality. Consider the strong support voters have given to recent ballot questions raising state minimum wages and the extensive coverage of economic inequality that has suddenly begun to appear in mainstream news outlets like the *New York Times*, the *Los Angeles Times*, and the *Wall Street Journal*, all of which published lengthy article series on the topic in the past few years. Just last month, news outlets around the country spotlighted the extravagant bonuses paid out by investment firm Goldman Sachs, including a $53.4 million bonus to the firm's CEO.

By now, economists and others who do pay attention to the issue are aware that income and wealth inequality in the United States rose steadily during the last three decades of the 20th century. But now that we are several years into the 21st, what do we know about income and wealth distribution today? Has the trend toward inequality continued, or are there signs of a reversal? And what can an understanding of the entire post-World War II era tell us about how to move again toward greater economic equality?

The short answers are: (1) Income distribution is even more unequal than we thought; (2) The newest data suggest the trend toward greater inequality continues, with no signs of a reversal; (3) We all do better when we all do better. During the 30 or so years after World War II the economy boomed and every stratum of society did better—pretty much at the same rate. When the era of shared growth ended, so too did much of the growth: the U.S. economy slowed down and recessions were deeper, more frequent, and harder to overcome. Growth spurts that did occur left most people out: the bottom 60% of U.S. households earned only 95 cents in 2004 for every dollar they made in 1979. A quarter century of falling incomes for the vast majority, even though average household income rose by 27% in real terms. Whew!

THE CLASSLESS SOCIETY?

Throughout the 1950s, 1960s, and 1970s, sociologists preached that the United States was an essentially "classless" society in which everyone belonged to the middle class. A new "mass market" society with an essentially affluent, economically homogeneous population, they claimed, had emerged. Exaggerated as these claims were in the 1950s, there was some reason for their popular acceptance. Union membership reached its peak share of the private-sector labor force in the early 1950s; unions were able to force corporations of the day to share the benefits of strong economic growth. The union wage created a target for non-union workers as well, pulling up all but the lowest of wages as workers sought to match the union wage and employers often granted it as a tactic for keeping unions out. Under these circumstances, millions of families entered the lower middle class and saw their standard of living rise markedly. All of this made the distribution of income more equal for decades until the late 1970s. Of course there were outliers—some millions of poor, disproportionately blacks, and the rich family here and there.

Something serious must have happened in the 1970s as the trend toward greater economic equality rapidly reversed. Here are the numbers. The share of income received by the bottom 90% of the population was a modest 67% in 1970, but by 2000 this had shrunk to a mere 52%, according to a detailed study of U.S. income distribution conducted by Thomas Piketty and Emmanuel Saez, published by the prestigious National Bureau of Economic Research in 2002. Put another way, the top 10% increased their overall share

of the nation's total income by 15 percentage points from 1970 to 2000. This is a rather astonishing jump—the *gain* of the top 10% in these years was equivalent to more than the *total income received* annually by the bottom 40% of households.

To get on the bottom rung of the top 10% of households in 2000, it would have been necessary to have an adjusted gross income of $104,000 a year. The real money, though, starts on the 99th rung of the income ladder—the top 1% received an unbelievable 21.7% of all income in 2000. To get a handhold on the very bottom of this top rung took more than $384,000.

The Piketty-Saez study (and subsequent updates), which included in its measure of annual household income some data, such as income from capital gains, that generally are not factored in, verified a rising *trend* in income inequality which had been widely noted by others, and a *degree* of inequality which was far beyond most current estimates.

The Internal Revenue Service has essentially duplicated the Piketty-Saez study. They find that in 2003, the share of total income going to the "bottom" four-fifths of households (that's 80% of the population!) was only slightly above 40%. (See Figure 1.) Both of these studies show much higher levels of inequality than were previously thought to exist based on widely referenced Census Bureau studies. The Census studies still attribute 50% of total income to the top fifth for 2003, but this number appears to understate what the top fifth now receives—nearly 60%, according to the IRS.

A BRAVE NEW (GLOBALIZED) WORLD FOR WORKERS

Why the big change from 1970 to 2000? That is too long a story to tell here in full. But briefly, we can say that beginning in the early 1970s, U.S. corporations and the wealthy individuals who largely own them had the means, the motive, and the opportunity to garner a larger share of the nation's income—and they did so.

Let's start with the motive. The 1970s saw a significant slowdown in U.S. economic growth, which made corporations and stockholders anxious to stop sharing the benefits of growth to the degree they had in the immediate postwar era.

Opportunity appeared in the form of an accelerating globalization of economic activity. Beginning in the 1970s, more and more U.S.-based corporations began to set up production operations overseas. The trend has only accelerated since, in part because international communication and transportation costs have fallen dramatically. Until the 1970s, it was very difficult—essentially unprofitable—for giants like General Electric or General Motors to operate plants offshore and then import their foreign-made products into the United States. So from the 1940s to the 1970s, U.S. workers had a geographic lever, one they have now almost entirely lost. This erosion in workers' bargaining power has undermined the middle class and decimated the unions that once managed to assure the working class a generally comfortable economic existence. And today, of course, the tendency to send jobs offshore is affecting many highly trained professionals such as engineers. So this process of gutting the middle class has not run its course.

Given the opportunity presented by globalization, companies took a two-pronged approach to strengthening their hand vis-à-vis workers: (1) a frontal assault on unions, with decertification elections and get-tough tactics during unionization attempts, and (2) a debilitating war of nerves whereby corporations threatened to move offshore unless workers scaled back their demands or agreed to givebacks of prior gains in wage and benefit levels or working conditions.

A succession of U.S. governments that pursued conservative—or pro-corporate—economic policies provided the means. Since the 1970s, both Republican and Democratic administrations have tailored their economic policies to benefit corporations and shareholders over workers. The laundry list of such policies includes

- new trade agreements, such as NAFTA, that allow companies to cement favorable deals to move offshore to host nations such as Mexico;

- tax cuts for corporations and for the wealthiest households, along with hikes in the payroll taxes that represent the largest share of the tax burden on the working and middle classes;

- lax enforcement of labor laws that are supposed to protect the right to organize unions and bargain collectively.

EXPLODING MILLIONAIRISM

Given these shifts in the political economy of the United States, it is not surprising that economic inequality in 2000 was higher than in 1970. But at this point, careful readers may well ask whether it is misleading to use data for the year 2000, as the studies reported above do, to demonstrate rising inequality. After all, wasn't 2000 the year the NASDAQ peaked, the year the dot-com bubble reached its maximum volume? So if the wealthiest households received an especially large slice of the nation's total income that year, doesn't that just reflect a bubble about to burst rather than an underlying trend?

To begin to answer this question, we need to look at the trends in income and wealth distribution *since* 2000. And it turns out that after a slight pause in 2000-2001, inequality has continued to rise. Look at household income, for example. According to the standard indicators, the U.S. economy saw a brief recession in 2000-2001 and has been in a recovery ever since. But the median household income has failed to recover.* In 2000 the median household had an annual income of $49,133; by 2005, after adjusting for inflation, the figure stood at $46,242. This 6% drop in median household income occurred while the inflation-adjusted Gross Domestic Product *expanded* by 14.4%.

When the Census Bureau released these data, it noted that median household income had gone up slightly between 2004 and 2005. This point was seized upon by Bush administration officials to bolster their claim that times are good for American workers. A closer look at the data, however, revealed a rather astounding fact: Only 23 million households moved ahead in 2005, most headed by someone aged 65 or above. In other words, subtracting out the cost-of-living increase in Social Security benefits and increases in investment income (such as profits, dividends, interest, capital gains, and rents) to the over-65 group, workers again suffered a *decline* in income in 2005.

Another bit of evidence is the number of millionaire households—those with net worth of $1 million or more excluding the value of a primary residence and any IRAs. In 1999, just before the bubbles burst, there were 7.1 million millionaire households in the United States. In 2005, there were 8.9 million, a record number. Ordinary workers may not have recovered from the 2000-2001 rough patch yet, but evidently the wealthiest households have!

Many economists pay scant attention to income distribution patterns on the assumption that those shifts merely reflect trends in the productivity of labor or the return to risk-taking. But worker productivity *rose* in the 2000-2005 period, by 27.1% (see Figure 2). At the same time, from 2003 to 2005 average hourly pay fell by 1.2%. (Total compensation, including all forms of benefits, rose by 7.2% between 2000 and 2005. Most of the higher compensation spending merely reflects rapid increases in the health insurance premiums that employers have to pay just to maintain the same levels of coverage. But even if benefits are counted as part of workers' pay—a common and questionable practice—productivity growth outpaced this elastic definition of "pay" by 50% between 1972 and 2005.)

And at the macro level, recent data released by the Commerce Department demonstrate that the share of the country's GDP going to wages and salaries sank to its lowest postwar level, 45.4%, in the third quarter of 2006 (see Figure 3). And this figure actually overstates how well ordinary workers are doing. The "Wage & Salary" share includes all income of this type, not just production workers' pay. Corporate executives' increasingly munificent salaries are included as well. Workers got roughly 65% of total wage and salary income in 2005, according to survey data from the U.S. Department of Labor; the other 35% went to salaried professionals—medical doctors and technicians, managers, and lawyers—who comprised only 15.6% of the sample.

Moreover, the "Wage & Salary" share shown in the National Income and Product Accounts includes bonuses, overtime, and other forms of payment not included in the Labor Department survey. If this income were factored in, the share going to nonprofessional, nonmanagerial workers would be even smaller. Bonuses and other forms of income to top employees can be ma*ny times* base pay in important areas such as law and banking. Goldman Sachs's notorious 2006 bonuses are a case in point; the typical managing director on Wall Street garnered a bonus ranging between $1 and $3 million.

So, labor's share of the nation's income is falling, as Figure 3 shows, but it is actually falling much faster than these data suggest. Profits, meanwhile, are at their highest level as a share of GDP since the booming 1960s.

These numbers should come as no surprise to anyone who reads the paper: story after story illustrates how corporations are continuing to squeeze workers. For instance, workers at the giant auto parts manufacturer Delphi have been told to prepare for a drop in wages from $27.50 an hour in 2006 to $16.50 an hour in 2007. In order to keep some of Caterpillar's manufacturing work in the United States, the union was cornered into accepting a contract in 2006 that limits new workers to a maximum salary of $27,000 a year—no matter how long they work there—compared to the $38,000 or more that long-time Caterpillar workers make today. More generally, for young women with a high school diploma, average entry-level pay fell to only $9.08 an hour in 2005, down by 4.9% just since 2001. For male college graduates, starter-job pay fell by 7.3% over the same period.

AIDING AND ABETTING

And the federal government is continuing to play its part, facilitating the transfer of an ever-larger share of the nation's income to its wealthiest households. George W. Bush once joked that his constituency was "the haves and the have-mores"—this may have been one of the few instances in which he was actually leveling with his audience. Consider aspects of the four tax cuts for individuals that Bush has implemented since taking office. The first two cut the top *nominal* tax rate from 39.6% to 35%. Then, in 2003, the third cut benefited solely those who hold wealth, reducing taxes on dividends from 39.6% to 15% and on capital gains from 20% to 15%. (Bush's fourth tax cut—in 2006—is expected to drop taxes by 4.8% percent for the top one tenth of one percent of all households, while the median household will luxuriate with an extra nickel per day.)

So, if you make your money by the sweat of your brow and you earned $200,000 in 2003, you paid an *effective* tax rate of 21%. If you earned a bit more, say another $60,500, you paid an effective tax rate of 35% on the additional income. But if, with a flick of the wrist on your laptop, you flipped some stock you had held for six months and cleared $60,500 on the transaction, you paid the IRS an effective tax rate of only 15%. What difference does it make?

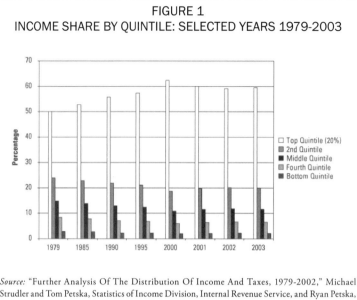

FIGURE 1
INCOME SHARE BY QUINTILE: SELECTED YEARS 1979-2003

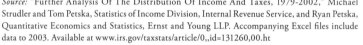

Source: "Further Analysis Of The Distribution Of Income And Taxes, 1979-2002," Michael Strudler and Tom Petska, Statistics of Income Division, Internal Revenue Service, and Ryan Petska, Quantitative Economics and Statistics, Ernst and Young LLP. Accompanying Excel files include data to 2003. Available at www.irs.gov/taxstats/article/0,,id=131260,00.ht

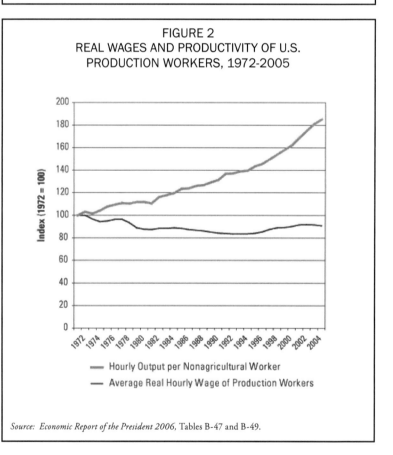

FIGURE 2
REAL WAGES AND PRODUCTIVITY OF U.S. PRODUCTION WORKERS, 1972-2005

Source: Economic Report of the President 2006, Tables B-47 and B-49.

Well, in 2003 the 6,126 households with incomes over $10 million saw their taxes go down by an average of $521,905 from this one tax cut alone.

These tax cuts represent only one of the many Bush administration policies that have abetted the ongoing shift of income away from most households and toward the wealthiest ones. And what do these top-tier households do with all this newfound money? For one thing, they save. This is in sharp contrast to most households. While the top fifth of households by income has a savings rate of 23%, the bottom 80% as a group dissave—in other words, they go into debt, spending more than they earn. Households headed by a person under 35 currently show a negative savings rate of 16% of income. Today *overall* savings—the savings of the top fifth minus the dis-savings of the bottom four-fifths—are slightly negative, for the first time since the Great Depression.

Here we find the crucial link between income and wealth accumulation. Able to save nearly a quarter of their income, the rich search out financial assets (and sometimes real assets such as houses and businesses) to pour their vast funds into. In many instances, sometimes with inside information, they are able to generate considerable future income from their invested savings. Like a snowball rolling downhill, savings for the rich can have a turbo effect—more savings generates more income, which then accumulates as wealth.

FIGURE 3
WAGES/SALARIES VS. CORPORATE PROFITS AS
SHARES OF U.S. INCOME, 1972-2006

— Wages/Salaries as share of GDI (%)
— Corporate Profits as share of GDI (%)

Source: U.S. Dept. of Commerce, Bureau of Economic Analysis, *National Income and Product Accounts 2006*, Table 1.10.

LIFESTYLES OF THE RICH

Make the rich even richer and the creative forces of market capitalism will be unleashed, resulting in more savings and consequently more capital investment, raising productivity and creating abundance for all. At any rate, that's the supply-side/neoliberal theory. However—and reminiscent of the false boom that defined the Japanese economy in the late 1980s—the big money has not gone into productive investments in the United States. Stripping out the money pumped into the residential real estate bubble, inflation-adjusted investment in machinery, equipment, technology, and structures increased only 1.4% from 1999 through 2005—an average of 0.23% per year. Essentially, productive investment has stagnated since the close of the dot-com boom.

Instead, the money has poured into high-risk hedge funds. These are vast pools of unregulated funds that are now generating 40% to 50% of the trades in the New York Stock Exchange and account for very large portions of trading in many U.S. and foreign credit and debt markets.

And where is the income from these investments going? Last fall media mogul David Geffen sold two paintings at record prices, a Jasper Johns ($80 million) and a Willem de Kooning ($63.5 million), to two of "today's crop of hedge-fund billionaires" whose cash is making the art market "red-hot," according to the *New York Times.*

Other forms of conspicuous consumption have their allure as well. Boeing and Lufthansa are expecting brisk business for the newly introduced 787 airplane. The commercial version of the new Boeing jet will seat 330, but the VIP version offered by Lufthansa Technik (for a mere $240

million) will have seating for 35 or fewer, leaving room for master bedrooms, a bar, and the transport of racehorses or Rolls Royces. And if you lose your auto assembly job? It should be easy to find work as a dog walker: High-end pet care services are booming, with sales more than doubling between 2000 and 2004. Opened in 2001, Just Dogs Gourmet expects to have 45 franchises in place by the end of 2006 selling hand-decorated doggie treats. And then there is Camp Bow Wow, which offers piped-in classical music for the dogs (oops, "guests") and a live Camper Cam for their owners. Started only three years ago, the company already has 140 franchises up and running.

According to David Butler, the manager of a premiere auto dealership outside of Detroit, sales of Bentleys, at $180,000 a pop, are brisk. But not many $300,000 Rolls Royces are selling. "It's not that they can't afford it," Butler told the New York Times, "it's because of the image it would give." Just what is the image problem in Detroit? Well, maybe it has something to do with those Delphi workers facing a 40% pay cut. Michigan's economy is one of the hardest-hit in the nation. GM, long a symbol of U.S. manufacturing prowess, is staggering, with rumors of possible bankruptcy rife. The best union in terms of delivering the goods for the U.S. working class, the United Auto Workers, is facing an implosion. Thousands of Michigan workers at Delphi, GM, and Ford will be out on the streets very soon. (The top three domestic car makers are determined to permanently lay off three-quarters of their U.S. assembly-line workers—nearly 200,000 hourly employees. If they do, then the number of autoworkers employed by the Big Three—Ford, Chrysler, and GM—will have shrunk by a staggering 900,000 since 1978.) So, this might not be the time to buy a Rolls. But a mere $180,000 Bentley—why not?

HAD ENOUGH OF THE "HAVES"?

In the era Twain decried as the "great barbeque," the outrageous concentration of income and wealth eventually sparked a reaction and a vast reform movement. But it was not until the onset of the Great Depression, decades later, that massive labor/social unrest and economic collapse forced the country's political elite to check the growing concentration of income and wealth.

Today, it does not appear that there are, as yet, any viable forces at work to put the brakes on the current runaway process of rising inequality. Nor does it appear that this era's power elite is ready to accept any new social compact. In a recent report on the "new king of Wall Street" (a co-founder of the hedge fund/private-equity buyout corporation Blackstone Group) that seemed to typify elite perspectives on today's inequality, the *New York Times* gushed that "a crashing wave of capital is minting new billionaires each year." Naturally, the *Times* was too discreet to mention is that those same "crashing waves" have flattened the middle class. And their backwash has turned the working class every-which-way while pulling it down, down, down.

But perhaps those who decry the trend can find at least symbolic hope in the new boom in yet another luxury good. Private mausoleums, in vogue during that earlier Gilded Age, are back. For $650,000, one was recently constructed at Daytona Memorial Park in Florida—with matching $4,000 Medjool date palms for shade. Another, complete with granite patio, meditation room, and doors of hand cast bronze, went up in the same cemetery. Business is booming, apparently, with 2,000 private mausoleums sold in 2005, up from a single-year peak of 65 in the 1980s. Some cost "well into the millions," according to one the nation's largest makers of cemetery monuments. Who knows: maybe the mausoleum boom portends the ultimate (dead) end for the neo-Gilded Age.

Resources: Jenny Anderson, "As Lenders, Hedge Funds Draw Insider Scrutiny," *NY Times* 10/16/06; Steven Greenhouse, "Many Entry-Level Workers Feel Pinch of Rough Market," *NY Times* 9/4/06; Greenhouse and David Leonhardt, "Real Wages Fail to Match a Rise in Productivity," *NY Times* 8/28/06; Paul Krugman, "Feeling No Pain," *NY Times* 3/6/06; Krugman, "Graduates vs. Oligarchs," *NY Times* 2/27/06; David Cay Johnston, *Perfectly Legal* (Penguin Books, 2003); Johnston, "Big Gain for Rich Seen in Tax Cuts for Investments," *NY Times* 4/5/06; Johnston, "New Rise in Number of Millionaire Families," *NY Times* 3/28/06; Johnston, "'04 Income in US was Below 2000 Level," *NY Times* 11/28/06; Leonhardt, "The Economics of Henry Ford May Be Passé," *NY Times* 4/5/06; Rick Lyman, "Census Reports Slight Increase in '05 Incomes," *NY Times* 8/30/06; Micheline Maynard and Nick Bunkley, "Ford is Offering 75,000 Employees Buyout Packages," *NY Times* 9/15/06; Jeremy W. Peters, "Delphi Is Said to Offer Union a One-Time Sweetener," *NY Times* 3/28/06; Joe Sharky, "For the Super-Rich, It's Time to Upgrade the Old Jumbo Jet," *NY Times* 10/17/06; Guy Trebay, "For a Price, Final Resting Place that Tut Would Find Pleasant" *NY Times* 4/17/06.

WHAT'S GOOD FOR WAL-MART

BY JOHN MILLER

"Is Wal-Mart Good for America?"

It is a testament to the public relations of the anti-Wal-Mart campaign that the question above is even being asked.

By any normal measure, Wal-Mart's business ought to be noncontroversial. It sells at low costs, albeit in mind-boggling quantities....

The company's success and size ... do not rest on monopoly profits or price-gouging behavior. It simply sells things people will buy at small markups and, as in the old saw, makes it up on volume.... You may believe, as do service-workers unions and a clutch of coastal elites—many of whom, we'd wager, have never set foot in Wal-Mart—that Wal-Mart "exploits" workers who can't say no to low wages and poor benefits. You might accept the canard that it drives good local businesses into the ground, although both of these allegations are more myth than reality.

But even if you buy into the myths, there's no getting around the fact that somewhere out there, millions of people are spending billions of dollars on what Wal-Mart puts on its shelves. No one is making them do it.... Wal-Mart can't make mom and pop shut down the shop anymore than it can make customers walk through the doors or pull out their wallets.

What about the workers? ... Wal-Mart's average starting wage is already nearly double the national minimum of $5.15 an hour. The company has also recently increased its health-care for employees on the bottom rungs of the corporate ladder.

—Wall Street Journal *editorial, December 3, 2005*

Who's Number One? The Customer! Always!" The last line of Wal-Mart's company cheer just about sums up the *Wall Street Journal* editors' benign view of the behemoth corporation. But a more honest answer would be Wal-Mart itself: not the customer, and surely not the worker.

The first retail corporation to top the Fortune 500, Wal-Mart trailed only Exxon-Mobil in total revenues last year. With 1.6 million workers, 1.3 million in the United States and 300,000 offshore, Wal-Mart is the largest private employer in the nation and the world's largest retailer.

Being number one has paid off handsomely for the family of Wal-Mart founder Sam Walton. The family's combined fortune is now an estimated $90 billion, equal to the net worth of Bill Gates and Warren Buffett combined.

But is what's good for the Walton family good for America? Should we believe the editors that Wal-Mart's unprecedented size and market power have redounded not only to the Walton family's benefit but to ours as well?

LOW WAGES AND MEAGER BENEFITS

Working for the world's largest employer sure hasn't paid off for Wal-Mart's employees. True, they have a job, and others without jobs line up to apply for theirs. But that says more about the sad state of today's labor market than the quality of Wal-Mart jobs. After all, less than half of Wal-Mart workers last a year, and turnover at the company is twice that at comparable retailers.

Why? Wal-Mart's oppressive working conditions surely have something to do with it. Wal-Mart has admitted to using minors to operate hazardous machinery, has been sued in six states for forcing employees to work off the books (i.e., unpaid) and without breaks, and is currently facing a suit brought by 1.6 million current and former female employees accusing Wal-Mart of gender discrimination. At the same time, Wal-Mart workers are paid less and receive fewer benefits than other retail workers.

Wal-Mart, according to its own reports, pays an average of $9.68 an hour. That is 12.4% below the average wage for retail workers even after adjusting for geography, according to a recent study by Arindrajit Dube and Steve Wertheim, economists at the University of California's Institute of Industrial Relations and long-time Wal-Mart researchers. Wal-Mart's wages are nearly 15% below the average wage of workers at large retailers and about 30% below the average wage of unionized grocery workers. The average U.S. wage is $17.80 an hour; Costco, a direct competitor of Wal-Mart's Sam's Club warehouse stores, pays an average wage of $16 an hour (see box on p. 32).

Wal-Mart may be improving its benefits, as the *Journal*'s editors report, but it needs to. Other retailers provide health care coverage to over 53% of their workers, while Wal-Mart covers just 48% of its workers. Costco, once again, does far better, covering 82% of its employees. Moreover, Wal-Mart's coverage is far less comprehensive than the plans offered by other large retailers. Dube reports that according to 2003 IRS data, Wal-Mart paid 59% of the health care costs of its workers and dependents, compared to the 77% of health care costs for individuals and 68% for families the average retailer picks up.

A recent internal Wal-Mart memo leaked to the *New York Times* confirmed the large gaps in Wal-Mart's health care coverage and exposed the high costs those gaps impose on government programs. According to the memo, "Five percent of our Associates are on Medicaid compared to an average for national employees of 4 percent. Twenty-seven percent of Associates' children are on such programs, compared to a national average of 22 percent. In total, 46 percent of Associates' children are either on Medicaid or are uninsured."

A considerably lower 29% of children of all large-retail workers are on Medicaid or are uninsured. Some 7% of the children of employees of large retailers go uninsured, compared to the 19% reported by Wal-Mart.

Wal-Mart's low wages drag down the wages of other retail workers and shutter downtown retail businesses. A 2005 study by David Neumark, Junfu Zhang, and Stephen Ciccarella, economists at the University of California at Irvine, found that Wal-Mart adversely affects employment and wages. Retail workers in a community with a Wal-Mart earned 3.5% less because Wal-Mart's low prices force other businesses to lower prices, and hence their wages, according to the Neumark study. The same study also found that Wal-Mart's presence reduces retail employment by 2% to 4%. While other studies have not found this negative employment effect, Dube's research also reports fewer retail jobs and lower wages for retail workers in metropolitan counties with a Wal-Mart. (Fully 85% of Wal-Mart stores are in metropolitan counties.) Dube figures that Wal-Mart's presence costs retail workers, at Wal-Mart and elsewhere, $4.7 billion a year in lost earnings.

In short, Wal-Mart's "everyday low prices" come at the expense of the compensation of Wal-Mart's own employees and lower wages and fewer jobs for retail workers in the surrounding area. That much remains true no matter what weight we assign to each of the measures that Wal-Mart uses to keep its costs down: a just-in-time inventory strategy, its ability to use its size to pressure suppliers for large discounts, a routinized work environment that requires minimal training, and meager wages and benefits.

HOW LOW ARE WAL-MART'S EVERYDAY LOW PRICES?

Even if one doesn't subscribe to the editors' position that it is consumers, not Wal-Mart, who cause job losses at downtown retailers, it is possible to argue that the benefit of Wal-Mart's low prices to consumers, especially low-income consumers, outweighs the cost endured by workers at Wal-Mart and other retailers. Jason Furman, New York University economist and director of economic policy for the 2004 Kerry-Edwards campaign, makes just such an argument. Wal-Mart's "staggering" low prices are 8% to 40% lower than people would pay elsewhere, according to Furman. He calculates that those low prices on average boost low-income families' buying power by 3% and more than offset the loss of earnings to retail workers. For Furman, that makes Wal-Mart "a progressive success story."

But exactly how much savings Wal-Mart affords consumers is far from clear. Estimates vary widely. At one extreme is a study Wal-Mart itself commissioned by Global Insight, an economic forecasting firm. Global Insight estimates

Wal-Mart created a stunning savings of $263 billion, or $2,329 per household, in 2004 alone.

At the other extreme, statisticians at the U.S. Bureau of Labor Statistics found no price savings at Wal-Mart. Relying on Consumer Price Index data, the BLS found that Wal-Mart's prices largely matched those of its rivals, and that instances of lower prices at Wal-Mart could be attributed to lower quality products.

Both studies, which rely on the Consumer Price Index and aggregate data, have their critics. Furman himself allows that the Global Insight study is "overly simplistic" and says he "doesn't place as much weight on that one." Jerry Hausman, the M.I.T. economist who has looked closely at Wal-Mart's grocery stores, maintains that the CPI data that the Bureau of Labor Statistics relies on systematically miss the savings offered by "supercenters" such as Wal-Mart. To show the difference between prices at Wal-Mart and at other grocers, Hausman, along with Ephraim Leibtag, USDA Economic Research Service economist, used supermarket scanner data to examine the purchasing patterns of a national sample of 61,500 consumers from 1988 to 2001. Hausman and Leibtag found that Wal-Mart offers many identical food items at an average price about 15%-25% lower than traditional supermarkets.

While Hausman and Leibtag report substantial savings from shopping at Wal-Mart, they fall far short of the savings alleged in the Global Insight study. The Hausman and Leibtag study suggests a savings of around $550 per household per year, or about $56 billion in 2004, not $263 billion. Still, that is considerably more than the $4.7 billion a year in lost earnings to retail workers that Dube attributes to Wal-Mart.

But if "Wal-Mart hurts wages, not so much in retail, but across the whole country," as economist Neumark told *Business Week*, then the savings to consumers from Wal-Mart's everyday low prices might not outweigh the lost wages to all workers. (Retail workers make up just 11.6% of U.S. employment.)

Nor do these findings say anything about the sweatshop conditions and wages in Wal-Mart's overseas subcontractors. One example: A recent Canadian Broadcasting Corporation investigative report found that workers in Bangladesh were being paid less than $50 a month (below even the United Nation's $2 a day measure of poverty) to make clothes for the Wal-Mart private label, Simply Basic. Those workers included 10- to 13-year-old children forced to work long hours in dimly lit and dirty conditions sewing "I Love My Wal-Mart" t-shirts.

MAKING WAL-MART DO BETTER

Nonetheless, as Arindrajit Dube points out, the relevant question is not whether Wal-Mart creates more savings for consumers than losses for workers, but whether the corporation can afford to pay better wages and benefits.

Dube reasons that if the true price gap between Wal-Mart

and its retail competitors is small, then Wal-Mart might not be in a position to do better—to make up its wage and benefit gap and still maintain its price advantage. But if Wal-Mart offers consumers only minor price savings, then its lower wages and benefits hardly constitute a progressive success story that's good for the nation.

If Wal-Mart's true price gap is large (say, the 25% price advantage estimated by Hausman), then Wal-Mart surely is in a position to do better. For instance, Dube calculates that closing Wal-Mart's 16% overall compensation gap with other large retailers would cost the company less than 2% of sales. Raising prices by two cents on the dollar to cover those increased compensation costs would be "eminently absorbable," according to Dube, without eating away much of the company's mind-boggling $10 billion profit (2004).

Measures that set standards to force Wal-Mart and all big-box retailers to pay decent wages and provide benefits are beginning to catch on. Chicago, New York City, and the state of Maryland have considered or passed laws that would require big-box retailers to pay a "living wage" or to spend a minimum amount per worker-hour for health benefits. The Republican board of Nassau County on Long Island passed an ordinance requiring that all big-box retailers pay $3 per hour toward health care. Wal-Mart's stake in making sure that such proposals don't become law or spread nationwide goes a long way toward explaining why 80% of Wal-Mart's $2 million in political contributions in 2004 went to Republicans.

Henry Ford sought to pay his workers enough so they could buy the cars they produced. Sam Walton sought to pay his workers so little that they could afford to shop nowhere else. And while what was good for the big automakers was probably never good for the nation, what is good for Wal-Mart, today's largest employer, is undoubtedly bad for economic justice.

Resources: "Is Wal-Mart Good for America?" *Wall Street Journal*, 12/3/05; "Gauging the Wal-Mart Effect," *WSJ*, 12/03/05; Arindrajit Dube & Steve Wertheim, "Wal-Mart and Job Quality—What Do We Know, and Should We Care?" 10/05; Jason Furman, "Wal-Mart: A Progressive Success Story," 10/05; Leo Hindery Jr., "Wal-Mart's Giant Sucking Sound," 10/05; A. Bernstein, "Some Uncomfortable Findings for Wal-Mart," *Business Week Online*, 10/26/05, and "Wal-Mart: A Case for the Defense, Sort of," *Business Week Online*, 11/7/05; Dube, Jacobs, and Wertheim, "The Impact of Wal-Mart Growth on Earnings throughout the Retail Sector in Urban and Rural Counties," *Institute of Industrial Relations Working Paper*, U-C Berkeley, 10/05; Dube, Jacobs, and Wertheim, "Internal Wal-Mart Memo Validates Findings of UC Berkeley Study," 11/26/05; Jerry Hausman and Ephraim Leibtag, "Consumer Benefits from Increased Competition in Shopping Outlets: Measuring the Effect of Wal-Mart," 10/05; Hausman and Leibtag, "CPI Bias from Supercenters: Does the BLS Know that Wal-Mart Exists?" *NBER Working Paper No. 10712*, 8/04; David Neumark, Junfu Zhang, and Stephen Ciccarella, "The Effects of Wal-Mart on Local Labor Markets," *NBER Working Paper No. 11782*, 11/05; Erin Johansson, "Wal-Mart: Rolling Back Workers' Wages, Rights, and the American Dream," (American Rights at Work, 11/05); Wal-Mart Watch, "Spin Cycle"; CBC News, "Wal-Mart to cut ties with Bangladesh factories using child labour," 11/30/05; National Labor Committee, "10 to 13-year-olds Sewing 'I Love My Wal-Mart' Shirts," 12/05; Global Insight. "The Economic Impact of Wal-Mart," 2005.

THE COSTCO ALTERNATIVE? WALL STREET PREFERS WAL-MART

BY ESTHER CERVANTES

Average Hourly Wage		Percentage of U.S. Workforce in Unions		Employees Covered by Company Health Insurance		Employees Who Leave After One Year	
						Sam's Club*	Costco
Wal-Mart	Costco	Wal-Mart	Costco	Wal-Mart	Costco		
$9.68	$16.00	0.0%	17.9%	48%	82%	21%	6%
* Sam's Club is the Wal-Mart unit that competes directly with Costco.							

In an April 2004 online commentary, *Business Week* praised Costco's business model but pointed out that Costco's wages cause Wall Street to worry that the company's "operating expenses could get out of hand." How does Costco compare to low-wage Wal-Mart on overhead expenses? At Costco, overhead is 9.8% of revenue; at Wal-Mart, it is 17%. Part of Costco's secret is that its better paid workers are also more efficient: Costco's operating profit per hourly employee is $13,647; each Wal-Mart employee only nets the company $11,039. Wal-Mart also spends more than Costco on hiring and training new employees: each one, according to Rutgers economist Eileen Appelbaum, costs the company $2,500 to $3,500. Appelbaum estimates that Wal-Mart's relatively high turnover costs the company $1.5 to $2 million per year.

Despite Costco's higher efficiency, Wall Street analysts like Deutsche Bank's Bill Dreher complain that "Costco's corporate philosophy is to put its customers first, then its employees, then its vendors, and finally its shareholders. Shareholders get the short end of the stick." Wall Street prefers Wal-Mart's philosopy: executives first, then shareholders, then customers, then vendors, and finally employees.

In 2004, Wal-Mart paid CEO Lee Scott $5.3 million, while a full-time employee making the average wage would have received $20,134. Costco's CEO Jim Senegal received $350,000, while a full-time average employee got $33,280. And *Business Week* intimates that the top job at Costco may be tougher than at Wal-Mart. "Management has to hustle to make the high-wage strategy work. It's constantly looking for ways to repackage goods into bulk items, which reduces labor, speeds up Costco's just-in-time inventory, and boosts sales per square foot. Costco is also savvier ... about catering to small shop owners and more affluent customers, who are more likely to buy in bulk and purchase higher-margin goods."

Costco's allegedly more affluent clientele may be another reason that its profit per employee is higher than Wal-Mart's and its overhead costs a lower percentage of revenue. However, Costco pays its employees enough that they could afford to shop there. As the *Business Week* commentary noted, "the low-wage approach cuts into consumer spending and, potentially, economic growth."

MEASURES OF POVERTY

BY ELLEN FRANK

Dear Dr. Dollar:

Can you explain how poverty is defined in government statistics? Is this a realistic definition?

—*Susan Balok, Savannah, Ga.*

Each February, the Census Bureau publishes the federal poverty thresholds—the income levels for different sized households below which a household is defined as living "in poverty." Each August, the bureau reports how many families, children, adults, and senior citizens fell below the poverty threshold in the prior year. As of 2005, the federal poverty thresholds were as follows:

Household Size	Federal Poverty Threshold
1 person	$ 10,210
2 people	$ 13,690
3 people	$ 17,170
4 people	$ 20,650
5 or more	Add $3,480 per person

Using these income levels, the Census Bureau reported that 12.6% percent of U.S. residents and 17.6% of U.S. children lived in poverty in 2005. Black Americans experience poverty at nearly double these rates: 24.9% of all Blacks and 33.5% of Black children live in households with incomes below the poverty line.

The poverty threshold concept was originally devised by Social Security analyst Mollie Orshansky in 1963. Orshansky estimated the cost of an "economy food plan" designed by the Department of Agriculture for "emergency use when funds are low." Working from 1955 data showing that families of three or more spent one-third of their income on food, Orshansky multiplied the food budget by three to calculate the poverty line. Since the early 1960s, the Census Bureau has simply recalculated Orshansky's original figures to account for inflation.

The poverty line is widely regarded as far too low for a household to survive on in most parts of the United States. For one thing, as antipoverty advocates point out, since 1955 the proportion of family budgets devoted to food has fallen from one-third to one-fifth. Families expend far more on nonfood necessities such as child care, health care, transportation, and utilities today than they did 50 years ago, for obvious reasons: mothers entering the work force, suburbanization and greater dependence on the auto, and

soaring health care costs, for example. Were Orshansky formulating a poverty threshold more recently, then, she would likely have multiplied a basic food budget by five rather than by three.

Furthermore, costs—particularly for housing and energy—vary widely across the country, so that an income that might be barely adequate in Mississippi is wholly inadequate in Massachusetts. Yet federal poverty figures make no adjustment for regional differences in costs.

A number of state-level organizations now publish their own estimates of what it takes to support a family in their area, in conjunction with the national training and advocacy group Wider Opportunities for Women. Using local data on housing costs, health care premiums, taxes, and child care costs as well as food, transportation and other necessities, these "self-sufficiency standards" estimate that a two-parent two-child family needs between $40,000 and $50,000 a year, depending on the region, to cover basic needs.

State and federal officials often implicitly recognize that official poverty thresholds are unrealistically low by setting income eligibility criteria for antipoverty programs higher than the poverty level. Households with incomes of 125%, 150%, or even 185% of the federal poverty line are eligible for a number of federal and state programs. In addition, the Census Bureau publishes figures on the number of households with incomes below 200% of the federal poverty line—a level many social scientists call "near poor" or "working poor."

Poverty calculations also have critics on the right. Conservative critics contend that the official poverty rate overstates poverty in the United States. While the Census Bureau's poverty-rate calculations include Social Security benefits, public assistance, unemployment and workers' compensation, SSI (disability) payments, and other forms of cash income, they exclude noncash benefits from state and federal antipoverty programs like Food Stamps, Medicaid, and housing subsidies. If the market value of these benefits were counted in family income, fewer families would count as "poor." On the other hand, by not counting such benefits, policymakers have a better grasp of the number of Americans in need of such programs.

Resources: For background information on poverty thresholds and poverty rate calculations, see <aspe.hhs.gov/poverty/papers/hptgssiv. htm>. Self-sufficiency standards for different states can be found at <www.sixstrategies.org/states/states.cfm>. In addition, the Economic Policy Institute has calculated family budgets for the 435 metropolitan areas: <www.epi.org/content.cfm/datazone_fambud_budget>.

ACCESS TO PAID SICK DAYS VASTLY UNEQUAL

BY ELISE GOULD

Just 57% of private-industry workers in the United States have access to paid sick leave; 43% have no paid sick days. When these workers get sick, they are forced either to stay home, without pay and, in many cases, with some risk of losing their job, or else to go to work.

What this number masks, however, is how vastly unequal access to paid sick leave is for workers at different wage levels. Workers at the bottom of the wage scale, those making less than $7.38 an hour, are five times less likely to have sick days than workers at the top of the scale, those making greater than $29.47 an hour. As the figure reveals, only 16% of low-wage workers have access to paid sick days, versus 79% of high-wage workers.

In recent months, legislation has been introduced that would level the playing field and provide much needed paid leave for all workers who are sick. Such legislation—as exists in other advanced economies—would not only give workers an important benefit. Universal paid sick leave could increase productivity by strengthening worker loyalty, decreasing turnover, and cutting down on the number of sick employees who show up to work and infect others.

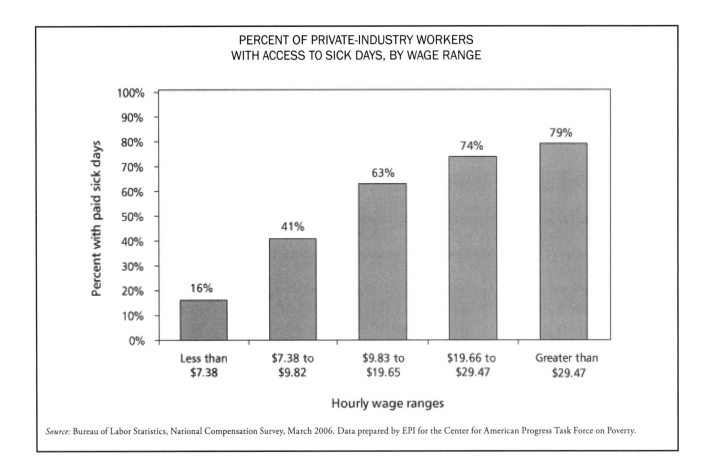

PERCENT OF PRIVATE-INDUSTRY WORKERS
WITH ACCESS TO SICK DAYS, BY WAGE RANGE

Source: Bureau of Labor Statistics, National Compensation Survey, March 2006. Data prepared by EPI for the Center for American Progress Task Force on Poverty.

EDUCATION AND INCARCERATION
LIMITED ACCESS TO EDUCATION FOR PEOPLE IN PRISON LEADS TO ECONOMIC EXCLUSION.

BY WILL GOLDBERG

It's tough to get an education in prison. People in prison tend to start with lower educational levels than the general population, and spending time behind bars generally makes matters worse. Because schooling is a major factor in earnings potential, the incarcerated are being left farther and farther behind.

In New York State, 48.6% of people in prison do not have a high school diploma, as compared to 27.8% of the general population. From 1980 to 2000, the number of incarcerated black and white high school dropouts both tripled, and other disparities are immense. The rate of imprisonment among black men with college degrees has fallen, while a full 60% of black high school dropouts are now prisoners or ex-cons by the time they reach their mid-30s.

Lower levels of education already translate directly into lower earnings over a lifetime, as a 2002 Census Bureau study found (see figure).

This is compounded by the worsened prospects for employment and greater obstacles to job success that result from incarceration.

The economic penalties of incarceration begin with the stigma of a criminal record and snowball from there. A study conducted by sociologist Devah Pager found that applicants are much less likely to receive callbacks from potential employers if their resumes indicate that they have been incarcerated. Furthermore, each month someone cannot work because of incarceration, he or she loses ground in experience and personal connections; research indicates that the people serving the longest sentences suffer the largest loss in earnings. Sociologist Bruce Western has found that important survival skills for prison—"suspicion of strangers, aggressiveness, withdrawal from social interaction"—are detrimental to success at work. Western also found that Latino workers' average hourly wages dropped from $12.30 to $10.31 following incarceration; black workers' from $10.25 to $9.25.

GED programs have helped offset some of these effects. The Florida Department of Corrections found that recidivism, or repeat criminal offending, was 8.7% lower among graduates of GED programs; the benefits of education extended to groups at greatest risk for recidivism, including prior recidivists, black prisoners, and young males. Florida calculated that its GED program prevented the recidivism of approximately 100 people in prison annually, saving that state about $1.9 million a year.

Post-secondary education has been shown to be even more effective than the GED in reducing recidivism. James Gilligan, a director of mental health for the Massachusetts prison system and a prison psychiatrist for 25 years, found that a program through which hundreds of people in prison earned a college degree was *100%* effective in preventing recidivism. The N.Y. Department of Correctional Services found that only 26.4% of people in prison who had earned a college degree re-offended, far lower than the recidivism rates of people in prison who had never enrolled in the program (47.4%) or those who had not completed it (44.6%).

William Weld, Republican governor of Massachusetts from 1991 to 1997, previously unaware that college classes were available in prisons, responded to this news by declaring that Massachusetts should not grant the "privilege" of a college education to the incarcerated, or poor people would end up committing crimes in hopes of getting free higher education. This came at the same time as Jesse Helms and other "tough on crime" senators began to imply that awarding Pell grants to people in prison cut into federal funding set aside for unincarcerated students' education, though this was not the case. In 1994, Congress passed a crime bill that eliminated prisoner eligibility for the grants, a considerable setback for people in prison wishing to pursue a college education.

The alarmingly disproportionate levels of incarceration among black and Latino populations, in combination with all of these obstacles to future financial success upon release, result in troubling economic disadvantages. Giving people in prison, and released from prison, the tools they need to support themselves and to contribute meaningfully is both economically advantageous and morally necessary. Annette Johnson, member of the Board of Directors of the Prisoners' Reading Encouragement Project, testified in 2000 that education was an important part of criminal justice reform that would "make it more effective—indeed, more cost-effective—in preventing crime and restoring convicted persons to the community with a positive attitude and

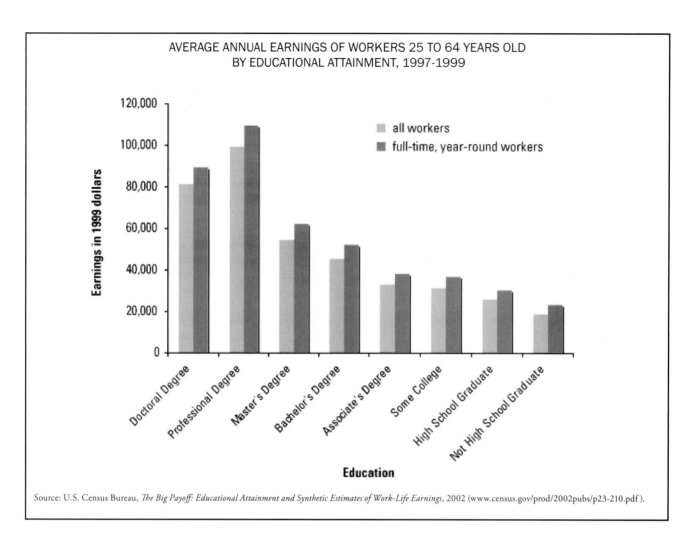

AVERAGE ANNUAL EARNINGS OF WORKERS 25 TO 64 YEARS OLD
BY EDUCATIONAL ATTAINMENT, 1997-1999

Earnings in 1999 dollars

- all workers
- full-time, year-round workers

Education

Source: U.S. Census Bureau, *The Big Payoff: Educational Attainment and Synthetic Estimates of Work-Life Earnings*, 2002 (www.census.gov/prod/2002pubs/p23-210.pdf).

positive skills that will allow them to contribute to the economy and reclaim a wholesome place in family life."

Apart from the obvious advantage that education offers people who have been in prison in finding employment after release, quality educational programs help people in prison to have a better mindset both during and after incarceration. And prison education programs save money: the reductions in crime, incarceration, and social welfare costs, plus increased payroll and income tax revenues from employing people who would otherwise likely be re-imprisoned, more than compensate for their costs.

With the expansion of distance-learning technologies, it is easier and cheaper than ever to provide education to people in prison. The missing ingredient is the political will to view incarceration not just as punishment but also as an opportunity for recovery.

Resources: Devah Pager, "The Mark of a Criminal Record," *American Journal of Sociology*, 108(5), 2003; Bruce Western, *Punishment and Inequality in America*, Russell Sage, 2006; Follow-Up Study of a Sample of Offenders Who Earned High School Equivalency Diplomas (GEDs) While Incarcerated in DOCS, www.prison-policy.org/scans/ny_ged.shtml; Annette Johnson, Testimony concerning the positive correlation between inmate education and reduction of recidivism, www.prisonreader.org/TestimonyEduc. html.

THE DEATH OF HORATIO ALGER

BY PAUL KRUGMAN

The other day I found myself reading a leftist rag that made outrageous claims about America. It said that we are becoming a society in which the poor tend to stay poor, no matter how hard they work; in which sons are much more likely to inherit the socioeconomic status of their fathers than they were a generation ago.

The name of the leftist rag? *Business Week*, which published an article titled "Waking Up From the American Dream." The article summarizes recent research showing that social mobility in the United States (which was never as high as legend had it) has declined considerably over the past few decades. If you put that research together with other research that shows a drastic increase in income and wealth inequality, you reach an uncomfortable conclusion: America looks more and more like a class-ridden society.

And guess what? Our political leaders are doing everything they can to fortify class inequality, while denouncing anyone who complains—or even points out what is happening—as a practitioner of "class warfare."

Let's talk first about the facts on income distribution. Thirty years ago we were a relatively middle-class nation. It had not always been thus: Gilded Age America was a highly unequal society, and it stayed that way through the 1920s. During the 1930s and '40s, however, America experienced what the economic historians Claudia Goldin and Robert Margo have dubbed the Great Compression: a drastic narrowing of income gaps, probably as a result of New Deal policies. And the new economic order persisted for more than a generation. Strong unions, taxes on inherited wealth, corporate profits and high incomes, and close public scrutiny of corporate management all helped to keep income gaps relatively small. The economy was hardly egalitarian, but a generation ago the gross inequalities of the 1920s seemed very distant.

Now they're back. According to estimates by the economists Thomas Piketty and Emmanuel Saez—confirmed by data from the Congressional Budget Office—between 1973 and 2000 the average real income of the bottom 90% of American taxpayers actually fell by 7%. Meanwhile, the income of the top 1% rose by 148%, the income of the top 0.1% rose by 343% and the income of the top 0.01% rose 599%. (Those numbers exclude capital gains, so they're not an artifact of the stock-market bubble.) The distribution of income in the United States has gone right back to Gilded Age levels of inequality.

Never mind, say the apologists, who churn out papers with titles like that of a 2001 Heritage Foundation piece, "Income Mobility and the Fallacy of Class-Warfare Arguments." America, they say, isn't a caste society—people with high incomes this year may have low incomes next year and vice versa, and the route to wealth is open to all. That's where those commies at *Business Week* come in. As they point out (and as economists and sociologists have been pointing out for some time), America actually is more of a caste society than we like to think. And the caste lines have lately become a lot more rigid.

The myth of income mobility has always exceeded the reality. As a general rule, once they've reached their 30s, people don't move up and down the income ladder very much. Conservatives often cite studies like a 1992 report by Glenn Hubbard, a Treasury official under the elder Bush who later became chief economic adviser to the younger Bush, that purport to show large numbers of Americans moving from low-wage to high-wage jobs during their working lives. But what these studies measure, as the economist Kevin Murphy put it, is mainly "the guy who works in the college bookstore and has a real job by his early 30s." Serious studies that exclude this sort of pseudo-mobility show that inequality in average incomes over long periods isn't much smaller than inequality in annual incomes.

It is true, however, that America was once a place of substantial intergenerational mobility—sons often did much better than their fathers. A classic 1978 survey found that among adult men whose fathers were in the bottom 25% of the population as ranked by social and economic status, 23% had made it into the top 25%. In other words, during the first thirty years or so after World War II, the American dream of upward mobility was a real experience for many people.

Now for the shocker: The *Business Week* piece cites a new survey of today's adult men, which finds that this number has dropped to only 10%. That is, over the past generation upward mobility has fallen drastically. Very few children of the lower class are making their way to even moderate affluence. This goes along with other studies indicating that rags-to-riches stories have become vanishingly rare, and that the correlation between fathers' and sons' incomes has risen in recent decades. In modern America, it seems, you're quite likely to stay in the social and economic class into which you were born.

Business Week attributes this to the "Wal-Martization" of the economy, the proliferation of dead-end, low-wage jobs and the disappearance of jobs that provide entry to the middle class. That's surely part of the explanation. But public policy plays a role—and will, if present trends continue, play an even bigger role in the future.

Put it this way: Suppose that you actually liked a caste

society, and you were seeking ways to use your control of the government to further entrench the advantages of the haves against the have-nots. What would you do?

One thing you would definitely do is get rid of the estate tax, so that large fortunes can be passed on to the next generation. More broadly, you would seek to reduce tax rates both on corporate profits and on unearned income such as dividends and capital gains, so that those with large accumulated or inherited wealth could more easily accumulate even more. You'd also try to create tax shelters mainly useful for the rich. And more broadly still, you'd try to reduce tax rates on people with high incomes, shifting the burden to the payroll tax and other revenue sources that bear most heavily on people with lower incomes.

Meanwhile, on the spending side, you'd cut back on healthcare for the poor, on the quality of public education and on state aid for higher education. This would make it more difficult for people with low incomes to climb out of their difficulties and acquire the education essential to upward mobility in the modern economy.

And just to close off as many routes to upward mobility as possible, you'd do everything possible to break the power of unions, and you'd privatize government functions so that well-paid civil servants could be replaced with poorly paid private employees.

IT ALL SOUNDS SORT OF FAMILIAR, DOESN'T IT?

Where is this taking us? Thomas Piketty, whose work with Saez has transformed our understanding of income distribution, warns that current policies will eventually create "a class of rentiers in the U.S., whereby a small group of wealthy but untalented children controls vast segments of the US economy and penniless, talented children simply can't compete." If he's right—and I fear that he is—we will end up suffering not only from injustice, but from a vast waste of human potential.

Goodbye, Horatio Alger. And goodbye, American Dream.

Reprinted with permission from the January 5, 2004 issue of *The Nation*. For subscription information call 1-800-333-8536. Portions of each week's *Nation* Magazine can be accessed at www.thenation.com

---

AMERICA'S GROWING FRINGE ECONOMY

BY HOWARD KARGER

Ron Cook is a department manager at a Wal-Mart store in Atlanta. Maria Guzman is an undocumented worker from Mexico; she lives in Houston with her three children and cleans office buildings at night. Marty Lawson works for a large Minneapolis corporation.* What do these three people have in common? They are all regular fringe economy customers.

The term "fringe economy" refers to a range of businesses that engage in financially predatory relationships with low-income or heavily indebted consumers by charging excessive interest rates, superhigh fees, or exorbitant prices for goods or services. Some examples of fringe economy businesses include payday lenders, pawnshops, check-cashers, tax refund lenders, rent-to-own stores, and "buy-here/pay-here" used car lots. The fringe economy also includes credit card companies that charge excessive late payment or over-the-credit-limit penalties; cell phone providers that force less credit worthy customers into expensive prepaid plans; and subprime mortgage lenders that gouge prospective homeowners.

The fringe economy is hardly new. Pawnshops and informal high-interest lenders have been around forever. What we see today, however, is a fringe-economy sector that is growing fast, taking advantage of the ever-larger part of the U.S. population whose economic lives are becoming less secure. Moreover, in an important sense the sector is no longer "fringe" at all: more and more, large mainstream financial corporations are behind the high-rate loans that anxious customers in run-down storefronts sign for on the dotted line.

---

*The names have been changed to protect the privacy of the individuals.

THE PAYDAY LENDING TRAP

Ron and Deanna Cook have two children and a combined family income of $48,000—more than twice the federal poverty line but still $10,000 below Georgia's median income. They are the working poor.

To make ends meet, the Cooks borrow from payday lenders. When Ron and Deanna borrow $300 for 14 days they pay $60 in interest—an annual interest rate of 520%! If they can't pay the full $360, they pay just the $60 interest fee and roll over the loan for another two weeks. The original $300 loan now costs $120 in interest for 30 days. If they roll over the loan for another two-week cycle, they pay $180 in interest on a $300 loan for 45 days. If the payday lender permits only four rollovers, the Cooks sometimes take out a payday loan from another lender to repay the original loan. This costly cycle can be devastating. The Center for Responsible Lending tells the tale of one borrower who entered into 35 back-to-back payday loans over 17 months, paying $1,254 in fees on a $300 loan.

The Cooks take out about ten payday loans a year, which is close to the national average for payday loan customers. Although the industry claims payday loans are intended only for emergencies, a 2003 study of Pima County, Ariz., by the Southwest Center for Economic Integrity found that 67% of borrowers used their loans for general non-emergency bills. The Center for Responsible Lending found that 66% of borrowers initiate five or more loans a year, and 31% take out twelve or more loans yearly. Over 90% of payday loans go to borrowers with five or more loans a year. Customers who take out 13 or more loans a year account for over half of payday lenders' total revenues.

THE UNBANKED

Maria Guzman and her family are part of the 10% of U.S. households—more than 12 million—that have no relationship with a bank, savings institution, credit union, or other mainstream financial service provider. Being "unbanked," the Guzmans turn to the fringe economy for check cashing, bill payment, short-term pawn or payday loans, furniture and appliance rentals, and a host of other financial services. In each case, they face high user fees and exorbitant interest rates.

Without credit, the Guzmans must buy a car either for cash or through a "buy-here/pay-here" (BHPH) used car lot. At a BHPH lot they are saddled with a 28% annual percentage rate (APR) on a high-mileage and grossly overpriced vehicle. They also pay weekly, and one missed payment means a repossession. Since the Guzmans have no checking account, they use a check-casher who charges 2.7% for cashing their monthly $1,500 in payroll checks, which costs them $40.50 a month or $486 a year.

Like many immigrants, the Guzmans send money to relatives in their home country. (Money transfers from the United States to Latin America are expected to reach $25 billion by 2010.) If they sent $500 to Mexico on June 26, 2006, using Western Union's "Money in Minutes," they would have paid a $32 transfer fee. Moreover, Western Union's exchange rate for the transaction was 11.12 pesos for the U.S. dollar, while the official exchange rate that day was 11.44. The difference on $500 was almost $14, which raised the real costs of the transaction to $46, or almost 10% of the transfer amount.

Without a checking account, the Guzmans turn to money orders or direct bill pay, both of which add to their financial expenses. For example, ACE Cash Express charges 79 cents per money order and $1 or more for each direct bill payment. If the Guzmans use money orders to pay six bills a month, the fees total nearly $57 a year; using direct bill pay, they would pay a minimum of $72 in fees per year.

All told, the Guzmans spend more than 10% of their income on alternative financial services, which is average for unbanked households. To paraphrase James Baldwin, it is expensive to be poor and unbanked in America.

The Cooks and the Guzmans, along with people like Marty Lawson caught in a cycle of credit card debt (see sidebar on next page), may not fully appreciate the economic entity they are dealing with. Far from a mom-and-pop industry, America's fringe economy is largely dominated by a handful of large, well-financed multinational corporations with strong ties to mainstream financial institutions. It is a comprehensive and fully formed parallel economy that addresses the financial needs of the poor and credit-challenged in the same way as the mainstream economy meets the needs of the middle class. The main difference is the exorbitant interest rates, high fees, and onerous loan terms that mark fringe economy transactions.

THE SCOPE OF THE FRINGE ECONOMY

The unassuming and often shoddy storefronts of the fringe economy mask the true scope of this economic sector. Check-cashers, payday lenders, pawnshops, and rent-to-own stores alone engaged in at least 280 million transactions in 2001, according to Fannie Mae Foundation estimates, generating about $78 billion in gross revenues. By comparison, in 2003 combined state and federal spending on the core U.S. social welfare programs—Temporary Aid to Needy Families (AFDC's replacement), Supplemental Security Income, Food Stamps, the Women, Infants and Children (WIC) food program, school lunch programs, and the U.S. Department of Housing and Urban Development's (HUD) low-income housing programs—totaled less than $125 billion. Revenues in the combined sectors of the fringe economy—including subprime home mortgages and refinancing, and used car sales—would inflate the $78 billion several times over and eclipse federal and state spending on the poor.

There can be no doubt that the scope of the fringe economy is enormous. The Community Financial Services Association of America claims that 15,000 payday lenders extend more than $25 billion in short-term loans to millions of households each year. According to Financial Service Cen-

CREDIT CARDS, COLLEGE STUDENTS, AND THE FRINGE ECONOMY

Marty Lawson is one of the growing legions of the credit poor. Although he earns $65,000 a year, his $50,000 credit card debt means that he can buy little more than the essentials. This cycle of debt began when Marty received his first credit card in college.

Credit cards are the norm for today's college students. A 2005 Nellie Mae report found that 55% of college students get their first credit card during their freshman year; by senior year, 91% have a credit card and 56% carry four or more cards.

College students are highly prized credit card customers because of their high future earnings and lifetime credit potential. To ensnare them, credit card companies actively solicit on campus through young recruiters who staff tables outside university bookstores and student centers. Students are baited with free t-shirts, frisbees, candy, music downloads, and other come-ons. Credit card solicitations are stuffed into new textbooks and sent to dormitories, electronic mailboxes, and bulletin boards. According to Junior Achievement, the typical college freshman gets about eight credit card offers in the first week of the fall semester. The aggressiveness of credit card recruiters has led several hundred colleges to ban them from campus.

Excited by his newfound financial independence, Marty overlooked the fine print explaining that cash advances carried a 20% or more APR. He also didn't realize how easily he could reach the credit limit, and the stiff penalties incurred for late payments and over-the-credit-limit transactions. About one-third of credit card company profits come from these and other penalties.

Marty applied for a second credit card after maxing out his first one. The credit line on his second card was exhausted in only eight months. Facing $4,000 in high-interest credit card bills, Marty left college to pay off his debts. He never returned. Dropping out to repay credit card debt is all too common, and according to former Indiana University administrator John Simpson, "We lose more students to credit card debt than academic failure." Not coincidentally, by graduation the average credit card debt for college seniors is almost $3,000. Credit card debt worsens the longer a student stays in school. A 2004 Nellie Mae survey found the average credit card debt for graduate students was a whopping $7,831, a 59% increase over 1998. Fifteen percent of graduate students carry credit card balances of $15,000 or more.

---

ters of America, 10,000 check-cashing stores process 180 million checks with a face value of $55 billion.

The sheer number of fringe economy storefronts is mind-boggling. For example, ACE Cash Express—only one of many such corporations—has 68 locations within 10 miles of my Houston zip code. Nationwide there are more than 33,000 check-cashing and payday loan stores, just two parts of the fringe economy. That's more than the all the McDonald's and Burger King restaurants and all the Target, J.C. Penney, and Wal-Mart retail stores in the United States combined.

ACE Cash Express is the nation's largest check-casher and exemplifies the growth and profitability of the fringe economy. In 1991 ACE had 181 stores; by 2005 it had 1,371 stores with 2,700 employees in 37 states and the District of Columbia. ACE's revenues totaled $141 million in 2000 and by 2005 rose to $268.6 million. In 2005 ACE:

- cashed 13.3 million checks worth approximately $5.3 billion (check cashing fees totaled $131.6 million);

- served more than 40 million customers (3.4 million a month or 11,000 an hour) and processed $10.3 billion in transactions;

- processed over 2 million loan transactions (worth $640 million) and generated interest income and fees of $91.8 million;

- added a total of 142 new locations (in 2006 the company anticipates adding 150 more);

- processed over $410 million in money transfers and 7.6 million money orders with a face value of $1.3 billion;

- processed over 7.8 million bill payment and debit card transactions, and sold approximately 172,000 prepaid debit cards.

Advance America is the nation's leading payday lender, with 2,640 stores in 36 states, more than 5,500 employees, and $630 million this year in revenues. Dollar Financial Corporation operates 1,106 stores in 17 states, Canada, and the United Kingdom. Their 2005 revenues were $321 million. Check-into-Cash has more than 700 stores; Check N' Go has 900 locations in 29 states. Almost all of these are publicly traded NASDAQ corporations.

There were 4,500 pawnshops in the United States in 1985; now there are almost 12,000, including outlets owned by five publicly traded chains. In 2005 the three big chains—Cash America International (a.k.a Cash America Pawn and SuperPawn), EZ Pawn, and First Cash—had combined annual revenues of nearly $1 billion. Cash America is the largest pawnshop chain, with 750 locations; the company also makes payday loans through its Cash America Payday Advance, Cashland, and Mr. Payroll stores. In 2005, Cash America's revenues totaled $594.3 million.

The Association of Progressive Rental Organizations claims that the $6.6 billion a year rent-to-own (RTO) industry serves 2.7 million households through 8,300 stores in 50 states. Many RTOs rent everything from furniture, electronics, major appliances, and computers to jewelry. Rent-A-Center is the largest RTO corporation in the world. In 2005 it employed 15,000 people; owned or operated 3,052 stores in the United States and Canada; and had revenues of $2.4 billion. Other leading RTO chains include Aaron Rents (with 1,255 stores across the United States and Canada and gross revenues of $1.1 billion in 2005) and RentWay (with 788 stores in 34 states and revenues of almost $516 million in 2005).

These corporations represent the tip of the iceberg. Low-income consumers spent $1.75 billion for tax refund loans in 2002. Many lost as much as 16% of their tax refunds because of expensive tax preparation fees and/or interest incurred in tax refund anticipation loans. The interest and fees on such loans can translate into triple-digit annualized interest rates, according to the Consumer Federation of America, which has also reported that 11 million tax filers received refund anticipation loans in 2000, almost half through H&R Block. According to a Brookings Institution report, the nation's largest tax preparers earned about $357 million from fringe economy "fast cash" products in 2001, more than double their earnings in 1998. All for essentially lending people their own money!

The fringe economy plays a big role in the housing market, where subprime home mortgages rose from 35,000 in 1994 to 332,000 in 2003, a 25% a year growth rate and a tenfold increase in just nine years. (A subprime loan is a loan extended to less creditworthy customers at a rate that is higher than the prime rate.) According to Edward Gramlich, former member of the Board of Governors of the Federal Reserve System, subprime mortgages accounted for almost $300 billion or 9% of all mortgages in 2003.

While the fringe economy squeezes its customers, it is generous to its CEOs. According to Forbes, salaries in many fringe economy corporations rival those in much larger companies. In 2004 Sterling Brinkley, chairman of EZ Corp, earned $1.26 million; ACE's CEO Jay Shipowitz received $2.1 million on top of $2.38 million in stocks; Jeffrey Weiss, Dollar Financial Group's CEO, earned $1.83 million; Mark Speese, Rent-A-Center's CEO, made $820,000 with total stock options of $10 million; and Cash America's CEO Daniel Feehan was paid almost $2.2 million in 2003 plus the $9 million he had in stock options.

Fringe-economy corporations argue that the high interest rates and fees they charge reflect the heightened risks of doing business with an economically unstable population. While fringe businesses have never made their pricing criteria public, some risks are clearly overstated. For example, ACE assesses the risk of each check-cashing transaction and reports losses of less than 1%. Since tax preparers file a borrower's taxes, they are reasonably assured that refund antic-

ipation loans will not exceed refunds. To further guarantee repayment, they often establish an escrow account into which the IRS directly deposits the tax refund check. Pawnshops lend only about 50% of a pawned item's value, which leaves them a large buffer if the pawn goes unclaimed (industry trade groups claim that 70% of customers do redeem their goods). The rent-to-own furniture and appliance industry charges well above the "street price" for furniture and appliances, which is more than enough to offset any losses. Payday lenders require a post-dated check or electronic debit to assure repayment. Payday loan losses are about 6% or less, according to the Center for Responsible Lending.

Much of the profit in the fringe economy comes from financing rather than the sale of a product. For example, if a used car lot buys a vehicle for $3,000 and sells it for $5,000 cash, their profit is $2,000. But if they finance that vehicle for two years at a 25% APR, the profit jumps to $3,242. This dynamic is true for virtually every sector of the fringe economy. A customer who pays off a loan or purchases a good or service outright is much less profitable for fringe economy businesses than customers who maintain an ongoing financial relationship with the business. In that sense, profit in the fringe economy lies with keeping customers continually enmeshed in an expensive web of debt.

FUNDING AND EXPORTING AMERICA'S FRINGE ECONOMY

Fringe economy corporations require large amounts of capital to fund their phenomenal growth, and mainstream financial institutions have stepped up to the plate. ACE Cash Express has a relationship with a group of banks including Wells Fargo, JP Morgan Chase Bank, and JP Morgan Securities to provide capital for acquisitions and other activities. Advance America has relationships with Morgan Stanley, Banc of America Securities LLC, Wachovia Capital Markets, and Wells Fargo Securities, to name a few. Similar banking relationships exist throughout the fringe economy.

The fringe economy is no longer solely a U.S. phenomenon. In 2003 the HSBC Group purchased Household International (and its subsidiary Beneficial Finance) for $13 billion. Headquartered in London, HSBC is the world's second largest bank and serves more than 90 million customers in 80 countries. Household International is a U.S.-based consumer finance company with 53 million customers and more than 1,300 branches in 45 states. It is also a predatory lender. In 2002, a $484 million settlement was reached between Household and all 50 states and the District of Columbia. In effect, Household acknowledged it had duped tens of thousands of low-income home buyers into loans with unnecessary hidden costs. In 2003, another $100 million settlement was reached based on Household's abusive mortgage lending practices.

A GLOSSARY OF THE FRINGE ECONOMY

Payday loans are small, short-term loans, usually of no more than $1,500, to cover expenses until the borrower's next payday. These loans come with extremely high interests rates, commonly equivalent to 300% APR. The Center for Responsible Lending conservatively estimates that predatory payday lending practices cost American families $3.4 billion annually.

Refund anticipation loans (RALs), provided by outlets of such firms as H&R Block, Western Union, and Liberty Tax Service, are short-term loans, often with high interest rates or fees, secured by an expected tax refund. Interest rates can reach over 700% APR-equivalent.

Check cashing stores (ACE Cash Express is the biggest chain) provide services for people who don't have checking accounts. These stores are most often located in low-income neighborhoods and cash checks for a fee, which can vary greatly but is typically far higher than commercial banks charge for the same service. Check cashing fees have steadily increased over the past ten years.

Money Transfer companies (outlets of such companies as Western Union, Moneygram, and Xoom) allow people to make direct bill payments and send money either to a person or bank account for a fee, typically 10% of the amount being sent, not including the exchange rate loss for money sent internationally. the total cost can reach up to 25% of the amount sent.

Pawnshops give loans while holding objects of value as collateral. The pawnbroker returns the object when the loan is repaid, usually at a high interest rates. If the borrower doesn't repay the loan within a specified period, the pawnbroker sells the item. For example, the interest charge on a 30-day loan of $10 could be $2.20, equivalent to a 264% APR. Most pawnshops are individually owned but regional chains are now appearing.

Rent-to-own (RTO) stores—two leading chains are Rent-A-Center and Aaron Rents—rent furniture, electronics, and other consumer goods short-term or long-term. The consumer can eventually own the item after paying many times the standard retail price through weekly rental payments with an extremely high interest rate, commonly around 300% APR. If the consumer misses a payment, the item is repossessed.

Buy here/pay here (BHPH) car lots offer car loans on used cars on-site, with interest rates much higher than auto loans issued by commercial banks. Customers are often saddled with high-interest loans for high-mileage, overpriced vehicles. If a customer misses one payment, the car is repossessed. The largest BHPH company is the J.D. Byrider franchise, with 124 dealerships throughout the country.

—Barbara Sternal

HSBC plans to export Household's operations to Poland, China, Mexico, Britain, France, India, and Brazil, for starters. One shudders to think how the fringe economy will develop in nations with even fewer regulatory safeguards than the United States. Presumably, HSBC also believes that predatory lending will not tarnish the reputation of the seven British lords and one baroness who sit on its 20-member board of directors.

WHAT CAN BE DONE?

The fringe economy is one of the few venues that credit-challenged or low-income families can turn to for financial help. This is especially true for those facing a penurious welfare system with a lifetime benefit cap and few mechanisms for emergency assistance. In that sense, enforcing strident usury and banking laws to curb the fringe economy while providing no legal and accessible alternatives would hurt the very people such laws are intended to help by driving these transactions into a criminal underground. Instead of ending up in court, non-paying debtors would wind up in the hospital. Simply outlawing a demand-driven industry is rarely successful.

One strategy to limit the growth of the fringe economy is to develop more community-based lending institutions modeled on the Grameen Bank or on local cooperatives. Although community banks might charge a higher interest rate than commercial banks charge prime rate customers, the rates would still be significantly lower than in the existing fringe sector.

Another policy option is to make work pay, or at least make it pay better. In other words, we need to increase the minimum wage and the salaries of the lower middle class and working poor. One reason for the rapid growth of the fringe economy is the growing gap between low and stagnant wages and higher prices, especially for necessities like housing, health care, pharmaceuticals, and energy.

Stricter usury laws, better enforcement of existing banking regulations, and a more active federal regulatory system to protect low-income consumers can all play a role in taming the fringe economy. Concurrently, federal and state governments can promote the growth of non-predatory community banking institutions. In addition, commercial banks can provide low-income communities with accessible and inexpensive banking services. As the "DrillDown" studies conducted in recent years by the Washington, D.C., non-profit Social Compact suggest, low-income communities contain more income and resources than one might think. If fringe businesses can make billions in low-income neighborhoods, less predatory economic institutions should be able to profit there too. Lastly, low and stagnant wages make it difficult, if not impossible, for the working poor to make ends meet without resorting to debt. A significant increase in wages would likely result in a significant decline in the fringe economy. In the end, several concerted strategies will be required to restrain this growing and out-of-control economic beast.

Resources: "2003 Credit Card Usage Analysis" (2004) and "Undergraduate Students and Credit Cards in 2004" (2005) (Nellie Mae); Alan Berube, Anne Kim, Benjamin Forman, and Megan Burns, "The Price of Paying Taxes: How Tax Preparation and Refund Loan Fees Erode the Benefits of the EITC" (Brookings Institution and Progressive Policy Institute, May 2002); James H. Carr and Jenny Shuetz, "Financial Services in Distressed Communities: Framing the Issue, Finding Solutions," *Financial Services in Distressed Communities: Issues and Answers* (2001, Fannie Mae Foundation); "Making the Case for Financial Literacy: A Collection of Current Statistics Regarding Youth and Money" (Junior Achievement); Amanda Sapir and Karen Uhlich, "Pay Day Lending in Pima County Arizona" (Southwest Center for Economic Integrity, 2003); Keith Urnst, John Farris, and Uriah King, "Quantifying the Economic Cost of Predatory Payday Lending" (Center for Responsible Lending, 2004).Organizations working on these issues include U.S. Public Interest Research Group, www.uspirg.org; Association of Community Organizations for Reform Now (ACORN), www.acorn.org; Coalition for Responsible Credit Practices, www.responsible-credit.net; Community Financial Services Association of America, www.cfsa.net; Consumer Federation of America, www.consumerfed.org; Harvard University, Joint Center for Housing Studies, www.jchs.harvard.edu; National Consumer Law Center, www.consumerlaw.org.

GEESE, GOLDEN EGGS, AND TRAPS
WHY INEQUALITY IS BAD FOR THE ECONOMY

BY CHRIS TILLY

Whenever progressives propose ways to redistribute wealth from the rich to those with low and moderate incomes, conservative politicians and economists accuse them of trying to kill the goose that lays the golden egg. The advocates of unfettered capitalism proclaim that inequality is good for the economy because it promotes economic growth. Unequal incomes, they say, provide the incentives necessary to guide productive economic decisions by businesses and individuals. Try to reduce inequality, and you'll sap growth. Furthermore, the conservatives argue, growth actually promotes equality by boosting the have-nots more than the haves. So instead of fiddling with who gets how much, the best way to help those at the bottom is to pump up growth.

But these conservative prescriptions are absolutely, dangerously wrong. Instead of the goose-killer, equality turns out to be the goose. Inequality stifles growth; equality gooses it up. Moreover, economic expansion does not necessarily promote equality—instead, it is the types of jobs and the rules of the economic game that matter most.

INEQUALITY: GOOSE OR GOOSE-KILLER?

The conservative argument may be wrong, but it's straightforward. Inequality is good for the economy, conservatives say, because it provides the right incentives for innovation and economic growth. First of all, people will only have the motivation to work hard, innovate, and invest wisely if the economic system rewards them for good economic choices and penalizes bad ones. Robin Hood-style policies that collect from the wealthy and help those who are worse off violate this principle. They reduce the payoff to smart decisions and lessen the sting of dumb ones. The result: people and companies are bound to make less efficient decisions. "We must allow [individuals] to fail, as well as succeed, and we must replace the nanny state with a regime of self-reliance and self-respect," writes conservative lawyer Stephen Kinsella in The Freeman: Ideas on Liberty (not clear how the free woman fits in). To prove their point, conservatives point to the former state socialist countries, whose economies had become stagnant and inefficient by the time they fell at the end of the 1980s.

If you don't buy this incentive story, there's always the well-worn trickle-down theory. To grow, the economy needs productive investments: new offices, factories, computers, and machines. To finance such investments takes a pool of savings. The rich save a larger fraction of their incomes than those less well-off. So to spur growth, give more to the well-heeled (or at least take less away from them in the form of taxes), and give less to the down-and-out. The rich will save their money and then invest it, promoting growth that's good for everyone.

Unfortunately for trickle-down, the brilliant economist John Maynard Keynes debunked the theory in his *General Theory of Employment, Interest, and Money* in 1936. Keynes, whose precepts guided liberal U.S. economic policy from the 1940s through the 1970s, agreed that investments must be financed out of savings. But he showed that most often it's changes in investment that drive savings, rather than the other way around. When businesses are optimistic about the future and invest in building and retooling, the economy booms, all of us make more money, and we put some of it in banks, 401(k)s, stocks, and so on. That is, saving grows to match investment. When companies are glum, the process runs in reverse, and savings shrink to equal investment. This leads to the "paradox of thrift": if people try to save too much, businesses will see less consumer spending, will invest less, and total savings will end up diminishing rather than growing as the economy spirals downward. A number of Keynes's followers added the next logical step: shifting money from the high-saving rich to the high-spending rest of us, and not the other way around, will spur investment and growth.

Of the two conservative arguments in favor of inequality, the incentive argument is a little weightier. Keynes himself agreed that people needed financial consequences to steer their actions, but questioned whether the differences in payoffs needed to be so huge. Certainly state socialist countries' attempts to replace material incentives with moral exhortation have often fallen short. In 1970, the Cuban government launched the Gran Zafra (Great Harvest), an attempt to reap 10 million tons of sugar cane with (strongly encouraged) volunteer labor. Originally inspired by Che Guevara's ideal of the New Socialist Man (not clear how the New Socialist Woman fit in), the effort ended with Fidel Castro tearfully apologizing to the Cuban people in a nationally broadcast speech for letting wishful thinking guide economic policy.

But before conceding this point to the conservatives, let's look at the evidence about the connection between equality and growth. Economists William Easterly of New York University and Gary Fields of Cornell University have recently summarized this evidence:

- Countries, and regions within countries, with more equal incomes grow faster. (These growth figures do not include environmental destruction or improvement. If they knocked off points for environmental destruction and added points for environmental improvement, the correlation between equality and growth would be even stronger, since desperation drives poor people to adopt environmentally destructive practices such as rapid deforestation.)
- Countries with more equally distributed land grow faster.
- Somewhat disturbingly, more ethnically homogeneous countries and regions grow faster—presumably because there are fewer ethnically based inequalities.

In addition, more worker rights are associated with higher rates of economic growth, according to Josh Bivens and Christian Weller, economists at two Washington think tanks, the Economic Policy Institute and the Center for American Progress.

These patterns recommend a second look at the incentive question. In fact, more equality can actually *strengthen* incentives and opportunities to produce.

EQUALITY AS THE GOOSE

Equality can boost growth in several ways. Perhaps the simplest is that study after study has shown that farmland is more productive when cultivated in small plots. So organizations promoting more equal distribution of land, like Brazil's Landless Workers' Movement, are not just helping the landless poor—they're contributing to agricultural productivity!

Another reason for the link between equality and growth is what Easterly calls "match effects," which have been highlighted in research by Stanford's Paul Roemer and others in recent years. One example of a match effect is the fact that well-educated people are most productive when working with others who have lots of schooling. Likewise, people working with computers are more productive when many others have computers (so that, for example, e-mail communication is widespread, and know-how about computer repair and software is easy to come by). In very unequal societies, highly educated, computer-using elites are surrounded by majorities with little education and no computer access, dragging down their productivity. This decreases young people's incentive to get more education and businesses' incentive to invest in computers, since the payoff will be smaller.

Match effects can even matter at the level of a metropolitan area. Urban economist Larry Ledebur looked at income and employment growth in 85 U.S. cities and their neighboring suburbs. He found that where the income gap between those in the suburbs and those in the city was largest, income and job growth was slower for everyone.

"Pressure effects" also help explain why equality sparks growth. Policies that close off the low-road strategy of exploiting poor and working people create pressure effects, driving economic elites to search for investment opportunities that pay off by boosting productivity rather than squeezing the have-nots harder. For example, where workers have more rights, they will place greater demands on businesses. Business owners will respond by trying to increase productivity, both to remain profitable even after paying higher wages, and to find ways to produce with fewer workers. The CIO union drives in U.S. mass production industries in the 1930s and 1940s provide much of the explanation for the superb productivity growth of the 1950s and 1960s. (The absence of pressure effects may help explain why many past and present state socialist countries have seen slow growth, since they tend to offer numerous protections for workers but no right to organize independent unions.) Similarly, if a government buys out large land-holdings in order to break them up, wealthy families who simply kept their fortunes tied up in land for generations will look for new, productive investments. Industrialization in Asian "tigers" South Korea and Taiwan took off in the 1950s on the wings of funds freed up in exactly this way.

INEQUALITY, CONFLICT, AND GROWTH

Inequality hinders growth in another important way: it fuels social conflict. Stark inequality in countries such as Bolivia and Haiti has led to chronic conflict that hobbles economic growth. Moreover, inequality ties up resources in unproductive uses such as paying for large numbers of police and security guards—attempts to prevent individuals from redistributing resources through theft.

Ethnic variety is connected to slower growth because, on the average, more ethnically diverse countries are also more likely to be ethnically divided. In other words, the problem isn't ethnic variety itself, but racism and ethnic conflict that can exist among diverse populations. In nations like Guatemala, Congo, and Nigeria, ethnic strife has crippled growth—a problem alien to ethnically uniform Japan and South Korea. The reasons are similar to some of the reasons that large class divides hurt growth. Where ethnic divisions (which can take tribal, language, religious, racial, or regional forms) loom large, dominant ethnic groups seek to use government power to better themselves at the expense of other groups, rather than making broad-based investments in education and infrastructure. This can involve keeping down the underdogs—slower growth in the U.S. South for much of the country's history was linked to the Southern system of white supremacy. Or it can involve seizing the surplus of ethnic groups perceived as better off—in the extreme, Nazi Germany's expropriation and genocide of the Jews, who often held professional and commercial jobs.

Of course, the solution to such divisions is not "ethnic cleansing" so that each country has only one ethnic group—in addition to being morally abhorrent, this is simply impossible in a world with 191 countries and 5,000 ethnic groups. Rather, the solution is to diminish ethnic inequalities. Once the 1964 Civil Rights Act forced the South to drop racist laws, the New South's economic growth spurt began. Easterly reports that in countries with strong rule of law, professional bureaucracies, protection of contracts, and freedom from expropriation—all rules that make it harder for one ethnic group to economically oppress another—ethnic diversity has no negative impact on growth.

If more equality leads to faster growth so everybody benefits, why do the rich typically resist redistribution? Looking at the ways that equity seeds growth helps us understand why. The importance of pressure effects tells us that the wealthy often don't think about more productive ways to invest or reorganize their businesses until they are forced to. But also, if a country becomes very unequal, it can get stuck in an "inequality trap." Any redistribution involves a trade-off for the rich. They lose by giving up part of their wealth, but they gain a share in increased economic growth. The bigger the disparity between the rich and the rest, the more the rich have to lose, and the less likely that the equal share of boosted growth they'll get will make up for their loss. Once the gap goes beyond a certain point, the wealthy have a strong incentive to restrict democracy, and to block spending on education which might lead the poor to challenge economic injustice—making reform that much harder.

DOES ECONOMIC GROWTH REDUCE INEQUALITY?

If inequality isn't actually good for the economy, what about the second part of the conservatives' argument—that growth itself promotes equality? According to the conservatives, those who care about equality should simply pursue growth and wait for equality to follow.

"A rising tide lifts all boats," President John F. Kennedy famously declared. But he said nothing about which boats will rise fastest when the economic tide comes in. Growth does typically reduce poverty, according to studies reviewed by economist Gary Fields, though some "boats"—especially families with strong barriers to participating in the labor force—stay "stuck in the mud." But inequality can increase at the same time that poverty falls, if the rich gain even faster than the poor do. True, sustained periods of low unemployment, like that in the late 1990s United States, do tend to raise wages at the bottom even faster than salaries at the top. But growth after the recessions of 1991 and 2001 began with years of "jobless recoveries"—growth with inequality.

For decades the prevailing view about growth and inequality within countries was that expressed by Simon Kuznets in his 1955 presidential address to the American Economic Association. Kuznets argued that as countries grew, inequality would first increase, then decrease. The reason is that people will gradually move from the low-income agricultural sector to higher-income industrial jobs—with inequality peaking when the workforce is equally divided between low- and high-income sectors. For mature industrial economies, Kuznets's proposition counsels focusing on growth, assuming that it will bring equity. In developing countries, it calls for enduring current inequality for the sake of future equity and prosperity.

But economic growth doesn't automatically fuel equality. In 1998, economists Klaus Deininger and Lyn Squire traced inequality and growth over time in 48 countries. Five followed the Kuznets pattern, four followed the reverse pattern (decreasing inequality followed by an increase), and the rest showed no systematic pattern. In the United States, for example:

- incomes became more equal during the 1930s through 1940s New Deal period (a time that included economic decline followed by growth)
- from the 1950s through the 1970s, income gaps lessened during booms and expanded during slumps
- from the late 1970s forward, income inequality worsened fairly consistently, whether the economy was stagnating or growing.

The reasons are not hard to guess. The New Deal introduced widespread unionization, a minimum wage, social security, unemployment insurance, and welfare. Since the late 1970s, unions have declined, the inflation-adjusted value of the minimum wage has fallen, and the social safety net has been shredded. In the United States, as elsewhere, growth only promotes equality if policies and institutions to support equity are in place.

TRAPPED?

Let's revisit the idea of an inequality trap. The notion is that as the gap between the rich and everybody else grows wider, the wealthy become more willing to give up overall growth in return for the larger share they're getting for themselves. The "haves" back policies to control the "have-nots," instead of devoting social resources to educating the poor so they'll be more productive.

Sound familiar? It should. After two decades of widening inequality, the last few years have brought us massive tax cuts that primarily benefit the wealthiest, at the expense of investment in infrastructure and the education, child care, and income supports that would help raise less well-off kids to be productive adults. Federal and state governments have cranked up expenditures on prisons, police, and "homeland security," and Republican campaign organizations have devoted major resources to keeping blacks and the poor away from the polls. If the economic patterns of the past are any indication, we're going to pay for these policies in slower growth and stagnation unless we can find our way out of this inequality trap.

TRANSFORMING THE ENGINES OF INEQUALITY

BY WILLIAM GREIDER

American politics has always involved a struggle between "organized money" and "organized people." It's a neglected truth that has resurfaced with ironic vengeance in our own time—ironic because the 20th century produced so much progress toward political equality among citizens, and because the emergence of a prosperous and well-educated middle class was expected to neutralize the overbearing political power of concentrated wealth. Instead, Americans are reminded, almost any time they read a newspaper, that the rich do indeed get richer and that our political system is, as Greg Palast put it, "the best democracy money can buy."

What should we make of this retrogressive turn—a nation of considerable abundance still ruled by gilded-age privilege? A cynic would say it was ever thus, end of story. Political commentators argue it's a sign of the country's maturation that its citizens now accept what they once resisted—gross and growing inequalities of wealth. And many economists simply avert their gaze from the troubling consequences of maldistribution for economic progress and the well-being of society.

I stake out a contrary claim: The United States remains an unfinished nation—stunted in its proclaimed values—so long as it fails to confront the enduring contradictions between wealth and democracy. That is not a utopian lament for radical change, but simply an observation of what our own era has taught us.

Inequality retains its crippling force over society and politics and the lives of citizens, despite the broader distribution of material comforts. We are not the nation of 80 or 100 years ago, when most Americans struggled in very modest circumstances, often severe deprivation. Yet, despite the nation's wealth (perhaps also because of it), the influence of concentrated economic power has grown stronger and more intimate in our lives. Today the social contract is determined more by the needs and demands of corporations and finance than by government or the consensual will of the people.

The federal government and several generations of liberal and labor reformers did achieve great, life-improving gains during the last century. But those reforms and redistributive programs did not succeed in altering the root sources of economic inequality, much less taming them. On the contrary, the U.S. economic system recreates and even expands the maldistribution of incomes and wealth in each new generation.

The root sources of inequality are located within the institutions of advanced capitalism—in the corporation and financial system—with their narrow operating values and the peculiar arrangements that consign enormous decision-making power to a remarkably small number of people. The problem of inequality is essentially a problem of malformed power relationships: Advanced capitalism deprives most people of voice and influence, while it concentrates top-down authority among the insiders of finance and business. Ameliorative interventions by government (for example, through regulation, taxation, and reform) have never succeeded in overcoming the tendency within capitalism toward increased concentrations of economic power.

The drive for greater equality must involve governmental actions, of course, but it cannot succeed unless it also confronts the engines of inequality within the private realm and forces deep changes in how American capitalism functions. The challenge is nothing less than to rearrange power relationships within the corporation and finance capital.

Who has the power to restructure capitalist institutions? In my view, ordinary people do—at least potentially—acting collectively as workers, investors, consumers, managers or owners and, above all, as citizens, to force change. Many are, in small and different ways, already at work on the task of reinventing capitalism.

TRANSFORMING THE WORKPLACE

The workplace is perhaps the most effective engine of inequality, since it teaches citizens resignation and subservience, while it also maldistributes the returns of enterprise. For most Americans, the employment system functions on the archaic terms of the master-servant relationship inherited from feudalism. The feudal lord commanded the lives and livelihoods of serfs on his land and expelled those who disobeyed. The corporate employer has remarkably similar powers, restrained only by the limited prohibitions in law or perhaps by the terms of a union contract. Elaine Bernard, director of Harvard's trade union studies program, described the blunt reality:

As power is presently distributed, workplaces are factories of authoritarianism polluting our democracy. Citizens cannot spend eight hours a day obeying orders and being shut out of important decisions affecting them, and then be expected to engage in a robust, critical dialogue about the structure of our society.

Where did people learn to accept their powerlessness? They learned it at work. Nor is this stunted condition confined to assembly lines and working-class occupations. The degradation of work now extends very far up the job ladder, including even well-educated professionals whose expert judgments have been usurped by distant management systems.

In most firms, only the insiders at the top of a very steep command-and-control pyramid will determine how the economic returns are distributed among the participants. Not surprisingly, the executives value their own work quite generously while regarding most of the employees below as mere commodities or easily interchangeable parts. More importantly, these insiders will harvest the new wealth generated by an enterprise, while most workers will not. In the long run, this arrangement of power guarantees the permanence of wealth inequalities.

Joseph Cabral, CEO of Chatsworth Products Inc., a successful employee-owned computer systems manufacturer in California, is an accountant, not a political philosopher, but he understands the wealth effects of closely held control in private businesses. "The wealth that's created ends up in too few hands," he said. "The entrepreneur who's fortunate enough to be there at the start ends up really receiving a disproportionate amount of wealth. And the working folks who enabled that success to take place share in little of that wealth. At some point, capitalism is going to burst because we haven't done right for the folks who have actually created that wealth."

But there are other, more democratic, ways to structure the work environment. At Chatsworth, where the workers collectively purchased the enterprise, "Everyone is sharing in the wealth they're creating. … We're not just doing this for some outside shareholder. We're doing it because we are the shareholders."

Employee ownership, worker-management, and other systems of worker self-organization provide a plausible route toward reforming workplace power relations and spreading financial wealth among the many instead of the few.

TRANSFORMING FINANCE CAPITAL

The top-down structure of how Wall Street manages "other people's money" ensures the maldistribution of financial returns. As wealthy people know, those who bring major money to the table are given direct influence over their investments and a greater return on their risk-taking. The rank-and-file investors—because their savings are modest and they lack trustworthy intermediaries to speak for them—are regarded as passive and uninformed, treated more or less like "widows and orphans," and blocked from exerting any influence over how their wealth is invested. To put the point more crudely, the stock market is a casino, and the herd of hapless investors is always the "mark."

Nevertheless, finance capital is, I predict, the realm of capitalism most vulnerable to reform pressures. That's mainly because it operates with other people's money, and most of that money belongs not to the wealthiest families but to the broad ranks of ordinary working people. A historic shift in the center of gravity has occurred in U.S. finance over the past decade: Fiduciary institutions like pension funds and mutual funds have eclipsed individual wealth as the largest owner of financial assets. Their collectivized assets now include 60% of the largest 1,000 corporations. Because these funds invest across the broad stock market, they literally own the economy.

Public pension funds, union-managed pension funds, and shareholder activists are already working to forge an engaged voice for the individuals whose wealth is in play, and to force the fiduciary institutions to take responsibility for the social and environmental effects of how these trillions in savings are invested. The collapse of the stock-market bubble and subsequent corporate scandals have accelerated these reform efforts.

Some of the largest public-employee pension funds including the California Public Employees' Retirement System and the New York State public employees fund, joined by state officials who sit on supervisory boards, are aggressively leading the fight for corporate-governance reform and for stricter social accountability on urgent matters like workers' rights and global warming. The labor movement is organizing proxy battles to press for corporate reforms at individual companies including the Disney Corporation and Royal Dutch Shell, while the AFL's Office of Investment won a victory for mutual-fund investors in early 2003 when it persuaded the Securities and Exchange Commission to require mutual funds to disclose their proxy votes in corporate-governance shareholder fights. (The mutual fund industry is working to resist the measure, and for good reason. Investment firms regularly vote against the interests of their own rank-and-file investors in order to curry favor with the corporations that hire them to manage corporate-run pension funds and 401(k) plans.)

The major banks and brokerages cannot brush aside these new critics as easily as corporate directors often do. Wall Street will respond to fiduciary concerns because it must. It needs the rank-and-file's capital to operate. When six or seven major funds, collectively holding nearly $1 trillion, speak to Wall Street, things do change. Their unspoken threat to scorn companies or financial firms that ignore

THE DRIVE FOR GREATER EQUALITY MUST INVOLVE GOVERNMENTAL ACTIONS, BUT IT CANNOT SUCCEED UNLESS IT ALSO CONFRONTS THE ENGINES OF INEQUALITY WITHIN THE PRIVATE REALM.

larger social obligations and shift their money elsewhere sends broad shockwaves across both financial markets and corporate boardrooms.

The more profound tasks are to challenge fraudulent economic valuations (think Enron) and to account for (and internalize) the true costs of products and production processes. Both steps would refocus capital investing toward creating real, long-term value and away from the transient thrill of quarterly returns. The fiduciary funds have the potential power to enforce this new economic perspective, though it is not yet widely understood or accepted by them. As universal owners of the economy, their own portfolios are the losers when individual corporations throw off externalities in order to boost their bottom lines. The costs will be borne by every other firm, by the economy as a whole, or by taxpayers who have to clean up the mess. The compelling logic of this new economic argument is this: what is bad for society cannot be good for future retirees or for their communities and their families.

Citizens, in other words, have more power than they imagine. If they assert influence over these intermediaries, they have the power to punish rogue corporations for antisocial behavior and block the low-road practices that have become so popular in business circles. In coalition with organized labor, environmentalists, and other engaged citizens, they have the capacity to design—and enforce—a new social contract that encourages, among other things, participatory management systems and worker ownership, loyalty to community, and respect for our deeper social values.

While none of this promises a utopian outcome of perfect equality, the redistribution of power within capitalism is certainly a predicate for the creation of a more equitable society.

My conviction is that we are on the brink of a broad new reform era, in which reorganizing capitalism becomes the principal objective. What I foresee is a long, steady mobilization of people attempting to do things differently, often in small and local settings, trying out new arrangements, sometimes failing, then trying again. As these inventive departures succeed, others will emulate them. In time, an alternative social reality will emerge with different values, alongside the archaic and destructive system that now exists. When that begins to happen and gains sufficient visibility, the politics is sure to follow. If all this sounds too remote to the present facts, too patient for our frenetic age, remember that this is how deep change has always occurred across American history.

This article is adapted from *The Soul of Capitalism* (Simon & Schuster, 2003).

ARTICLE 2.11   *March/April 2005*

RICH AND POOR IN THE GLOBAL ECONOMY

INTERVIEW WITH BOB SUTCLIFFE

Whether economic inequality is rising or falling globally is a matter of intense debate, a key question in the larger dispute over how three decades of intensified economic globalization have affected the world's poor. Bob Sutcliffe is an economist at the University of the Basque Country in Bilbao, Spain, and the author of 100 Ways of Seeing an Unequal World. *He has been analyzing both the statistical details and the broader political-economic import of the debate and shared some of his insights in a recent interview with* Dollars & Sense.

DOLLARS & SENSE: If someone asked you whether global inequality has grown over the past 25 years, I assume you'd say, "It depends—on how inequality is defined, on what data is used, on how that data is analyzed." Is that fair?

BOB SUTCLIFFE: Yes, it's fair, but it's not enough. First, the most basic fact about world inequality is that it is monstrously large; that result is inescapable, whatever the method or definition. As to its direction of change in the last 25 years, to some extent there are different answers. But also there are different questions. Inequality is not a simple one-dimensional concept that can be reduced to a single number. Single overall measures of world inequality (where all incomes are taken into account) give a different result from measures of the relation of the extremes (the richest compared with the poorest). Over the last 25 years, you find that the bottom half of world income earners seems to have gained something in relation to the top half (so, in this sense, there is less inequality), but the bottom 10% have lost seriously in comparison with the top 10% (thus, more inequality), and the bottom 1% have lost enormously in relation to the top 1% (much more inequality). None of these measures is a single true measure of inequality; they are all part of a complex structure of inequalities, some of which can lessen as part of the same overall process in which others increase.

We do have to be clear about one data-related question that has caused huge confusion. To look at the distribution of income in the world, you have to reduce incomes of different countries to one standard. Traditionally it has been done by using exchange rates; this makes inequality appear to change when exchange rates change, which is misleading. But now we have data based on "purchasing power parity" (the comparative buying power, or real equivalence, of currencies). Using PPP values achieves for comparisons over space what inflation-adjusted index numbers have achieved for comparisons over time. Although many problems remain with PPP values, they are the only way to make coherent comparisons of incomes between countries. But they produce estimates that are astonishingly different from exchange rate-based calculations. For instance, U.S. income per head is 34 times Chinese income per head using exchange rates, but only 8 times as great using PPP values. (And, incidentally, on PPP estimates the total size of the U.S. economy is now only 1.7 times that of China, and is likely to be overtaken by it by 2011.) So when you make this apparently technical choice between two methods of converting one currency to another, you come up not only with different figures on income distribution but also with two totally different world economic, and thus political, perspectives.

D&S: So even if some consensus were reached on the choices of definition, data, and method, you're urging a complex, nuanced portrait of what is happening to global inequality, rather than a yes or no answer. Could you give a brief outline of what you think that portrait looks like?

BS: Most integral measures—integral meaning including the entire population rather than comparing the extremes—that use PPP figures suggest that overall income distribution at the global level during the last 25 years has shown a slight decline in inequality, though there is some dissent on this. In any event this conclusion is tremendously affected by China, a country with a fifth of world population which has been growing economically at an unprecedented rate. Second, there seems to me little room for debate over the fact that the relative difference between the very rich and the very poor has gotten worse. And the smaller the extreme proportions you compare, the greater the gap. So the immensely rich have done especially well in the last 25 years, while the extremely poor have done very badly. The top one-tenth of U.S. citizens now receive a total income equal to that of the poorest 2.2 billion people in the rest of the world.

There have also been clear trends within some countries. Some of the fastest growing countries have become considerably more unequal. China is an example, along with some other industrializing countries like Thailand. The most economically liberal of the developed countries have also become much more unequal—for instance, the United States, the United Kingdom, and Australia—and so have the post-communist countries. The most extreme figures for inequality are found in a group of poor countries including

Namibia and Botswana in southern Africa and Paraguay and Panama in Latin America.

Finally, the overall index of world inequality (measured by the Gini coefficient, a measure of income distribution) is about the same as that for two infamously unequal countries, South Africa and Brazil. And in the last few years it has shown no signs of improvement whatsoever.

D&S: People use the terms "unimodal" and "bimodal" to describe the global distribution of income. Can you explain what these mean? Also, you have referred elsewhere to a possible trimodal distribution—what does that refer to?

BS: The mode of a distribution is its most common value. In many countries there is one level of income around which a large proportion of the population clusters; at higher or lower levels of income there are progressively fewer people, so the distribution curve rises to a peak and then falls off. That is a unimodal distribution. But in South Africa, for example, due to the continued existence of entrenched ethnic division and economic inequality, the curve of distribution has two peaks—a low one, the most common income received by black citizens, and another, higher one, the the most common received by whites. This is a bimodal distribution because there are two values that are relatively more common than those above or below them. Because of its origins you could call it the "Apartheid distribution." The world distribution is in many respects uncannily like that of South Africa. It could be becoming trimodal in the sense that the frequency distribution of income has three peaks—one including those in very poor countries which have not been growing economically (e.g., parts of Africa), one in those developing countries which really have been developing (e.g., in South and East Asia), and one in the high-income industrialized countries. It's a kind of "apartheid plus" form of distribution.

D&S: In 2002, you wrote that many institutions, like the United Nations and the World Bank, were not being exactly honest in this debate—for example, emphasizing results based on data or methods that they elsewhere acknowledged to be poor. Has this changed over the past few years? Has the quality of the debate over trends in global income inequality improved?

BS: The most egregious pieces of statistical opportunism have declined. But I think there is a strong tendency in general for institutions to seize on optimistic conclusions regarding distribution in order to placate critics of the present world order. This increasingly takes the form of putting too much weight on measures of welfare other than income, for instance, life expectancy, for which there has been more international convergence than in the case of income. But there has been very little discussion of the philosophical basis for using life expectancy instead of or combined with income to measure inequality. If poor people live longer but in income terms remain as relatively poor as ever, has the world become less unequal?

The problem of statistical opportunism is not confined to those who are defending the world economic order; it also exists on the left. So, on the question of inequality, there is a tendency to accept whatever numerical estimate shows greatest inequality on the false assumption that this confirms the wickedness of capitalism. But capitalist inequality is so great that the willful exaggeration of it is not needed as the basis of anti-capitalist propaganda. It is more important for the left to look at the best indicators of the changing state of capitalism, including indicators of inequality, in order to intervene more effectively.

Finally, the quality of the debate, regardless of the intentions of the participants, is still greatly restricted by the shortage of available statistics about inequalities. That has improved somewhat in recent years although there are many things about past and present inequalities which we shall probably never know.

D&S: Do you see any contexts in which it's more important to focus on absolute poverty levels and trends in those levels rather than on inequality?

BS: The short answer is no, I do not. Plans for minimum income guarantees or for reducing the number of people lacking basic necessities can be important. But poverty always has a relative as well as an absolute component. It is a major weakness of the Millenium Development Goals, for example, that they talk about halving the number of people in absolute extreme poverty without a single mention of inequality. [The Millenium Development Goals is a U.N. program aimed at eliminating extreme poverty and achieving certain other development goals worldwide by 2015. —Eds.] And there is now a very active campaign on the part of anti-egalitarian, pro-capitalist ideologues in favor of the complete separation of the two. That is wrong not only because inequality is what partly defines poverty but more importantly because inequality and poverty reduction are inseparable. To separate them is to say that redistribution should not form part of the solution to poverty. Everyone is prepared in some sense to regard poverty as undesirable. But egalitarians see riches as pathological too. The objective of reducing poverty is integrally linked to the objective of greater equality and social justice.

D&S: Can you explain the paradox that China's economic liberalization since the late 1970s has increased inequality within China and at the same time reduced global inequality? Some researchers and policymakers interpret China's experience over this period as teaching us that it may be necessary for poor countries to sacrifice some equality in order to fight poverty. Do you agree with this—if not, how would you respond?

BS: When you measure *global* inequality, you are not just totalling the levels of inequality in individual countries. In theory all individual countries could become more unequal and yet the world as a whole become more equal, or vice versa. In China, a very poor country in 1980, average incomes have risen much faster than the world average and this has reduced world inequality. But different sections of the population have done much better than others so that inequality within China has grown. If and when China becomes on average a richer country than it is now, further unequal growth there may contribute to increasing rather than decreasing world inequality.

China's growth has been very inegalitarian, but it has been very fast. And the proportion of the population in poverty seems to have been reduced. But it is possible to envisage a more egalitarian growth path which would have been slower in aggregate but which would have reduced the number of poor people at least as much if not more than China's actual record. So I do not think it is right to say that higher inequality is the cause of reduced poverty, though it may for a time be a feature of the rapid growth which in turn creates employment and reduces poverty.

This does not mean that all increases in inequality are necessarily pathological. The famous Kuznets curve sees inequality first rising and then falling during economic growth as an initially poor population moves by stages from low-income, low-productivity work into high-income, high-productivity work, until at the end of the process 100% of the population is in the second group. If you measure inequality during such a process, it does in fact rise and then fall again to its original level—in this example at the start everyone is equally poor, at the end everyone is equally richer. That might be called transitional inequality; many growth processes may include an element of it. In that case equality is not really being "sacrificed" to reduce poverty—poverty is reduced by a process which increases inequality and then eliminates it again. But at the same time inequality may be growing for many other reasons which are not, like the Kuznets effect, self-eliminating, but rather cumulative. When inequality grows, this malign variety tends to be more important than the self-eliminating variety. But many economists are far too ready to see growing inequality as the more benign, self-eliminating variety.

D&S: Where do you think the question of what is happening to global income inequality fits into the broader debate over neoliberalism and globalization?

BS: Many people say that since some measures of inequality started to improve in about 1980 and that is also when neoliberalism and globalization accelerated, it is those processes which have produced greater equality. There are many problems with this argument, among them the fact that at least on some measures global inequality has grown since 1980. In any case, measures which show global inequality falling in this period are, as we have seen, very strongly influenced by China. China's extraordinary growth has, of course, in part been expressed in and permitted by greater globalization (its internationalization has grown faster than its production), and it is also clear that liberalization of economic policy has played a role, though China hardly has a neoliberal economy. But to permit is not to cause. The real cause is surely to be found not so much in economic policy as in a profound social movement in which a new and highly dynamic capitalist class (combined with a supportive authoritarian state) has once again become an agent of massive capitalist accumulation, as seen before in Japan, the United States, and Western Europe. So, an important part of what we are observing in figures which show declining world inequality is not any growth of egalitarianism, but the dynamic ascent of Chinese and other Asian capitalisms.

This interview also appears on the website of the Political Economy Research Institute at the University of Massachusetts-Amherst, along with Bob Sutcliffe's working paper "A More or Less Unequal World? World Income Distribution in the 20th Century." See <www.umass. edu/peri>.

CHAPTER 3
SAVINGS AND INVESTMENT

INTRODUCTION

Never a slip from the savings cup to the investment lip. That is the orderly world of classical macroeconomics, where every cent of household savings is neatly transferred to corporate investment. In the classical world, savings markets—governed by all-powerful interest rates—work seamlessly to assure that savings are matched by investments, fueling growth in the private economy, which in turn guarantees full employment. Should the flow of savings exceed the uptake of corporate investment, falling interest rates automatically solve the problem.

In the real world, macroeconomies are far messier than classical macroeconomics suggests. Keynes argued that there is no neat connection, or nexus, between savings and investment in a modern financial economy. Savings often sit, hoarded and uninvested. And interest rates, no matter how low, seldom coax balky investors to lay out their money in a weak economy. In the Keynesian world, economies regularly suffer from investment shortfalls that lead to recessions and cost workers their jobs.

In this chapter, Gretchen McClain and Randy Albelda report on one critical test of the classical and Keynesian visions, conducted by economist Steven Fazzari. In a massive study of 5,000 manufacturing firms, Fazzari rated the influence of interest rates, business cycle conditions, and firms' financial conditions on their investment in plant and equipment. He concluded that the influence of interest rates is overrated, putting him squarely in the Keynesian camp (Article 3.1).

KEY TO COLANDER

E = *Economics*   M = *Macroeconomics*

This chapter takes up topics in chapters E24-E26 or M8-M10; and prefigures the policy debates in chapters E28 and E33, or M12 and M18.

Article 3.1 discusses investment, the subject of chapter E24 or M8; the macro models in chapters E25-E26 or M9-M10; and the effectiveness of lowering interest rates to encourage investment, the topic of chapter E29 or M13.

Articles 3.2 and 3.3 fit with the discussion of growth in chapter E24 or M8, and the box on the stock boom in chapter E33 or M18.

Articles 3.4, 3.5, and 3.6 fit with chapters E24-E26 or M8-M10, which rely on an understanding of household savings.

According to conventional wisdom, the stock market boom of the last decade and last year's market high should have benefited most people in the United States who own corporate stock either directly or indirectly through mutual funds or retirement accounts. But, as Sylvia Allegretto shows, the number of households that own stock has been *falling* in recent years, and the wealthiest Americans own the great bulk of stock by value (Article 3.2). Also, as Ellen Frank explains, there is no logical connection between rising stock prices and rising investment. Stock prices are based on traders' guesses about which stocks are likely to catch the eye of other traders—guesses that can have little to do with actual economic conditions (Article 3.3).

But residential investment, a housing boom followed by a mortgage crisis and housing bust, is the chief source of instability and uncertainty in today's economy. The crisis in the subprime mortgage market has hit low-income homeowners especially hard. Howard Karger throws into sharp relief the downsides that come with the well-known benefits of homeownership for low-income households (Article 3.4). A low income often affords these buyers no more than rundown houses located in distressed neighborhoods and leaves them just a heartbeat away from financial disaster if their wages decline, property taxes or insurance rates rise, or if expensive repairs are needed. Economist John Miller looks at the macroeconomic effects of the housing crisis. He tracks the rash of foreclosures, the nationwide decline in housing prices, the lack of housing starts, and the insolvency problems that began in the subprime mortgage market and are now spreading throughout the economy. Miller notes that the bursting of the housing bubble will likely put more of a dent in consumer spending than the bursting of the stock market bubble at the beginning of the decade, leaving the economy in an economic malaise immune to any quick cure at the hands of the Federal Reserve Board. Worse yet, the economic slowdown comes on the heels on economic expansion that did little to benefit most people (Article 3.5).

There are alternatives to the instability of the bubble economy. Daniel Fireside reports on how one Vermont city managed to provide affordable housing despite skyrocketing real estate prices through a community housing trust (Article 3.6). Finally, Adria Scharf describes how pension wealth, labor's capital, can be used to fund investments that generate good jobs and empower workers (Article 3.7).

DISCUSSION QUESTIONS

1. (Articles 3.1) Keynes argued that savings and investment were not balanced by the interest rate but by changes

in the level of aggregate output. How does the essay by McClain and Albelda support Keynes' claim about investment?

2. (Article 3.1) According to McClain and Albelda, how did Fazzari rate the influence of interest rates, business cycle conditions, and firms' financial conditions on corporate investment? What do his findings suggest about Keynesian and classical theories of investment? Based on his findings, what stabilization policies might be appropriate to promote investment?

3. (Article 3.2) If nearly one half of U.S. households own stock either directly or indirectly, why would the recent highs on the Dow be inconsequential for them?

4. (Article 3.3) During the 1930s, Keynes compared the stock market to a newspaper beauty contest that asked readers to pick the photo of the contestant that other readers would pick as the prettiest. Frank suggests that Keynes' analogy still holds for today's stock market. How does Frank's explanation of stock prices compare with those in your textbook? Do you find it convincing?

5. (Article 3.4) Is homeownership a good investment for low-income households? What is the upside? What is the downside?

6. (Article 3.5) At the end of 2007 and the beginning of 2008, the *Economist* magazine, several prominent economists, and some major Wall Street brokerage houses warned that the U.S. economy was heading toward, or was already in, a recession. Were they right?

7. (Article 3.5) How has the mortgage crisis spread through the U.S. economy? How big of a threat is it to the U.S. and global economies?

8. (Article 3.6) How did the Burlington Community Land Trust (BCLT) allow the city to increase the supply of affordable housing? Can the BCLT model be applied successfully to housing markets in other cities?

9. (Article 3.7) What is the legal space that would allow the custodians of workers' pensions to invest them in a way that creates good jobs and empowers workers? Give examples of pension investments that have benefited workers. How effective do you think pension fund investing can be at making the U.S. economy more worker-friendly?

ARTICLE 3.1

July 1993, revised April 2001

BOOSTING INVESTMENT

THE OVERRATED INFLUENCE OF INTEREST RATES

BY GRETCHEN McCLAIN AND RANDY ALBELDA

Few economists or politicians would disagree that an economy's prospects for long-term growth depend on the productive capacity of its people and its physical equipment. But what to invest in—and how to get the appropriate economic actors to invest—is a matter of much debate.

All economies face a choice between using their productive resources to produce goods and services to be consumed now, and forsaking today's consumption to produce more goods for the future. While catering to consumption today may be more satisfying for wealthier countries and absolutely vital for poor countries, it fails to provide for future growth.

Investing in new plant and equipment can stimulate growth over time, as it provides the physical capacity for new production. Moreover, new plant and equipment tend to be better designed than the existing capital stock, and the improvement usually helps to boost output per worker. If this new productivity translates into higher wages, investment can also increase a country's standard of living and improve employment pos-

sibilities. In turn, improving human productive capacity—through training and education—can lead to growth and increased productivity in the long run.

Investment, and the consequent increase in productivity, is critical for international economic success. The more efficiently a country can produce a product, the more competitive that country will be in the world market. Since international markets provide an avenue of demand for our goods, the more domestically produced products and services we can sell abroad, the more jobs we can support here.

Investment can also help stimulate the economy in the short run. During an economic downturn, increased investment will yield more jobs and income for workers who would otherwise be unemployed. They will then return their income to the market when they purchase goods and services, which will boost demand for those products. Economists call this the "multiplier effect." The increase in demand in turn encourages firms to invest more so that they can meet that demand—

known to economists as the "accelerator effect." All in all, such a cycle creates more jobs, income, and spending.

While few economists dispute the importance of investment, many disagree on what type is needed, which sectors of the economy are best able to provide it, and what are the best ways to encourage investment. Typically, these debates have revolved around the government's role in encouraging private investment in new plant and equipment. But the role that public investment in infrastructure and education plays in promoting not only our economic well-being and growth, but also in encouraging private investment, could and should widen the terms of the debate.

THE BACKDROP

The traditional economic argument about investment—and the prevailing conservative line espoused by elected officials at the federal and state levels—has been that the most important fiscal policies to encourage privately owned firms to invest are those which boost profits. If the government helps provide the conditions for profitability, the argument goes, firms will be encouraged to make the right types of investment.

Government tax-and-spend policies during the 1980s and 1990s have often tried to promote investment by reducing corporate taxes, in order to boost profits and stimulate savings. Such measures were supposed to leave firms with a bigger bottom line, in the hope that they would turn profits into new plant and equipment. Cuts in personal income tax rates—especially for the wealthiest—were intended to leave people with more after-tax income that they could save. Higher savings, according to this logic, translates into lower interest rates which in turn lead to more investment. While such policies have been very effective in redistributing money from the poor to the wealthy, they did not do much for investment. For example, the amount of new fixed investment (i.e., new plant and equipment) relative to the total amount of plant and equipment actually sank to its lowest post-World War II mark between 1989 and 1991.

Merely providing the conditions for profit-making does not mean that private firms will plow those profits back into new plant and equipment. Speculation on real-estate markets, the value of foreign currencies, or the price of silver and gold could easily eat up new profits. Much of the money generated for investment in the 1980s financed mergers and acquisitions, which generally resulted in less employment and little new physical productive capacity. And, perhaps even more important, new investment by U.S. firms may not take place in the United States. Investing abroad has been the trend since the 1970s. Finally, even if there is domestic investment and it increases productivity, unless workers share in those gains it may not promote robust growth or increase the standard of living of the country as a whole.

In the face of the failure of the 1980s policies to promote investment, conservatives came up with a new explanation of why the economy was so sluggish: the deficit. Ironically, the conservative policies mentioned above were largely responsible for the public debt, but nonetheless Republicans, along with many Democrats galvanized by billionaire Ross Perot, latched onto deficit reduction as the most important fiscal policy of the 1990s.

The deficit, they argued, kept long-term interest rates high because it created competition for precious funds. The result was that federal borrowing, necessitated by debt-financed government spending and tax cuts, "crowded out" private investment. The best solution, they said, was to reduce the deficit and bring down long-term interest rates so that private investment would thrive.

IDENTIFYING INFLUENCE

Economist Steven Fazzari tackled these assumptions in a study of the influence of the federal government's taxing and spending policies on private investment. Using a large data base from Standard and Poor on over 5,000 manufacturing firms from 1971 to 1990, Fazzari tested three different factors for their effects on levels of investment in plant and equipment: interest rates, the business cycle, and the financial conditions of the firms.

According to Fazzari, these three "channels of influence" shape patterns of investment. First, he takes on the traditionalists, by addressing the costs associated with investment: the price of borrowing money (i.e., interest rates), depreciation (how fast the new piece of equipment or building will lose its value), and taxes affecting both corporate profits and dividends. To measure this channel, Fazzari employs the interest rate on one type of corporate bond.

Next, he considers the influence of the business cycle by looking at sales growth. Traditional economic theory tends to assume a ready market, but Fazzari suggests instead that firms make investment decisions based on their perception of their ability to sell their products. The more robust current sales are and are expected to be, the more likely firms will be willing to risk new investment—regardless of the interest rate. Since the general condition of the economy influences sales levels, it also has an impact on investment.

In Fazzari's examination of the third channel of influence—the financial condition of firms—he again questions conventional wisdom, this time about the supply and demand for loans. Most economists assume that if the expected return on an investment exceeds the interest rate, then the project is profitable and will be undertaken. This is most likely to be true when the firm in question has enough cash on hand from prior profits to make the investment without asking a bank for a loan. Many firms, though, need to borrow money, and some are unable to persuade banks to loan it to them. Banks often refuse loan applications from new businesses with few assets, or charge them prohibitively high interest rates. Even if a young firm finds a potentially profitable investment, severe constraints on raising capital may prevent the firm from pursuing it. A firm's financial condition—not the projected rate of return on the new investment—can thus end up determining whether or not investment takes place.

PERFECTING POLICY

After looking at the importance of interest rates, the business cycle, and the financial conditions of firms in determining investment, Fazzari found that interest rates exert the weakest influence of the three factors. He concludes that there is no evidence that interest rates significantly affect investment for the fastest growing firms in his sample. Based on these findings, Fazzari claims that "it would be speculative to base policy on the assumption that interest rates drive investment to an important extent, especially for growing firms."

So, what kinds of fiscal policies should we adopt? If we believe Fazzari's results, we should be looking for those that attend to the financial conditions of firms and stimulate demand for products.

A tax cut targeted not at the very rich but at the "middle class" would probably give investment at least a temporary boost by generating increased consumption. Increased sales from a temporary tax cut create the illusion of a permanent increase in demand, and the multiplier and accelerator effects discussed earlier come into play. In order to meet what firms believe is a permanent increase in demand for their goods, they make investments in more equipment, more factories, and more employees.

Another means of encouraging investment that Fazzari evaluates is cutting corporate income taxes. Such cuts increase firms' after-tax profits, leaving them with a larger pool of funds to invest if they so choose. Since there is no guarantee that they will invest the savings from reduced taxes, though, Fazzari prefers investment tax credits (ITCs) to cuts in taxes for all firms. Only if firms invested would they be able to reduce their corporate tax bills. In Fazzari's view, ITCs will effectively encourage investment whether it is sensitive to interest rates or not.

The most important lesson from Fazzari's analysis is that concerns about investment should not stand in the way of policy initiatives that are important for society, such as spending on education and job training, simply because they may increase the federal budget deficit and cause interest rates to rise. Government investments in public works and education will likely increase productivity in the long run, and this can only be good for investment. Moreover, if investment is not sensitive to interest rates, then the much-discussed "crowding out" effect of deficit spending on private business is bound to be very small. And as Fazzari points out, when unemployment is high, the stimulative effects of deficit spending on sales may far outweigh the impacts of increased interest rates.

The focus on balanced budgets should be tempered by a thorough analysis of what this policy implies for society's immediate and long-term welfare. When we underinvest in the economy during a recession by eliminating educational and social investments, the foregone technical innovation resulting from this underinvestment may lead to less efficient workers, and lower productivity, for many years.

Fazzari's results not only repudiate the traditional answer to lagging investment—tax cuts for the wealthy and the lowering of interest rates. Instead, the government should be trying to stimulate the economy through improved physical and social infrastructure, which will boost not only sales but investment and incomes.

March/April 2007

THE DOW HIGH AND STOCK OWNERSHIP

BY SYLVIA ALLEGRETTO

In April the Dow Jones Industrial Average rose above 13,000 for the first time ever, an event marked with great fanfare in some quarters. "Dow 13,000" may be a milestone on Wall Street, but it is a relatively insignificant blip on the radar screen of average working families. Fostered by the constant focus and widespread attention given to the performance of the stock market, conventional wisdom has it that everyone in the United States is heavily invested in the stock market—and so is poised to benefit when stock prices rise. However, the data tell a different story.

In recent decades the share of U.S. households owning any stock, whether directly (owning shares in a particular company) or indirectly (owning shares through a mutual fund or a retirement account) has indeed increased. But the most recent triennial data from the Survey of Consumer Finances show that this trend has actually reversed course: just over half of households (51.9%) owned any stock in 2001, but just under half (48.6%) in 2004—the first such decline on record (see Figure 1). In 2004, only about a third of U.S. households had stock holdings valued at more than $5,000.

The distribution of stocks by value is heavily tilted to the wealthiest Americans, as shown in Figure 2. In 2004, the wealthiest 1% of households owned 36.9% of the value of all stocks, while the next 9% owned 41.9%. Hence, the wealthiest 10% owned about 80% of all wealth in stocks. Between 2001 and 2004, while the wealthiest 1% of households increased their share of total stock value, the share held by the bottom 80% fell from just above 10% (10.7%) to just below (9.4%).

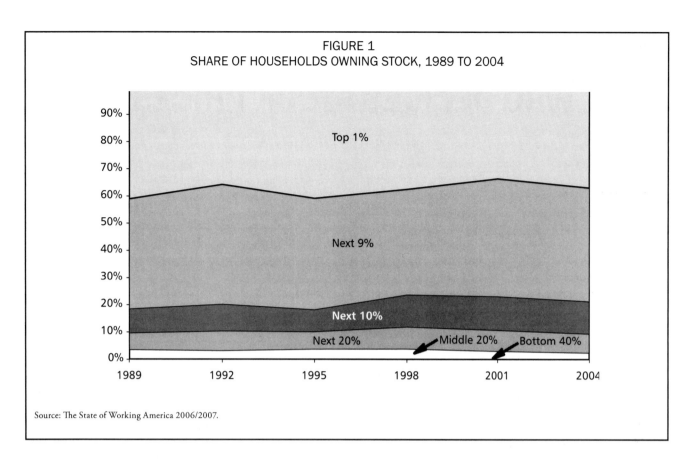

FIGURE 1
SHARE OF HOUSEHOLDS OWNING STOCK, 1989 TO 2004

Top 1%

Next 9%

Next 10%

Next 20%

Middle 20%   Bottom 40%

Source: The State of Working America 2006/2007.

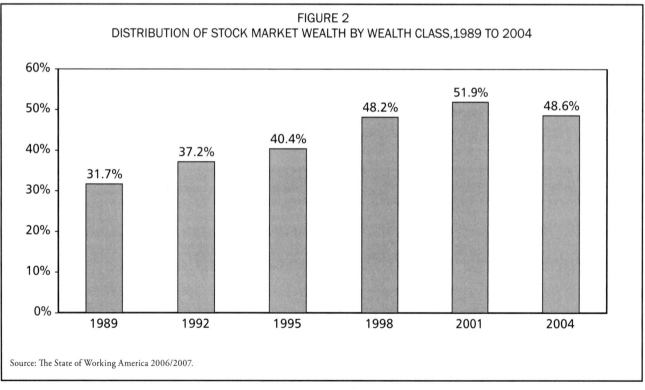

FIGURE 2
DISTRIBUTION OF STOCK MARKET WEALTH BY WEALTH CLASS,1989 TO 2004

1989: 31.7%
1992: 37.2%
1995: 40.4%
1998: 48.2%
2001: 51.9%
2004: 48.6%

Source: The State of Working America 2006/2007.

For the most part, lower-, middle-, and even upper-middle-income working-age households depend on their paychecks, not stock portfolios, to meet their everyday needs. Typical working families that own stock do so in retirement plans that are costly to turn into cash. So higher stock prices do little to help them make ends meet at a time when inflation-adjusted wages for most workers have been stagnant for many years now.

WHO DECIDES STOCK PRICES?

BY ELLEN FRANK

Dear Dr. Dollar:

During the course of a single day, a stock can go up and down frequently. These changes supposedly reflect the changing demand for that stock (and its potential resale value) or changing expectations of a company's profitability. But this seems too vague to me. How can these factors be so volatile? Who actually decides, or what is the mechanism for deciding, when a stock price should go up or down and by how much?

—*Joseph Balszak, Muskegon, Michigan*

Let's start with your last question first—how are stock prices determined? Shares in most large established corporations are listed on organized exchanges like the New York or American Stock Exchanges. Shares in most smaller or newer firms are listed on the NASDAQ—an electronic system that tracks stock prices.

Every time a stock is sold, the exchange records the price at which it changes hands. If, a few seconds or minutes later, another trade takes place, the price at which that trade is made becomes the new market price, and so on. Organized exchanges like the New York Stock Exchange will occasionally suspend trading in a stock if the price is excessively volatile, if there is a severe mismatch between supply and demand (many people wanting to sell, no one wanting to buy) or if they suspect that insiders are deliberately manipulating a stock's price. But in normal circumstances, there is no official arbiter of stock prices, no person or institution that "decides" a price. The market price of a stock is simply the price at which a willing buyer and seller agree to trade.

Why then do prices fluctuate so much? The vast bulk of stock trades are made by professional traders who buy and sell shares all day long, hoping to profit from small changes in share prices. Since these traders do not hold stocks over the long haul, they are not terribly interested in such long-term considerations as a company's profitability or the value of its assets. Or rather, they are interested in such factors mostly insofar as news that would affect a company's long-term prospects might cause *other traders* to buy the stock, causing its price to rise. If a trader believes that others will buy shares (in the expectation that prices will rise), then she will buy as well, hoping to sell when the price rises. If others believe the same thing, then the wave of buying pressure will, in fact, *cause* the price to rise.

Back in the 1930s, economist John Maynard Keynes compared the stock market to a contest then popular in British tabloids, in which contestants had to look at photos and choose the faces that *other contestants* would pick as the prettiest. Each contestant had to look for photos "likeliest to catch the fancy of the other competitors, all of whom are looking at the problem from the same point of view." Similarly, stock traders try to guess which stocks other traders will buy. The successful trader is the one who anticipates and outfoxes the market, buying before a stock's price rises and selling before it falls.

Financial firms employ thousands of market strategists and technical analysts who spend hours poring over historical stock data, trying to divine the logic behind these price changes. If they could unlock the secret of stock prices, they could arm their traders with the ability to always buy low and sell high. So far, no one has found this particular holy grail. And by continuing to guess and gamble, traders send prices gyrating.

For small investors, who do hold stock for the long term and will need to cash in their stocks at some point to finance their retirements, the volatility of the market can be a source of constant anxiety. Every time a share in, say, General Electric is traded, the new price is used to revalue *all* outstanding shares—just as the value of your home appreciates when the house down the block sells for more than a similar house sold last week. But the value of your home wouldn't be so high if every house on your block were suddenly put up for sale. Similarly, if all ten billion outstanding shares of General Electric—or even a small fraction of them—were put up for sale, they wouldn't fetch anywhere near the current market price. Small investors need to keep in mind that the gains and losses on their 401(k) statements are just hypothetical paper gains and losses. You won't know the true value of your stocks until you actually try to sell them.

THE HOMEOWNERSHIP MYTH

BY HOWARD KARGER

Anyone who has given the headlines even a passing glance recently knows the subprime mortgage industry is in deep trouble. Since 2006 more than 20 subprime lenders have quit the business or gone bankrupt. Many more are in serious trouble, including the nation's number two subprime lender, New Century Financial. The subprime crisis is also hitting Wall Street brokerages that invested in these loans, with reverberations from Tokyo to London. And the worst may be yet to come. At least $300 billion in subprime adjustable-rate mortgages will reset this year to higher interest rates. CNN reports that one in five subprime mortgages issued in 2005-2006 will end up in foreclosure. If these dire predictions come true, it will be the equivalent of a nuclear meltdown in the mortgage and housing industries.

What's conspicuously absent from the news reports is the effect of the subprime lending debacle on poor and working-class families who bought into the dream of homeownership, regardless of the price. Sold a false bill of goods, many of these families now face foreclosure and the loss of the small savings they invested in their homes. It's critical to examine the housing crisis not only from the perspective of the banks and the stock market, but also from the perspective of the families whose homes are on the line. It is also critical to uncover the systemic reasons for the recent burst of housing-market insanity that saw thousands upon thousands of families getting signed up for mortgage loans that were highly likely to end in failure and foreclosure.

Like most Americans, I grew up believing that buying a home represents a rite of passage in U.S. society. Americans widely view homeownership as the best choice for everyone, everywhere and at all times. The more people who own their own homes, the common wisdom goes, the more robust the economy, the stronger the community, and the greater the collective and individual benefits. Homeownership is the ticket to the middle class through asset accumulation, stability, and civic participation.

For the most part, this is an accurate picture. Homeowners get a foothold in a housing market with an almost infinite price ceiling. They enjoy important tax benefits. Owning a home is often cheaper than renting. Most important, homeownership builds equity and accrues assets for the next generation, in part by promoting forced savings. These savings are reflected in the data showing that, according to the National Housing Institute's Winton Picoff, the median

wealth of low-income homeowners is 12 times higher than that of renters with similar incomes. Plus, owning a home is a status symbol: homeowners are seen as winners compared to renters.

Homeownership may have positive effects on family life. Ohio University's Robert Dietz found that owning a home contributes to household stability, social involvement, environmental awareness, local political participation and activism, good health, low crime, and beneficial community characteristics. Homeowners are better citizens, are healthier both physically and mentally, and have children who achieve more and are better behaved than those of renters.

Johns Hopkins University researchers Joe Harkness and Sandra Newman looked at whether homeownership benefits kids even in distressed neighborhoods. Their study concluded that "[h]omeownership in almost any neighborhood is found to benefit children. ... Children of most low-income renters would be better served by programs that help their families become homeowners in their current neighborhoods instead of helping them move to better neighborhoods while remaining renters." (Harkness and Newman also found, however, that the positive effects of homeownership on children are weaker in unstable low-income neighborhoods. Moreover, the study cannot distinguish whether homeownership leads to positive behaviors or whether owners were already predisposed to these behaviors.)

Faith in the benefits of homeownership—along with low interest rates and a range of governmental incentives—have produced a surge in the number of low-income homeowners. In 1994 Bill Clinton set—and ultimately surpassed—a goal to raise the nation's overall homeownership rate to 67.5% by 2000. There are now 71 million U.S. homeowners, representing close to 68% of all households. By 2003, 48% of black households owned their own homes, up from 34.5% in 1950. Much of this gain has been among low-income families.

Government efforts to increase homeownership for low-income families include both demand-side (e.g., homeowner tax credits, housing cost assistance programs) and supply-side (e.g., developer incentives) strategies. Federal housing programs insure more than a million loans a year to help low-income homebuyers. Fannie Mae and Freddie Mac—the large, federally chartered but privately held corporations that buy mortgages from lenders, guarantee the notes, and then resell them to investors—have increasingly turned their attention to low-income homebuyers as the upper-income housing market becomes more saturated. Banking industry regulations such as the Community Reinvestment Act and the Home Mortgage Disclosure Act encourage homeownership by reducing lending discrimination in underserved markets.

The Housing and Urban Development department (HUD) has adapted some of its programs originally designed to help renters to focus on homeownership. For instance, cities and towns can now use the federal dollars they receive through HOME (the Home Investment Partnerships Act) and Community Development Block Grants to provide housing grants, down payment loans, and closing cost assistance. The American Dream Downpayment Initiative, passed by Congress in 2003, authorized up to $200 million a year for down payment assistance to low-income families. Private foundations have followed suit. The Ford Foundation is currently focusing its housing-related grants on homeownership rather than rental housing; the foundation views homeownership as an important form of asset-building and the best option for low-income people.

While homeownership has undeniable benefits, that doesn't mean it is the best option for everyone. For many low-income families, buying a home imposes burdens that end up outweighing the benefits. It is time to reassess the policy emphasis on homeownership, which has been driven by an honest belief in the advantages of homeownership, but also by a wide range of business interests who stand to gain when a new cohort of buyers is brought into the housing market.

THE DOWNSIDES OF HOMEOWNERSHIP

Low-income families can run into a range of pitfalls when they buy homes. These pitfalls may stem from the kinds of houses they can afford to buy (often in poor condition, with high maintenance costs); the neighborhoods they can afford to buy in (often economically distressed); the financing they can get (often carrying high interest rates, high fees, and risky gimmicks); and the jobs they work at (often unstable). Taken together, these factors can make buying a home a far riskier proposition for low-income families than it is for middle- and upper-income households.

Most low-income families only have the financial resources to buy rundown houses in distressed neighborhoods marked by few jobs, high crime rates, a dearth of services, and poor schools. Few middle-class homebuyers would hitch themselves to 30-year mortgages in these kinds of communities; poor families, too, have an interest in making the home-buying commitment in safe neighborhoods with good schools.

Homeownership is no automatic hedge against rising housing costs. On the contrary: lower-end affordable housing stock is typically old, in need of repair, and expensive to maintain. Low-income families often end up paying inflat-

ed prices for homes that are beset with major structural or mechanical problems masked by cosmetic repairs. A University of North Carolina study sponsored by the national non-profit organization NeighborWorks found that almost half of low-income homebuyers experienced major unexpected costs due to the age and condition of their homes. If you rent, you can call the landlord; but a homeowner can't take herself to court because the roof leaks, the plumbing is bad, or the furnace or hot water heater quits working.

Besides maintenance and repairs, the expenses of homeownership also include property taxes and homeowners insurance, both of which have skyrocketed in cost in the last decade. Between 1997 and 2002 property tax rates rose nationally by more than 19%. Ten states (including giants Texas and California) saw their property tax rates rise by 30% or more during that period. In the suburbs of New York City, property tax rates grew two to three times faster than personal income from 2000 to 2004.

Nationally, the average homeowner's annual insurance premiums rose a whopping 62% from 1995 to 2005—twice as fast as inflation. Low-income homeowners in distressed neighborhoods are hit especially hard by high insurance costs. According to a Conning and Co. study, 92% of large insurance companies run credit checks on potential customers. These credit checks translate into insurance scores that are used to determine whether the carrier will insure an applicant at all, and if so, what they will cover and how much they will charge. Those with poor or no credit are denied coverage, while those with limited credit pay high premiums. Needless to say, many low-income homeowners do not have stellar credit scores. Credit scoring may also partly explain why, according to HUD, "Recent studies have shown that, compared to homeowners in predominantly white-occupied neighborhoods, homeowners in minority neighborhoods are less likely to have private home insurance, more likely to have policies that provide less coverage in case of a loss, and are likely to pay more for similar policies."

With few cash reserves, low-income families are a heartbeat away from financial disaster if their wages decline, property taxes or insurance rates rise, or expensive repairs are needed. With most—or all—of their savings in their homes, these families often have no cushion for emergencies. HUD data show that between 1999 and 2001, the only group whose housing conditions worsened—meaning, by HUD's definition, the only group in which a larger share of households spent over 30% of gross household income on housing in 2001 than in 1999—were low- and moderate-income homeowners. The National Housing Conference reports that 51% of working families with critical housing needs (i.e., those spending more than 50% of gross household income on housing) are homeowners.

Most people who buy a home imagine they will live there for a long time, benefiting from a secure and stable housing situation. For many low-income families, this is not what happens. Nationwide data from 1976 to 1993 reveal that 36% of low-income homeowners gave up or lost their homes within two years and 53% exited within five years, according to a 2005 study by Carolina Katz Reid of the University of Washington. Reid found that very few low-income families ever bought another house after returning to renting. A 2004 HUD research study by Donald Haurin and Stuart Rosenthal reached similar conclusions. Following a national sample of African Americans from youth (ages 14 to 21) in 1979 to middle age in 2000, the researchers found that 63% of the sample owned a home at some point, but only 34% still did in 2000.

Low-income homeowners, often employed in unstable jobs with stagnant incomes, few health care benefits, limited or no sick days, and little vacation time, may find it almost impossible to keep their homes if they experience a temporary job loss or a change in family circumstances, such as the loss of a wage earner. Homeownership can also limit financial opportunities. A 1999 study by economists Richard Green (University of Wisconsin) and Patric Hendershott (Ohio State University) found that states with the highest homeownership rates also had the highest unemployment rates. Their report concluded that homeownership may constrain labor mobility since the high costs of selling a house make unemployed homeowners reluctant to relocate to find work.

Special tax breaks have been a key selling point of homeownership. If mortgage interest and other qualifying expenses come to less than the standard deduction ($10,300 for joint filers in 2006), however, there is zero tax advantage to owning. That is one reason why only 34% of taxpayers itemize their mortgage interest, local property taxes, and other deductions. Even for families who do itemize, the effective tax saving is usually only 10 to 35 cents for every dollar paid in mortgage interest. In other words, the mortgage deduction benefits primarily those in high income brackets who have a need to shelter their income; it means little to low-income homeowners.

Finally, homeownership promises growing wealth as home prices rise. But the homes of low-income, especially minority, homeowners generally do not appreciate as much as middle-class housing. Low-income households typically purchase homes in distressed neighborhoods where significant appreciation is unlikely. Among other reasons, if financially-stressed property owners on the block can't afford to maintain their homes, nearby property values fall. For instance, Reid's longitudinal study surveyed low-income minority homeowners from 1976 to 1994 and found that they realized a 30% increase in the value of their homes after owning for 10 years, while middle- and upper-income white homeowners enjoyed a 60% jump.

"FUNNY MONEY" MORTGAGES AND OTHER TRAVESTIES

Buying a home and taking on a mortgage are scary, and people often leave the closing in a stupor, unsure of what they signed or why. My partner and I bought a house a few years ago; like many buyers, we didn't retain an attorney. The title company had set aside one hour for the closing. During that time more than 125 single-spaced pages (much of it in small print) were put in front of us. More than 60 required our signature or initials. It would have been difficult for us to digest these documents in 24 hours, much less one. When we asked to slow down the process, we were met with impatience. After the closing, Anna asked, "What did we sign?" I was clueless.

Yet buying a home is the largest purchase most families will make in their lifetimes, the largest expenditure in a family budget, and the single largest asset for two-thirds of homeowners. It's also the most fraught with danger.

For low-income families in particular, homeownership can turn out to be more a crushing debt than an asset-building opportunity. The primary reason for this is the growing chasm between ever-higher home prices and the stagnant incomes of millions of working-class Americans. The last decade has seen an unprecedented surge in home prices, which have risen 35% nationally. While the housing bubble is largely confined to specific metropolitan areas in the South, the Southwest, and the two coasts (home prices rose 50% in the Pacific states and 60% in New England), there are also bubbles in midwestern cities like Chicago and Minneapolis. And although the housing bubble is most pronounced in high-end properties, the prices of low-end homes have also spiked in many markets.

Current incomes simply do not support these inflated home prices. For example, only 18% of Californians can afford the median house in the state using traditional loan-affordability calculations. Even the fall in mortgage interest rates in the 1990s and early 2000s was largely neutralized by higher property taxes, higher insurance premiums, and rising utility costs.

This disparity might have put a dent in the mortgage finance business. But no: in 2005, Americans owed $5.7 trillion in mortgages, a 50% increase in just four years. Over the past decade the mortgage finance industry has developed creative schemes designed to squeeze potential homebuyers, albeit often temporarily, into houses they cannot afford. It is a sleight of hand that requires imaginative and risky financing for both buyers and financial institutions.

Most of the "creative" new mortgage products fall into the category of subprime mortgages—those offered to people whose problematic credit drops them into a lower lending category. Subprime mortgages carry interest rates ranging from a few points to ten points or more above the prime or market rate, plus onerous loan terms. The subprime mortgage industry is growing: lenders originated $173 billion in subprime loans in 2005, up from only $25 billion in 1993. By 2006 the subprime market was valued at $600 billion, one-fifth of the $3 trillion U.S. mortgage market.

Subprime lending can be risky. In the 37 years since the

Mortgage Bankers Association (MBA) began conducting its annual national mortgage delinquency survey, 2006 saw the highest share of home loans entering foreclosure. In early 2007, according to the MBA, 13.5% of subprime mortgages were delinquent (compared to 4.95% of prime-rate mortgages) and 4.5% were in foreclosure. By all accounts, this is just the tip of the iceberg. However, before the current collapse the rate of return for subprime lenders was spectacular. *Forbes* claimed that subprime lenders could realize returns up to six times greater than the best-run banks.

In the past there were two main kinds of home mortgages: fixed-rate loans and adjustable-rate loans (ARMs). In a fixed-rate mortgage, the interest rate stays the same throughout the 15- to 30-year loan term. In a typical ARM the interest rate varies over the course of the loan, although there is usually a cap. Both kinds of loans traditionally required borrowers to provide thorough documentation of their finances and a down payment of at least 10% of the purchase price, and often 20%.

Adjustable-rate loans can be complicated, and a Federal Reserve study found that fully 25% of homeowners with ARMs were confused about their loan terms. Nonetheless, ARMs are attractive because in the short run they promise a home with an artificially low interest rate and affordable payments.

Even so, traditional ARMs proved inadequate to the tasks of ushering more low-income families into the housing market and generally keeping home sales up in the face of skyrocketing home prices. So in recent years the mortgage industry created a whole range of "affordability" products with names like "no-ratio loans," "option ARMS," and "balloon loans" that it doled out like candy to people who were never fully apprised of the intricacies of these complicated loans. (See sidebar for a glossary of the new mortgage products.) These new mortgage options have opened the door for almost anyone to secure a mortgage, whether or not their circumstances auger well for repayment. They also raise both the costs and risks of buying a home—sometimes steeply—for the low- and moderate-income families to whom they're largely marketed.

Beyond the higher interest rates (at some point in the loan term if not at the start) that characterize the new "affordability" mortgages, low-income homebuyers face other costs as well. For instance, predatory and subprime lenders often require borrowers to carry credit life insurance, which pays off a mortgage if the homeowner dies. This insurance is frequently sold either by the lender's subsidiary or else by a company that pays the lender a commission. Despite low payouts, lenders frequently charge high premiums for this insurance.

As many as 80% of subprime loans include prepayment penalties if the borrower pays off or refinances the loan early, a scam that costs low-income borrowers about $2.3 billion a year and increases the risk of foreclosure by 20%. Prepayment penalties lock borrowers into a loan by making it dif-

ficult to sell the home or refinance with a different lender. And while some borrowers face penalties for paying off their loans ahead of schedule, others discover that their mortgages have so-called "call provisions" that permit the lender to accelerate the loan term even if payments are current.

And then there are all of the costs outside of the mortgage itself. Newfangled mortgage products are often sold not by banks directly, but by a rapidly growing crew of mortgage brokers who act as finders or "bird dogs" for lenders. There are approximately 53,000 mortgage brokerage companies in the United States employing an estimated 418,700 people, according to the National Association of Mortgage Brokers; *BusinessWeek* notes that brokers now originate up to 80% of all new mortgages.

Largely unregulated, mortgage brokers live off loan fees. Their transactions are primed for conflicts of interest or even downright corruption. For example, borrowers pay brokers a fee to help them secure a loan. Brokers may also receive kickbacks from lenders for referring a borrower, and many brokers steer clients to the lenders that pay them the highest kickbacks rather than those offering the lowest interest rates. Closing documents use arcane language ("yield spread premiums," "service release fees") to hide these kickbacks. And some hungry brokers find less-than-kosher ways to make the sale, including fudging paperwork, arranging for inflated appraisals, or helping buyers find co-signers who have no intention of actually guaranteeing the loan.

Whether or not a broker is involved, lenders can inflate closing costs in a variety of ways: charging outrageous document preparation fees; billing for recording fees in excess of the law; "unbundling," whereby closing costs are padded by duplicating charges already included in other categories.

All in all, housing is highly susceptible to the predations of the fringe economy. Unscrupulous brokers and lenders have considerable latitude to ply their trade, especially with vulnerable low-income borrowers.

TIME TO CHANGE COURSE

Despite the hype, homeownership is not a cure-all for low-income families who earn less than a living wage and have poor prospects for future income growth. In fact, for some low-income families homeownership only leads to more debt and financial misery. With mortgage delinquencies and foreclosures at record levels, especially among low-income households, millions of people would be better off today if they had remained renters. Surprisingly, rents are generally more stable than housing prices. From 1995 to 2001 rents rose slightly faster than inflation, but not as rapidly as home prices. Beginning in 2004 rent increases began to slow—even in hot markets like San Francisco and Seattle—and fell below the rate of inflation.

In the mid-1980s, low- and no-downpayment mortgages led to increased foreclosures when the economy tanked. Today, these mortgages are back, along with a concerted effort to drive economically marginal households into hom-

THE NEW WORLD OF HOME LOANS

The new home loan products, marketed widely in recent years but especially to low- and moderate-income families, are generally adjustable-rate mortgages (ARMs) with some kind of twist. Here are a few of these "creative" (read: confusing and risky) mortgage options.

Option ARM: With this loan, borrowers choose each month which of three or four different—and fluctuating—payments to make:

- full (principal+interest) payment based on a 30-year or 15-year repayment schedule.
- interest-only payment—does not reduce the loan principal or build homeowner equity. Borrowers who pay only interest for a period of time then face a big jump in the size of monthly payments or else are forced to refinance.
- minimum payment—may be lower than one month's interest; if so, the shortfall is added to the loan balance. The result is "negative amortization": over time, the principal goes up, not down. Eventually the borrower may have an "upside down" mortgage where the debt is greater than the market value of the home.

According to the credit rating firm Fitch Ratings, up to 80% of all option ARM borrowers choose the minimum monthly payment option. So it's no surprise that in 2005, 20% of option ARMs were "upside down." When a negative amortization limit is reached, the minimum payment jumps up to fully amortize the loan for the remaining loan term. In other words, borrowers suddenly have to start paying the real bill.

Even borrowers who pay more than the monthly minimums can face payment shocks. Option ARMs often start with a temporary super-low teaser interest rate (and correspondingly low monthly payments) that allows borrowers to qualify for "more house." The catch? Since the low initial monthly payment, based on interest rates as low as 1.25%, is not enough to cover the *real* interest rate, the borrower eventually faces a sudden increase in monthly payments.

Balloon Loan: This loan is written for a short 5- to 7-year term during which the borrower pays either interest and principal each month or, in a more predatory form, interest only. At the end of the loan term, the borrower must pay off the entire loan in a lump sum—the "balloon payment." At that point, buyers must either refinance or lose their homes. Balloon loans are known to real estate pros as "bullet loans," since if the loan comes due—forcing the owner to refinance—during a period of high interest rates, it's like getting a bullet in the heart. According to the national organizing and advocacy group ACORN, about 10% of all subprime loans are balloons.

Balloon loans are sometimes structured with monthly payments that fail to cover the interest, much less pay down the principal. Although the borrower makes regular payments, her loan balance increases each month: negative amortization. Many borrowers are unaware that they have a negative amortization loan until they have to refinance.

Shared Appreciation Mortgage (SAM): These are fixed-rate loans for up to 30 years that have easier credit qualifications and lower monthly payments than conventional mortgages. In exchange for a lower interest rate, the borrower relinquishes part of the future value of the home to the lender. Interest rate reductions are based on how much appreciation the borrower is willing to give up. SAMs discourage "sweat equity" since the homeowner receives only some fraction of the appreciation resulting from any improvements. Not surprisingly, these loans have been likened to sharecropping.

Stated-Income Loan: Aimed at borrowers who do not draw regular wages from an employer but live on tips, casual jobs that pay under the table, commissions, or investments, this loan does not require W-2 forms or other standard wage documentation. The trade-off: higher interest rates.

No-Ratio Loan: The debt-income ratio (the borrower's monthly payments on debt, including the planned mortgage, divided by her monthly income) is a standard benchmark that lenders use to determine how large a mortgage they will write. In return for a higher interest rate, the no-ratio loan abandons this benchmark; it is aimed at borrowers with complex financial lives or those who are experiencing divorce, the death of a spouse, or a career change.

—*Amy Gluckman*

---

eownership and high levels of unsustainable debt. To achieve this goal, the federal government spends $100 billion a year for homeownership programs (including the $70-plus billion that the mortgage interest deduction costs the Treasury).

Instead of focusing exclusively on homeownership, a more progressive and balanced housing policy would address the diverse needs of communities for both homes and rental units, and would facilitate new forms of ownership such as community land trusts and cooperatives. A balanced policy

would certainly aim to expand the stock of affordable rental units. Unfortunately, just the opposite is occurring: rental housing assistance is being starved to feed low-income homeownership programs. From 2004 to 2006, President Bush and the Congress cut federal funding for public housing alone by 11%. Over the same period, more than 150,000 rental housing vouchers were cut.

And, of course, policymakers must act to protect those consumers who do opt to buy homes: for instance, by requiring mortgage lenders to make certain not only that a borrower is eligible for a particular loan product, but that the loan is suitable for the borrower.

The reason the United States lacks a sound housing policy is obvious if we follow the money. Overheated housing markets and rising home prices produce lots of winners. Real estate agents reap bigger commissions. Mortgage brokers, appraisers, real estate attorneys, title companies, lenders, builders, home remodelers, and everyone else with a hand in the housing pie does well. Cities raise more in property taxes, and insurance companies enroll more clients at higher premiums. Although housing accounts for only 5% of GDP, it has been responsible for up to 75% of all U.S. job growth in the last four years, according to the consulting firm Oxford Analytica. Housing has buffered the economy, and herding more low-income families into homes, regardless of the consequences, helps keep the industry ticking in the short run. The only losers? Renters squeezed by higher rents and accelerating conversion of rental units into condos. Young middle-income families trying to buy their first house. And, especially, the thousands of low-income families for whom buying a home turns into a financial nightmare.

Resources: Carolina Katz Reid, *Studies in Demography and Ecology: Achieving the American Dream? A Longitudinal Analysis of the Homeownership Experiences of Low-Income Households,* Univ. of Washington, CSDE Working Paper No. 04-04; Dean Baker, "The Housing Bubble: A Time Bomb in Low-Income Communities?" *Shelterforce Online*, Issue #135, May/June 2004, www.nhi.org/online/issues/135/bubble.html; Howard Karger, *Shortchanged: Life and Debt in the Fringe Economy* (Berrett-Koehler, 2005); National Multi Housing Council (www.nmhc.org).

STORMIER WEATHER

THE ECONOMIC RECOVERY IS OVER—
TOO BAD MANY AMERICANS NEVER GOT TO EXPERIENCE IT.

BY JOHN MILLER

It's not only radical economists and cyberspace Cassandras uttering the "r"-word nowadays. Just what are we to make of it when Harvard economists, *The Economist* magazine, and Morgan Stanley followed by Goldman Sachs and Merrill Lynch say the economy is headed toward, or already in, a recession?

You can bet the house, whatever its current value, that hard times are on the way—more layoffs, fewer new jobs, lower wages, tighter family budgets, more debt, and higher poverty levels. This year will see rising economic hardship even if the U.S. economy scrapes by without sinking into an official recession, usually defined as two straight quarters of declining output.

How do I know this? Hard times have been the hallmark of the U.S. economy during this decade, even as the economy expanded. We will be in for more of the same, but worse, as the economy slows and the inevitable downturn in the business cycle exacerbates the economic injuries many people have already sustained thanks to long-term shifts in the U.S. economic system.

AND THOSE WERE THE GOOD TIMES

For a while now, there have been plenty of signs that the overall U.S. economy is headed south. Economic growth stalled in the last three months of 2007, adding only 0.6% to output after correcting for inflation. In December, job growth ground to a near halt, and the economy lost 17,000 jobs in January, as construction suffered large job losses. The unemployment rate jumped to 5.0% for the first time in three years, and would be much higher if the labor force participation rate—the fraction of the population either working or actively looking for work—were at the same level as when George Bush took office. On top of that, retail sales tanked in December as worried consumers cut back on holiday spending. Finally, the terminally volatile stock market registered one of its worst Januaries on record, enough to induce a panicked Fed to make an emergency interest-rate cut.

But even leaving these and other recent numbers aside, U.S. economic performance this decade has been nothing to write home about. The economy has now expanded for 74 straight months, from November 2001 to December 2007, far longer than the usual 51-month post-WWII expansion. But economic growth has been the slowest of any post-WWII expansion, averaging just 2.8% a year, far below the 4.3% average posted by earlier post-WWII business cycles of similar length. Worse yet, the economic growth that has occurred has done so little for so many—and so much for so few.

- Employment expanded by just 0.9% a year since the recovery began, compared with an average of 2.5% for all recoveries that have lasted at least this long.

- After correcting for inflation, weekly wages were just 1.9% higher in October 2007 than at the onset of the last recession in March 2001. The average post-WWII expansion drove wages up by twice that amount, 3.8%.

- Seven million more people were without health insurance in 2006 than when the expansion began in 2001.

- Median household income actually *fell* during this recovery. After correcting for inflation, median household income in 2006 (the latest year for which data are available) was down 2.0% from its 2000 level, and down 8.0% for black families.

- The poverty rate was 12.3% in 2006 (again the latest year available), down from 12.6% in 2005, but still a full percentage point above the 11.3% rate at the onset of the last recession.

- U.S. inequality reached levels not seen since the 1920s as the average real (inflation-adjusted) income of the richest 1% of households rose 34.8% from 2001 to 2005, while rising just 0.8% for the middle fifth of the population and *falling* by 3.0% for the poorest fifth.

- And corporate profits skyrocketed. Inflation-adjusted corporate profits rose 12.8% a year during the first five years of this recovery, compared to an 8.3% average growth rate in the other post-WWII recoveries lasting at least as long.

No wonder 7 out of 10 people think the U.S. economy is heading into a recession, according to a recent poll conducted by the Economic Cycle Research Institute, a New York-based independent think tank. For many, the recession that began in March 2001 and ended, officially, that October has in reality continued straight through the decade.

POP GOES THE HOUSING BUBBLE

Besides punishing people who work for a living and those who can't even find a job, the 2008 economy will face a financial crisis brought on by the bursting of the housing bubble. How bad will it get? Pretty bad. A decade long stagnation, as Harvard economist Larry Summers suggests, or "the worst housing bust ever," as NYU professor Noureil Roubini suggests, are not out of the question. Here is why.

To begin with, subprime borrowers are not the only ones in trouble. The same types of loans that imposed inordinate risks on subprime borrowers have left many other homeowners vulnerable to foreclosure as well.

Defaults are now engulfing even better-off borrowers saddled with adjustable rate mortgages (ARMs), subprime or not, whose low introductory monthly payments are reset upward as interest rates rise in the economy. About one-quarter (24%) of *all* home loans are ARMs. Merrill Lynch economists have called ARM mortgages "ticking time bombs" that they suspect will add another $100 billion in losses, on top of an estimated $400 billion in losses on subprime and other mortgages. Lehman Brothers estimates that nearly $156 billion worth of one particular type of ARM (so-called option ARMs) will face payment resets between 2008 and the second quarter of 2012. If home prices fall by 6% or more in both 2008 and 2009, the borrowers in over $90 billion of these loans would owe as much as or more than the market value of their homes. With a growing number of borrowers already owing more than their houses are worth and, so, unable to refinance, foreclosure and delinquency rates have soared. By the third quarter of 2007, the percentage of home owners behind in their mortgage payments on all one- to four-unit residential loans already stood at a 19-year high, according to a Mortgage Bankers Association survey, and the percent of loans in the process of foreclosure was the highest ever.

As of October, home prices in the ten major metropolitan areas that make up the S&P/Case-Shiller home-price index were down a record 6.7% from a year earlier. In Las Vegas, Miami, San Diego, and Phoenix, cities whose housing markets were sizzling just a few years ago, housing prices have fallen even faster, dropping by 10% or more over the same period. Existing home sales were at their lowest rate on record, and down about one-third from their mid-2005 peak.

Not surprisingly, then, the supply of detached single-family homes listed for sale in October 2007 was at its highest (relative to the pace of sales) since 1985, according to the National Association of Realtors. A glut of unsold houses has in turn squashed housing starts, which hit a 16-year low in December.

How much more will housing prices drop and when will they hit bottom? While one real estate economist suggests that "parts of the housing market are scratching bottom right now," others think housing prices won't bottom out until 2009 or even 2010 and forecast prices at that point may be 12% lower than their peak levels. Summers points to one property derivatives market indicating that over the next several years, house prices could fall by as much as 25% from their previous peaks nationwide.

For anyone who doesn't believe that housing prices can fall for a long time, the recent history of the Japanese housing market suggests otherwise. So does the size of the U.S. housing bubble, which drove home prices up further and for longer than any period since 1890, according to Yale economist Robert Shiller's long-term U.S. house price index. Economic journalist Doug Henwood, publisher of the *Left Business Observer*, calculates that housing prices at their peak were 40% above Schiller's long-term trend line, and notes that a 20% to 25% drop in housing prices would be "in line with past experience."

During the bubble, housing prices rose far more quickly than income; the resulting imbalance is another reason to expect home prices to keep falling. From 2000 to 2006 nationwide housing prices jumped 74%, while median household income rose just 15% (*before* correcting for inflation). To restore a historically normal ratio of housing prices to incomes, average home prices would have to fall by more than 30% percent from their peak levels, according to Princeton economist Paul Krugman.

CONSUMERS TO THE RESCUE?

The bursting of the housing bubble will likely put more of a dent in consumer spending than the stock market collapse of 2001. The two bubbles are of comparable size. But historically, a $100 rise in housing wealth leads to about a $6 increase in long-run consumption, one and a half times the $4 gain from the same increase in stock wealth. Likewise, the current fall in housing wealth will likely translate into a sharper dropoff in consumer spending than would an equal-size fall in stock wealth.

And household consumption has been especially important in this decade's expansion. It now represents a record 72% of GDP, up from about 67% in the late 1990s. So you can expect a collapse of consumer spending to trigger a deeper recession than the 2001 downturn set off by the dot-com bust and a collapse in business capital spending, which at the time accounted for only 13% of GDP. In November, a report by the forecasting firm Global Insight for the U.S. Conference of Mayors predicted that "the deepening housing crisis will cut economic growth by more than 25 percent in 143 U.S. metropolitan areas by next year."

Meanwhile, as house prices fall and unemployment rises, defaults on consumer loans and credit cards, which put a sizeable dent in even American Express's earnings last year, will spike in 2008. And since consumer debt is chopped up, bundled, and resold much like mortgages are, bad consumer debt will add to the fragility of the financial system as far-flung creditors take further losses.

While more and more business economists now foresee recession in 2008, many remain convinced the U.S. economy will get through the year without lapsing into a recession. Most of the optimists are betting that foreign economies will provide enough stimulus to keep the U.S. economy out of recession. Recent Fed interest-rate cuts have reduced the value of the dollar, which in turn lowers the price of U.S. products to foreign consumers. This should spur U.S. export growth and buoy the economy. Indeed, in a recent note Morgan Stanley economists told their clients that their "meager" growth forecast for 2008 would be negative if not for export growth.

Perhaps the fast-growing emerging economies in the developing world offer some hope. In 2007 emerging economies contributed half of the globe's GDP growth measured at market exchange rates, over three times as much as the United States' did. In addition, emerging markets, which buy more than half of U.S. exports, continue to grow, some at an accelerating pace, even as industrialized economies cool. "This time," *The Economist* proposed in November, "they could be the rescuers."

"Don't count on it," says economist Stephen Roach, chairman of Morgan Stanley Asia. "American consumers spent close to $9.5 trillion over the last year. Chinese consumers spent around $1 trillion and Indians spent $650 billion. It is almost mathematically impossible for China and India to offset a pullback in American consumption."

FALSE SAVIOR

All eyes are now on the Fed as it tries to prevent the housing slump from dragging down the broader economy by cutting interest rates and pumping liquidity into the system—as it has following other financial crises. The Fed has cut interest rates repeatedly since the middle of last year and two times in January alone, including an extraordinary three-quarters of a percentage point cut to prop up the teetering stock market.

But because the current problem is not liquidity but solvency, the Fed's actions will likely be ineffective this time around. Injecting money into the economy won't solve today's credit problem because banks are reluctant to lend, even to other banks, when they don't know how much of the economy's bad mortgage debt any borrower may be holding. So when the Fed adds liquidity to the system, banks either hoard the money or, like everyone else, buy safe Treasury bills. With few willing buy to other bonds, long-term interest

rates, or the yields on those bonds, have not dropped, despite repeated liquidity injections by the Fed. For instance, the interbank lending rate is still well above the rates on much safer government bond yields of similar maturity.

Economist and *American Prospect* editor Robert Kuttner likens the situation to "[t]he financial system holding a $400,000 mortgage on a $300,000 house. Lower interest rates can't fix that problem nor give people the confidence to lend."

The ability of the Fed to pull the U.S. economy's fat out of this fire is constrained in other ways as well. At the end of last year, higher energy costs and imports made more expensive by the declining value of the dollar pushed up consumer prices. The pick-up in inflation will make the Fed reluctant to cut interest rates further.

So too will the massive U.S. current account deficit. Each year the United States finances the huge gap between its imports and exports by enticing Asian and other foreign investors to buy dollar-denominated assets such as government bonds and corporate stocks and bonds. When the Fed cuts interest rates, that lowers the rate of return on U.S. assets and makes them less attractive to foreign investors—especially as the U.S. economy falters. Should purchases of U.S. securities by foreign investors slow dramatically, then the dollar would crash, stock values would plummet, and a far more severe economic downturn would surely follow.

THE "D" WORD

With the sharp tightening of credit brought on by the bursting of the housing bubble, and with the Fed's ability to affect the picture highly limited, chilling comparisons between today's rocky economy and the 1920s economy prior to the onset of the Great Depression are now commonplace. No one has beaten that drum louder than Kuttner. "Future historians are likely to look back on the final year of the Bush administration as a moment not unlike 1930, when government dithered while a financial crisis deepened," he warns.

The comparison is an apt one. Reckless private borrowing and gaping inequality defined both periods. What's more, in both periods a borrowing binge pushed up asset prices, first stock prices and then housing prices in the current period, to historically unprecedented levels compared to economic growth and incomes, saddling the economy with unsustainable levels of debt.

At some point that mounting debt will cut the economy down to size, perhaps in a sudden debt deflation similar to the Great Depression, in which the value of most assets, not just housing, sinks below the value of the debt on those assets. More likely the post-stock market crash, post-housing bubble U.S. economy will sink into a lengthy period of economic malaise that looks as dismal as the economic prospects that most working people have already faced over the last decade.

It doesn't have to be that way. But much will have to be done to rescue today's economy from its free-market excesses and to improve the life chances of those who have suffered as a few have enriched themselves. Spending and tax relief targeted at the most hard-pressed, who can be counted on to spend any extra money they get and immediately boost consumption, is not a bad place to start. Other good, quick stimulus measures include expanding unemployment insurance, cutting payroll taxes for families of modest incomes, getting funds to cash-strapped state governments so they can continue to deliver services, and providing mortgage relief for low-income homeowners. But the economic stimulus package the Bush administration and the Democratic leadership of the House recently agreed on does not cover even this modest agenda: it fails to extend unemployment insurance or funnel monies to state governments, and it wastes one-third of its $150 billion price tag on accelerated-depreciation tax breaks for business that have no track record of inducing new investment, especially in a timely way. And whatever the specifics, a $150 billion package is far too small to change to the direction of the $14 trillion U.S. economy.

Massive social investment and fundamental financial reform are needed to put the bubble economy out of business and to create a housing market that serves the needs of most people, not speculators. Back in December, former democratic presidential candidate John Edwards proposed a progressive stimulus package that would also address some of the country's long-term environmental and energy needs. The Edwards plan would build a clean energy infrastructure, provide relief to states, expand unemployment insurance, and help families facing foreclosures. Nobel Prize-winning economist and mainstream rebel Joseph Stiglitz proposes some additional worthy projects: more federal support for state education budgets, tax breaks and spending to lower

emissions. While it would take a while to get those programs in place, Stiglitz warns that this downturn is likely to last longer than other recent downturns.

Until those measures and many more are undertaken, the macroeconomy will lurch from bubble to bubble, while most people endure unrelenting economic hardship that intensifies when in an economic downturn but persists even when the economy grows.

Resources: "America's Economy: Recession in America looks increasingly likely," *The Economist*, 11/15/07; Lawrence Summers, "Wake up to the dangers of a deepening crisis," *Financial Times*, 11/25/07; "False Savior," Review and Outlook, *Wall Street Journal*, 12/12/07; Richard Berner and David Greenshaw, "Recession Coming," *Morgan Stanley Global Economic Forum*, 12/10/07; "Goldman Sees Recession This Year," Real Time Economics, *WSJ* Online, 1/9/08, 9:34am; James Quinn, "U.S. recession is already here, warns Merrill," *Daily Telegraph*, 01/08/08; Nouriel Roubini, "Risk of U.S. Recession and Implications for Financial Markets," 01/09/08; "Economy–Housing Crisis Ushers in Economic Downturn," Center for American Progress, 11/27/07; Christian Weller, "Economic snapshot for December 2007," *American Prospect*, 12/11/07; Sudeep Reedy, "Why Economists Are Betting A Recession Won't Happen," *WSJ*, 12/17/07; "A Better Fed Idea," Review & Outlook, *WSJ*, 12/13/07; Kelly Evans, "Exports May Provide Economy a Safety Net," *WSJ*, 12/13/07; Paul Krugman, "After the Money's Gone," *New York Times*, 12/14/07; Doug Henwood, "Reflections on the recent crisis," *Left Business Observer*, no. 116, 10/19/07; Stephen S. Roach, "You Can Almost Hear It Pop," *New York Times*, 12/16/07; Robert Kuttner, "The Bubble Economy," American Prospect, 9/24/07; Robert Kuttner, "America's economic perfect storm," *Boston Globe*, 12/21/07; James Hagerty and Kelly Evans, "Pace of Decline In Home Prices Sets a Record," *WSJ*, 12/27/07; Gene Sperling, "Ways to Get Economic Stimulus Right This Time," Bloomberg, 12/27/07.

BURLINGTON BUSTS THE AFFORDABLE HOUSING DEBATE

BY DANIEL FIRESIDE

"Housing used to be an opportunity ladder in our country. You started out in a rental and began to save. Then you bought a small home, and eventually you moved up. Today, housing prices are so high that if you're renting an apartment, you can't possibly save," says Brenda Torpy, executive director of the Burlington Community Land Trust.

With housing prices skyrocketing beyond the means of the average worker, rents eating up a greater share of household income, and HUD funding on the chopping block, local governments have few tools at their disposal to create affordable housing. Too often, mayors are reduced to offering tax breaks to big developers in exchange for a few token "below market rate" apartments. In the old debate between supply-siders and government interventionists, it's clear who has the momentum.

Undaunted by these grim trends, community leaders in Burlington, Vt., are continuing to carry out a 20-year experiment in affordable housing based on the radical precept that housing should not be treated as a market commodity. The Burlington Community Land Trust (BCLT) represents an altogether different approach to housing security—and one that holds important lessons for community organizers around the country.

BCLT IS BORN

In the early 1980s, wealthy out-of-town speculators began driving up the cost of housing in Burlington. Harried New York City yuppies saw the bucolic college town of 40,000 as an ideal place for their vacation homes, and longtime working class residents were being rapidly priced out of their own neighborhoods. Housing prices in Burlington were rising at twice the national rate.

Frustration over housing issues came to a boiling point when the political establishment cut a deal with big-time developers to put an upscale apartment complex on the city's scenic waterfront. Voter disgust with this plan to privatize public space led to an upset victory in the mayoral race by Socialist gadfly Bernie Sanders and his ragtag Progressive Coalition in 1981.

Sanders and the Progressive Coalition quickly sought to develop institutions and programs that would have a lasting impact on the community. The Progressives decided to make affordable housing a signature issue. Things got off to a rough start when their proposal for rent control was voted

down after a coalition of property owners and establishment politicians hired a professional consultant to defeat it. With rent control off the table, and federal funding in short supply, the Progressives had to turn to more creative measures to address the housing crisis.

In 1983, they created the Community and Economic Development Office (CEDO), a permanent community-development office that would set development goals and initiate creative projects. CEDO initially focused on three areas of housing policy: protecting the vulnerable, preserving affordable housing, and producing affordable housing. While these goals sound typical of many municipal development authorities, CEDO's strategy was distinctive. It sought to decommodify residential property, ensure its housing projects would be permanently affordable, and actually empower residents. Its most important initiative, and the key to all of these goals, was the Burlington Community Land Trust.

RETHINKING PRIVATE PROPERTY

In the late 1970s, Vermont environmentalist Rick Carbin had formed the Vermont Land Trust (VLT) in an effort to preserve open space as developers bought up farms. Instead of buying and holding land, as some land trusts do, the VLT used its resources to buy undeveloped properties at the edge of urban areas and resell them, often at a profit, but with strict conservation easements that prohibited future development. (For more on easements, see "Land Trusts Ease Control of U.S. Farmland Away from Developers," p. 16.) The VLT's successful track record paved the way for Burlington's housing land trust program.

The Institute for Community Economics, a thinktank based in Springfield, Mass., approached CEDO planners with a proposal to use the land trust model as a tool to address Burlington's housing crisis. Much as the VLT program "unbundled" the ownership of property from its function in the future, the housing land trust separated the ownership of a house from the land it sits on. As Brenda Torpy summarizes, "Conservation land trusts take land out of the market to protect the natural environment. Community land trusts take land out of market to protect the urban environment including the people who live there."

CEDO established the Burlington Community Land Trust as an independent nonprofit corporation in 1984, with official backing from the Burlington City Council and $200,000 in seed money. The trust was viewed as an integral part of the city's affordable housing program. Even traditional politicians came to see the land trust model as an acceptable compromise between a flawed free market approach and heavy-handed government intervention, especially as it promoted the popular concept of home ownership. Democratic and Republican politicians have found it difficult to oppose a program that offered life-long renters a "piece of the American Dream."

At its founding, the BCLT was the first municipally funded community land trust in the country. Today it is the nation's largest community land trust, with over 2,500 members.

HOUSING TRUST 101

Buying land through a housing trust involves several steps. To start, the trust acquires a parcel of land through purchase, foreclosure, tax abatements, or donation, and then arranges for a housing unit to be built on the parcel if one does not yet exist. The trust sells the building but retains ownership of the land underneath. It leases the land to the homeowner for a nominal sum (e.g., $25 per month), generally for 99 years or until the house is sold again.

This model supports affordable housing in several ways. First, homebuyers have to meet low-income requirements. Second, the buying price of the home is reduced because it does not include the price of the land. Third, the trust works with lenders to reduce the cost of the mortgage by using the equity of the land as part of the mortgage calculation. This reduces the size of the down payment and other closing costs and eliminates the need for private mortgage insurance. In all, the trust can cut the cost of home ownership by at least 25%.

For longtime BCLT member Bob Robbins, purchasing a home through the trust "was the only affordable option. We did not have access to money for a down payment on a regular home, and at our income level, we wouldn't have qualified for a mortgage. Through the BCLT, we were able to purchase a $99,000 home with just $2,500 down."

Unlike federal programs that only help the initial buyer, the BCLT keeps the property affordable in perpetuity by imposing restrictions on the resale of the house. Specifically, the contract restricts the profit buyers are able to take when they later sell the house. According to the terms of the BCLT leases, homeowners get back all of their equity from their mortgage plus the market value of any capital improvements they made. However, they only get 25% of any increase in the value of the house (which constitutes 75% of the total value of the property), and none of the increase in the value of the land.

Since buyers keep a portion of the housing value appreciation, families do accumulate some wealth through BCLT homeownership. And as time passes, if the surrounding housing prices continue to rise, the trust prices become even more affordable relative to market housing, and the trust captures more wealth on behalf of the community.

When the homeowner sells, the new buyer must agree to the same terms. If no buyers are interested or the owners default on the mortgage, the BCLT retains the option to buy the property.

This model gives the buyer the benefits of homeownership (including the tax deduction for mortgage interest, wealth accumulation through equity, and stable housing costs) that would otherwise be beyond her means. In return, she gives up the potential of windfall profits if the market keeps rising. BCLT recently published a study of the first 100 trust homes that were sold to a second generation. "The implications were very powerful," says Brenda Torpy. "The initial homebuyers realized a net gain of 29% on the money they had invested. Our homeowners were taking an average of $6,000 with them. These aren't the sky-high returns that some people have come to expect from the housing market, but these were people who would never have entered it in the first place." That's because most BCLT homeowners "would never have been able to buy homes otherwise, even with existing federal and state programs," explains Torpy. "For many, we are a stepping stone between renting and homeownership."

Urban land is not a normal economic good because it exists in a fixed quantity. (They're not making any more of it, as realtors say.) Since the supply cannot rise to meet growing demand, the price is subject to speculative forces. The housing supply can be increased by building in greater density, but this does not happen quickly. When a normal home is offered for sale on the usual terms, it does virtually nothing to make the overall housing market more affordable. A land trust home, by contrast, creates a permanently affordable property because the land it sits on is removed from the speculative market. Most of the appreciation is retained by the housing trust (and by extension, the community), rather than the individual. In this way the trust model creates a bridge between purely public and purely private property. "We're trying to stop the concentration of land in the hands of a wealthy minority," says Torpy.

The land trust program was designed to outlast any change in city hall. This was an important strategy in the Progressive Coalition's early years. As it turned out, the Progressives hung on to control, with the exception of a single Republican administration in the mid-1990s. As a result, they have been able to expand on the aims of their original programs and establish a broad base of support for their housing agenda.

The BCLT has become an important force in Burlington's housing market. After 20 years, the trust controls almost 650 housing units, including over 270 rental apartments and 370 shared-appreciation single-family homes and condominiums—about 4% of Burlington's total housing stock. The process is "buyer initiated"; the buyer picks out the house and asks the trust to incorporate it. Therefore the units are dotted all over the city. The trust has also built a wide variety of homes in various styles to fit into particular neighborhoods. "Most of them are modest," says Torpy. "We've found that condos are good starter homes. They're something new but are still affordable. But we're also building modular homes and 2- and 3-bedroom homes." The BCLT's programs also include tenant-owned cooperatives, a family shelter, a transitional shelter, and housing for homeless youth, the mentally ill, and people with HIV/AIDS.

The BCLT is remarkable not only for its size, but as an organizing structure that promotes community empowerment. Tenants and owners of BCLT units vote for and serve on its governing board, along with government officials and other residents with technical expertise, such as architects and urban planners. The system is designed so that the BCLT doesn't play the role of landlord to tenants and homeowners. Rather, all interested parties have a voice and a vote. In this way it's also an experiment in democratic self-governance.

By looking at housing as a fundamental human right rather than a market good that goes to the highest bidder, and with shrewd political organizing in a hostile environment, housing advocates in Burlington have created a sustainable model for affordable housing that deserves to be emulated across the country. Others are catching on. Since the BCLT published its study, the Fannie Mae Corporation, other city planning offices, and state financing offices have all contacted the BCLT for information about how to use housing trusts in an environment of shrinking funds. Today there are 130 community land trusts in more than 30 states, including in large cities like Atlanta and Cincinnati. The largest growth has been in California and the Pacific Northwest. BCLT itself is expanding into the surrounding counties.

BCLT homeowner Bob Robbins says, "I think every community should have a land trust—not just as a fringe option but as the dominant model to keep housing affordable."

September/October 2005

LABOR'S CAPITAL

PUTTING PENSION WEALTH TO WORK FOR WORKERS

BY ADRIA SCHARF

Pension fund assets are the largest single source of investment capital in the country. Of the roughly $17 trillion in private equity in the U.S. economy, $6 to 7 trillion is held in employee pensions. About $1.3 trillion is in union pension plans (jointly trusteed labor-management plans or collectively bargained company-sponsored plans) and $2.1 trillion is in public employee pension plans. Several trillion more are in defined contribution plans and company-sponsored defined benefit plans with no union representation. These vast sums were generated by—and belong to—workers; they're really workers' deferred wages.

Workers' retirement dollars course through Wall Street, but most of the capital owned *by* working people is invested with no regard *for* working people or their communities. Pension dollars finance sweatshops overseas, hold shares of public companies that conduct mass layoffs, and underwrite myriad anti-union low-road corporate practices. In one emblematic example, the Florida public pension system bought out the Edison Corporation, the for-profit school operator, in November 2003, with the deferred wages of Florida government employees—including public school teachers. (With just three appointed trustees, one of whom is Governor Jeb Bush, Florida is one of the few states with no worker representation on the board of its state-employee retirement fund.)

The custodians of workers' pensions—plan trustees and investment managers—argue that they are bound by their "fiduciary responsibility" to consider only narrow financial factors when making investment decisions. They maintain they have a singular obligation to maximize financial returns and minimize financial risk for beneficiaries—with no regard for broader concerns. But from the perspective of the teachers whose dollars funded an enterprise that aims to privatize their jobs, investing in Edison, however promising the expected return (and given Edison's track record, it wasn't very promising!), makes no sense.

A legal concept enshrined in the 1974 Employee Retirement Income Security Act (ERISA) and other statutes, "fiduciary responsibility" does constrain the decision-making of those charged with taking care of other people's money. It obligates fiduciaries (e.g., trustees and fund managers) to invest retirement assets for the exclusive benefit of the pension beneficiaries. According to ERISA, fiduciaries must act with the care, skill, prudence, and diligence that a "prudent man" would use. Exactly what that means, though, is contested.

The law does *not* say that plan trustees must maximize short-term return. It does, in fact, give fiduciaries some leeway to direct pension assets to worker- and community-friendly projects. In 1994, the U.S. Department of Labor issued rule clarifications that expressly permit fiduciaries to make "economically targeted investments" (ETIs), or investments that take into account collateral benefits like good jobs, housing, improved social service facilities, alternative energy, strengthened infrastructure, and economic development. Trustees and fund managers are free to consider a double bottom line, prioritizing investments that have a social pay-off so long as their expected risk-adjusted financial returns are equal to other, similar, investments. Despite a backlash against ETIs from Newt Gingrich conservatives in the 1990s, Clinton's Labor Department rules still hold.

Nevertheless, the dominant mentality among the asset management professionals who make a living off what United Steelworkers president Leo Gerard calls "the deferred-wage food table" staunchly resists considering any factors apart from financial risk and return.

This is beginning to change in some corners of the pension fund world, principally (no surprise) where workers and beneficiaries have some control over their pension capital. In jointly managed union defined-benefit (known as "Taft-Hartley") plans and public-employee pension plans, the ETI movement is gaining ground. "Taft-Hartley pension trustees have grown more comfortable with economically targeted investments as a result of a variety of influences, one being the Labor Department itself," says Robert Pleasure of the Center for Working Capital, an independent capital stewardship-educational institute started by the AFL-CIO. Concurrently, more public pension fund trustees have begun adopting ETIs that promote housing and economic development within state borders. Most union and public pension trustees now understand that, as long as they follow a careful process and protect returns, ETIs do not breach their fiduciary duty, and may in certain cases actually be sounder investments than over-inflated Wall Street stocks.

SAVING JOBS: HEARTLAND LABOR CAPITAL NETWORK

During the run-up of Wall Street share prices in the 1990s, investment funds virtually redlined basic industries, preferring to direct dollars into hot public technology stocks and emerging foreign markets, which despite the rhetoric of fiduciary responsibility were often speculative, unsound, investments. Even most collectively bargained funds put their assets exclusively in Wall Street stocks, in part because some pension trustees feared that if they didn't, they could be held liable. (During an earlier period, the Labor Department aggressively pursued union pension trustees for breaches of fiduciary duty. In rare cases where trustees were found liable, their personal finances and possessions were at risk.) But in the past five years, more union pension funds and labor-friendly fund managers have begun directing assets into

investments that bolster the "heartland" economy: worker-friendly private equity, and, wherever possible, unionized industries and companies that offer "card-check" and "neutrality." ("Card-check" requires automatic union recognition if a majority of employees present signed authorization cards; "neutrality" means employers agree to remain neutral during organizing campaigns.)

The Heartland Labor Capital Network is at the center of this movement. The network's Tom Croft says he and his allies want to "make sure there's an economy still around in the future to which working people will be able to contribute." Croft estimates that about $3 to $4 billion in new dollars have been directed to worker-friendly private equity since 1999—including venture capital, buyout funds, and "special situations" funds that invest in financially distressed companies, saving jobs and preventing closures. Several work closely with unions to direct capital into labor-friendly investments.

One such fund, New York-based KPS Special Situations, has saved over 10,000 unionized manufacturing jobs through its two funds, KPS Special Situations I and II, according to a company representative. In 2003, St. Louis-based Wire Rope Corporation, the nation's leading producer of high carbon wire and wire rope products, was in bankruptcy with nearly 1,000 unionized steelworker jobs in jeopardy. KPS bought the company and restructured it in collaboration with the United Steelworkers International. Approximately 20% of KPS's committed capital is from Taft-Hartley pension dollars; as a result, the Wire Rope transaction included some union pension assets.

The Heartland Labor Capital Network and its union partners want to expand this sort of strategic deployment of capital by building a national capital pool of "Heartland Funds" financed by union pension assets and other sources. These funds have already begun to make direct investments in smaller worker-friendly manufacturing and related enterprises; labor representatives participate alongside investment experts on their advisory boards.

"It's simple. Workers' assets should be invested in enterprises and construction projects that will help to build their cities, rebuild their schools, and rebuild America's infrastructure," says Croft.

"CAPITAL STEWARDSHIP": THE AFL-CIO

For the AFL-CIO, ETIs are nothing new. Its Housing Investment Trust (HIT), formed in 1964, is the largest labor-sponsored investment vehicle in the country that produces collateral benefits for workers and their neighborhoods. Hundreds of union pension funds invest in the $2 billion trust, which leverages public financing to build housing, including low-income and affordable units, using union labor. HIT, together with its sister fund the Building Investment Trust (BIT), recently announced a new investment program that is expected to generate up to $1 billion in investment in apartment development and rehabilitation by

2005 in targeted cities including New York, Chicago, and Philadelphia. The initiative will finance thousands of units of housing and millions of hours of union construction work. HIT and BIT require owners of many of the projects they help finance to agree to card-check recognition and neutrality for their employees.

HIT and BIT are two examples of union-owned investment vehicles. There are many others—including the LongView ULTRA Construction Loan Fund, which finances projects that use 100% union labor; the Boilermakers' Co-Generation and Infrastructure Fund; and the United Food and Commercial Workers' Shopping Center Mortgage Loan Program—and their ranks are growing.

Since 1997, the AFL-CIO and its member unions have redoubled their efforts to increase labor's control over its capital through a variety of means. The AFL-CIO's Capital Stewardship Program promotes corporate governance reform, investment manager accountability, pro-worker investment strategies, international pension fund cooperation, and trustee education. It also evaluates worker-friendly pension funds on how well they actually advance workers' rights, among other criteria. The Center for Working Capital provides education and training to hundreds of union and public pension fund trustees each year, organizes conferences, and sponsors research on capital stewardship issues including ETIs.

PUBLIC PENSION PLANS JOIN IN

At least 29 states have ETI policies directing a portion of their funds, usually less than 5%, to economic development within state borders. The combined public pension assets in ETI programs amount to about $55 billion, according to a recent report commissioned by the Vermont state treasurer. The vast majority of these ETIs are in residential housing and other real estate.

The California Public Employees' Retirement System (CalPERS) is an ETI pioneer among state pension funds. The single largest pension fund in the country, it has $153.8 billion in assets and provides retirement benefits to over 1.4 million members. In the mid-1990s, when financing for housing construction dried up in California, CalPERS invested hundreds of millions of dollars to finance about 4% of the state's single-family housing market. Its ETI policy is expansive. While it requires economically targeted investments earn maximum returns for their level of risk and fall within geographic and asset-diversification guidelines, CalPERS also considers the investments' benefits to its members and to state residents, their job creation poten-

tial, and the economic and social needs of different groups in the state's population. CalPERS directs about 2% of its assets—about $20 billion as of May 2001—to investments that provide collateral social benefits. It also requires construction and maintenance contractors to provide decent wages and benefits.

Other state pension funds have followed CalPERs' lead. In 2003, the Massachusetts treasury expanded its ETI program, which is funded by the state's $32 billion pension. Treasurer Timothy Cahill expects to do "two dozen or more" ETI investments in 2004, up from the single investment made in 2003, according to the *Boston Business Journal*. "It doesn't hurt our bottom line, and it helps locally," Cahill explained. The immediate priority will be job creation. Washington, Wisconsin, and New York also have strong ETI programs.

In their current form and at their current scale, economically targeted investments in the United States are not a panacea. Pension law does impose constraints. Many consultants and lawyers admonish trustees to limit ETIs to a small portion of an overall pension investment portfolio. And union trustees must pursue ETIs carefully, following a checklist of "prudence" procedures, to protect themselves from liability. The most significant constraint is simply that these investments must generate risk-adjusted returns equal to alternative investments—this means that many deserving not-for-profit efforts and experiments in economic democracy are automatically ruled out. Still, there's more wiggle room in the law than has been broadly recognized. And when deployed strategically to bolster the labor movement, support employee buyouts, generate good jobs, or build affordable housing, economically targeted investments are a form of worker direction over capital whose potential has only begun to be realized. And (until the day that capital is abolished altogether) that represents an important foothold.

As early as the mid-1970s, business expert Peter Drucker warned in *Unseen Revolution* of a coming era of "pension-fund socialism" in which the ownership of massive amounts of capital by pension funds would bring about profound changes to the social and economic power structure. Today, workers' pensions prop up the U.S. economy. They're a point of leverage like no other. Union and public pension funds are the most promising means for working people to shape the deployment of capital on a large scale, while directing assets to investments with collateral benefits. If workers and the trustees of their pension wealth recognize the power they hold, they could alter the contours of capitalism.

CHAPTER 4

FISCAL POLICY, DEFICITS, AND DEBT

INTRODUCTION

Most textbooks depict a macroeconomy stabilized by government intervention. Reflecting the influence of Keynes, they look at ways that the government can use fiscal policy—government spending and taxation—to bolster a flagging economy. Despite record corporate profits and five years of economic growth, the current economic expansion has created fewer jobs and done less to raise wages than any other economic expansion since World War II (see Article 1.1). What is the role of fiscal policy in this context? How is the federal government, under an administration committed to shrinking the size of government, using fiscal tools?

Our coverage of the Bush administration's reversal of fiscal fortune, which turned unprecedented projected budget surpluses into deficits likely to persist until 2013, begins with "The Tax Cut Time Bomb" by Adria Scharf. Scharf documents (Article 4.1) the devastating fiscal effects of the Bush tax cuts—making those cuts permanent would cost more than the money necessary to keep Social Security solvent in the decades ahead.

Tax cuts for the rich are the hallmark of Bush's fiscal policy. Ramaa Vasudevan responds to the Bush administration's claim that the rich are "double-taxed," noting that all taxpayers face double-taxation (Article 4.2). While the editors of the Wall Street Journal argue that the well-to-do pay more than their fair share of taxes, John Miller shows that U.S. tax policy actually does little to redistribute income and lessen today's mind-boggling inequality (Article 4.3). Finally, Paul Krugman's article explains that the 2001-2003 tax cuts can only be sustained by shredding the social safety net. Unfortunately, Krugman shows that that's exactly the point (Article 4.4).

One of the key debates in policy circles today is whether to privatize programs that have long been the responsibility of the government. The Bush administration's current proposal to privatize social security is the foremost example. Our authors take on that proposal. Doug Orr shows that left alone, Social Security is unlikely to suffer a shortfall in revenues, let alone a crisis. He shows that proposals to privatize social security are not designed to make the system solvent, but rather, are aimed at propping up the prices of financial assets (Article 4.5). John Miller takes a close-up look at the macroeconomic projections that underlie the Social Security Administration's claim that the system will suffer a shortfall of revenues. Miller argues that even conservative estimates of future immigration, productivity, and economic growth would keep the system solvent (Article 4.6). Finally, William Spriggs debunks the myth that social security is a bad deal for African Americans, and shows how privatization

would exacerbate racial differences in benefits of retirees and leave African-American retirees worse off than before (Article 4.7).

Other programs are also suffering under the slash-and-burn approach of privatization. James Woolman looks into Health Savings Accounts (HSAs), created by Congress in 2003 and backed by the Bush Administration. Woolman finds that HSAs are putting consumers with families, health problems, or low incomes at risk of large out of pocket expenditures, while awarding high-income healthy purchasers with tax breaks (Article 4.8). And even the military, despite a massive influx of funds, is feeling the negative effects of privatization. Ann Markusen takes a close look at the Pentagon's large-scale effort to outsource its operations to private corporations. Markusen argues that there is little evidence that the privatization of military contracts has generated efficiencies (Article 4.9).

DISCUSSION QUESTIONS

1. (Article 4.1) What is the cost of making the Bush tax cuts permanent? What would be the likely impact on social spending if this were to happen?

2. (Article 4.2) Why does Vasudevan argue that taxing dividends is fair? What is the basis of her claim that the tax code treats investment income more favorably than wage income?

3. (Article 4.3) According to Miller, how significantly does the U.S. tax code redistribute income and reduce inequality? What evidence does he use to respond to the *Wall Street Journal* editors' contention that the tax code is already highly progressive?

4. (Article 4.4) What does Krugman think is the hidden agenda of those currently pushing for tax cuts? Do you agree with his analysis? Expalin why or why not.

5. (Article 4.5) What convinces Orr that the Social Secu-

> ## KEY TO COLANDER
>
> E = *Economics*   M = *Macroeconomics*
>
> Article 4.1 addresses topics from E31 or M15. Articles 4.2, 4.3, and 4.4 go with chapters E25-E26 or M9-M10, or the macro policy discussions in E30, E31, and E33, or M14, M15, and M18. Articles 4.5, 4.6, 4.7, and 4.8 add to the discussion of Social Security and social spending in E31 and M15. Article 4.9 also illustrates macroeconomic policy issues in chapters E30, E31, and E33, or M14, M15, and M18.

rity system is not suffering a crisis? What is the looming bond market crisis that Orr says is the real concern of those who want to privatize Social Security?

6. (Article 4.6) How do changes in immigration levels and productivity growth affect the production possibilities of the nation and the solvency of the Social Security system?

7. (Article 4.7) Spriggs identifies three myths used by those who claim that social security is bad for African Americans. How does he debunk them? Do you find his arguments convincing?

8. (Article 4.8) According to Woolman, what has been the track record of Health Savings Accounts? Have they worked for employees? Which ones? Have HSAs worked for employers?

9. (Article 4.9) What evidence does Markusen present to call into question the claim that privatizing military spending will create competition and improve the efficiency of military services?

March/April 2004

TAX CUT TIME BOMB

BY ADRIA SCHARF

President George W. Bush and Congress planted a time bomb in the federal budget, and they're about to light the fuse. The largest parts of the tax cuts passed in 2001 and 2003 didn't activate immediately, but were designed to kick in later this decade. If they go forward, the cuts will likely cripple or destroy the social programs that form the cornerstone of the federal welfare state. Even worse, the Bush administration is now pushing to make permanent virtually all of the 2001 and 2003 tax cuts, which were originally set to expire by 2010.

In 2001, Bush sought and won the largest income tax rollback in two decades—it reduced tax rates on the top four income brackets and gave advance refunds of $300 to $600 to 94 million taxpayers. In 2003, despite the growing budget deficit, the administration secured a second tax cut—the third largest in U.S. history. The 2003 package shrank dividend and capital gains taxes and accelerated the 2001 rate cut for top income brackets. Combined, the 2001 and 2003 tax cuts will cost at least $824.1 billion between 2001 and 2010, even if Republicans don't succeed in renewing the provisions scheduled to expire, or "sunset," according to Citizens for Tax Justice (CTJ). If the cuts are extended, CTJ estimates they will cost more than $1 trillion between 2004 and 2014, with over 80% of the revenue loss hitting after 2009. (See Figure 1.)

Aside from their sheer size, the 2001 and 2003 packages were notable for a couple of reasons: First, their major provisions were deliberately scheduled to hit later in the decade. Republican congressional leaders delayed the largest cuts to protect the bills from filibuster and deflect attention from

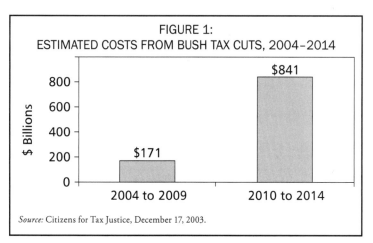

FIGURE 1:
ESTIMATED COSTS FROM BUSH TAX CUTS, 2004–2014

Source: Citizens for Tax Justice, December 17, 2003.

their long-term effects on the budget and inequality. Second, they were frontloaded with tiny morsels for the middle class and backloaded with enormous benefits for the top 1%. (See Figure 2 and Table 1, which are conservative in that they assume expiring provisions will in fact "sunset.")

Over the next 75 years, the cost of extending the 2001 and 2003 tax cuts would amount to $5.9 trillion, or 1.1% of gross domestic product (GDP), according to William G. Gale and Peter R. Orszag of the Brookings Institution. To put that figure into perspective, the expected costs of funding Social Security during that same period are just $3.8 trillion (or 0.7% of GDP). Gale and Orszag warn the new Bush budget plan will necessitate one of the following changes, or a "change of a similar magnitude," within the decade, and argue that even deeper cuts may be required:

- A 29% cut in Social Security benefits;
- A 70% cut in federal Medicaid benefits;
- A 49% cut in all domestic discretionary spending, or
- A 21% increase in payroll taxes.

Resources: William G. Gale and Peter R. Orszag, "Should the President's Tax Cuts be Made Permanent?" Brookings, Washington, D.C., February 24, 2004; "The Bush Tax Cuts: The Most Recent CTJ Data," Citizens for Tax Justice, December 17, 2003, <www.ctj.org>; "Details of the Administration's Budget Proposals," Citizens for Tax Justice, February 3, 2004, <www.ctj.org>.

TABLE 1 AVERAGE TAX CUTS UNDER THE 2001-2003 BUSH TAX CUTS BY CALENDAR YEAR*			
	2001	2005	2010
Top 1%	$3,221	$41,264	$85,002
Next 4%	$1,015	$3,913	$2,780
Next 15%	$742	$2,015	$1,225
Fourth 20%	$572	$971	$1,081
Middle 20%	$403	$563	$791
Second 20%	$266	$371	$508
Lowest 20%	$57	$77	$98

*with sunsets
Source: Citizens for Tax Justice, December 17, 2003.

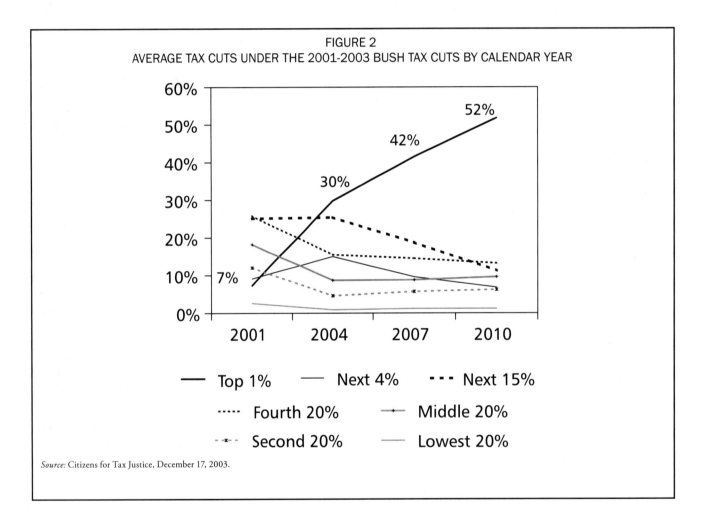

FIGURE 2
AVERAGE TAX CUTS UNDER THE 2001-2003 BUSH TAX CUTS BY CALENDAR YEAR

Source: Citizens for Tax Justice, December 17, 2003.

THE DOUBLE TAXATION OF CORPORATIONS

BY RAMAA VASUDEVAN

Dear Dr. Dollar:
My congressman, John Mica (R-Fla.), sent me a letter claiming that "the high income tax rate of 40% for U.S. corporations, unlike most competitors, does not provide relief for the double taxation of corporate income." Like the double talk? He wants to reduce the incentives for companies to move offshore by lowering corporate income taxes. But what's the best response to this claim about "double-taxation"? I don't know much about economics, but I do know enough to know that this position is a con job.

—*Sandra Holt, Casselberry, Fla*

When corporations and their friends in Washington go on about "double taxation," what they're referring to is the notion that if corporations are taxed on their income and shareholders on their dividends, then the same income is getting taxed twice, with the implication that this is unfair or unduly burdensome. You're right to view this idea as a con job. Here's why:

First, the corporation as an entity is legally distinct from its shareholders. This distinction lies at the core of the notion of limited liability and protects individual shareholders from liability for damages caused by the corporation's pursuit of profits. The claim of "double-taxation" is bogus because the two taxes apply to different taxpayers—corporations versus individual shareholders.

Second, the double taxation claim is a bit of a red herring since many kinds of income are in effect double taxed. For instance, along with the income tax, workers also have to pay Medicare and Social Security taxes on their earnings.

In fact, investment income is currently treated more favorably by the tax code than wage income. Investment income is taxed at an average rate of 9.6%, compared to 23.4 % for wages. One reason for this disparity is that investment income is exempt from Medicare and Social Security taxes. But a second key reason is the reduced special tax rate for investment income approved by Congress during Bush's first term. This includes cutting the top tax rate on dividends from around 35% to 15%. As David Cay Johnston of *The New York Times* has observed, "the wealthiest Americans now pay much higher direct taxes on money they work for than on money that works for them."

Who benefits when the tax code rewards investment rather than wage earning? The wealthy, who garner most investment income: about 43% of total investment income goes to the top 1% of taxpayers.

Repealing the dividend tax would only exacerbate that disparity. According to Federal Reserve Board data, fewer than 20% of families hold stocks outside of retirement accounts. Individual stockholdings are concentrated among the richest families, who would be the real beneficiaries of a dividend tax break. Some 42% of benefits from repealing the dividend tax would go to the richest 1% of taxpayers, and about 75% would go to the richest 10% of taxpayers.

In contrast, the vast majority of those who own any stock at all hold their stocks in retirement accounts. They neither receive dividends on these shares directly nor pay a dividend tax—but they'll find themselves paying the normal income tax as soon as they begin drawing on their retirement accounts.

Do taxes impose a disproportionately heavy burden on U.S. corporations? The oft-quoted 40% tax rate applies only to a tiny proportion of corporate income. The official tax rate for most corporate profits is 35%; the very smallest corporations (those with income under $50,000 per year) are subject to a rate of only 15%. Moreover, the official tax rates are higher than the effective tax rates that corporations actually end up paying. A variety of tax breaks allow corporations to reap tremendous tax savings, estimated at $87 billion to $170 billion in 2002-2003 alone, according to a study by Citizens for Tax Justice. The double-taxation argument would have meaning only if the actual burden of corporate taxes were excessive. But it is not. In 2002-03, U.S. corporations paid an effective tax rate of only about 23%. Forty-six large corporations, including Pfizer, Boeing, and AT&T, actually received tax rebates (negative taxes)! Far from being a crushing burden, corporate income tax in the United States has fallen from an average of nearly 5% of GDP in the fifties to 2% in the nineties and about 1.5% (projected) in 2005-2009.

Is the U.S. corporate tax burden higher that that of its competitors? Comparisons of 29 developed countries reveal that only three—Iceland, Germany, and Poland—collected less corporate income tax as a share of GDP than the United States. This represents a reversal from the 1960s, when corporate income tax as a share of GDP in the United States was nearly double that of other developed countries.

The demand for cutting dividend taxes needs to be exposed for what it is: an attempt to create yet another windfall for upper income families who earn the bulk of their income from financial investments. It would not stimulate business investment. And it would exacerbate, rather than redress, the many *real* inequities in the tax code.

Resources: John Miller, "Double Taxation Double Speak: Why repealing the dividend tax is unfair," *Dollars & Sense,* March-April 2003; Dean Baker "The Dividend Taxbreak; Taxing Logic," Center for Economic and Policy Research, 2003; Joel Friedman, "The Decline of Corporate income tax revenues," Center on Budget and Policy Priorities, 2003; David Cay Johnston, *Perfectly Legal: The Covert Campaign to Rig our Tax System to Benefit the Super-Rich—and Cheat Everybody Else,* Portfolio, 2003.

ARTICLE 4.3   *November/December 2005*

MIND BOGGLING INEQUALITY: ENOUGH TO MAKE EVEN ADAM SMITH WORRY

BY JOHN MILLER

Do soaring corporate profits (higher as a share of national income than at any time since 1950) and a green Christmas on Wall Street (green as in record-setting multimillion dollar bonuses for investment bankers) have you worried about economic inequality? How about real wages that are lower and poverty rates higher than when the current economic expansion began five years ago? If that is not enough to make you worry, try this. The editors of the *Wall Street Journal* are spilling a whole lot of ink these days to convince their readers that today's inequality is just not a problem. Besides that, there is not much to be done about inequality, say the editors, since taxes are already soaking the rich.

Not even Ben Bernanke, the new head of the Fed, is prepared to swallow the editors' line this time. Inequality in the U.S. economy "is increasing beyond what is healthy," Bernanke told Congress, although like the editors he finds it a "big challenge to think about what to do about it."

There is real reason to worry. By nearly every measure, inequality today is at a level not seen since the Great Depression. And by historical standards, the rich have hardly overpaid in taxes for their decades-long economic banquet.

Once you remove the Journal editors' spin, the "actual evidence" from the Congressional Budget Office (CBO) makes clear that the charge of worsening inequality and a declining tax burden on the rich is anything but "trumped up." The CBO's latest numbers document a lopsided economic growth that has done little to improve the lot of most households while it has paid off handsomely for those at the top. From 1979 to 2004, the poorest quintile saw their average real (i.e., inflation-adjusted) income barely budge, increasing just 2.0% over the entire period. The middle-income quintile enjoyed a larger but still modest real-income gain of 14.6% over the 25-year span, while the best-off fifth

enjoyed a 63.0% gain. But the 153.9% jump in the real income of the richest 1% far outdistanced even the gains of the near rich. (see Figure 1)

The *Journal's* editors are right about one thing: a widening income gap is a long-term trend that has persisted regardless of the party in power. The well-to-do made out like bandits during the Clinton years as well as the Bush years. In fact, postwar inequality, after peaking in 2000, did retreat somewhat in the first four Bush years as the stock market bubble burst, cutting into the income share of the most well-off, who hold the vast majority of corporate stock. (In 2004, the wealthiest 1% of U.S. households held 36.9% of common stock by value; the wealthiest 10% held 78.7%.)

The increase in the gulf between the haves and the have-nots during the Bush years, however, has hardly been modest. In 2004, as in 1999 and in 2000, the share of pre-tax income going to the richest 1% is greater than the share they received in any year since 1929, according to the ground-breaking historical study of inequality by economists Thomas Piketty and Emmanuel Saez. (See "The Long U.S. Barbeque," p. 14, for further discussion of the study.) *Barron's* magazine, the Dow Jones business and financial weekly, put it succinctly in their recent cover story, "Rich America, Poor America": "never in history have the haves had so much."

FEAST AND FAMINE

The editors' banquet scenario is unconvincing, to say the least. First off, before we examine the bill for the banquet, we ought to look at what the 100 guests were served. Not everyone got the same meal; in fact, the economic banquet of the last two and a half decades was a feast for some and a famine for others. Most people got modest portions indeed. The income, or serving size if you will, of the average guest

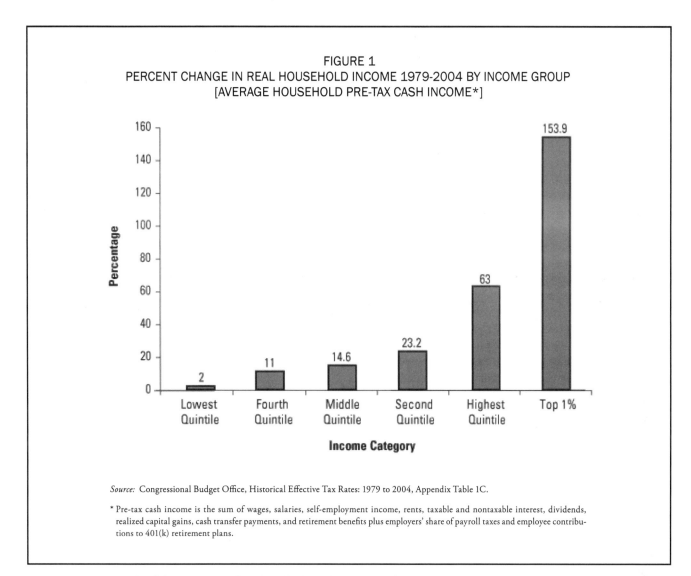

FIGURE 1
PERCENT CHANGE IN REAL HOUSEHOLD INCOME 1979-2004 BY INCOME GROUP
[AVERAGE HOUSEHOLD PRE-TAX CASH INCOME*]

Source: Congressional Budget Office, Historical Effective Tax Rates: 1979 to 2004, Appendix Table 1C.

* Pre-tax cash income is the sum of wages, salaries, self-employment income, rents, taxable and nontaxable interest, dividends, realized capital gains, cash transfer payments, and retirement benefits plus employers' share of payroll taxes and employee contributions to 401(k) retirement plans.

was just one sixteenth of the economic feast lavished on the richest 1%. Surely even *Wall Street Journal* editors wouldn't expect the average taxpayer to subsidize the culinary indulgences of the rich.

Second, the well-to-do picked up much less of the tab for their banquet than the *Journal's* editorials suggest. True enough, the richest 1% of taxpayers now pay more than one-third of all income taxes. But the federal tax bill is not confined to income taxes alone. It also includes payroll taxes (like FICA, the Social Security tax) and excise taxes (for example, on cars) that fall more heavily on low-income households than the income tax does, making up much of their tax bill. Taking those taxes into account does make a substantial difference in the share of the total federal tax bill shouldered by the rich. In 2004, the richest 1% paid just over one-quarter (25.3%), not one-third, of all federal taxes. (see Table 1) No working American ate for free.

Beyond federal tax liabilities, the banquet tab also includes state and local taxes. Those taxes, especially state sales taxes, fall most heavily on those who were served the smallest portions: low-income earners. Once state and local taxes are included, the tax share of the richest 1% falls to just over

one-fifth, not much more than their share of national income as calculated by the IRS. According to these estimates, provided by the Washington-based think tank Citizens for Tax Justice, the U.S. tax code taken in its entirety does little to redistribute income. By any definition, our tax system is at best mildly progressive, and surely not "highly progressive" as the Journal claims.

On top of all that, when the bill for today's economic banquet came due, the Bush administration somehow decided that the guests as a group had overpaid. The purported excess over the amount of the bill should, at least according to the Bush administration's reasoning, go back to each member of the group in tax cuts, in proportion with what they contributed toward paying the bill. Those who contributed the most should get the most back; those who contributed less should get less back. And those whom the rest are treating to dinner, of course, should get nothing back.

But the Bush tax cuts don't manage to conform to even this version of fairness, at least not when it comes to the share of the cuts going to the super-rich. The richest 1% of taxpayers, with average household income well over $1 million, get a whopping 35.9% of the benefits of the Bush tax cuts,

TABLE 1
SHARE OF TOTAL TAX LIABILITIES AND EFFECTIVE TAX RATES PAID BY DIFFERENT INCOME GROUPS, 2004

Income Category	Share of Total Tax Liabilities		Effective Tax Rate	
	Federal	Federal, State, and Local	Federal	Federal, State, and Local
Lowest Quintile	0.9%	2.2%	7.9%	19.7%
Second Quintile	4.5%	5.5%	11.4%	23.3%
Middle Quintile	9.7%	10.5%	15.8%	27.0%
Fourth Quintile	17.6%	19.0%	18.7%	29.8%
Highest Quintile	67.1%	62.6%	21.6%	31.8%
TOP 1%	25.3%	20.8%	24.6%	32.8%

Sources: Congressional Budget Office, *Historical Effective Tax Rates: 1979 to 2004*, Appendix Tables 1b. Citizens for Tax Justice, "Overall Tax Rates Have Flattened Sharply Under Bush," 4/13/04.

or an annual tax cut of $48,311 during this decade, well in excess of their one-quarter (or 25.3% to be exact) share of the federal tax burden.

All told, the U.S. tax system does not soak the rich, especially after the Bush tax cuts. In 2004, the effective federal tax rate—that is, the share of total income anyone hands over to the government in federal taxes—for the richest 1% was 24.6%, according to Citizens for Tax Justice, far lower than it was in the 1970s. By historical standards, or by any reasonable definition, taxes on the rich have not reached the saturation point.

On top of that, the effective tax rate for all federal, state, and local taxes combined for the poorest fifth of households is 19.7%—well over half the effective tax rate of 32.8% that the richest 1% pay—and that's *after* taking into account the Earned Income Tax Credit that some low-income households receive. With an average income of $1,259,700, as opposed to $15,400, that rate falls far short of exhausting the ability of the superrich to pay. It hardly represents a contribution to the bill for the economic banquet of the last two and a half decades that is in proportion to the large and lavish meal they've enjoyed.

WHAT WOULD ADAM SMITH SAY?

There is no reason to be flummoxed about how to address worsening inequality, even in the short run. Wall Street Journal columnist David Wessel, in a November 2006 article on how Democrats might tackle the wealth gap, had no problem enumerating several measures that would lessen inequality. Those included raising the minimum wage, restraining CEO pay, expanding the earned-income tax credit, and rolling back President Bush's upper-income tax cuts.

Just the thought that Congress might actually pass some of these measures was enough for the Journal's editors to minimize the reality of rising inequality and to extol the supposed tax generosity of the rich.

Too bad. Unlike the Wall Street Journal's editors, even Adam Smith, the patron saint of capitalism, recognized the corrupting effect of inequality in a market economy. As Smith put it in The Theory of Moral Sentiments, his often overlooked lectures on ethics, the "disposition to admire, and almost to worship, the rich and the powerful, and to despise, or, at least, to neglect persons of poor and mean condition is the great and most universal cause of the corruption of our moral sentiments."

A fitting description of the attitude the Wall Street Journal's editors seem to have toward the rich and the poor. Business executives and policymakers would do well to skip the Journal and go back to Smith.

Resources: Congressional Budget Office, "Historical Effective Federal Tax Rates: 1979 to 2004," 12/04; Citizens for Tax Justice, "Overall Tax Rates Have Flattened Sharply Under Bush," 4/13/04; David Wessel, "Fed Chief Warns of Widening Inequality," *Wall Street Journal*, 2/7/07; David Wessel, "Democrats target wealth gap and hope not to hit economy," *Wall Street Journal*, 11/21/06; Adam Smith, The Theory of Moral Sentiments, Sec. III, Chap. III, in The Essential Adam Smith ed. Robert Heilbroner (Norton, 1986), p. 86; "Incomes and Politics," *Wall Street Journal* editorial, 9/2/06; "The Top 1% Pay 35%," *Wall Street Journal* editorial, 12/20/06.

THE TAX-CUT CON

BY PAUL KRUGMAN

Bruce Tinsley's comic strip, "Mallard Fillmore," is, he says, "for the average person out there: the forgotten American taxpayer who's sick of the liberal media." In June 2003, that forgotten taxpayer made an appearance in the strip, attacking his TV set with a baseball bat and yelling: "I can't afford to send my kids to college, or even take 'em out of their substandard public school, because the federal, state and local governments take more than 50% of my income in taxes. And then the guy on the news asks with a straight face whether or not we can 'afford' tax cuts."

Nobody likes paying taxes, and no doubt some Americans are as angry about their taxes as Tinsley's imaginary character. But most Americans also care a lot about the things taxes pay for.

All politicians say they're for public education; almost all of them also say they support a strong national defense, maintaining Social Security and, if anything, expanding the coverage of Medicare. When the "guy on the news" asks whether we can afford a tax cut, he's asking whether, after yet another tax cut goes through, there will be enough money to pay for those things. And the answer is no.

But it's very difficult to get that answer across in modern American politics, which has been dominated for 25 years by a crusade against taxes.

I don't use the word "crusade" lightly. The advocates of tax cuts are relentless, even fanatical. An indication of the movement's fervor—and of its political power—came during the Iraq war. War is expensive and is almost always accompanied by tax increases. But not in 2003. "Nothing is more important in the face of a war," declared Tom DeLay, the House majority leader, "than cutting taxes." And sure enough, taxes were cut, not just in a time of war but also in the face of record budget deficits.

A result of the tax-cut crusade is that there is now a fundamental mismatch between the benefits Americans expect to receive from the government and the revenues government collect. This mismatch is already having profound effects at the state and local levels: teachers and policemen are being laid off and children are being denied health insurance. The federal government can mask its problems for a while by running huge budget deficits, but it, too, will eventually have to decide whether to cut services or raise taxes. And we are not talking about minor policy adjustments. If taxes stay as low as they are now, government as we know it cannot be maintained. In particular, Social Security will have to become far less generous; Medicare will no longer be able to guarantee comprehensive medical care to older Americans; Medicaid will no longer provide basic medical care to the poor.

How did we reach this point? What are the origins of the antitax crusade? And where is it taking us?

SUPPLY-SIDERS, STARVE-THE-BEASTERS, AND LUCKY DUCKIES

It is often hard to pin down what antitax crusaders are trying to achieve. The reason is not, or not only, that they are disingenuous about their motives—though as we will see, disingenuity has become a hallmark of the movement in recent years. Rather, the fuzziness comes from the fact that today's antitax movement moves back and forth between two doctrines. Both doctrines favor the same thing: big tax cuts for people with high incomes. But they favor it for different reasons.

One of those doctrines has become famous under the name "supply-side economics." It's the view that the government can cut taxes without severe cuts in public spending. The other doctrine is often referred to as "starving the beast," a phrase coined by David Stockman, Ronald Reagan's budget director. It's the view that taxes should be cut precisely in order to force severe cuts in public spending. Supply-side economics is the friendly, attractive face of the tax-cut movement. But starve-the-beast is where the power lies.

The starting point of supply-side economics is an assertion that no economist would dispute: taxes reduce the incentive to work, save and invest. A businessman who knows that 70 cents of every extra dollar he makes will go to the IRS is less willing to make the effort to earn that extra dollar than if he knows that the IRS will take only 35 cents. So reducing tax rates will, other things being the same, spur the economy.

This much isn't controversial. But the government must pay its bills. So the standard view of economists is that if you want to reduce the burden of taxes, you must explain what government programs you want to cut as part of the deal. There's no free lunch.

What the supply-siders argued, however, was that there was a free lunch. Cutting marginal rates, they insisted, would lead to such a large increase in gross domestic product that it wouldn't be necessary to come up with offsetting spending cuts. What supply-side economists say, in other words, is, "Don't worry, be happy and cut taxes." And when they say cut taxes, they mean taxes on the affluent: reducing the top marginal rate means that the biggest tax cuts go to people in the highest tax brackets.

The other camp in the tax-cut crusade actually welcomes the revenue losses from tax cuts. Its most visible spokesman today is Grover Norquist, president of Americans for Tax Reform, who once told National Public Radio: "I don't want to abolish government. I simply want to reduce it to the size where I can drag it into the bathroom and drown it in the bathtub." And the way to get it down to that size is to starve it of revenue. "The goal is reducing the size and scope of government by draining its lifeblood," Norquist told *U.S. News & World Report*.

What does "reducing the size and scope of government" mean? Tax-cut proponents are usually vague about the details. But the Heritage Foundation, ideological headquarters for the movement, has made it pretty clear. Edwin Feulner, the foundation's president, uses "New Deal" and "Great Society" as terms of abuse, implying that he and his organization want to do away with the institutions Franklin Roosevelt and Lyndon Johnson created. That means Social Security, Medicare, Medicaid—most of what gives citizens of the United States a safety net against economic misfortune.

The starve-the-beast doctrine is now firmly within the conservative mainstream. George W. Bush himself seemed to endorse the doctrine as the budget surplus evaporated: in August 2001 he called the disappearing surplus "incredibly positive news" because it would put Congress in a "fiscal straitjacket."

Like supply-siders, starve-the-beasters favor tax cuts mainly for people with high incomes. That is partly because, like supply-siders, they emphasize the incentive effects of cutting the top marginal rate; they just don't believe that those incentive effects are big enough that tax cuts pay for themselves. But they have another reason for cutting taxes mainly on the rich, which has become known as the "lucky ducky" argument.

Here's how the argument runs: to starve the beast, you must not only deny funds to the government; you must make voters hate the government. There's a danger that working-class families might see government as their friend: because their incomes are low, they don't pay much in taxes, while they benefit from public spending. So in starving the beast, you must take care not to cut taxes on these "lucky duckies." (Yes, that's what the *Wall Street Journal* called them in a famous editorial.) In fact, if possible, you must raise taxes on working-class Americans in order, as the *Journal* said, to get their "blood boiling with tax rage."

So the tax-cut crusade has two faces. Smiling supply-siders say that tax cuts are all gain, no pain; scowling starve-the-beasters believe that inflicting pain is not just necessary but also desirable. Is the alliance between these two groups a marriage of convenience? Not exactly. It would be more accurate to say that the starve-the-beasters hired the supply-siders—indeed, created them—because they found their naive optimism useful.

A look at who the supply-siders are and how they came to prominence tells the story. The supply-side movement likes to present itself as a school of economic thought like Keynesianism or monetarism—that is, as a set of scholarly ideas that made their way, as such ideas do, into political discussion. But the reality is quite different. Supply-side economics was a political doctrine from Day 1; it emerged in the pages of political magazines, not professional economics journals.

That is not to deny that many professional economists favor tax cuts. But they almost always turn out to be starve-the-beasters, not supply-siders. And they often secretly—or sometimes not so secretly—hold supply-siders in contempt. N. Gregory Mankiw, now chairman of George W. Bush's Council of Economic Advisers, is definitely a friend to tax cuts; but in the first edition of his economic-principles textbook, he described Ronald Reagan's supply-side advisers as "charlatans and cranks."

> ## TO STARVE THE BEAST, YOU MUST MAKE VOTERS HATE THE GOVERNMENT.

It is not that the professionals refuse to consider supply-side ideas; rather, they have looked at them and found them wanting. A conspicuous example came earlier this year when the Congressional Budget Office tried to evaluate the growth effects of the Bush administration's proposed tax cuts. The budget office's new head, Douglas Holtz-Eakin, is a conservative economist who was handpicked for his job by the administration. But his conclusion was that unless the revenue losses from the proposed tax cuts were offset by spending cuts, the resulting deficits would be a drag on growth, quite likely to outweigh any supply-side effects.

But if the professionals regard the supply-siders with disdain, who employs these people? The answer is that since the 1970s almost all of the prominent supply-siders have been aides to conservative politicians, writers at conservative publications like *National Review,* fellows at conservative policy centers like Heritage or economists at private companies with strong Republican connections. Loosely speaking, that is, supply-siders work for the vast right-wing conspiracy. What gives supply-side economics influence is its connection with a powerful network of institutions that want to shrink the government and see tax cuts as a way to achieve that goal.

Supply-side economics is a feel-good cover story for a political movement with a much harder-nosed agenda.

A PLANNED CRISIS

Right now, much of the public discussion of the Bush tax cuts focuses on their short-run impact. Critics say that the 2.7 million jobs lost since March 2001 prove that the administration's policies have failed, while the administration says that things would have been even worse without the tax cuts and that a solid recovery is just around the corner.

But this is the wrong debate. Even in the short run, the right question to ask isn't whether the tax cuts were better than nothing; they probably were. The right question is whether some other economic-stimulus plan could have achieved better results at a lower budget cost. And it is hard to deny that, on a jobs-per-dollar basis, the Bush tax cuts have been extremely ineffective. According to the Congressional Budget Office, half of this year's $400 billion budget deficit is due to Bush tax cuts. Now $200 billion is a lot of money; it is equivalent to the salaries of four million average workers. Even the administration doesn't claim its policies have created four million jobs. Surely some other policy—aid to state and local governments, tax breaks for the poor and middle class rather than the rich, maybe even WPA-style public works— would have been more successful at getting the country back to work.

Meanwhile, the tax cuts are designed to remain in place even after the economy has recovered. Where will they leave us?

Here's the basic fact: partly, though not entirely, as a result of the tax cuts of the last three years, the government of the United States faces a fundamental fiscal shortfall. That is, the revenue it collects falls well short of the sums it needs to pay for existing programs. Even the U.S. government must, eventually, pay its bills, so something will have to give.

The numbers tell the tale. This year and next, the federal government will run budget deficits of more than $400 billion. Deficits may fall a bit, at least as a share of gross domestic product, when the economy recovers. But the relief will be modest and temporary. As Peter Fisher, undersecretary of the treasury for domestic finance, puts it, the federal government is "a gigantic insurance company with a sideline business in defense and homeland security." And about a decade from now, this insurance company's policyholders will begin making a lot of claims. As the baby boomers retire, spending on Social Security benefits and Medicare will steadily rise, as will spending on Medicaid (because of rising medical costs). Eventually, unless there are sharp cuts in benefits, these three programs alone will consume a larger share of GDP than the federal government currently collects in taxes.

THE LOOMING FISCAL CRISIS ISN'T A DEFEAT FOR THE LEADERS OF THE TAX-CUT CRUSADE. IT'S EXACTLY WHAT THEY HAD IN MIND.

Alan Auerbach, William Gale, and Peter Orszag, fiscal experts at the Brookings Institution, have estimated the size of the "fiscal gap"—the increase in revenues or reduction in spending that would be needed to make the nation's finances sustainable in the long run. If you define the long run as 75 years, this gap turns out to be 4.5% of GDP. Or to put it another way, the gap is equal to 30% of what the federal government spends on all domestic programs. Of that gap, about 60% is the result of the Bush tax cuts. We would have faced a serious fiscal problem even if those tax cuts had never happened. But we face a much nastier problem now that they are in place.

And more broadly, the tax-cut crusade will make it very hard for any future politicians to raise taxes.

So how will this gap be closed? The crucial point is that it cannot be closed without either fundamentally redefining the role of government or sharply raising taxes.

Politicians will, of course, promise to eliminate wasteful spending. But take out Social Security, Medicare, defense, Medicaid, government pensions, homeland security, interest on the public debt and veterans' benefits—none of them what people who complain about waste usually have in mind—and you are left with spending equal to about 3% of gross domestic product. And most of that goes for courts, highways, education and other useful things. Any savings from elimination of waste and fraud will amount to little more than a rounding-off error.

So let's put a few things back on the table. Let's assume that interest on the public debt will be paid, that spending on defense and homeland security will not be compromised and that the regular operations of government will continue to be financed. What we are left with, then, are the New Deal and Great Society programs: Social Security, Medicare, Medicaid and unemployment insurance. And to close the fiscal gap, spending on these programs would have to be cut by around 40%.

It's impossible to know how such spending cuts might unfold, but cuts of that magnitude would require drastic changes in the system. It goes almost without saying that the age at which Americans become eligible for retirement benefits would rise, that Social Security payments would fall sharply compared with average incomes, that Medicare patients would be forced to pay much more of their expenses out of pocket—or do without. And that would be only a start.

All this sounds politically impossible. In fact, politicians of both parties have been scrambling to expand, not reduce, Medicare benefits by adding prescription drug coverage. It's hard to imagine a situation under which the entitlement programs would be rolled back sufficiently to close the fiscal gap.

Yet closing the fiscal gap by raising taxes would mean rolling back all of the Bush tax cuts, and then some. And that also sounds politically impossible.

For the time being, there is a third alternative: borrow the difference between what we insist on spending and what we're willing to collect in taxes. That works as long as lenders believe that someday, somehow, we're going to get our fiscal act together. But this can't go on indefinitely.

Eventually—I think within a decade, though not everyone agrees—the bond market will tell us that we have to make a choice.

In short, everything is going according to plan.

For the looming fiscal crisis doesn't represent a defeat for the leaders of the tax-cut crusade or a miscalculation on their part. Some supporters of President Bush may have really believed that his tax cuts were consistent with his promises to protect Social Security and expand Medicare; some people may still believe that the wondrous supply-side effects of tax cuts will make the budget deficit disappear. But for starve-the-beast tax-cutters, the coming crunch is exactly what they had in mind.

WHAT KIND OF COUNTRY?

The astonishing political success of the antitax crusade has, more or less deliberately, set the United States up for a fiscal crisis. How we respond to that crisis will determine what kind of country we become.

If Grover Norquist is right—and he has been right about a lot—the coming crisis will allow conservatives to move the nation a long way back toward the kind of limited government we had before Franklin Roosevelt. Lack of revenue, he says, will make it possible for conservative politicians—in the name of fiscal necessity—to dismantle immensely popular government programs that would otherwise have been untouchable.

In Norquist's vision, America a couple of decades from now will be a place in which elderly people make up a disproportionate share of the poor, as they did before Social Security. It will also be a country in which even middle-class elderly Americans are, in many cases, unable to afford expensive medical procedures or prescription drugs and in which poor Americans generally go without even basic health care. And it may well be a place in which only those who can afford expensive private schools can give their children a decent education.

But that's a choice, not a necessity. The tax-cut crusade has created a situation in which something must give. But what gives—whether we decide that the New Deal and the Great Society must go or that taxes aren't such a bad thing after all—is up to us. The American people must decide what kind of a country we want to be.

Excerpted from the *New York Times* Magazine, September 14, 2003.

SOCIAL SECURITY ISN'T BROKEN

SO WHY THE RUSH TO "FIX" IT?

BY DOUG ORR

Federal Reserve Chairman Alan Greenspan told Congress earlier this year that everyone knows there's a Social Security crisis. That's like saying "everyone knows the earth is flat."

Starting with a faulty premise guarantees reaching the wrong conclusion. The truth is there is no Social Security crisis, but there is a potential crisis in retirement income security and there may be a crisis in the future in U.S. financial markets. It's this latter crisis that Greenspan actually is worried about.

Social Security is the most successful insurance program ever created. It insures millions of workers against what economists call "longevity risk," the possibility they will live "too long" and not be able to work long enough, or save enough, to provide their own income. Today, about 10% of those over age 65 live in poverty. Without Social Security, that rate would be almost 50%.

Social Security was originally designed to supplement, and was structured to resemble, private-sector pensions. In the 1930s, all private pensions were defined-benefit plans. The retirement benefit was based on a worker's former wage and years of service. In most plans, after 35 years of service the monthly benefit, received for life, would be at least half of the income received in the final working year.

Congress expected that private-sector pensions eventually would cover most workers. But pension coverage peaked at 40% in the 1960s. Since then, corporations have systematically dismantled pension systems. Today, only 16% of private-sector workers are covered by defined-benefit pensions. Rather than supplementing private pensions, Social Security has become the primary source of retirement income for almost two-thirds of retirees. Thus, Congress was forced to raise benefit levels in 1972.

What has happened to private-sector defined benefit pensions? They've been replaced with defined-contribution (DC) savings plans such as 401(k)s and 403(b)s. These plans provide some retirement income but offer no real protection from longevity risk. Once a retiree depletes the amount saved in the plan, their retirement income is gone.

In a generous DC plan, a firm might match the worker's contribution up to 3% of his or her pay. With total contributions of 6%, average wage growth of 2% a year, and an average return on the investment portfolio of 5%, after 35 years of work, a retiree would exhaust the plan's savings in just 8.5 years even if her annual spending is only half of her final salary. If she restricts spending to just one-third of the final salary, the savings can stretch to 14 years.

At age 65, life expectancy for women today is about 20 years, and for men about 15 years, so DC savings plans will not protect the elderly from longevity risk. The conversion of defined-benefit pensions to defined-contribution plans is the source of the real potential crisis in retirement income. Yet Greenspan did not mention this in his testimony to Congress.

NO CRISIS

Opponents of Social Security have hated it since its creation in 1935. The first prediction of a Social Security crisis was published in 1936! The Heritage Foundation and Cato Institute are home to many of the program's opponents today, and they fixate on the concept of a "demographic imperative." In 1960, the United States had 5.1 workers per retiree, in 1998 we had 3.4, and by 2030 we will have only 2.1. Opponents claim that with these demographic changes, revenues will eventually be insufficient to pay Social Security retirement benefits.

The logic is appealingly simple, but wrong for two reasons. First, this "old-age dependency" ratio in itself is irrelevant. No amount of financial manipulation can change this fact: all current consumption must come from current physical output. The consumption of all dependents (non-workers) must come from the output produced by current workers. It's the overall dependency ratio—the number of workers relative to all non-workers, including the aged, the young, the disabled, and those choosing not to work—that determines whether society can "afford" the baby boomers' retirement years. In the 1960s we had only 0.62 workers for each dependent, and we were building new schools and the interstate highway system and getting ready to put a man on the moon. No one bemoaned a demographic crisis or looked for ways to cut the resources allocated to children; in fact, the living standards of most families rose rapidly. In 2030, we will have 0.98 workers per dependent. We'll have more workers per dependent in the future than we did in the past. While it is true a larger share of total output will be allocated to the aged, just as a larger share was allocated to children in the 1960s, society will easily produce adequate output to support all workers and dependents, and at a higher standard of living.

Second, the "demographic imperative" ignores productivity growth. Average worker productivity has grown by about 2% per year, adjusted for inflation, for the past half-century. That means real output per worker doubles every 36 years. This productivity growth is projected to continue, so by 2040, each worker will produce twice as much as today. Suppose each of three workers today produces $1,000 per week and one retiree is allocated $500 (half of his final salary)—then each worker gets $833. In 2040, two such workers will produce $2,000 per week each (after adjusting for inflation). If each retiree gets $1,000, each worker still gets

$1,500. The incomes of both workers and retirees go up. Thus, paying for the baby boomers' retirement need not decrease their children's standard of living. A larger share of output going to retirees does not imply that the standard of living of those still working will be lower. Those still working will have a slightly smaller share of a much larger pie.

So why the talk of a Social Security crisis? Social Security always has been a pay-as-you-go system. Current benefits are paid out of current tax revenues. But in the 1980s, a commission headed by Greenspan recommended raising payroll taxes to expand the trust fund in order to supplement tax revenues when the baby boom generation retires. Congress responded in 1984 by raising payroll taxes significantly. As a result, the Social Security trust fund, which holds government bonds as assets, has grown every year since. As the baby boom moves into retirement, these assets will be sold to help pay their retirement benefits.

Each year, Social Security's trustees must make projections of the system's status for the next 75 years. In 1996, they projected the trust fund balance would go to zero in 2030. In 2000, they projected a zero balance in 2036 and today they project a zero balance in 2042. The projection keeps changing because the trustees continue to make unrealistic assumptions about future economic conditions. The current projections are based on the assumption that annual GDP growth will average 1.8 % for the next 75 years. In no 20-year period, even including the Great Depression, has the U.S. economy grown that slowly. Each year the economy grows faster than 1.8%, the zero balance date moves further into the future. But the trustees continue to suggest that if we return to something like the Great Depression, the trust fund will go to zero.

Opponents of Social Security claim the system will then be "bankrupt." Bankruptcy implies ceasing to exist. But if the trust fund goes to zero, Social Security will not shut down and stop paying benefits. It will simply revert to the pure pay-as-you-go system that it was before 1984 and continue to pay current benefits using current tax revenues. Even if the trustees' worst-case assumptions come true, the payroll tax paid by workers would need to increase by only about 2% points, and only in 2042, not today.

If the economy grows at 2.4%—which is still slower than the stagnant growth of the 1980s—the trust fund never goes to zero. The increase in real output and real incomes will generate sufficient revenues to pay promised benefits. By 2042, we will need to lower payroll taxes or raise benefits to reduce the surplus.

The claim that benefits of future retirees must be reduced in order to not reduce the standard of living of future workers is simply wrong. It is being used to drive a wedge between generations and panic younger workers into supporting Bush's plan to destroy Social Security. Under the most likely version of his privatization proposal, according to Bush's own Social Security Commission, the guaranteed benefits from Social Security of a 20-year-old worker joining the

HOW DOES THE BOND MARKET WORK?

A bond is nothing more than an IOU. A company or government borrows money and promises to pay a certain amount of interest annually until it repays the loan. When you buy a newly issued bond, you are making a loan. The amount of the loan is the "face value" of the bond. The initial interest rate at which the bond is issued, the "face rate," multiplied by this face value determines the amount of interest paid each period. Until the debt is paid back, events in the financial markets affect the bond's value.

If market interest rates fall, prices of existing bonds rise. Why? Suppose you buy a bond with a face value of $100 that pays 10%. You then collect $10 per year. If the current interest rate falls to 5%, newly issued bonds will pay that new rate. Since your bond pays 10%, people would rather buy that one than one paying 5%. They are willing to pay more than the face value to get it, so the price will be bid up until interest rates equalize. The price at which you could sell your bond will rise to $200, since $10 is 5% of $200.

But changes in bond prices also affect interest rates. If more people are selling bonds than buying them, an excess supply exists, and prices will fall. If you need to sell your bond to get money to pay your rent, you might have to lower the price of the bond you hold to $50. Because the bond still pays $10 per year to the owner, the new owner gets a 20% return on the $50 purchase. Anyone trying to issue new bonds will have to match that return, so the new market interest rate becomes 20%.

---

labor force today would be reduced by 46%. That Commission also admitted that private accounts are unlikely to make up for this drop in benefits. An estimate made by the Goldman-Sacks brokerage firm suggests that even with private accounts, retirement income of younger workers would be reduced by 42% compared to what they would receive if nothing is done to change the Social Security system. Private accounts are a losing proposition for younger workers.

THE REAL FEAR: AN OVERSUPPLY OF BONDS

So why did Greenspan claim cutting benefits would become necessary? To understand the answer, we need to take a side trip to look at how bonds and the financial markets affect each other. It turns out that rising interest rates reduce the selling price of existing financial assets, and falling asset prices push up interest rates (see box "How Does the Bond Market Work?").

For example, in the 1980s, President Reagan cut taxes and created the largest government deficits in history up to that point. This meant the federal government had to sell lots of bonds to finance the soaring government debt; to attract enough buyers, the Treasury had to offer very high interest rates. During the 1980s, real interest rates (rates adjusted for inflation) were almost four times higher than the historic average. High interest rates slow economic growth by making it more expensive for consumers to buy homes or for businesses to invest in new infrastructure. The GDP growth rate in the 1980s was the slowest in U.S. history apart from the Great Depression.

But high interest rates also depress financial asset prices. A five percentage point rise in interest rates reduces the selling price of a bond (loan) that matures in 10 years by 50%. It was the impact of the record-high interest rates of the 1980s on the value of the loan portfolios of the savings and loan industry that caused the S&L crisis and the industry's collapse.

Greenspan is worried because he sees history repeating itself in the form of President Bush's tax cuts. In his testimony, Greenspan expressed concern over a potentially large rise in interest rates. This is his way of warning about an excess supply of bonds. Starting in 2020, Social Security will have to sell about $150 billion (in 2002 dollars) in trust fund bonds each year for 22 years. At the same time, private-sector pension funds will be selling $100 billion per year of financial assets to make their pension payments. State and local governments will be selling $75 billion per year to cover their former employees' pension expenses, and holdings in private mutual funds will fall by about $50 billion per year as individual retirees cash in their 401(k) assets. Private firms will still need to issue about $100 billion of new bonds a year to finance business expansion. Combined, these asset sales could total $475 billion per year.

This level of bond sales is more than double the record that was set in the 1980s following the Reagan tax cuts. But back then, the newly issued bonds were being purchased by "institutional investors" such as private-sector pension funds and insurance companies. After 2020, these groups will be net sellers of bonds. The financial markets will strain to absorb this level of asset sales. It's unlikely they will be able to also absorb the extra $400 billion per year of bond sales needed to cover the deficit spending that will occur if the new Bush tax cuts are made permanent. This oversupply of bonds will drive down the value of all financial assets.

In a 1994 paper, Sylvester Schieber, a current advisor to President Bush on pension and Social Security reform, predicted this potential drop in asset prices. After 2020, the value of assets held in 401(k) plans, already inadequate, will be reduced even more. More importantly, at least to Greenspan, the prices of assets held by corporations to fund their defined benefit pension promises will fall. Thus, pension payments will need to come out of current revenues, reducing corporate profits and, in turn, driving down stock prices.

It's this potential collapse in the prices of financial assets that worries Greenspan most. In order to reduce the run-up of long-term interest rates, some asset sales must be eliminated. Greenspan said, "You don't have the resources to do it all." But rather than rescinding Bush's tax cuts, Greenspan favors reducing bond sales by the Social Security trust fund. Doing that requires a reduction in benefits and raising payroll taxes even more.

Framing a question incorrectly makes it impossible to find a solution. The problem is not with Social Security, but rather with blind reliance on financial markets to solve all economic problems. If the financial markets are likely to fail us, what is the solution? The solution is simple once the question is framed correctly: where will the real output that baby boomers are going to consume in retirement come from?

The federal budget surplus President Bush inherited came entirely from Social Security surpluses resulting from the 1984 payroll tax increase. Bush gave away revenues meant to provide for workers' retirement as tax cuts for the wealthiest 10% of the population.

We should rescind Bush's tax cuts and use the Social Security surpluses to really prepare for the baby boom retirement. Public investment or targeted tax breaks could be used to encourage the building of the hospitals, nursing homes, and hospices that aging baby boomers will need. Such investment in public and private infrastructure would also stimulate the real economy and increase GDP growth.

Surpluses could be used to fund the training of doctors, nurses and others to staff these facilities, and of other high skilled workers more generally. The higher wages of skilled labor will help generate the payroll tax revenues needed to fund future benefits. If baby boomers help to fund this infrastructure expansion through their payroll taxes while they are still working, less output will need to be allocated when they retire. These expenditures will increase the productivity of the real economy, which will help keep the financial sector solvent to provide for retirees.

Destroying Social Security in order to "save" it is not a solution.

Sources: Dean Baker and Mark Weisbrot, *Social Security: The Phony Crises*, University of Chicago Press, 1999; William Wolman and Anne Colamosca, *The Great 401(k) Hoax*, Perseus Publishing, 2002; Sylvester J. Schieber and John B. Shoven, "The Consequences of Population Aging on Private Pension Fund Saving and Asset Markets," National Bureau of Economic Research, Working Paper No. 4665, 1994.

ARTICLE 4.6

November/December 2004

THE SOCIAL SECURITY ADMINISTRATION'S CRACKED CRYSTAL BALL

BY JOHN MILLER

2042. That's the year the Social Security Trust Fund will run out of money, according to the Social Security Administration (SSA). But its doomsday prophesy is based on overly pessimistic assumptions about our economic future: The SSA expects the U.S. economy to expand at an average annual rate of just 1.8% from 2015 to 2080—far slower than the 3.0% average growth rate the economy posted over the last 75 years.

What's behind the gloomy growth projections? Is there anything to them—or has the SSA's economic crystal ball malfunctioned?

FLAWED FORECAST

The Social Security Administration foresees a future of sluggish economic growth in which labor productivity, or output per worker, improves slowly; total employment barely grows; and workers put in no additional hours on the job. (It reasons that economic growth, or growth of national output, must equal the sum of labor productivity increases, increases in total employment, and increases in the average hours worked.)

In its widely cited "intermediate" 1.8% growth scenario,

labor productivity improves by just 1.6% a year and workforce growth slows almost to a standstill at 0.2% a year—rates well below their historical averages. (See Table 1.) Under these assumptions, and if average work time holds steady, Social Security exhausts its trust fund in the year 2042, at which point it faces an initial shortfall of 27% of its obligations. After that, Social Security would be able to pay out just 70% of the benefits it owes to retirees.

The problem is not with the logic of the method the Social Security Administration uses to make its projections, but rather with its demographic and economic assumptions. Its forecast of 1.6% annual labor productivity growth is especially suspect. When the nonpartisan Congressional Budget Office (CBO) assessed the financial health of Social Security earlier this year, it assumed that productivity would improve at a rate of 1.9% per year. In the CBO forecast, faster productivity growth, along with a lower unemployment rate, boosts wages—the tax base of the system—allowing Social Security to remain solvent until 2052, 10 years longer than the SSA had projected just a few months earlier.

TABLE 1:
SOCIAL SECURITY ADMINISTRATION'S
PRINCIPAL ECONOMIC ASSUMPTIONS[a]

Annual Percentage Increase

Year	Real Gross Domestic Product[b]	Productivity (Total U.S. Economy)	Total Employment[c]	Average Hours Worked
2004	4.4%	2.7%	1.7%	0.0%
2005	3.6%	1.8%	1.7%	0.0%
2006	3.2%	1.9%	1.3%	0.0%
2007	3.0%	1.9%	1.1%	0.0%
2008	1.0%	1.8%	2.8%	0.0%
2009	2.7%	1.8%	0.9%	0.0%
2010	2.6%	1.7%	0.8%	0.0%
2011	2.4%	1.7%	0.8%	0.0%
2012	2.3%	1.6%	0.6%	0.0%
2013	2.2%	1.6%	0.6%	0.0%

Average Annual Percentage Increase

2010 to 2015	2.2%	1.6%	0.6%	0.0%
2015 to 2080	1.8%	1.6%	0.2%	0.0%

[a] These are the "intermediate economic assumptions" that the Social Security Administration regards as most plausible. The SSA also reports a "low cost" forecast that projects a 2.6% real growth rate from 2015 to 2080 and a "high cost" forecast that projects a 1.1% real growth rate from 2015 to 2080.
[b] Real Gross Domestic Product is calculated in constant 1996 dollars.
[c] Total employment is the total of civilian and military employment in the U.S. economy.
Source: Social Security Administration, 2004 Annual Report of the Board of Trustees (March 23, 2004), Table V.B.1 and Table V.B.2, pp. 89 and 94.

One doesn't have to buy into the hype about the magic of the new economy to conclude that the CBO came closer to getting the projected productivity growth rates right than the SSA did. The federal government's own Bureau of Labor Statistics estimates that productivity rates in the nonfarm sector improved at a 2.3% average pace from 1947 through 2003. Adjusting for the gap of 0.2 percentage points between the productivity growth of the nonfarm business sector and the economy as a whole still leaves productivity across the economy growing by a healthy 2.1% over the postwar period. That historical record convinces economist Dean Baker, from the Washington-based Center for Economic and Policy Research, that a productivity growth rate of 2.0% a year is a "very reasonable" assumption.

The drastic deceleration of employment growth, from its historic (1960 to 2000) average of 1.78% to 0.2% per year, is also overstated. As the trustees see it, employment will grow far more slowly as the baby-boomers leave the labor force. That is true as far as it goes. But if their projections are correct, the country will soon face a chronic labor shortage. And in that context, the immigration rate is unlikely to slow, as they assume, to 900,000 a year. Rather, future immigration rates would likely be at least as high as they were in the 1990s, when 1.3 million people entered the United States annually, and possibly even higher if immigration laws are relaxed in response to a labor shortage. Faster immigration would boost employment growth and add workers, who would pay into Social Security, helping to relieve the financial strain on the system created by the retirement of the baby-boom generation.

In its own optimistic or "low cost" scenario, the SSA erases the shortfall in the trust fund by assuming a faster productivity growth rate (of 1.9%), a lower unemployment rate (of 4.5% per year), and higher net immigration (of 1.3 million people per year). The still rather sluggish 2.6% average growth rate that results would wipe out the rest of the imbalance in the system and leave a sizeable surplus in the trust fund—0.15% of GDP over the next 75 years.

MAKING SHORT WORK OF THE SHORTFALL

Even in the unlikely event that the pessimistic predictions the SSA has conjured up actually do come to pass, the Social Security imbalance could be easily remedied.

The Social Security Trust Fund needs $3.7 trillion to meet its unfunded obligations over the next 75 years. That is a lot of money—about 1.89% of taxable payroll and about 0.7% of GDP over that period. But it's far less than the 2.0% of GDP the 2001 to 2003 tax cuts will cost over the next 75 years if they are made permanent. (Many of the tax cuts are currently scheduled to sunset in 2010.) The portion of the Bush tax cuts going to the richest 1% of taxpayers alone will cost 0.6% of GDP—more than the CBO projected shortfall of 0.4% of GDP.

Here are a few ways to make short work of any remaining shortfall without cutting retirement benefits or raising taxes for low- or middle-income workers. First, newly hired state and local government workers could be brought into the system. (About 3.5 million state and local government workers are not now covered by Social Security.) That move alone would eliminate about 30% of the projected deficit.

In addition, we could raise the cap on wages subject to payroll taxes. Under current law, Social Security is funded by a payroll tax on the first $87,900 of a person's income. As a result of this cap on covered income, the tax applies to just 84.5% of all wages today—but historically it applied to 90%. Increasing the cap for the next decade so that the payroll tax covers 87.3% of all wages, or halfway back to the 90% standard, would eliminate nearly one-third of the SSA's projected deficit.

Finally, stopping the repeal of the estate tax, a tax giveaway that benefits only the richest taxpayers, would go a long way toward closing the gap. Economists Peter Diamond and

Peter Orszag, writing for The Century Fund, advocate dedicating the revenues generated by renewing the estate tax to the Social Security Trust Fund. They suggest an estate tax set at its planned 2009 level, which would exempt $3.5 million of an individual's estate. The tax would fall exclusively on the wealthiest 0.3% of taxpayers. That alone would close another one-quarter of the SSA's projected shortfall. Returning the estate tax to its 2001 (pre-tax cut) level (with a $675,000 exemption for individuals) would do yet more to relieve any financial strain on Social Security.

Any way you look at it, Social Security can remain on sound financial footing even in the dreariest of economic futures, so long as alarmist reports like those of its trustees don't become an excuse to corrupt the system.

Sources: Congressional Budget Office, The Outlook for Social Security, June 2004; Social Security Administration, 2004 Annual Report of the Board of Trustees (March 23, 2004); "What the Trustees' Report Indicates About the Financial Status of Social Security," Robert Greenstein, Center on Budget and Policy Priorities (March 31, 2004); "The Implications of the Social Security Projections Issued By the Congressional Budget Office" Robert Greenstein, Peter Orszag, and Richard Kogan, Center on Budget and Policy Priorities (June 24, 2004); "Letter to Rudolph G. Penner" from Dean Baker, co-director of the Center For Economic and Policy Research (January 26, 2004); *Countdown to Reform: The Great Social Security Debate*, Henry Aaron and Robert Reischauer, The Century Foundation Press, 1998.

November/December 2004

AFRICAN AMERICANS AND SOCIAL SECURITY

WHY THE PRIVATIZATION ADVOCATES ARE WRONG

BY WILLIAM E. SPRIGGS

Proponents of Social Security privatization are trying to claim that the current program is unfair to African Americans and that a privatized program would serve African Americans better. This argument lends support to the privatization agenda while at the same time giving its advocates a compassionate gloss. But the claims about African Americans and Social Security are wrong.

The Old Age Survivors and Disability Insurance Program (OASDI), popularly known as Social Security, was put in place by Franklin Roosevelt to establish a solid bulwark of economic rights for the public—specifically, as he put it, "the right to adequate protection from the economic fears of old age, sickness, accident, and unemployment." Most Americans associate Social Security only with the retirement—or old age—benefit. Yet it was created to do much more, and it does.

As its original name suggests, Social Security is an insurance program that protects workers and their families against the income loss that occurs when a worker retires, becomes disabled, or dies. All workers will eventually either grow too old to compete in the labor market, become disabled, or die. OASDI insures all workers and their families against these universal risks, while spreading the costs and benefits of that insurance protection among the entire workforce. Currently, 70% of Social Security funds go to retirees, 15% to disabled workers, and 15% to survivors.

Social Security is a "pay as you go" system, which means the taxes paid by today's workers are not set aside to pay their own benefits down the road, but rather go to pay the benefits of current Social Security recipients. It's financed using the Federal Insurance Contribution Act (or FICA) payroll tax, paid by all working Americans on earnings of less than about $90,000 a year. While the payroll tax is not progressive, Social Security benefits are—that is, low-wage workers receive a greater percentage of pre-retirement earnings from the program than higher-wage workers.

In the 1980s, recognizing that the baby boom generation would strain this system, Congress passed reforms to raise extra tax revenues above and beyond the current need and set up a trust fund to hold the reserve. Trustees were appointed and charged with keeping Social Security solvent. Today's trustees warn that their projections, which are based on modest assumptions about the long-term growth of the U.S. economy, show the system could face a shortfall around 2042, when either benefits would have to be cut or the FICA tax raised.

Those who oppose the social nature of the program have pounced on its projected shortfall in revenues to argue that the program cannot—or ought not—be fixed, but should instead be fundamentally changed (see "Privatization Advocates.") Privatization proponents are seeking to frame the issue as a matter of social justice, as if Social Security "reform" would primarily benefit low-income workers, blue-collar workers, people of color, and women. Prompted by disparities in life expectancy between whites and African Americans and the racial wealth gap, a growing chorus within the privatization movement is claiming that privatizing Social Security would be beneficial to African Americans.

Opponents attack the program on the basis of an analogy to private retirement accounts. Early generations of Social Security beneficiaries received much more in benefits than they had paid into the system in taxes. Privatization proponents argue those early recipients received a "higher rate of return" on their "investment" while current and future generations are being "robbed" because they will see "lower rates of return." They argue the current system of social insurance—particularly the retirement program—should be privatized, switching from the current "pay-as-you-go" system to one in which individual workers claim their own contribution and decide where and how to invest it.

But this logic inverts the premise of social insurance. Rather than sharing risk across the entire workforce to ensure that all workers and their families are protected from the three inevitabilities of old age, disability, and death, privatizing Social Security retirement benefits would enable high-wage workers to reap gains from private retirement investment without having to help protect lower-wage workers from their (disproportionate) risks of disability and death. High-wage workers, who are more likely to live long enough to retire, could in fact do better on average if they opt out of the general risk pool and devote all their money to retirement without having to cover the risk of those who may become disabled or die, although they would of course be subjecting their retirement dollars to greater risk. But low-wage workers, who are far more likely to need disability or survivors' benefits to help their families and are less likely to live long enough to retire, would then be left with lower disability and survivors' benefits, and possibly no guaranteed benefits. This is what the Social Security privatization movement envisions. But you wouldn't know it from reading their literature.

And when the myths about Social Security's financial straits meet another American myth—race—even more confusion follows. Here is a look at three misleading claims by privatization proponents about African Americans and Social Security.

MYTH #1

Several conservative research groups argue that Social Security is a bad deal for African Americans because of their lower life expectancies. "Lifetime Social Security benefits depend, in large part, on longevity," writes the Cato Institute's Michael Tanner in his briefing paper "Disparate Impact: Social Security and African Americans." "At every age, African-American men and women both have shorter life expectancies than do their white counterparts. ... As a result, a black man or woman earning exactly the same lifetime wages, and paying exactly the same lifetime Social Security taxes, as his or her white counterpart will likely receive a far lower rate of return." Or as the Americans for Tax Reform web site puts it: "A black male born today has a life expectancy of 64.8 years. But the Social Security retirement age for that worker in the future will be 67 years. That means probably the majority of black males will never even receive Social Security retirement benefits."

The longevity myth is the foundation of all the race-based arguments for Social Security privatization. There are several problems with it.

First, the shorter life expectancy of African Americans compared to whites is the result of higher morbidity in midlife, and is most acute for African-American men. The life expectancies of African-American women and white men are virtually equal. So the life expectancy argument can really only be made about African-American men.

Second, the claim that OASDI is unfair to African Americans because their expected benefits are less than their expected payments is usually raised and then answered from the perspective of the retirement (or "old age") benefit alone. That is an inaccurate way to look at the problem. Because OASDI also serves families of workers who become disabled or die, a correct measure would take into account the probability of all three risk factors—old age, disability, and death. Both survivor benefits and disability benefits, in fact, go disproportionately to African Americans.

While African Americans make up 12% of the U.S. population, 23% of children receiving Social Security survivor benefits are African American, as are about 17% of disability beneficiaries. On average, a worker who receives disability benefits or a family that receives survivor benefits gets far more in return than the worker paid in FICA taxes, notwithstanding privatizers' attempts to argue that Social Security is a bad deal.

PRIVATIZATION ADVOCATES

Powerful advocates for privatization include libertarian and conservative think tanks and advocacy groups such as the Cato Institute, the Heritage Foundation, Americans for Tax Reform, and Citizens for a Sound Economy, all driven by an ideological commitment to the abolition of federal social programs.

Wall Street too is thirsty for the $1.4 trillion that privatization would funnel into equities if the taxes collected to support the Social Security system were invested privately rather than reinvested in federal government bonds. That's not to mention the windfall of fees privatization would deliver for banks, brokerage houses, and investment firms.

Just after he took office, President Bush appointed a commission to examine privatizing the Social Security system. The commission could not figure out how to maintain payments to current recipients while diverting tax dollars to the savings of current workers, nor could it resolve how to cover the benefits of the disabled or resolve issues surrounding survivors' benefits. Although the president did not succeed in carrying out Social Security privatization in his first term, he has made the partial privatization of Social Security retirement accounts the top priority of his second-term domestic agenda.

Survivors' benefits also provide an important boost to poor families more generally. A recent study by the National Urban League Institute for Opportunity and Equality showed that the benefit lifted 1 million children out of poverty and helped another 1 million avoid extreme poverty (living below half the poverty line).

Finally, among workers who do live long enough to get the retirement benefit, life expectancies don't differ much by racial group. For example, at age 65, the life expectancies of African-American and white men are virtually the same.

President Bush's Social Security commission proposed the partial privatization of Social Security retirement accounts, but cautioned that it could not figure out how to maintain equal benefits for the other risk pools. The commission suggested that disability and survivor's benefits would have to be reduced if the privatization plan proceeds.

This vision is of a retirement program designed for the benefit of the worker who retires—only. A program with that focus would work against, not for, African Americans because of the higher morbidity rates in middle age and the smaller share of African Americans who live to retirement.

MYTH #2

African Americans have less education, and so are in the work force longer, than whites, and yet Social Security only credits 35 years of work experience in figuring benefits. Tanner says, "benefits are calculated on the basis of the highest 35 years of earnings over a worker's lifetime. Workers must still pay Social Security taxes during years outside those 35, but those taxes do not count toward or earn additional benefits. Generally, those low-earnings years occur early in an individual's life. That is particularly important to African Americans because they are likely to enter the workforce at an earlier age than whites...."

This claim misinterprets the benefit formula for Social Security. Yes, African Americans on average are slightly less educated than whites. The gap is mostly because of a higher college completion rate for white men compared to African-American men. But the education argument fails to acknowledge that white teenagers have a significantly higher labor force participation rate (at 46%) than do African-American teens (29%). The higher labor force participation of white teenagers helps to explain why young white adults do better in the labor market than young African-American adults. (The racial gaps in unemployment are considerably greater for teenagers and young adults than for those over 25.)

These differences in early labor market experiences mean that African-American men have more years of zero earnings than do whites. So while the statement about education is true, the inference from education differences to work histories is false. By taking only 35 years of work history into account in the benefit formula, the Social Security formula is progressive. It in effect ignores years of zero or very low earnings. This levels the playing field among long-time workers, putting African Americans with more years of zero earnings

on par with whites. By contrast, a private system based on total years of earnings would exacerbate racial labor market disparities.

MYTH #3

A third claim put forward by critics of Social Security is that African-American retirees are more dependent on Social Security than whites. Tanner writes: "Elderly African Americans are much more likely than their white counterparts to be dependent on Social Security benefits for most or all of their retirement income." Therefore, he concludes, "African Americans would be among those with the most to gain from the privatization of Social Security—transforming the program into a system of individually owned, privately invested accounts." Law professor and senior policy advisor to Americans for Tax Reform Peter Ferrara adds, "the personal accounts would produce far higher returns and benefits for lower-income workers, African Americans, Hispanics, women and other minorities."

It's true that African-American retirees are more likely than whites to rely on Social Security as their only income in old age. It's the sole source of retirement income for 40% of elderly African Americans. This is a result of discrimination in the labor market that limits the share of African Americans with jobs that offer pension benefits. Privatizing Social Security would not change labor market discrimination or its effects.

Privatizing Social Security would, however, exacerbate the earnings differences between African Americans and whites, since benefits would be based solely on individual savings. What would help African-American retirees is not privatization, but rather changing the redistributive aspects of Social Security to make it even more progressive.

The current formula for Social Security benefits is progressive in two ways: low earners get a higher share of their earnings than do higher wage earners and the lowest years of earning are ignored. Changes in the formula to raise the benefits floor enough to lift all retired Social Security recipients out of poverty would make it still more progressive. Increasing and updating the Supplemental Security Income payment, which helps low earners, could accomplish the same goal for SSI recipients. (SSI is a program administered by Social Security for very low earners and the poor who are disabled, blind, or at least 65 years old.)

The proponents of privatization argue that the heavy reliance of African-American seniors on Social Security requires higher rates of return—returns that are only possible by putting money into the stock market. Yet given the lack of access to private pensions for African-American seniors and their low savings from lifetimes of low earnings, such a notion is perverse. It would have African Americans gamble with their only leg of retirement's supposed three-legged stool—pension, savings, and Social Security. And, given the much higher risk that African Americans face of both death before retirement and of disability, it would be a risky gamble indeed to lower those benefits while jeopardizing their only retirement leg.

Privatizing the retirement program, and separating the integrated elements of Social Security, would split America. The divisions would be many: between those more likely to be disabled and those who are not; between those more likely to die before retirement and those more likely to retire; between children who get survivors' benefits and the elderly who get retirement benefits; between those who retire with high-yield investments and those who fare poorly in retirement. The "horizontal equity" of the program (treating simi-

lar people in a similar way) would be lost, as volatile stock fluctuations and the timing of retirement could greatly affect individuals' rates of return. The "vertical equity" of the program (its progressive nature, insuring a floor for benefits) would be placed in greater jeopardy with the shift from social to private benefits.

Social Security works because it is "social." It is America's only universal federal program. The proposed changes would place Social Security in the same political space as the rest of America's federal programs—and African Americans have seen time and again how those politics work.

November/December 2006

THE OPPOSITE OF INSURANCE
UNLESS YOU'RE RICH, HEALTHY, OR BOTH,
HEALTH SAVINGS ACCOUNTS ARE BAD NEWS.

BY JAMES WOOLMAN

Congress created Health Savings Accounts (HSAs) in 2003 as tax-advantaged savings accounts linked to the purchase of a high-deductible health plan. But the scheme is not a new idea. HSA proponents, including many health economists, have long argued that standard "comprehensive" insurance policies are too generous, sheltering consumers from the true cost of medical care. "Empowering" consumers to decide for themselves how much money to save for medical expenses, the theory goes, will unleash the magic of the market; costs will decline and quality will improve as doctors, hospitals, and other providers compete for discriminating customers.

New research on consumer and employer experiences with HSAs, however, confirms many of the fears cited by critics of the plans. The evidence shows that these plans attract relatively high-income, healthy people who are attracted to the tax benefits, while they place other consumers—including those with families, health problems, or low incomes—at risk for steep increases in out-of-pocket spending.

THE MECHANICS OF HSAS
Workers can contribute pre-tax income to an HSA and can withdraw from it at any time for health-related spending. Employers may also contribute to employees' HSAs. Any money remaining at the end of the year stays in the account, enjoys tax benefits, and can be invested just like money in an Individual Retirement Account.

To open an HSA, however, you must have a high-deductible health insurance plan, and you *cannot* have ordinary

health coverage. To qualify, a plan must have a deductible of at least $1,050 for an individual or $2,100 for a family. (HSA-qualified plans are allowed to cover some preventive care without a deductible.) Actual deductibles are much higher: in 2006 HSA-qualified plans had average deductibles of around $2,000 (individual) or $4,000 (family). Under the HSA scheme, in other words, a family typically has to pay the first $4,000 in medical bills each year out of pocket; their insurance plan kicks in—with all of the usual co-pays, exclusions, etc.—only after annual medical expenses exceed that amount.

The funds in the HSA are supposed to cover a portion of these out-of-pocket expenses, but workers are wholly responsible for any gap between the amount in their HSA and the amount of the deductible. The gap can be sizeable. A national survey by the Kaiser Family Foundation found the average deductible for a family HSA plan was $4,008, while the average employer HSA contribution was $1,139. Enrollees are fully responsible for the $2,869 gap, in addition to their premium payments and additional co-pays (see Figure 1).

By reducing employers' premium costs, limiting the amount of services employees are likely to use, and increasing the likelihood that employees will pay more out of pocket for health care, high-deductible plans shift financial risk from employers onto employees. Monthly premiums are lower under these plans than for comprehensive insurance, but high-deductible plan enrollees are still much more likely to spend a substantial amount of their income

FIGURE 1
THE HEALTH SAVINGS ACCOUNT/HIGH DEDUCTIBLE HEALTH PLAN SCHEME: WORKERS PAY MORE, EMPLOYERS PAY LESS

Annual Worker Contribution Comparison

	Single		Family	
	All Plans	*HDHP*	*All Plans*	*HDHP*
Worker Premium Contribution	$624	$467	$2,976	$2,115
Deductible	$508	$2,011	$1,099	$4,008
Employer HSA Contribution		($988)		($1,139)
Total Employer Spending	$1,132	$1,490	$4,075	$4,984

Annual Worker Contribution Comparison

	Single		Family	
	All Plans	*HDHP*	*All Plans*	*HDHP*
Employer Premium Contribution	$4,248	$2,709	$7,756	$6,400
Employer HSA Contribution		$988		$1,139
Total Employer Spending	$1,132	$1,490	$4,075	$4,984

* Totals do not include coinsurance.
Source: The Kaiser Family Foundation and The Health Research and Education Trust 2006 Employer Benefits Survey.

by working-age households with health insurance were made by those who spend above the minimum HSA deductibles, and that overall, nearly 79% of total medical expenditures occurred above the minimum HSA deductibles. In fact, the only type of spending HSAs are likely to reduce is the kind we want to encourage: primary and preventive care. According to the Commonwealth Fund, enrollees with deductibles over $1,000 were twice as likely as enrollees with deductibles under $500 to avoid seeing the doctor for a medical problem, avoid seeing a specialist, or skip a recommended treatment due to cost.

Moreover, people do not and cannot shop for health care services as they do for other goods. Most people do not have adequate information on the cost and quality of care to make informed purchasing decisions. Nor are they inclined to do so when they are sick or in distress, which is when health care decisions are typically made. Most people enrolled in high-deductible plans do not, in fact, shop for less expensive care, although many shop for better prescription drug prices, according to a 2006 Government Accountability Office (GAO) report.

The GAO found that current HSA participants are disproportionately high on health expenses than people enrolled in comprehensive plans. For instance, 31% of enrollees in HSA-type plans spent over 5% of their income on medical expenses, including premiums, compared with only 12% of enrollees in comprehensive plans, according to a recent survey conducted by the Employee Benefits Research Institute and the Commonwealth Fund (see Figure 2).

FLAWED PLAN

Proponents of HSAs would say this shifting of risk is a good thing: a market-based reform to address escalating health care costs. But this is a deeply flawed view.

For one thing, high-deductible plans are unlikely to have much impact on overall health care spending, most of which results from expensive treatments for serious illnesses whose costs exceed the high deductibles. One recent study found that more than 95% of medical expenditures

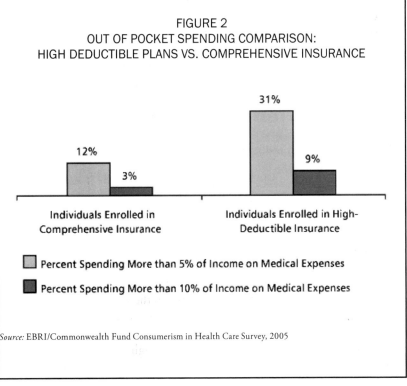

FIGURE 2
OUT OF POCKET SPENDING COMPARISON:
HIGH DEDUCTIBLE PLANS VS. COMPREHENSIVE INSURANCE

Source: EBRI/Commonwealth Fund Consumerism in Health Care Survey, 2005

income, healthy people who will benefit from the tax advantages and are unlikely to need much health care. Although generally satisfied with their own experience, HSA enrollees polled by the GAO said they would *not* recommend high-deductible plans for people with families, health problems, maintenance medications, or moderate incomes—in other words, most people.

So HSAs represent a double-edged sword. If large numbers of people are forced to switch from comprehensive health coverage to high-deductible plans, they will likely face significantly higher out-of-pocket costs. On the other hand, if HSAs continue to attract the healthiest enrollees, the exit of this healthy segment from the comprehensive coverage pool will likely drive up health insurance costs for everyone else.

HSAs and high-deductible plans appeal to employers looking to cut health care costs, high-income earners looking for more tax breaks, and younger workers willing to gamble they won't get sick. For most people, however, they are the opposite of insurance: they concentrate the financial risk of illness instead of spreading it, and they increase the likelihood of incurring medical debt instead of reducing it.

Resources: "Consumer-Directed Health Plans: Early Enrollee Experiences with Health Savings Accounts and Eligible Health Plans," GAO, 8/06; Kaiser Family Foundation and Health Research and Educational Trust, "Employer Health Benefits: 2006 Annual Survey," 9/06; Paul Fronstin and Sara R. Collins, "Early Experience With High-Deductible and Consumer-Driven Health Plans," Employee Benefits Research Institute and the Commonwealth Fund, 12/05; Edwin Park and Robert Greenstein, "Latest Enrollment Data Still Fail to Dispel Concerns about Health Savings Accounts," Center on Budget and Policy Priorities, 1/30/06.

ARTICLE 4.9

May/June 2004

THE CASE AGAINST PRIVATIZING NATIONAL SECURITY

BY ANN MARKUSEN

In the past 20 years, this country has undergone a transformation in the way it prepares for, conducts, and mops up after war. The Pentagon has overseen a large-scale effort to outsource all aspects of its operations to private corporations. But despite the claims of privatization proponents, there's scant evidence that private firms perform better or at lower cost than public-sector agencies. More troubling, as corporations cash in on lucrative contracts, they encroach on the political process, driving up military spending and influencing military and foreign policy.

THE GROWING "SHADOW PENTAGON"

National defense is one of the most heavily outsourced activities in the U.S. federal government. From 1972 to 2000, private contractors' share of all defense-related jobs climbed from 36% to 50%. While the country's public-sector defense workforce remains large—about 2.2 million in 2000—its "shadow workforce," the true number of people supported by federal government spending and mandates, is far larger. (See Table 1.)

Of the dozens of major military contract firms in the United States today, Lockheed Martin, Boeing, and Northrop Grumman are the largest three—they divvied up $50 billion of the $209 billion the Pentagon awarded in prime contracts in 2003, according to defense analyst William Hartung—but lesser-known info-tech and engineering companies like Computer Sciences Corporation, BDM International, and Science Applications International Corporation are emerging as major Department of Defense (DOD) suppliers, each with billions of dollars in defense business annually.

Despite the popular image of a defense contract as a contract for building large weapons systems like aircraft, missiles, or tanks, contracts for services are actually more typical. Service workers—not production workers—accounted for nearly three out of four contract-created jobs in 1996, up more than 50% since 1984. A growing legion of contracted employees install, maintain, trouble-shoot, operate, and integrate military hardware. Similarly, research and development work is increasingly farmed out. (Navy technical centers outsourced 50% of research, development, test, and evaluation work by 1996, up from 30% in 1970.) And other, lower-skill, service contract firms perform a panoply of other functions, from base maintenance and catering and support, to security detail and military training.

TABLE 1 ESTIMATED FULL-TIME EQUIVALENT FEDERAL CIVIL SERVICE, CONTRACT, AND GRANT JOBS BY CATEGORY, 1996				
Federal Agency	Civil Service Jobs	Contract Jobs	Grant Jobs*	Ratio of Civil Service to Contract + Grant Jobs
Defense	778,900	3,634,000	53,000	1:4.7
Energy	19,100	633,000	40,200	1:37
NASA	20,100	350,600	26,900	1:19
Total Defense-Related	818,100	4,617,600	120,100	1:5.8
All Other Federal	1,073,900	1,017,400	2,292,900	1:3.1

*Jobs created by money given as a grant rather than a contract for performance of services. The grant category includes research grants to universities.

Source: Paul Light, *The True Size of Government*, Washington, DC: Brookings Institution Press, 1999.

ECONOMIC EXPECTATIONS

According to economic theory, it's competition, not privatization per se, that is expected to produce cost savings and performance improvements. Competition is key because private contractors are profit-seeking firms whose first loyalties are to their shareholders. Without competition, and in the absence of close monitoring, the corporations have every incentive to raise prices and hide information about their products and services. Defense economists suggest competition should generate efficiencies, but only under certain conditions: four or more firms competing for a given job, ongoing competition over time, clarity by the government buyer about task and performance requirements, and active, sustained government monitoring.

That's the theory. In the real world of military contracting, these conditions are rarely met. Most contracts that are opened to competing bids have fewer than three bidders. Once signed, contracts last for long periods, insulating firms from ongoing competitive pressures. The bidding process itself may be distorted in that firms "low-ball" bids, knowing they can negotiate add-ons later. And with the dramatic consolidation of the industry in the mid-1990s, and the shrinking number of large prime contractors, collusion among firms is a recurrent problem.

Several Pentagon contracts are "cost-plus," meaning the companies recoup their costs, including a portion of overhead, and are guaranteed a percentage of the costs as profit—a recipe for cost inflation. For example, Halliburton subsidiary Kellogg Brown & Root was given a 10-year multibillion dollar contract to provide logistical support services to U.S. troops overseas. The contract guarantees the firm will receive 1% of total costs as profit. In addition, KBR is eligible for a bonus payment of up to 2%. The firm has a long record of cost overruns in Kosovo, and its performance to date in Iraq has been weak. KBR admitted to overcharging the government by $61 million for gasoline, and its own internal audit of its Iraq operations reveals serious problems including a failure to control subcontractor costs and widespread loss of supplies and equipment, according to the *Wall Street Journal*.

THE EVIDENCE ON EXPECTED GAINS FROM PRIVATIZATION

Given the colossal sum of government dollars doled out in defense contracts, you'd think Congress and the Pentagon would carefully track cost and performance outcomes. But Pentagon records are sketchy and largely hidden from public view. Even the U.S. General Accounting Office (GAO), the investigative arm of Congress, has had difficulty prying data from the Pentagon. What's more, the few assessments that do exist focus on competitions between public and private bidders (where a government agency bids for work in competition with a private entity), and not private-private competitions, or the 50% of DOD purchases that are sole-sourced, simply given to a contractor with no competitive bidding process at all.

Some have estimated that the DOD saves 20% to 30% from public-private competitions, but those approximations are based on savings estimates at the initial bidding stage. In other words, they look at the promise of savings, not actual savings over time—a poor measure, since cost overruns are common and contracts are often renegotiated or otherwise changed after they're awarded.

The few existing studies of longer-term outcomes—conducted mainly by the Center for Naval Analysis (CNA), a federally funded research and development center, and the GAO—offer mixed results.

A CNA study of surface ships found that readiness was about the same whether the work was done in a public Navy yard or a private yard; a study of Navy maintenance work over time found that for a period of around two years, the contractors' performance was worse than that of the Navy in-house team, but that overall, the contractors performed better than the Navy team.

CNA insists that public-private competitions do generate bids and plans which would, if implemented, save the Pentagon money. But CNA analyses are emphatic that "competition produces the savings and not outsourcing per se." Its simulations suggest that 65% of total savings should in theory be achieved simply by the exercise of competing, even if no private firm receives a contract.

GAO is less sanguine about the potential for cost savings. The agency investigated some of the Pentagon's savings estimates and concluded that they were overstated because "DOD has not fully calculated either the investment costs associated with undertaking these competitions or the personnel separation costs likely to be associated with implementing them." DOD had assumed it would cost just $2,000 per position to conduct a competition, but in actuality the costs run from $7,000 to $9,000. In a later review of the Pentagon's claim that it had saved $290 million through public-private competition in 1999, the GAO concluded that it was difficult to determine how much had actually been saved. A large part of the problem, again, is that the DOD does not systematically track or update its savings estimates once contracts are underway.

GAO also cautions that savings from outsourcing come chiefly from cuts in personnel costs. We cannot know whether these cuts normally take the form of wage and benefit reductions, the use of temporary workers, cuts to the full-time workforce, or some combination, because private-sector firms refuse to share personnel information, calling it proprietary.

The large role of labor-cost savings in Pentagon outsourcing should give policymakers pause. It's troubling that the Pentagon does not monitor the pay and working conditions of its "shadow employees." If private prison administrators are required to share employment data with evaluators, why shouldn't Pentagon contractors face the same requirement?

In sum, the jury's still out on whether outsourcing military work produces efficiencies, and little is known about how savings that are achieved may result from cutting wages. Furthermore, no study has included the cost of competent oversight in the outsourcing calculus, or looked systematically at performance outcomes.

CORRUPTION AND POLICY INFLUENCE

Beyond efficiency and performance concerns, the increasing reliance on for-profit firms for national defense creates deeper political and institutional problems—namely, the capture of public decision-making by private military interests.

Through lobbying, advertising, and heavy campaign contributions, the private defense sector calls for weapons systems and defense initiatives that generate lucrative contracts. Since the end of the Cold War, private military contractors have formed a powerful lobby to protect obsolete Cold War weapons systems. For example, during the Reagan years, strenuous lobbying overcame even the highly mobilized and scientifically well-informed opposition to the B-1 bomber and the Star Wars program, two of the most costly weapons programs in the postwar period. In the 1990s, lobbyists undermined important initiatives to control the export of conventional arms, and recently the aerospace industry—led by Lockheed Martin—pushed hard to bring Poland, Hungary, and the Czech Republic into NATO in the expectation that these countries would then upgrade their militaries with costly new hardware. In general, the defense industry's leverage in Congress makes it difficult for the nation to shift resources toward peace-keeping missions, negotiated settlements, and the use of economic development in place of regional warfare.

As John Donahue summarizes in *The Privatization Decision*:

In any contractual relationship between government and private business, a key question becomes who is representing the broader public interests. Unless there are sturdy provisions to prevent it—and even if all parties are immune to corruption—the natural outcome is an alliance between private-sector suppliers and government officials at the taxpayers' expense.

Less visible than the congressional lobbyists and trade groups, but just as significant, contractors employ their superior technical expertise to sell Pentagon procurement managers and top military leaders on pricey and risky new projects. Sitting on Pentagon advisory committees helps, as does the firms' insulation from public scrutiny. The quickening pace of privatization in research and development has left the government without the expertise to assess and monitor contractors' proposals.

WHAT'S DRIVING DEFENSE PRIVATIZATION?

The political, intellectual, and financial impetus for government privatization began in the 1970s and received its major political boost from the Reagan administration, which shrank government even as it increased defense expenditures by 50% in real terms. The Clinton administration's reversal of the Carter-Reagan military buildup had the unintended consequence of unleashing a hungry pro-privatization lobby onto the political scene—the mid-1990s reduction of the defense budget sent private contractors scrambling for new markets. At the same time, a raft of mergers consolidated the industry into a powerful handful of giant firms, all focused on developing new streams of government revenue. Their efforts on Capitol Hill dovetailed with and drew life from the 20-year ideological assault on public-sector provision of goods and services. During the Clinton years, insiders also adopted and capitalized on the "reinventing government" agenda spearheaded by Vice President Al Gore at the federal level.

Since the 1990s, private business groups, DOD advisory boards and key managers, and both the Clinton and Bush administrations have heightened calls to privatize national-security activity. For Pentagon managers, privatization offers a means of coping with a "go it alone" defense doctrine that deploys U.S. armed forces around the world with little international support.

Advocacy groups heavily populated by large defense contractors issue a stream of pronouncements and publications urging privatization. They recommend outsourcing functions outright rather than relying on public-private competitions (which give public agencies a chance to bid for projects), and back the wholesale privatization of complex business areas that currently involve large numbers of government employees.

One such task force, the Defense Science Board Task Force on Outsourcing and Privatization, issued studies in 1996 claiming that $10 billion to $30 billion could be saved through privatizing DOD's support and maintenance services.

Needless to say, they offered inadequate evidence to support these multibillion-dollar savings estimates. The panel that released the first study was headed by the CEO of military contractor BDM International.

At about the same time, Business Executives for National Security (BENS), a group founded in 1982 as a watchdog organization to monitor the Pentagon on weapons costs and nuclear, chemical, and biological warfare, transformed itself into an outspoken advocate of outsourcing. In 1996, BENS launched a high-profile commission to "promote outsourcing and privatization, closing unneeded military bases and implementing acquisition reform" with a self-described membership of "business leaders, former government officials and retired military officers." The commission published op-eds and position papers claiming the Pentagon civilian workforce is bloated. It decried what it misleadingly described as the bleeding away of private-sector defense jobs. (BENS used 1988 as its baseline; the year was an anomaly that included a spike in Reagan-era defense contracts.) It also claimed the Pentagon lags behind private corporations in outsourcing, and that the United States lags behind Europeans in privatization. Neither assertion is borne out by the evidence.

Under Clinton, Secretary of Defense William Cohen and other top DOD officials echoed BENS' calls for a "Revolution in Military Business Affairs." Dr. Jacques Gansler, President Clinton's undersecretary of defense for acquisition and technology, frequently spoke out in favor of outsourcing and a business approach:

> To meet the challenge of modernization, the Department of Defense ... must do business more like private business.... My top priority, as Under Secretary of Defense, is to make the Pentagon look much more like a dynamic, restructured, reengineered, world-class commercial sector business.

In February 2001, just after George W. Bush took office, a defense reform conference organized by the Aerospace Industries Association of America and Boeing, Lockheed Martin, Northrop Grumman, Raytheon, TRW, Inc., and BAE Systems met to set the agenda for the new administration. It attracted 500 participants and drew up a "Blueprint for Action" to slash bureaucracies, reduce "cycle times" and restore operational and financial strength to the defense industrial base. Also in February 2001, a BENS initiative, "Improving the Business End of the Military," identified activities the DOD can discontinue and "replace with world class business models," turning entire functions (housing, communications, power utilities, logistics systems) over to the private sector.

Since George W. Bush took office, the military budget has grown from $300 billion to $400 billion, not counting the $200 billion in supplemental expenditures for Iraq and Afghanistan. The spending hike has set off a feeding frenzy among contractors, some of which have seen double-digit growth in profits.

The Bush administration is intensifying efforts to transfer work from inside the Pentagon to private contractors. The DOD is expected to put 225,000 jobs up for competition between public employee groups and private companies by the end of Bush's first term. Many more jobs have been displaced through direct outsourcing. The Bush push appears to be driven by a combination of ideology and political calculation, reinforced by defense-sector campaign contributions and the accelerating revolving door between the Pentagon and private contractors.

But this strategy poses serious risks and may threaten the possibility of society exercising democratic control over the evolution and use of military force. George Washington University political scientist Deborah Avant stresses that privatizing security "almost inevitably redistributes power over the control of violence both within governments and between states and non-state actors." In the United States, the private delivery of services has strengthened the executive branch, diminished the control of Congress, and reduced transparency. And, she warns, the process is cumulative— as private security companies are integrated into military efforts, the companies gain greater influence over foreign and military policy-making.

Resources: Deborah Avant, The Market for Force: Private Security and Political Change, manuscript under review, 2004; "The Revolution in Business Affairs: Realizing the Potential," Conference Summary, CNA Corporation, Alexandra, VA: 1998; John Donahue, *The Privatization Decision: Public Ends, Private Means,* New York: Basic Books, 1989; William D. Hartung, "Making Money on Terrorism," *The Nation,* February 5, 2004; Paul Light, The True Size of Government, Washington, DC: Brookings Institution Press, 1999.

CHAPTER 5
MONETARY POLICY AND FINANCIAL MARKETS

INTRODUCTION

Ben Bernanke has replaced Alan Greenspan as the man behind the curtain of the Federal Reserve Board. But unless he actually possesses the wizard-like powers the business press sometimes attributed to Greenspan, it is doubtful that working people will fare any better. In his final year, Greenspan himself worried that under his tenure inequality had worsened to levels that threaten our democratic institutions, and that the unprecedented level of U.S. reliance on foreign borrowing has become unsustainable. Bernanke has acknowledged the seriousness of both problems as well, but seems not more likely to be able to remedy them than his predecessor. And Bernanke is now saddled with a near intractable mortgage debt crisis that threatens to bring down the broader economy.

But why should it matter who chairs the Federal Reserve Board? The Fed is charged with using monetary policy to keep inflation in check and provide liquidity to keep the economy going, or bolster a flagging economy. The Fed is supposed to use its three tools—the reserve requirement, the discount and federal funds rates, and open market operations—to manipulate banking activity, control the money supply, and direct the economy to everyone's benefit.

It all sounds value-free. But what the Fed really does is serve those who hold financial assets. And that is just what's wrong with Fed monetary policy. When it comes to making monetary policy, the Fed puts the interests of bondholders first, well before those of job seekers and workers. Investors look to the Fed to protect the value of their stocks and bonds by keeping inflation low—and if that means keeping a cap on employment growth, so be it.

That is why monetary policy is not just a matter for financial market junkies, but for anyone concerned with the social policies it holds hostage. As Doug Orr and Ellen Frank argue in this chapter, "Whenever any policy is proposed, be it in health care, housing or transportation, the first question politicians ask is, 'What will the bond market think about it?'" The authors go on to show just how monetary policy under Greenspan has worked against most of us and even helped push the economy into a slowdown in 2000 (Article 5.3). Economist Tom Palley argues that monetary policy during the economic expansion, first under Alan Greenspan and then Ben Bernanke, followed the same pro-corporate globalization policy paradigm, thereby contributing to a fragile and shallow expansion that has created few jobs and helped to shrink domestic manufacturing (Article 5.5).

Other articles in this chapter look closely at diverse aspects of Fed policy-making. Doug Orr explains in everyday language what money is and how the Fed attempts to control the money supply (Article 5.1). Arthur MacEwan compares monetary and fiscal policy, highlighting the greater powers of fiscal policy to counteract recessions (Article 5.4). In a second article, MacEwan debunks the notion that a small cabal of bankers runs the world through the operations of the Fed, despite the powerful pro-corporate effect the Fed has on day-to-day economic life (Article 5.6).

The Fed is also charged with overseeing the regulation of U.S. financial institutions, including the stock market and home mortgages, as well as the banking industry. But with the blessing of most economists, Congress the Fed have done more to deregulate these institutions than to regulate them in a way that promotes the public interest. In a thoroughgoing article, William Black tells the story of how the banking industry became dysfunctional with deregulation, and how that deregulation enabled the current subprime mortgage crisis. Black worries that even the most recent international banking agreement (Basel Accord II, which makes banking regulations more uniform across nations) will fall prey to the deregulation craze and in the end do little to correct current banking excesses (Article 5.7). Economist Joseph Pluta offers a case study of the dark side of banking deregulation with his up-close look at the suspect practices of Chase Bank (Article 5.8).

The other two articles in the chapter address the context in which the Fed operates. In Article 5.2, James K. Galbraith explains how the value of the dollar, the world's reserve currency, depends on the willingness of foreign central banks and international investors to hold U.S. assets, and how that willingness is being eroded by the

---

KEY TO COLANDER

E = *Economics*   M = *Macroeconomics*

These readings complement E27, E28, and E33, or M11, M12, and M18.

Articles 5.1, 5.3, 5.4, 5.5, and 5.6 look at the working of monetary policy, who it serves, and the differences between monetary and fiscal policy. They fit with chapters E27 and E28 or M11 and M12. Article 5.2 takes up a complication of conducting monetary policy in an international economy, and fits with chapter E34 or M19. Pollin's discussion of transforming the Fed in Article 5.7 would work with any of these chapters.

deteriorating U.S. trade position. Bob Pollin closes the chapter with his proposal for transforming the Fed into a democratically controlled investment bank that serves the interests of all of us (Article 5.7).

DISCUSSION QUESTIONS

1. (Article 5.1) What are the mechanisms the Fed uses to "control" the creation of money by the banking system. Why, according to Orr, is the Fed's control over the creation of money "limited"?

2. (Article 5.2) According to Galbraith, how has the United States becoming a debtor nation threatened the status of the dollar as the world's reserve currency? How serious a threat is this for the U.S. economy?

3. (Article 5.3) According to Orr and Frank, monetary policy serves the interests of bondholders at the expense of people seeking work and of everyone who benefits from social spending. What evidence do they provide to show that Fed policy has this class character? Do you find it convincing?

4. (Article 5.4) What advantage is there in using monetary policy to slow down the economy? Why might fiscal policy be a more effective tool for lifting the economy out of a recession?

5. (Article 5.5) What evidence does economist Thomas Palley present to make the case that the Fed follows a pro-corporate globalization paradigm? And how, according to Palley, did Fed policies distort this decade's economic expansion?

6. (Article 5.6) Why is MacEwan unconvinced by those who argue that a small cabal of bankers runs the world through the Fed?

7. (Article 5.7) After reading Black's article, describe the measures that have led to the deregulation of the U.S. banking industry and the impact deregulation has had on the industry.

8. (Article 5.7) What is the Basel Accord II? How will Basel II affect the International banking industry? Is it likely to improve international banking?

9. (Article 5.7) How, according to Black, did the subprime crisis grow out of bank deregulation?

10. (Article 5.8) Identify the connections between banking deregulation and Chase's suspect banking practices documented in Pluta's article.

11. (Article 5.9) What are the chief elements of Pollin's proposal to transform the Fed and how would it affect the focus of the Fed and its decision-making? Do you think his proposals would be effective?

ARTICLE 5.1   *November/December 1993*

WHAT IS MONEY?

BY DOUG ORR

We all use money every day. Yet many people do not know what money actually is. There are many myths about money, including the idea that the government "prints" all of it and that it has some intrinsic value. But actually, money is less a matter of value, and more a matter of faith.

Money is sometimes called the universal commodity, because it can be traded for all other commodities. But for this to happen, everyone in society must believe that money will be accepted. If people stop believing that it will be accepted, the existing money ceases to be money. Recently in Poland, people stopped accepting the zloty, and used vodka as money instead.

In addition to facilitating exchanges, money allows us to "store" value from one point in time to another. If you sell your car today for $4,000, you probably won't buy that amount of other products today. Rather, you store the value as money, probably in a bank, until you want to use it.

The "things" that get used as money have changed over time, and "modern" people often chuckle when they hear about some of them. The Romans used salt (from which we get the word "salary"), South Sea Islanders used shark's teeth, and several societies actually used cows. The "Three Wise Men" brought gold, frankincense and myrrh, each of which was money in different regions at the time.

If money does not exist, or is in short supply, it will be created. In POW camps, where guards specifically outlaw its existence, prisoners use cigarettes instead. In the American colonies, the British attempted to limit the supply of British pounds, because they knew that by limiting the supply of money, they could hamper the development of independent markets in the colonies. Today, the United States uses a similar policy, through the International Monetary Fund, in dealing with Latin America.

To overcome this problem, the colonists began to use

tobacco leaves as money. This helped the colonies to develop, but it also allowed the holders of large plots of land to grow their own money! When the colonies gained independence, the new government decreed gold to be money, rather than tobacco, much to the dismay of Southern plantation owners. Now, rather than growing money, farmers had to find or buy it.

To aid the use of gold as money, banks would test its purity, put it in storage, and give the depositor paper certificates of ownership. These certificates, "paper money," could then be used in place of the gold itself. Since any bank could store gold and issue certificates, by the beginning of the Civil War, over 7,000 different types of "paper money" were in circulation in the United States, none of it printed by the government.

While paper money is easier to use than gold, it is still risky to carry around large amounts of cash. It is safer to store the paper in a bank and simply sign over its ownership to make a purchase. We sign over the ownership of our money by writing a check. Checking account money became popular when the government outlawed the printing of paper money by private banks in 1864.

HOW BANKS CREATE MONEY

Banks are central to understanding money, because in addition to storing it, they help to create it. Bankers realize that not everyone will withdraw their money at the same time, so they loan out much of the money that has been deposited. It is from the interest on these loans that banks get their profits, and through these loans the banking system creates new money.

If you deposit $100 cash in your checking account at Chase Manhattan Bank, you still have $100 in money to use, because checks are also accepted as money. Chase must set aside some of this cash as "reserves," in case you or other depositors decide to withdraw money as cash. Current regulations issued by the Federal Reserve Bank (the Fed) require banks to set aside three cents out of each dollar. So Chase can make a loan of $97, based on your deposit. Chase does not make loans by handing out cash but instead by putting $97 in the checking account of the person, say Emily, taking out the loan. So from your initial deposit of $100 in cash, the economy now has $197 in checking account money.

The borrower, Emily, pays $97 for some product or service by check, and the seller, say Ace Computers, deposits the money in its checking account. The total amount of checking account money is still $197, but its location and ownership have changed. If Ace Computer's account is at Citibank, $97 in cash is transferred from Chase to Citibank. This leaves just $3 in cash reserves at Chase to cover your original deposit. However, Citibank now has $97 in "new" cash on hand, so it sets aside three cents on the dollar ($2.91) and loans out the rest, $94.09, as new checking account money. Through this process, every dollar of "reserves" yields many dollars in total money.

If you think this is just a shell game and there is only $100 in "real" money, you still don't understand money. Anything that is accepted as payment for a transaction is "real" money. Cash is no more real than checking account money. In fact, most car rental companies will not accept cash as payment for a car, so for them, cash is not money!

Today, there is $292 billion of U.S. currency, i.e. "paper money," in existence. However, somewhere between 50% to 70% of it is held outside the United States by foreign banks and individuals. The vast majority of all money actually in use in the United States is not cash, but rather checking account money. This type of money, $726 billion, was created by private banks, and was not "printed" by anyone. In fact, this money exists only as electronic "bits" in banks' computers. (The less "modern" South Sea Islanders could have quite a chuckle about that!)

The amount of money that banks can create is limited by the total amount of reserves, and by the fraction of each deposit that must be held as reserves. Prior to 1914, bankers themselves decided what fraction of deposits to hold as reserves. Since then, this fraction has been set by the main banking regulator, the Fed.

Until 1934, gold was held as reserves, but the supply of gold was unstable, growing rapidly during the California and Alaska "gold rushes," and very slowly at other times. As a result, at times more money was created than the economy needed, and at other times not enough money could be created. Starting in 1934, the U.S. government decided that gold would no longer be used as reserves. Cash, now printed by the Fed, could no longer be redeemed for gold, and cash itself became the reserve asset.

Banks, fearing robberies, do not hold all of their cash reserves in their own vaults. Rather, they store it in an account at a regional Fed bank. These accounts count as reserves. What banks do hold in their vaults is their other assets, such as Treasury bonds and corporate bonds.

THE FED AND BANK RESERVES

The only role of the government in creating money is through the Fed. If the Fed wants to expand the money supply, it must increase bank reserves. To do this, the Fed buys Treasury bonds from a bank, and pays with a check drawn on the Fed itself. By depositing the check in its reserve account at the Fed, the bank now has more reserves, so the bank can now make more loans and create new checking account money.

By controlling the amount of reserves, the Fed attempts to control the size of the money supply. But as recent history has shown, this control is limited. During the recent recession, the Fed created reserves, but many banks were afraid to make loans, so little new money was created. During the late 1970s, the Fed tried to limit the amount of money banks could create by reducing reserves, but banks simply created new forms of money, just like the POW camp prisoners. In 1979, there was only one form of checking account money. Today, there are many, with odd names such as NOWs, ATSs, repos, and money market deposit accounts.

These amorphous forms of money function only because we believe they will function, which is why the continued stability of the banking system is so critical. Banks do not have cash reserves to cover all checking account money.

If, through a replay of the savings & loan debacle, we lose faith in the commercial banking system and all try to take out our "money" as cash, the banks will become insolvent (fail), and the money they have created will simply disappear. This would create a real crisis, since no market economy can function without its money.

ARTICLE 5.2

May/June 2003

THE DECLINE OF THE DOLLAR SYSTEM

BY JAMES K. GALBRAITH

Today, the U.S. dollar is the world's reserve currency. Nations around the world invest most of their foreign exchange reserves in dollar assets. The international economic position of the United States depends on this.

So long as foreign central banks and international investors are willing to take and hold U.S. assets (including stocks, bonds, and cash) this system works—and shamefully to the interest of Americans. Their demand keeps the value of the dollar high. This means that we have been able to consume comfortably, and in exchange for very little effort, the products of hard labor by poor people. (As the supplier of liquidity to the world system, our situation is akin to that of, say, Australia in the late 19th century when gold fields were discovered, except that, in our case, no actual effort is required to extract the gold.) And meanwhile (thanks to ample cheap imports), we are not obliged to invest unduly in maintaining our own industrial base, which has substantially eroded since the 1970s. We could afford to splurge on new technologies and telecommunications systems whose benefits were, to a very great extent, figments of the imagination. And even when the bubble burst in those sectors, life went on, for most Americans, substantially undisturbed—at least for now.

But for how long can this system endure? There can be no definitive answer; the few economists who have worried about this issue are far from being in agreement. On one side, it is argued that the dominant currency holds a "lock-in advantage"; that is, there are economies (reduced transaction costs and reduced risk) associated with keeping all reserves in one basket. The United States in particular is in a strong position to pressure foreign central banks—notably Japan's—to absorb the dollars that private parties may not wish to hold, at least within limits.

Furthermore, oil is bought and sold in dollars. As a result, oil importers must buy dollars in order to buy oil, and oil exporters accumulate dollars as they sell oil. To some extent this arrangement further strengthens the dollar—though it is not obvious why it requires anyone to hold dollars for very long, once they start falling in value.

Against this, the question remains: As the U.S. trade position continues to erode, will foreigners be willing to add to their holdings of dollar assets by enough to allow the United States to return to full employment? The amount to be absorbed at present—the trade deficit at full employment—is in the range of half a trillion dollars per year. This was easily handled when dollar asset prices were rising. But now that these prices are falling, they are not as attractive as they once were. If foreigners are not willing to absorb all the dollars we need to place, and if asset prices do not quickly fall to the point where U.S. stocks appear cheap to investors, dollar dumping is, sooner or later, inevitable.

To keep the dollar's fall from getting out of hand, the United States will be strongly tempted to slow the rate at which new U.S. assets reach the world system, by restricting its imports. Having renounced the traditional tools of trade protectionism, it can only do this by raising interest rates, holding down economic growth, and keeping incomes, and therefore imports, well below the full-employment level. In that situation—which may actually already have arrived—the United States joins Brazil and other developing nations as a country effectively constrained by its debts. Indeed, the world prognosis from that point forward becomes grim, since high levels of American demand have been just about the only motor of growth and development (outside, perhaps, of China and India) in recent years.

THE UNITED STATES AS A DEBTOR NATION

There are economists who advocate dollar devaluation, believing that the richer countries of the world would quickly rally to purchase increasing quantities of made-in-America exports, thus reversing the manufacturing decline of the past 20 years. But this is very unlikely. Exports to the rich regions may not be very price-sensitive.

And exports to the developing regions are very sensitive to income and credit conditions, which would get worse. At least in the short and medium term, there is no foolproof adjustment process to be had by these means. Where a high dollar provides U.S. consumers with cheap imports and capital inflows to finance domestic activity, a falling dollar would have opposite effects. A falling dollar would raise the price of imports into the United States, especially from the richer countries. Meanwhile, a declining dollar would hit at the value of developing countries' reserves and their access to credit, and so it would diminish their demand for our exports. (It would help, in some cases, on their debts.) The most likely outcome from dollar devaluation is a general deepening of the world slump, combined with pressure on American banks and markets as global investors seek safer havens in Europe.

This specter of financial vulnerability means that for the United States, the combination of falling internal demand, falling asset prices, and a falling dollar represents a threat that can best be described as millennial. (My colleague Randall Wray has called it the "perfect fiscal storm.") The consequences at home would include deepening unemployment. There would be little recovery of privately financed investment, amid a continued unraveling of plans—both corporate and personal—that had been based on the delirious stock market valuations of the late 1990s. The center of the world banking industry would move, presumably to continental Europe. Over time, the United States could lose both its position as the principal beneficiary of the world financial order and its margin of maneuver on the domestic scene. This would be not unlike what happened to the United Kingdom from 1914 to 1950.

It is not obvious that senior financial policymakers in the United States have yet grasped this threat, or that there is any serious planning under way to cope with it—apart from a simpleminded view among certain strategic thinkers about the financial advantages of the control of oil. Instead it appears that the responsible officials are confining themselves to a very narrow range of Third-World debt management proposals, whose premises minimize the gravity of the issue and whose purpose is to keep the existing bonds of debt peonage in place as long as possible.

The alternative? It would involve rebuilding a multilateral monetary system, demolished for the benefit of the private commercial banks in 1973. The way forward would probably entail new regional systems of financial stabilization and capital control, such as the Asian Monetary Fund proposed by Japan in 1997. Such a course would be unpalatable to current American leadership. But we may find, down the road, that for the sake of our own prosperity, let alone that of the rest of the world, there is no other way.

Adapted from "The Brazilian Swindle and The Larger International Monetary Problem," published by the Levy Economics Institute in 2002. The full article is available at <www.levy.org>.

FOCUS ON THE FED
THE BOND MARKET VERSUS THE REST OF US

BY DOUG ORR AND ELLEN FRANK

Why should anyone involved in environmental issues, or education reform efforts, or efforts to house the homeless, or anyone else, care about monetary policy? After all, it only affects the financial markets, right? *Wrong*. Monetary policy is holding all other social policy hostage, and is part of the cause of the rapid increase in income inequality in the United States. Whenever any policy change is proposed, be it in health care, housing or transportation, the first question politicians ask is, "What will the bond market think about this?"

"The bond market" is a euphemism for the financial sector of the U.S. economy and the Federal Reserve Bank (the Fed), which regulates that sector. The Fed is the central bank of the U.S. government. It controls monetary policy, and has been using its power to help the banking industry and the holders of financial assets, while thwarting government attempts to deal with pressing social problems.

Since 1979, the Fed has had an unprecedented degree of independence from government control. This independence had put it in a position to veto any progressive fiscal policy that the Congress might propose. To understand how this situation developed, we must understand the function of banks, the structure of the Fed, and the role of monetary policy.

BANKS AND INSTABILITY
Government regulates the banking industry because private sector, profit-driven banking is inherently unstable. Banks do more than just store money—they help create it. If you deposit a dollar in the bank, you still have that dollar. Commercial banks will set aside three cents as "reserves" to

"cover" your deposit, and the remaining 97 cents is loaned out to someone else who now has "new money." By making loans, banks create new money and generate profit. The drive to maximize profits often leads banks to become overextended: making too many loans and holding too few reserves. This drive for profits can undermine a bank's stability.

If depositors think the bank is holding too few reserves, or is making overly speculative loans, they might try to withdraw their money as cash. Large numbers of depositors withdrawing cash from a bank at the same time is called a "run on the bank." Since banks only hold 3% of their deposit liabilities as cash, even a moderate-sized "run" would be enough to drain the bank of its cash reserves. If a bank has no reserves, it is insolvent and is forced to close. At that point, all remaining deposits in the bank cease to exist, and depositors lose their money.

The failure of a bank affects more than just that bank's depositors. One bank's excesses tend to shake people's faith in other banks. If the run spreads, "bank panics" can occur. During the 1800s, such panics erupted every 10 to 15 years, bankrupting between 10% and 25% of the banks in the United States and creating a recession each time.

THE CREATION OF THE FED

The panic of 1907 bankrupted some of the largest banks and led to demands for bank reforms that would stabilize the system. Reform proposals ranged from doing almost nothing to nationalizing the entire banking industry. As a compromise, the Federal Reserve was created in 1913. The U.S. government saw the Fed as a way for bankers to regulate themselves, and structured the Federal Reserve System so that it could be responsive to its main constituents: banks and other financial-sector businesses that are now called, euphemistically, "the bond market." While ideally it should serve the interests of the general public when it conducts monetary policy, in reality the Fed balances two, occasionally conflicting goals: maintaining the stability of "the bond market" and maximizing financial-sector profits. Over time, Congress and the President have varied the degree of independence that they have given to the Fed to choose between these goals.

Initially, the Fed enjoyed a high degree of independence. Unfortunately, it was more successful in aiding bank profits than in stabilizing the system. During the 1920s, the Fed allowed member banks to engage in highly speculative activities, including using depositor's money to play the stock market. While many banks were very profitable, speculative excesses caused almost 20% of the banks in existence in 1920 to fail during the following decade. With the onset of the Great Depression, between 1929 and 1933, more than 9,000 banks, 38% of the total, failed. Since the Fed had not achieved its first goal, in 1935 Congress responded with laws that put many new regulations on banks, and reduced the Fed's independence.

FED INDEPENDENCE LOST

Under the new regulations, commercial banks were restricted to taking deposits and making commercial loans. Thus, the only opportunity for making a profit was to maintain a "spread" between the interest rate paid on deposits and that charged on loans. Loans are made for relatively long terms, and deposits are not. If the short-term interest rate on deposits varies widely, the spread will grow and shrink, which makes bank profits unstable. In order to stabilize bank profits, during the 30 years after 1935, the Treasury mandated that the Fed keep this rate approximately constant.

Under this arrangement, Congress indirectly controlled monetary policy. If Congress wanted to stimulate the economy it could increase government spending or cut taxes. Both led to an increase in spending and an increase in the demand for money. To keep interest rates, which are the price of money, from rising, the Fed must increase the supply of money. Thus, the Fed "accommodated" fiscal policy decisions made by Congress and the President.

During most of this period, growth was moderate and prices were stable. The Fed went along because this arrangement did not threaten bank profits. Starting in the mid-1960s, however, stimulative fiscal policy started to push up the inflation rate, which did threaten bank profits. A confrontation over Fed independence ensued and grew in intensity throughout the 1970s.

INFLATION'S IMPACT

Contrary to the view commonly propagated by the media, inflation does not affect everyone equally. In fact, there are very clear winners and losers. Inflation is an increase in the average level of prices, but some prices rise faster than average and some rise slower. If the price of something you are selling is rising faster than average, you win. Otherwise, you lose. Inflation redistributes income, but in an arbitrary manner. This uncertainty makes inflation unpopular, even to the winners. However, one industry always loses from unexpected inflation, and that industry is finance.

Banks make loans today that will be repaid, with interest, in the future. If inflation reduces the value of those future payments, the banks' profits will be reduced. So bankers are interested in the "real interest rate," that is, the actual (nominal) interest rate on the loan minus the rate of inflation. If the interest rate on commercial bank loans is 7% and the rate of inflation is 3%, the real rate of interest is 4%. In the early postwar period, real interest rates were relatively stable at about 2%.

From 1965 on, unexpected increases in inflation reduced the real interest rate. This cheap credit was a boon to home buyers, farmers, and manufacturers, but it greatly reduced bank profits. Banks wanted inflation cut. The Keynesian view of monetary policy offered a simple but unpopular solution: raise interest rates enough to cause a recession. High unemployment and falling incomes would take the steam out of inflation.

Putting people out of work to help bankers would be a hard sell. The Fed needed a different story to justify shifting its policy from stabilizing interest rates to fighting inflation. That story was monetarism, a theory that claims that changes in the money supply affect prices, but nothing else in the economy.

THE MONETARIST EXPERIMENT

On October 6, 1979, Fed Chair Paul Volcker, using monetarist theory as a justification, announced that the Fed would no longer try to keep interest rates at targeted levels. He argued that Fed policy should concentrate on controlling inflation, and to do so he would now focus on limiting the money supply growth rate. Since neither Congress nor the President attempted to overrule Volcker, this change ushered in an era of unprecedented independence for Fed monetary policy.

During the next three years, the Fed reduced the rate of growth in the money supply, but this experiment did not yield the results predicted by the monetarists. Instead of a swift reduction in the rate of inflation, the most immediate outcome was a rapid rise in the real interest rate and the start of the worst recession since the Great Depression.

As the Keynesian view predicted, the recession occurred because high interest rates slowed economic growth and increased unemployment. In 1979, the unemployment rate was 5.8%. By 1982 it had reached 10.7%, the first double-digit rate since the Depression. With fewer people working and buying products, the inflation rate, which had been 8.7% in 1979, finally started to slow in 1981 and was approaching 4% by the end of 1982. Tight money policies by the Fed kept nominal interest rates from falling as fast as inflation. This raised real interest rates (nominal rates minus inflation) on commercial loans from 0.5% in 1979 to 10% in 1982.

The Fed's fight against inflation had a severe impact on the entire economy. All businesses, especially farming and manufacturing, run on credit. The rise in interest rates, combined with lower prices, squeezed the profits of farmers and manufacturers.

Both of these industries rely heavily on exports, and so were also hurt by the negative effect of high interest rates on the competitiveness of U.S. exports. Real interest rates in the United States were the highest in the world, thereby attracting financial investment from abroad. In order for foreigners to buy financial assets in the United States, they first had to buy dollars. This demand for dollars drove up their value in international markets. While a "strong" dollar means imports are relatively cheap, it also means that U.S. exports are expensive. Foreign countries could not afford to buy our "costly" agricultural and manufactured exports. As a result, during this period, bankruptcy rates in these two industries were massive, higher than during the 1930s.

Despite its high cost to the rest of the economy, the monetarist experiment did not benefit many banks. Initially, the high real interest rates appeared to help bank profits. Regulations capped the interest rates banks could pay on deposits, but rates charged on loans were not regulated. This increased the profit on loans. Many investors, however, started moving their deposits to less regulated financial intermediaries, such as mutual funds, that could pay higher rates on deposits. In addition, the recession forced many borrowers to declare bankruptcy and default on their loans. Both of these factors pushed banks toward insolvency.

REVERSING COURSE

It was bank losses, rather than the pain in the rest of the economy, that led Volcker to announce in September 1982 that he was abandoning monetarism. His new policy aimed to provide enough reserves to keep most banks solvent and to allow a *slow* recovery from the recession. Unemployment remained high for the next five years, so inflation continued to slow. Real interest rates stayed near 8% through 1986, so interest-sensitive industries, such as farming and manufacturing, did not take part in the recovery.

Volcker made his allegiance to the banking industry very clear during a meeting, in February 1985, with a delegation of state legislators, laborers, and farmers who were demanding easier money and lower interest rates. He told them, "Look, your constituents are unhappy, mine aren't."

Yet by 1985, the crisis in the savings and loan industry was spreading into commercial banking. To provide cash ("liquidity") to the banks, Volcker allowed the money supply to grow by 12% during 1985 and by 17% in 1986. Monetarists raised the specter of a return to double-digit inflation. Instead, the rate of inflation continued to slow, demonstrating that a simple link between the money supply and inflation does not exist.

IN 1995 THE WEALTHIEST 10% OF HOUSEHOLDS OWNED 89.8% OF ALL BONDS, 88.4% OF ALL STOCKS, 88.5% OF FINANCIAL TRUSTS, AND 91% OF OTHER BUSINESS EQUITY.

THE VETO

Despite the failure and subsequent abandonment of monetarist policies, the Fed still uses monetarist *theory* to justify its continued focus on "fighting inflation." The myth that monetary policy only affects inflation provides a convenient "cover" that allows the Fed to serve its narrow constituency: "the bond market." During 1998, nominal interest rates appeared low, but because inflation is so low, real interest rates on commercial loans were 6.8%—3.2 times the post-World War II average. Real interest rates remain high because "the bond market" worries about any possible increase in future inflation.

Fighting inflation benefits the bond market. However, despite the near-depression that monetarism caused in the 1980s and the extremely slow rate of economic growth that has occurred in the 1990s, the Fed continues to claim that fighting inflation serves the interests of the entire country. The public's widespread belief in this myth denies progressives in Congress the support they need to force the Fed back into accommodating fiscal policy. It also provides support for those in Congress that want to block any expansion of social programs.

If Congress decides to spend more for environmental clean-up, housing the homeless, or education, "the bond market" will raise the specter of renewed inflation. The Fed will then raise interest rates, as it did in June 1999, as a "preemptive strike" to prevent inflation. The increase in interest rates, if large enough, will slow the economy, increase unemployment, reduce government revenues, and return the federal budget to a deficit. Since Congress is aware of this probable outcome, and knows it will be incorrectly blamed for it, Congress won't pass any legislation "the bond market" doesn't like. This is how the bond market holds Congress hostage. As long as Congress and the President allow the Fed to follow an inflation-fighting policy, the Fed can maintain a veto threat over the elected government.

The Fed has also played a large role in the rapid increase in income and wealth inequality that started in the 1980s and has accelerated in the 1990s. The two decades following World War II are often called the "golden age" of the U.S. economy. On average, Gross Domestic Product (GDP) grew 4.2% each year, unemployment averaged 4.6%, and real commercial interest rates averaged 2.1%. Average real wages, that is, wages adjusted for inflation, grew at an annual rate of 2.1%, rising from $8.34 an hour in 1950 to $12.75 in 1970 (both measured in 1998 dollars). This period saw the creation of a true middle class in the United States.

In the two decades since 1980, GDP growth has averaged 2.6% each year, unemployment has averaged 6.6%, and real interest rates have averaged 5.9%. Average real wages *declined* every year from 1980 to 1996. In fact, the real wage in 1996 was exactly the same as in 1968. If wages had continued to grow at 2.1%, the average wage today would be almost twice what it is. Without the slow growth policies of the Fed and the anti-labor policies started under Reagan, the average income of the majority of the people in the United States would be twice as large. Instead, we've seen a hollowing out of the middle class, and a rapid transfer of wealth and income to those already wealthy.

By focusing on inflation rather than interest rates, the media deflect attention from a critical social issue—how high interest rates transfer income from the indebted middle class to the very rich. The social consequences of high interest rates can be gauged by looking at the share of interest income in total U.S. personal income. Between 1980 and 1989, real interest rates rose from 1.8% to 6.1%. The share of income received as interest rose from 11% to 15.2%. As rates came back down slightly in the mid-1990s, so did the share of income going to interest.

WHERE DO INTEREST PAYMENTS GO?

If ownership of financial assets was evenly distributed among households, the growth in interest income would not be of much importance. When increases in interest rates outstripped wage and salary gains, the typical household would simply gain on the asset side what they were losing on the liability side. An increase in the size of their mortgage payment would be matched by an increase in their interest income.

But ownership of financial assets is heavily concentrated. A mere 7% of families with incomes of $100,000 or more control nearly half of total household net worth. Yet this number understates the concentration of financial wealth. Almost 80% of families in the United States have almost no assets, outside the equity in their homes and vehicles. As a result, despite the massive increase in financial asset values during the 1990s, median net worth was no higher in 1995 than it was in 1989. Almost all of the growth in net worth accrued to the few owners of financial assets.

Detailed studies of wealth data collected by the Fed report that in 1995 the wealthiest 10% of households owned 89.8% of all bonds, 88.4% of all stocks, 88.5% of financial trusts, and 91% of other business equity. Despite the media hype about the "democratization" of the stock market, between 1989 and 1995 the concentration of stock ownership increased. In 1995 only 15.3% of households held stocks directly and only 12% owned shares in mutual funds outside of their retirement accounts.

The "poorest" nine-tenths of the U.S. population—that is, most of us—have virtually no financial assets. Such families gain little from rising interest rates. But the higher mortgage, credit card, and auto payments that result take a real toll on living standards. Each uptick in the real interest rate entails a transfer of income from the lowest 90% of the population to the highest 10%. And most of that income goes to the very, very wealthy who are yet another part of "the bond market" served by the Fed.

Economist James Galbraith has called today's high interest rates a form of taxation without representation. The term is apt. Tax increases are passed by Congress, which has at least some public oversight. Interest rate hikes are decided by the Fed, an institution over which the President, Congress and the public have virtually no control.

Like taxes, rising interest rates are a drain on the resources and income of the vast majority of U.S. households. But unlike tax revenues that can be used to provide education, environmental clean-up, homeless shelters, roads, airports, and other infrastructure, interest payments flow into the pockets of the very rich, who become ever so much richer.

Resources: Arthur B. Kennickell, Martha Starr-McCluer, and Annika E. Sunden, "Family Finances in the U.S.: Recent Evidence from the Survey of Consumer Finances," *Federal Reserve Bulletin* (Jan. 1997); Lawrence Mishel, Jared Bernstein, and John Schmitt, *The State of Working America 1998-99*, 1999.

HOW DO FISCAL AND MONETARY POLICY COMPARE?

BY ARTHUR MacEWAN

The Federal Reserve influences the economy through monetary policy—the actions the Fed takes to affect the cost and availability of credit. For example, in March of this year, the Fed, led by its chairman Alan Greenspan, decided that it was time to slow economic growth. So it induced banks and other lenders to raise their interest rates. Higher interest rates mean fewer businesses and individuals will take out loans and spend the borrowed money. Lower spending means slower economic growth.

The federal government can also influence economic growth and the demand for goods and services through fiscal policy—the way it taxes and spends. If the government wants to slow down the economy, for example, it can raise taxes and reduce its own spending. Less money ends up in people's hands if the government hires fewer construction workers to build roads, or if it cuts back on education programs.

One problem with fiscal policy is that changing the budget takes time—except for programs whose spending levels change automatically when the economy does, like unemployment compensation. To slow down the economy, Congress has to pass new laws raising taxes—certainly a "no no" these days—or cutting spending. Then the President has to accept Congress's new law, which might require negotiations, or more legislative action. All this is to say that the political process involves considerable delays and might result in no action at all.

Monetary policy is different because the Fed does not have to bother with this messy political process that we call democracy. It is "independent" since its members, appointed by the President, serve long terms. They decide whether to ease or tighten the availability of credit, without any role for Congress or the President. To be sure, the "independence" of the Fed is not enshrined in the Constitution.

Yet for Congress and the President to pass new laws which directed or restricted the Fed's action would be a serious disruption of well-established policy.

The law governing the Fed says that it should pursue both stable prices (low inflation) and full employment. In fact, the Fed focuses almost exclusively on the goal of stable prices. If unemployment has to rise to meet this goal, well, too bad. It is easy to see why the Fed does its work best when it doesn't have to worry about getting democratic approval.

Fiscal policy is somewhat more constrained by democratic processes than is monetary policy. For example, conservative attacks on Medicare and Social Security have not gotten very far because these programs are very popular.

But the recent mania to balance the budget makes it difficult to use fiscal policy to stimulate economic expansion by increasing spending. This may present some serious problems during economic downturns. The monetary policy of the Fed, it turns out, is not nearly so effective in stimulating economic expansion during a recession as it is in slowing growth during relatively good times. In a recession, the Fed can induce commercial banks to lower their interest rates. But if the recession leads investors to worry that demand for products and services will fall, the lower interest rates might not reignite economic growth. What's the point, for example, in building a new office building when it doesn't look like it will be possible to rent out the space in existing buildings for quite a while?

In a recession, then, trying to use monetary policy to get the economy going can be like pushing on a string. It simply won't do any good. Fiscal policy, however, might directly create demand, present businesses with the reality of a new expansion, and generate a new period of investment and growth.

THE FED AND AMERICA'S DISTORTED EXPANSION

BY THOMAS I. PALLEY

The U.S. economy has been in expansion mode since November 2001. Though of reasonable duration, the expansion has been fragile and unbalanced. Now, with the subprime mortgage crisis and the ongoing deflation of the house price bubble, there are signs that the expansion may be ending.

Many observers blame the recent crises on the Federal Reserve, claiming the Fed promoted excess in the credit and housing markets by keeping interest rates too low for too long. However, the reality is that low interest rates were needed to sustain the expansion. Instead, the root problem has been a distorted expansion caused by record trade deficits and manufacturing's failure to fully participate in the expansion.

If the Fed deserves criticism, it is for endorsing the policy paradigm underlying these distortions. That paradigm rests on disregard of manufacturing and neglect of the adverse real consequences of trade deficits.

By almost every measure the current expansion has been fragile and shallow compared to previous business cycles. Following an extended period of jobless recovery, private sector job growth has been below par. Though the headline unemployment rate has fallen significantly, the percentage of the working age population that is employed remains far below its previous peak. Meanwhile, inflation-adjusted wages have barely changed despite rising productivity.

This gloomy picture justified the Fed in keeping interest rates low. But why the economic weakness—despite historically low interest rates, massive tax cuts in 2001, and huge increases in military and security spending triggered by 9/11 and the Iraq war?

The answer is the overvalued dollar and the trade deficit, which more than doubled between 2001 and 2006 to $838 billion or 6.5% of GDP. Increased imports have shifted spending away from domestic manufacturers, which explains manufacturing's weak participation in the expansion. Some firms have closed permanently, while others have grown less than they would have otherwise. Additionally, many have cut back on investment owing to weak demand or have moved their investment to China and elsewhere. These effects have then multiplied through the economy, with lost manufacturing jobs and reduced investment causing lost incomes that have further weakened consumer demand and, hence, job creation.

The evidence is clear. Manufacturing has *lost* an unprecedented 1.8 million jobs during the current expansion. Before 1980, manufacturing employment hit new peaks with every expansion. Since 1980 it has trended down, but it at least recovered somewhat during expansions. In this business cycle, manufacturing employment has fallen *during* the expansion. The business investment numbers tell a similar dismal story, with much weaker capital spending than in previous expansions.

These conditions compelled the Fed to keep interest rates low in order to maintain the expansion. That policy worked, but only by stimulating loose credit and a house price bubble that triggered a construction boom. Thus, residential investment never fell during the recession and has been stronger than normal during the expansion. Construction, which accounted for 5% of total employment, has provided over 12% of job growth. Meanwhile, higher house prices have fuelled a home-equity borrowing boom that has enabled consumption spending to grow despite stagnant wages. This explains both increased imports and job growth in the service sector.

The overall picture is one of a distorted expansion in which manufacturing continued to shrivel while imports and services expanded. The expansion was carried by the bubble in house prices and the rising burden of consumer debt, both unsustainable. That contradiction has surfaced with the implosion of the subprime mortgage market and deflation of the house price bubble.

The Fed is now trying to assuage markets to keep credit flowing. It has recently lowered interest rates and will lower them further if the economy continues to slow. On one level that is the right response, and it may even work again—though more and more it is coming to seem like sticking a finger in the dike. But the deeper problem is the policy paradigm behind the distorted expansion; this is where the Fed—along with a wide swath of federal policymakers and politicians—is at fault.

The ideological and partisan Alan Greenspan wholeheartedly endorsed corporate globalization and promoted the unbalanced expansion policies coming out of the White House and the Treasury Department. The Fed's professional economists also seem to have endorsed corporate globalization in the name of free trade, dismissing the sharp drop-off of domestic manufacturing as inconsequential. Thus, the Fed has tacitly supported the underlying policy paradigm that has given rise to the U.S. economy's distorted expansion. Despite talk about reducing global financial imbalances, the Fed under Chairman Ben Bernanke still seems locked into this paradigm, which is where constructive criticism should now be directed.

THE FED AND THE INTERNATIONAL BANKING CONSPIRACY

BY ARTHUR MacEWAN

Dear Dr. Dollar:
Some of my friends believe that the Federal Reserve and international bankers (Rothschilds, Rockefellers, etc.) run the world. They think the Federal Reserve was formed in secret and is pretty much a conspiracy. This is all hooked up with other conspiracy theories and right-wing views that make me uncomfortable. What do you think? Isn't the banking system part of the whole capitalist system? How does the Federal Reserve work; does it really have so much power?
—*Carol Brown, New York, N.Y.*

The Federal Reserve is a very powerful institution, and the people who run the world's large banks are a very powerful group of people. No one would claim otherwise. Also, the bankers have common interests, and, like any other group of people with common interests, they do what they can to bring about government policies that favor those interests.

Because the Federal Reserve (the "Fed"), as the central bank of the United States, implements policies that most directly affect the bankers, they of course are quite concerned with what the Fed does, how it is structured, and who runs it. And, like other elite groups, bankers certainly meet in private—in "secret," if one prefers—to figure out how best to get what they want.

With all that said, however, the idea that a small cabal of bankers runs the world through the operations of the Fed is wrong on several counts.

First of all, financial operatives are not the only powerful economic group. There are, for example, the people who run the large oil companies, the Silicon Valley operations, and the pharmaceutical firms, to name a few of the currently important capitalist clusters. These other groups have some common interests with the bankers, and they often all work together, both in private and in public, to achieve their common ends; they do not call in the press every time a few of them meet. (A recent example: when Vice President Cheney held a meeting to formulate the Bush administration's energy policy, the list of attendees—widely assumed to be top energy sector executives—was kept secret.) But to boil down this large class of people to a few bankers both distorts reality and obscures the conflicts that sometimes exist among them.

Second, not only are there often differences among these groups, but there are often contradictions between different things that they want. For example, they want a well-trained work force, but they do not want the high taxes that would be needed to pay for that training; they want freedom from government regulations, but they want the economic stability that often depends on government regulation; they want free access to international markets, but they want special preferences (as compared to foreign companies) within the United States; they want to pay low wages, but they want a populace with enough income to buy their products.

Third, while this set of people is undoubtedly very powerful in affecting the operation of our economic lives and in shaping history, they do not shape history just as they please. They simply can't control everything—as the problem that the Fed has with long-term interest rates illustrates (see below). They cannot control the economy just as they would like and they cannot control the rest of us just as they would like. Formal democracy, however limited, is a useful device. The power that the rest of us have can be a substantial constraint on the actions of big business—bankers, energy executives, and all the others.

But let's return to the Fed. What does it do, and how? The Fed has a variety of functions involving regulation of the banking system, including influencing the amount of money in circulation and interest rates (the price people pay to use other people's money). Of special importance, the Fed can influence the amount of loans that banks issue. When a bank issues a loan, this creates more spending power. This spending power (usually in the form of increasing the amount in the borrower's checking account) is the same thing as more money in circulation. So by influencing banks' loan actions, the Fed influences the money supply.

Right-wingers who view the Fed and the banks as an evil cabal tend to claim that by allowing banks to increase the money supply, the Fed is debasing our currency. The increased money supply lowers the value of money in relation to other goods, and the money prices of other goods rise—i.e., inflation. Moreover, they view this as a way of allowing the government to engage in excessive spending: the government can borrow from the public, but then, because of inflation, can repay in dollars that have less worth.

This fascination of some right-wingers with inflation and the debasement of the currency is ironic because, in fact, the Fed often (although not always) acts in exactly the opposite manner—*limiting* the growth of the money supply and *restricting* inflation. Banks, and businesses generally, like stable prices and stable interest rates. One reason is that a low-inflation policy keeps unemployment rates higher than they otherwise would be, weakening the bargaining power of workers and shifting the distribution of income in favor of capitalists.

A further irony: the Fed is not as powerful as either its proponents or its critics think. The Fed really has control only over short-term interest rates. Long-term interest rates, however, are more important (as they affect major investment decisions) and are influenced by many forces beyond the Fed's control. The expectations of business about future ups and downs of the economy—and about the myriad events that affect those fluctuations—are the central factors determining long-term interest rates. Neither capitalists' behavior nor capitalist economies are so easily controlled. If they were, then there would never be any stock market crashes, burst financial bubbles, or other serious disruptions.

By the way, the Fed was not formed in secret. The Fed was created by legislative action, formally and publicly. But there were certainly private (secret) meetings that laid the groundwork for it. Of course, the same is true of legislative actions affecting the pharmaceutical industry, Silicon Valley, insurance firms, and the list goes on. Nothing that special about the creation of the Fed.

Finally, while I am sure that there are many decent people who see the Fed and the bankers as the source of the world's problems, this view is often part of a larger anti-Semitism. The focus on "Jewish financiers" (the Rothschilds, for example) as the source of our economic and other problems is as old as it is wrong and offensive.

(MIS)UNDERSTANDING A BANKING INDUSTRY IN TRANSITION

BY WILLIAM K. BLACK

The U.S. financial system is, once again, in crisis. Or, more precisely, twin crises—first, huge numbers of defaults among subprime mortgage borrowers, and second, massive losses for the holders of new-fangled investments comprised of bundles of loans of varying risk, including many of those subprime mortgages.

These crises should shock the nation. Our largest, most sophisticated financial institutions have followed business practices that were certain to produce massive losses—practices so imprudent, in precisely the business task (risk management) that is supposed to be their greatest expertise, that they have created a worldwide financial crisis.

Why? Because their CEOs, acting on the perverse incentives created by today's outrageous compensation systems, engaged in practices that vastly increased their corporations' risk in order to drive up reported corporate income and thereby secure enormous increases in their own individual incomes. And those perverse incentives follow them out the door: CEOs Charles Prince, at Citicorp, and Stanley O'Neal, at Merrill Lynch, had dismal track records of similar failures prior to the latest disasters, but they collected massive bonuses for their earlier failures and will receive obscene termination packages now. Pay and productivity (and integrity) have become unhinged at U.S. financial institutions.

As this goes to print, Treasury Department officials are working with large financial institutions to cover up the scale of the growing losses. This is the same U.S. Treasury that regularly prates abroad about the vital need for transparency. And a former Treasury Secretary, Robert Rubin, who failed utterly in his fiduciary duty as lead board member at Citicorp to prevent the series of recent abuses, will become Citicorp's new CEO.

To even begin to understand events in the U.S. and global banking industries, you have to look back at the seismic shifts in the industry over the past 30 to 40 years, and at the interplay between those shifts and government policy. The story that continues to unfold is one of progressively worse policies that make financial crises more common and more severe.

These policies have their boosters, though. Chief among them are neoclassical banking and finance economists, whose ideology and methodologies lead them into blatant misreadings of the realities of the industry and the causes of its failures. When the history of this crisis-ridden era in global finance is written, the economists will no doubt be given a significant share of the blame.

A NEW ERA OF CRISIS

The changes in the U.S. banking industry in recent decades have been so great that a visitor from the 1950s would hardly recognize the industry. Over two decades of intense merger and acquisition activity has left a far smaller number of banks, with assets far more concentrated in the largest ones. Between 1984 and 2004, the number of banks on the FDIC's rolls fell from 14,392 to 7,511; the share of the U.S. banking industry's assets held by the ten largest banks rose from 21% in 1960 to nearly 60% in 2005. At the same time, nonbank businesses that lend, save, and invest money have proliferated, as have the products they sell: a vast array of new kinds of loans and exotic savings and investment vehicles. And the lines have blurred between all of the different players in the industry—between banks and thrifts (e.g., savings and loans), between commercial banks and investment banks.

These changes were made possible by the deregulation of the industry. Bit by bit, beginning in the 1970s, the banking regulations put into place in the wake of the Great Depression were repealed, culminating in the Gramm-Leach-Bliley Act in 1999, which removed the remaining legal barriers to combining commercial banking, investment banking, and insurance under one corporate roof. The new world of combined financial services is exemplified by the deal, inked (but ostensibly illegal) before the 1999 law was passed, that merged the insurance and investment-banking giant Travelers with Citibank, at the time the nation's number-one commercial bank.

These transformational changes in domestic banking, along with the related effects of economic globalization both in the United States and abroad, have produced recurrent crises in the financial sector. Indeed, the current era has seen over 100 major banking crises, in countries around the globe. Thomas Hoenig, head of the Kansas City Federal Reserve Bank, emphasized the remarkable and disturbing facts in a meeting with fellow heads of supervision:

> A 1996 survey by the IMF [International Monetary Fund] … found that 73 percent [133 of 181] of their member countries had experienced significant banking problems

during the preceding 15 years. Many of these problems led to substantial declines in GDP [and] serious disruptions in credit and capital markets. ...

To date none of these crises has led to a global Great Depression. Only a few were larger in absolute terms than the 1980s S&L debacle in the United States. Yet many imposed a much greater relative cost, measured as a percentage of the country's GDP. Some caused severe, depression-like economic problems in the affected nation. Some produced contagion effects that caused severe crises in other nations. And acute banking crises can cause long-term harm. Japan is a rich nation and can afford a 15-year banking crisis—but the world economy cannot. The crisis cut Japan's economic growth to near-zero for a decade, in turn creating contagion effects in the many countries for whom Japan was a major trading partner or a significant source of capital investment. Tens of millions of people remain in poverty in Asia and Africa as a result.

The recurrent banking crises have come as a shock to the United States, given the dearth of bank failures over the first three decades after World War II. The first severe postwar U.S. banking crisis was stemmed from the large loans that top U.S. banks made to sovereign borrowers (i.e., nations), largely in Latin America. The banks had claimed that sovereign loans offered high returns with minimal default risk because the nation could always repay the loan by printing more money. Citibank head Walter Wriston notoriously implied that countries could not go broke. The claim was absurd. However, banking regulators took no effective action to restrain this lending.

The 1982 Mexican default led to contagion and fears of an international meltdown, but the Federal Reserve and the Bank for International Settlements (BIS) took effective action. Brazil experienced a long economic slowdown that contributed to an imminent default on its loans from major U.S. banks. A Brazilian default could have rendered several of our largest banks insolvent. The banks were rescued by a combination of bailouts to Brazil through the IMF and the World Bank and flawed (albeit permissible under so-called Generally Accepted Accounting Principles, or GAAP) "troubled-debt restructuring" to cover up the losses. Brazil used the bailouts to pay minimal interest on the U.S. bank loans and ultimately recovered; while several U.S. banks took serious losses, none failed.

On the heels of this crisis came the savings and loan crisis, an unprecedented debacle which saw the collapse of some 1,000 S&Ls and which cost U.S. taxpayers about $125 billion dollars—primarily the cost of repaying to depositors money that criminal S&L heads had literally stolen from their institutions.

The causes of these crises are varied. They typically occur, however, when large banks are in essence looted by their owners and managers (a phenomenon known as "control fraud") or when there are financial bubbles in which assets become massively overvalued.

Economists who conduct case studies of banking crises commonly report the existence of substantial control fraud. Looting played a prominent role in the S&L debacle. Here is the conclusion of the National Commission on Financial Institution Reform, Recovery and Enforcement (NCFIRRE):

> The typical large failure was a stockholder-owned, state-chartered institution in Texas or California where regulation and supervision were most lax. ... The failed institution typically had experienced a change of control and was tightly held, dominated by an individual with substantial conflicts of interest. ... In the typical large failure, every accounting trick available was used to make the institution look profitable, safe, and solvent. Evidence of fraud was invariably present as was the ability of the operators to "milk" the organization through high dividends and salaries, bonuses, perks and other means. In short, the typical large failure was one in which management exploited virtually all the perverse incentives created by government policy.

Looting has played a significant role in banking crises around the world. It became so prevalent in the states of the former Soviet Union that it inspired a new term of art, "tunneling," to describe the process of the CEO and owners converting a company's funds to their private benefit.

In addition to the national banking crises, fraud has caused spectacular failures of large banks. The Bank for Credit and Commerce International (BCCI—known informally as the "Bank for Crooks and Criminals International"), Barings Bank, and Continental Bank all stunned the public when they failed. BCCI was the largest bank in the developing world, Barings was England's oldest bank, and Continental was America's third largest bank. Each one collapsed with minimal public warning.

And, of course, more recently control fraud played a role in a number of spectacular business failures outside of the banking industry including Enron, WorldCom, and Tyco. This fact makes it obvious that the conventional economic wisdom, which blames this era's wave of bank failures and banking crises on regulation and deposit insurance (which are specific to the banking industry) is just wrong. Despite this, mainstream economists persist in their diagnosis, rarely scrutinizing the deregulation and privatization that many observers believe in fact triggered these crises.

...THEY FIRST MAKE PROUD

Economists have dominated the creation of public policies to prevent banking crises. Their track record has been abysmal. They designed and implemented the disastrous deregulation that produced the U.S. S&L debacle, they praised Japan's and East Asia's banking structures just before they collapsed, and they designed the IMF's crisis intervention strategy that intensified losses and human misery. They also

DEPOSIT INSURANCE SPREADS DESPITE ECONOMISTS' PROTESTS

Banking economists now overwhelmingly criticize deposit insurance. This represents a major change. The prior consensus, shared by Milton Friedman and John Kenneth Galbraith alike, praised deposit insurance for ending the periodic runs on uninsured banks that helped cause the Great Depression. Today, however, the conventional economic wisdom is that deposit insurance may stop runs, but at the expense of encouraging banks to make imprudent loans and take excessive risks. (Neoclassical economists widely view insurance as inherently creating an incentive for insured parties to act in unduly risky ways because of the safety net that insurance provides—a phenomenon termed "moral hazard.")

This claim is dubious: economists do not offer a credible mechanism whereby deposit insurance could lead to the ills they claim it causes. Deposit insurance does not protect the shareholders or the CEO—the two groups (the first, in theory; the second, in practice) that control a bank. It is the depositors who are insured. Thus, they must be the ones who are subject to moral hazard—in other words, the argument against deposit insurance must be based on the claim that it reduces the incentive of depositors to exercise "private market discipline" by pulling their money out of a bank they believe is being poorly run or looted. But there is no credible evidence that depositors are capable of either discerning frauds or avoiding runs on healthy banks based on false rumors. Indeed, studies have shown that even private-sector financial experts who specialize in evaluating the health of banks cannot do so effectively.

Proponents of the view that deposit insurance causes banking failures display an unrecognized logical inconsistency. Their proposed reform is to rely on private market discipline to prevent management from looting the bank or lending imprudently in a bubble. But, if we assume hypothetically that private market discipline is effective against CEOs who would be so inclined, then it should normally be effective despite the presence of deposit insurance. Deposit insurance does *not* remove private market discipline where the bank is owned by shareholders (unless the CEO owns all the stock) or where the bank issues *uninsured* subordinated debt. Yet during the S&L crisis, control fraud (the looting of an institution by its own managers or owners) was most common in S&Ls owned in stock form, with the largest losses overwhelmingly among stock S&Ls. In these cases deposit insurance did not preclude private market discipline; market discipline was simply inadequate to prevent control fraud. Some opponents of deposit insurance proclaim the S&L debacle to be their primary example—a flat misreading of the facts.

The empirical evidence economists use to support their critique of deposit insurance is inconsistent. Moreover, even where the adoption of deposit insurance is correlated with a rise in bank failures, the causal relationship may be just the opposite of what economists claim. Nations with early signs of an impending banking crisis may adopt deposit insurance to reduce the risks of runs. Developing nations tend to adopt deposit insurance in conjunction with privatization—which itself often prompts a banking crisis. More broadly, in part because of the fall of the Soviet Union and the rise of the neoliberal "Washington Consensus," the number of nations adopting deposit insurance increased sharply in the last two decades. Banking crises have indeed been far more common over this same period—precisely because these radical transitions have been occurring in nations with weak institutions, too few regulators with too little experience, patterns of bank ownership that maximize conflicts of interest, and substantial corruption.

In addition, empirical studies rely on subjective coding of different countries' deposit insurance policies, often done by economists who oppose deposit insurance. In countries with no formal deposit insurance, *implicit* government guarantees for banks are common. There are good theoretical and historical reasons to argue that such implicit guarantees—common in crony capitalism and kleptocracies—create greater moral hazard than explicit deposit insurance does because they can be structured to bail out a bank's shareholders and CEO as well as its creditors (as was done in Chile). But there is no way to code accurately for whether there was an implicit guarantee (or whether bank CEOs *believed* there was an implicit guarantee) in a particular country at a particular time.

Despite these weaknesses in both evidence and analysis, World Bank economists draw firm conclusions, opposing the adoption of deposit insurance in any nation and clearly hoping for its elimination. But the world has rejected their advice. By 2006, 95 countries had deposit insurance, over four times the number in 1983. Moreover, economists' suggestions on how to "improve" deposit insurance (require banks to issue subordinated debt, charge variable rates for deposit insurance, or require private insurance of accounts) are rarely adopted and have proven unsuccessful in practice.

designed and praised privatization programs in many transition economies that led to banking crises; they planned (and in some cases profited from) the catastrophic failure of "shock therapy" in Russia. The irony is that when financial experts were most confident in their consensus, they erred the most grievously. As Mark Twain remarked: "It's not the things you *don't* know that cause disasters; it's the things you *do* know, *but aren't true.*"

This record of failure is disappointing and has caused great human suffering. Remarkably, the economists' hubris is unaffected by it. They are now engaged in a war against deposit insurance and regulation. At this juncture, they are

losing that war, but they are persevering in their effort to reclaim their domination over banking policy.

Neoclassical banking economists are failing in this arena for three reasons. First, they neither study nor understand fraud mechanisms and the institutions that are essential to limit fraud and corruption. Second, they are shackled by an ideology that *presumes* that unfettered markets always produce the best outcomes and that government intervention is always bad. For instance, in their writings many of the World Bank's banking economists display a passionate contempt for democratic government and banking regulators. Third, they are mono-disciplinary. They rarely cite (and no doubt

OFFSHORE BANKS

One particularly dark side of globalization is the rise of new offshore banks. While Switzerland now has reasonably workable procedures for tracking the funds of kleptocrats and drug traffickers, several small nations have adopted extreme forms of bank secrecy designed to cater to the needs of criminals and tax evaders. Corporations often incorporate in a tax haven because of the extremely low tax rates. In the late 1990s, the Organisation for Economic Co-operation and Development, an organization of the world's industrialized countries, created an initiative to try to curtail these abuses. Conservative think tanks sought to kill the OECD plan and convinced President Bush to block its implementation as one of his earliest actions. The administration reduced its opposition to the OECD initiative after the 9/11 attacks, when it became clear that terrorists used the offshore banks as their preferred means to move funds.

rarely examine) the literature in other relevant fields such as political science, sociology, and white-collar criminology.

Indeed, although it should be central to their study of crisis prevention, they rarely even cite the work of economist and 2001 Nobel Prize winner George Akerlof. Based on their study of the S&L crisis, which found that looting was a major cause of total S&L losses, Akerlof and Paul Romer developed an economic model of the looting control fraud.

Looters use accounting fraud to make a company *appear* extraordinarily profitable. Consider the S&L crisis. The worst S&L control frauds were the ones reporting the highest profitability. Moreover, the control frauds were routinely able to get a Big 8 audit firm to give them "clean" GAAP (or Generally Accepted Accounting Principles, the official standard of review in the U.S. accounting industry) opinions for false financial statements.

Economists, in turn, relied on *reported* accounting profits and share prices (which rose along with reported profits) to determine whether a given S&L was well run. But relying on reported accounting earnings or stock prices *must* lead to perverse results when a wave of looting control frauds is expanding. Thanks to their fraudulent accounting, whatever strategies control frauds follow will look profitable, and hence praiseworthy. In the S&Ls, this led economists to praise (1) domination by an owner/CEO; (2) extremely rapid growth; (3) changes of control; and (4) large investments in acquisition, development, and contruction (ADC) loans and direct investments. Lo and behold, these factors turned out to characterize the worst failures. In other words, standard econometrics techniques led economists to praise that which was fraudulent and fatal. The error was so great that they identified the worst S&L in the nation as the best.

Worse, economists persist in the same error. During the recent expansion of the even larger wave of looting control frauds such as Enron, economists touted (1) conflicts of interest at the top audit firms (which they euphemistically restyled as "synergies"); (2) using a top-tier auditor; (3) rapid growth; and (4) granting the CEO greater stock options as positive factors that were leading to increased profits and higher share prices. It was only after the looters began to collapse that variables like these reversed their sign (from a positive to a negative correlation) and displayed their true relationship to business failure. Economists are doomed to repeat these mistakes until they adopt statistical techniques that cannot be gamed by accounting fraud.

THE ECONOMISTS' WAR AGAINST BANKING REGULATION

In keeping with their skewed analysis of the recent wave of bank failures and banking crises, banking economists, including those at the World Bank and the IMF, have been waging a war against banking regulation. It is a curious assault that rests on implicit and false dichotomies between market and regulation and between types of regulation.

The World Bank economists recognize that regulation is vital to mandate accurate disclosure of corporate financial information and aid private market enforcement, but appear to believe that regulatory strength is unnecessary to induce banks to provide accurate information. That view is illogical and incorrect. Obtaining accurate information about banks is the heart of banking examination. Regulators use their powers primarily to pry out accurate information from the fraudulent; control frauds do not cooperate voluntarily.

Economists' rationale for opposing strong banking regulators typically rests on public choice theory, which holds that the actors in political systems act to maximize their own self-interest. This analysis paints politicians as corrupt and regulators as "captured" by the industries they are supposed to be regulating. World Bank economist Thorsten Beck and his colleagues summed up this view in 2003 and 2006 working papers:

> Politicians may induce banks to divert the flow of credit to politically connected firms, or powerful banks may "capture" politicians and induce official supervisors to act in the best interest of banks … .

> Government solutions to overcome market failures … have been proven wrong in Bangladesh as across the developed and developing world. … Indeed, powerful regulators are worse than futile—they are corrupt and harmful.

Again, this analysis is nonsensical. If banks can dominate politicians and strong regulators, they can certainly dominate the design of the disclosure standards they face. In that case, pursuant to the economists' own logic, the banks will submit, and politicians beholden to them will permit, deceptive financial reports that grossly overstate banks' value. (This has, in fact, been done in many cases.) Accounting fraud, in turn, renders markets deeply inefficient and causes private market discipline to become perverse. The looters report record profits. Credit is supposed to flow to the most profitable banks. So private markets *aid* the CEOs looting their banks by providing them with the funds to expand rapidly. Again, the failure to understand bank accounting fraud mechanisms, which have been well explained by Akerlof and Romer, leads to a deeply flawed analysis. (In lieu of Akerlof and Romer, the anti-regulation economists frequently cite work sponsored by Michael Milken's institute. Milken was the notorious junk-bond king and looter who caused large losses during the S&L crisis by recruiting and funding several of the worst control frauds, such as Charles Keating. Today, Milken's institute blames the S&L debacle on regulation and seeks to rehabilitate his reputation.

This overarching logical error, their hostility to democracy, and their view of public officials as inevitably rapacious leads economists to a claim that only *private* parties should exert discipline against banks. The view has a number of problems. First, it is overstated. Regulators in some nations do resist political pressure. In the S&L crisis, many regulators did their job despite intense political pressure and saved over a trillion dollars in the process. On the other hand: if, over time, people are taught to believe that it is normal and rational for public officials to be rapacious, this can become a self-fulfilling prophecy as those who aim to enrich themselves sign on to become officials.

Moreover, the argument proves too much. If the banks (or politicians) are powerful enough to act illegitimately *through* regulators, they are powerful enough to act illegitimately *without* regulators to achieve the same result. The argument is also based on a fundamental misunderstanding of control frauds. It is not the "powerful banks" Beck and his coauthors refer to that put pressure on regulators or politicians—it is the CEOs or their agents who do. They do not coerce regulators "to act in the best interest of banks." They coerce them in an attempt to act to help the CEO loot the bank.

In fact, the evidence shows that private parties are *more* subject to capture than public officials. Looting control frauds are routinely able to get top-tier audit firms to give their blessing to massive accounting fraud. The ratings agencies do no better against control fraud. Our most prestigious law firms have helped CEOs loot and destroy their clients. Private deposit insurance funds for thrifts used to exist in many states. None do now. The Maryland, Ohio, and Utah funds were each destroyed by the very first thrift that collapsed in their state thanks to control fraud. No private insurer made more than a feeble effort to exercise discipline. Instead, they acted as boosters for the CEOs who looted and destroyed their own thrifts and brought down the insurance funds with them.

Finally, the empirical studies on banking regulation rely on coding of data by economists who typically oppose regulation, rendering the results unreliable. The risks of subjective bias are acute. There is no objective measure of "strong" regulation, or capture, or "rent seeking behavior." We know that economists have claimed that the Bank Board under Chairman Edwin Gray was captured during the S&L crisis. Not so. In fact, *private* experts were routinely captured by the S&L control frauds. Plus, the studies focus on formal supervisory power, yet informal banking supervision is widespread and often a regulator's most effective tool.

Overall, empirical studies find that better quality regulation (again, to be fair, a subjective concept) reduces banking losses.

INTERNATIONAL CONVERGENCE

Despite the flawed logic and lack of empirical support for their views, conventional banking economists, including those at the World Bank, continue to voice opposition to the creation of strong supervisory agencies. For now, however, their call has been rejected.

In the 1980s, the U.S. government reacted to Japan's emergence as the new (apparent) dominant financial power by claiming that Japan gained an unfair advantage because its banks were permitted to operate with lower capital reserves. If all other factors are held constant, a bank held to a lower capital reserve requirement can grow more quickly, lend more cheaply, and finance greater economic growth. Complaining that the playing field was not level, the United States insisted on an international agreement to set minimum bank capital standards. The U.S. effort succeeded in 1988, when the largest industrial nations adopted the Basel Accord. More recently, the accord was revised and expanded ("Basel II") to include more closely calibrated minimum capital requirements as well as a supervisory strategy of "prompt corrective action" against banks that fail to meet the capital requirements and a strategy to make private market discipline more effective by requiring banks to disclose more information.

The Basel Accord was a major step towards greater international uniformity of banking regulation ("convergence") among developed nations. The expansion of the European Union is another major force for convergence, as candidate nations must adopt modern banking laws and regulatory structures meeting the EU's minimum standards.

Banks are also subject to an increasing number of international treaties designed to restrict money laundering and bribery. There are, however, very few enforcement actions or prosecutions, so enforcement does not appear to be effective at this time. In addition, offshore banks remain an enormous loophole limiting the effectiveness of convergence.

New banking crises have diminished substantially in nations complying with the Basel accords. Of course, it is too early to judge whether the Basel process is responsible for this success. However, we do have cross-country evidence showing that weak regulation leads to recurrent waves

THEY JUST NEVER LEARN

Today's financial crisis offers a superb example of how their methods lead mainstream economists to endorse both private practices and public policies that are perverse. The current crisis exemplifies a variant of accounting control frauds—one in which the CEO and top managers "skim" rather than loot the company—and demonstrates the unrecognized economic costs of obscenely high CEO pay. The incentives created by typical CEO compensation packages in the financial services industry produce bad investment decisions, decisions that increase the CEO's ability to skim, but that expose the financial institution to losses and the nation and world to recurrent financial crises.

Consider the plight of the honest chief financial officer (CFO) in the modern financial world. His counterparts at rival firms are earning record returns by investing in subprime mortgages. Economists trumpet studies showing that banks' income is boosted by practices he questions, including:

- Making more subprime mortgages
- Making more of the worst mortgages such as "Ninja" loans (no verification of income, job or assets), also known as "liars' loans"
- Making subprime loans at particularly high interest rates—which draws in the riskiest borrowers because only the worst credit risks and frauds will apply
- Making loans as quickly as possible
- Growing as quickly as possible
- Reducing internal controls against fraud
- Making loans in cities known to be "hot spots" for mortgage fraud
- Qualifying borrowers by offering "teaser" interest rates that will soon increase substantially
- Making loans in areas with rapidly inflation housing bubbles
- Purchasing and holding in portfolio high-yield CDOs (collateralized debt obligations, the investment instruments backed by bundles of mortgages and other loans, often of high risk)
- Keeping minimal reserves against losses

When a housing bubble is expanding, these practices dramatically increase fees and other noninterest income, minimize expenses, and produce relatively few losses. (Losses remain low as long as house prices are rising because borrowers who get in trouble can sell their house for more than they owe or else refinance based on its market value.) Note that this pretty income picture requires accounting and securities fraud, though: reserving properly for the future losses inherent in subjecting the financial institution to this vastly increased default risk would remove the fictional accounting gain.

The combination of dramatically increased revenue, moderately reduced expenses, and minimal loss means that financial institutions that invest heavily in subprime mortgages and CDOs *must* report record profits while the bubble is hyperinflating.

So what is our honest CFO to do? If she does not follow the pack, her company will report substantially lower income. Its stock price will fall relative to its rivals. The CEO's and CFO's compensation and wealth will fall sharply as raises disappear, bonuses decline, and the value of their shares and stock options falls. The CFO may be fired.

The upshot is that modern compensation systems and the short-term perspective of investors and senior managers all result in perverse incentives to make grossly imprudent investments in those assets experiencing the worst bubbles. This creates a destructive cycle in which large numbers of financial institutions follow the same dysfunctional strategy, which in turn extends and inflates the bubble and produces even more accounting control frauds.

---

of control fraud. Tests of Basel's effectiveness by one of the World Bank economists find positive relationships between stronger regulation and bank health. (These tests employed a methodology that posed less risk of subjective bias by the economists conducting the studies, but they remain inherently subjective.)

The economists' frustration, however, is understandable. They are skilled research scientists for whom econometric studies are the epitome of proof. Contrary case studies are mere "anecdotal evidence" that are fully encompassed within their data and, therefore, require no refutation. Moreover, their worldview is shaped by public choice theory. They view banking regulators as corrupt, "rent seeking" parasites who merely pretend to virtue. Alternatively, in their "capture" model, regulators are cowards who roll over to aid the control frauds. They have not been banking regulators, so they

are uncontaminated and can see the truth as the empirical data reveal it to them.

Regulators, however, dominate much of the Basel process. They view the economists' disdain as an inaccurate and insulting caricature that indicates their ignorance of the real-world banking business. Regulators tend to believe in their experiences, which overwhelmingly teach that control frauds exploit regulatory weaknesses and that normally honest, sober bankers act like frat boys on spring break during financial bubbles. Imprudent lending is the norm in bubbles. Regulators have seen many econometric "proofs" of propositions they know to be false from experience. Some of them have a reasonably sophisticated understanding of the illusion of precision in empirical work and the many opportunities for subjective coding to lead even the best scholars into error. To date, the regulators have staved off the economists' war against banking regulation, and even the World Bank's economists have had to concede that the *initial* results of the Basel process are extremely positive.

Basel II does have a worrying component. It encourages the large banks to value their assets (which implicitly means evaluating their risk) using their own proprietary models. It is easy for these models to be designed so as to dramatically overstate asset values. The problem is compounded by the nature of proprietary models: they are secret, complex, and (perhaps) subject to frequent adjustment. That makes them a nightmare to try to regulate. And in what is essentially a form of control fraud, modern compensation systems, especially in the United States, create powerful incentives for top managers to overstate banks' asset values in order to puff up their own pay packages. Such abuse is so common that instead of "mark to market," the usual term for bringing the valuation of an asset into line with its market price, the process is often known to insiders as "mark to myth."

In the United States, the word "deregulation" still has a positive ring for many despite the disastrous results of this country's experiment in loosening the reins on the banking industry. So perhaps it is ironic that it was the United States that instigated an international effort to develop convergent banking regulations worldwide. International convergence is moving forward, and for now the pace of new financial crises has slowed. The Basel process is indeed leveling the playing field among financial services companies around the world. But what kind of field will emerge? Does the Basel process offer any hope of reshaping the new world of banking into one that better meets consumer needs and better serves the broader public interest? If the banking economists, with their ideological commitment to oppose any regulation, are kept at bay, then at least we may find out.

Resources: C.E.V Borio and R. Filosa, "The Changing Borders of Banking: Trends and Implications," BIS Working Paper 23, 10/94; Ctr for Intl Private Enterprise, "Financial Reform: Paving the Way for Growth and Democracy," *Econ Reform Today,* 1995; J. Bisignano, "Precarious Credit Equilibria: Reflections on the Asian Financial Crisis," BIS Working Papers, 3/99; W. K. Black, *The Best Way to Rob a Bank is to Own One,* 2005; L.J. White, *The S&L Debacle: Public Policy Lessons for Bank and Thrift Regulation,* 1991; Federal Home Loan Bank Board, *Agenda for Reform: A Report on Deposit Insurance,* 1983; K. Calavita et al., *Big Money Crime: Fraud and Politics in the Savings and Loan Industry,* 1997; W. K. Black et al., "The Savings and Loan Debacle of the 1980's: White-Collar Crime or Risky Business?" *Law & Policy* 17; G. Akerlof and P. M. Romer, "Looting: The Economic Underworld of Bankruptcy for Profit," *Brookings Papers on Econ Activity,* 1993; M. Mayer, *The Greatest-Ever Bank Robbery,* 1990; T. Curry and L. Shibut, "The Cost of the Savings and Loan Crisis: Truth and Consequences," *FDIC Banking Review,* Fall 2000; W. K. Black, "Reexamining the Law-and-Economics Theory of Corporate Governance," *Challenge,* 1993; C-J Lindgren et al., *Bank Soundness and Macroeconomic Policy,* IMF, 1996; T. M. Hoenig, "Exploring the Macro-Prudential Aspects of Financial Sector Supervision," speech to the Meeting for Heads of Supervision, BIS, Basel, Switzerland, 4/27/04; V. A. Atanasov et al., "The Anatomy of Financial Tunneling in an Emerging Market," McCombs School of Business, Research Paper Fin-04-06; N. Passas, "The Genesis of the BCCI Scandal," *J Law and Soc,* 3/66; P. L. Zweig, *Belly Up: The Collapse of the Penn Square Bank,* 1986; R. J. Herring, "BCCI & Barings: Bank Resolutions Complicated by Fraud and Global Corporate Structure"; H.R. Davia et al., *Accountant's Guide to Fraud Detection and Control* (2nd ed.), 2000; P. Blustein, "The Chastening: Inside the Crisis that Rocked the Global Financial System and Humbled the IMF," *Public Aff,* 2001; W. K. Black, "A Tale of Two Crises," *Kravis Leadership Inst Rvw,* Fall 2002; Federal Reserve Bank of San Francisco, *Economic Letter,* 3/06; B. H. Soral et al., "Fraud, banking crisis, and regulatory enforcement: Evidence from micro-level transactions data," *Euro J Law and Econ,* 4/06; J. L. Pierce, *The Future of Banking,* 1991; E. J. Kane, *The Gathering Crisis in Federal Deposit Insurance,* MIT Univ Press, 1985; A. Demirguc-Kunt and E. Detragiache, "Does Deposit Insurance Increase Banking System Stability? An Empirical Investigation," *J Monetary Econ,* 10/02; D. Pyle, review of "The Gathering Crisis in Federal Deposit Insurance" in *J Econ Lit,* 9/86; J. Santos, "Bank Capital Regulation in Contemporary Banking Theory: A review of the literature," in *Financial Markets, Institutions & Instruments,* 2001; A.B. Ashcraft, "Does the Market Discipline Banks? New Evidence from Regulatory Capital Mix," 10/2/06; T. Beck et al., "Bank Supervision and Corporate Finance," World Bank Policy Research Working Paper, 5/03; D. R. Brumbaugh, Jr, *Thrifts Under Siege: Restoring Order to American Banking,* 1988; T. Beck et al., "Bank Supervision and Corruption in Lending," 9/3/05; A. Demirguc-Kunt et al., "Banking on the Principles: Compliance with Basel Core Principles and Bank Soundness," IMF Working Paper 10/06; R. La Porta et al., "Related Lending," *Quarterly J Econ,* 2003; S. Johnson et al., "Tunnelling," *Am Econ Assoc Papers & Proceedings,* 2000; R. Haselmann et al., "How Law Affects Lending," Columbia Law and Economics Working Paper, 9/06; J. D. Edwards and J. H. Godwin, "Why Sound Accounting Standards Count," *Econ Reform Today,* 1995; J. R. Barth, *The Great Savings and Loan Debacle,* 1991.

CHASE: A BANK FOR THE NEW CENTURY?

BY JOSEPH PLUTA

Here are a few items from the recent corporate history of JPMorgan Chase & Company:

October 2001: Chase quietly pays $1 million to settle Securities and Exchange Commission charges that it filed false reports while acting as a transfer agent for bond issues.

April 2002: Chase comes under investigation by the National Association of Securities Dealers (NASD) for charging customers extraordinarily large commissions for selling shares in initial public offerings—up to $3 a share, versus a typical fee of five cents a share—and is eventually fined.

2003-2004: Following large-scale job cuts in New York, Indianapolis, Tampa, Fla., and Findlay, Ohio, the company faces lawsuits alleging race and age discrimination in the layoffs.

January 2005: Chase is fined $400,000 by the NASD for illegal late trading of mutual fund shares and for falsely recording customer trading orders—the largest fine ever imposed for this type of violation.

January 2005: A Chase vice president pleads guilty to charges that he arranged to have the company pay $50,000 to a close friend of the Philadelphia mayor in order to seek favor with the city administration.

November 2005: Chase faces accusations of overcharging active-duty military personnel on loans, in direct violation of the Servicemembers Civil Relief Act, a 2003 law passed to ensure that military families could obtain low-interest loans to cover expenses while their service member is serving in a war zone.

March 2006: The Tokyo branch of JP Morgan Securities Asia is fined an undisclosed amount by Japan's Financial Services Agency for breaking securities laws. Accused of manipulating futures contracts, the Tokyo branch is also ordered to suspend its stock-futures trading temporarily.

This brief roster offers just a glimpse of the full range of Chase Bank's brushes with the law since 2000. And there is good reason to take a look at what megabanks such as Chase have been up to in the past seven years. The new century was ushered in by what may have seemed an obscure piece of legislation, but one that is significant in its impact on the U.S. financial system: the Gramm-Leach-Bliley Act, signed by Bill Clinton in November 1999. The new law repealed the remaining regulations of the 1933 Glass-Steagall Act and related Depression-era laws that had created a range of banking-industry regulations designed to prevent future financial meltdowns.

From the standpoint of the big bankers, the 1999 law meant their industry had finally turned a corner. Opponents of Glass-Steagall within the banking industry had sought its repeal for over six decades. While earlier laws had chipped away at its regulatory regime, the 1999 law finally reversed the most critical regulations.

Free to expand and diversify in new ways, many banks reacted cautiously. But not Chase. In September 2000, Chase Manhattan merged with JP Morgan to form J.P. Morgan Chase & Co. Then, in July 2004, Chase merged with Bank One, under the new name JPMorgan Chase & Co. (Yes, the same name minus some periods and spaces.) The roster of Chase's dubious practices over these seven years is one piece of the puzzle in coming to understand the new, post-Glass Steagall banking regime. Chase has clearly been a more frequent target of legal action in recent years than any other large bank, so it may not be typical—or perhaps fewer of the crimes and misdemeanors of the other megabanks have come to light. Either way, a portrait of the new 21st-century Chase bank illustrates the kinds of business practices that megabanks can now pursue.

DEREGULATION DILEMMAS

Probably the most significant change the 1999 law made was to allow commercial banks to pursue investment banking activities. Inevitable conflicts of interest arise when the same financial institution can engage in both commercial and investment banking, a point clearly understood by the Depression-era policymakers who wrote Glass-Steagall.

On its commercial banking side, a bank accepts deposits from customers and presumably looks out for their best interests, for instance, when it recommends various savings options. On its investment banking side, however, a bank has an incentive to downplay to customers the risks of investments such as stocks because it receives a brokerage commission when it buys stock for a customer—and when it resells a customer's stock as well, even if that stock has substantially plunged in value. There may be an even sharper conflict of interest when an investment bank is recommending specific stocks to individual investors while at the same time consulting for those same corporations and negotiating merger overtures for them.

CHASE AND ENRON

In 2000 and 2001, Chase and other investment banks became involved in a scheme which inflated Enron's reported profits and hid large amounts of its corporate debt. By April of 2002, Chase was the target of both Securities and Exchange Commission (SEC) charges and a class-action shareholder lawsuit, with the University of California as lead plaintiff. Both suits contended that the bank assisted Enron in maintaining its fraudulent image as a profitable firm. Their allegations were numerous and specific:

First, Chase loaned Enron $65 million to help a company subsidiary buy Enron assets and thereby make its 1999 profits look higher than they actually were. Formed by Merrill Lynch, this subsidiary was named LJM2—perhaps one of the many Enron offshoots with *Star Wars*-inspired names. In December of 2000, Mahonia Ltd., a firm controlled by Chase and located on the Channel Islands off the coast of England, purchased oil and gas contracts from Enron. Chase later sold these contracts back to Enron, which treated the dollar value of its repurchase as revenue.

But Chase was not only facilitating Enron's creation and manipulation of legally questionable partnerships. At the same time, the company was also selling Enron stock to investors—despite possessing insider information that would have given pause to any honest investment adviser. Chase and other banks, therefore, were charged with instigating fraud by helping Enron hide debt in off-balance-sheet partnerships and by providing false information to the public about Enron stock they knew was shaky.

Later in 2002, more federal and shareholder charges followed. The CEO of Chase was accused of lobbying Moody's Investor Service not to downgrade Enron's ratings while Chase tried to arrange a merger between Enron and Dynegy, Inc. The resulting false appearance of Enron's financial strength misled the public into investing billions of dollars. Three of Chase's "special purpose entities" (Choctaw Investors, Cherokee Finance, and Zephyrus) engaged in unusual lending transactions with Enron subsidiary Sequoia Financial Assets. These "loans" were repaid in full on the last day of the month, only to be loaned again the next day. The arrangement apparently was designed to allow Enron to covertly borrow hundreds of millions of dollars in undisclosed loans.

In June of 2005, Chase agreed to pay $2.2 *billion* to settle the class-action lawsuit over its role in assisting Enron in accounting fraud that cheated investors out of billions of dollars. (One month earlier, Chase agreed to pay $2 billion to settle similar claims by shareholders of WorldCom.) The $2.2 billion amount represents the largest settlement deal among all of Enron's criminal accomplices. During the following fourteen months, Chase also agreed to pay $80 million to settle regulatory charges that some of its employees helped Enron cook its books as well as another $350 million as part of a lawsuit Enron filed against ten banks. While Chase management still arrogantly denied any wrongdoing, most industry observers took the bank's willingness to pay such healthy sums as an implicit admission of guilt. Perhaps more importantly, these bank actions were a convenient way of avoiding lengthy court proceedings during which even more adverse information could have come to light.

Perhaps not surprisingly, many of the ethically-suspect actions Chase has been caught in since 2000 involve the interface between commercial and investment banking. Chase's involvement in the Enron scandal is the most prominent example: in 2002 Chase became the target of Securities and Exchange Commission (SEC) charges and a class-action shareholder lawsuit, both stemming from the myriad ways the bank had allegedly helped Enron maintain its fraudulent image as a profitable firm. (See "Chase & Enron," for more detail.)

Chase's new investment businesses engaged in some smaller-scale corporate misbehavior as well. The acquisition of J.P. Morgan in 2000 was intended to be part of Chase's move into investment banking, although ironically Morgan was another commercial bank, not an investment bank, and thus not likely to be a source of the kind of expertise Chase was seeking. So perhaps the company's problems with Texas customers beginning in 2000 were only a matter of inexperience. At that time, a number of investors in central Texas purchased mutual funds with a Chase investment services branch. In an effort to lure these customers away from their commercial banks, the investment advisors encouraged them to open checking

and savings accounts with Chase as well. Soon afterward, these customers began getting charged service fees because of supposedly inadequate balances. The checking and savings accounts, however, were backed by the money in their individual investment accounts, in some cases as much as several hundred thousand dollars. While the fees were removed when customers complained, the annoyance factor severely damaged the bank's reputation. The claim of a computer error for eight consecutive months in one case suggests ineptness, indifference, or both.

Alternatively, this behavior could be part of a larger pattern of extracting revenues intensively from small investors (as in the NASD investigation of Chase's exorbitant trading commissions noted above). Moreover, the performance of the mutual fund accounts was abysmal, with some losing more than a third of their value in less than a year. During this time, money managers serving the accounts in Texas changed frequently. None of the new managers contacted customers about possible concerns. All were difficult to reach and reluctant to meet with customers when they sought advice. When meetings finally occurred, investors were treated rudely and criticized for their alleged lack of knowledge about the complexities of the world of finance.

Predictably, investors began withdrawing funds at the earliest available opportunity.

Chase has engaged in plenty of questionable behavior (and gotten into plenty of legal scrapes) on other fronts as well. For one thing, it is the silent partner to a whole range of businesses—such as payday lenders, pawn shops, and check cashing stores—that prey on low-income households with little or no access to mainstream financial services. These businesses are part of a fringe banking system that has propped up the profits of Chase and the other "legitimate" financial corporations that finance the shabby storefronts. Consumer groups have criticized Chase for closing bank branches in low-income neighborhoods—South Bronx, for example—and then financing check cashing stores in those same neighborhoods.

Chase also engages heavily in subprime lending in low- and moderate-income neighborhoods—not only mortgages, but also auto, home equity, and other loans. Banks typically portray subprime loans as a legitimate attempt to provide credit to borrowers whose income or credit history prevent them from qualifying for loans at lower interest rates. But in many instances, the story is a shadier one. According to studies conducted by Inner City Press, a nonprofit watchdog group based in New York City, for instance, Chase disproportionately excludes blacks and Latinos from its conventional mortgage lending, a practice which has *worsened* since 1999. In the Boston area in 2002, for example, Chase's denial rates were nearly nine times greater for blacks and over six times greater for Latinos than for whites. Chase's lending in Washington, D.C., San Francisco, St. Louis, Little Rock, Detroit, Milwaukee, and Dallas shows a similar pattern, with variations in denial rates that far exceed the differences in income and credit history between the groups. Inner City Press reports thousands of consumer complaints against Chase on issues ranging from racially motivated loan denials to arrogant and indifferent treatment by bank personnel. Denied conventional mortgages, these home buyers have little choice but to turn to the subprime market, where Chase stands ready to "serve" them.

And then there are the charges of outright fraud. In 2001, a group of homeowners in the Poconos region of Pennsylvania went so far as to file a federal civil racketeering suit against Chase. Their complaint: local developers, in collusion with appraisers and Chase's mortgage division, had sold them houses overpriced by two-thirds or more. Unable to either sell or refinance, numerous homeowners ended up in foreclosure. In 2003 Chase faced a similar suit in Ohio. According to the complaint in the Ohio case:

> Rather than jeopardize its lucrative mortgage business, the Chase Defendants chose to ignore their own independent appraiser's warning and continued to purchase the Raintree mortgages [Raintree was the mortgage originator. —*Ed.*], knowing that they would be able to promptly

"flip" the loans to Freddie Mac and Fannie Mae before the Raintree customers began to default.

Chase vigorously denied the allegations in both the Pennsylvania and Ohio cases. In the Poconos, though, the company later acknowledged buying loans that it knew were based on fraudulent, inflated assessments and offered to reduce the mortgages of hundreds of homeowners by amounts ranging up to $50,000.

BIGGER AND BIGGER

Federal regulators had an opportunity to scrutinize Chase's record in 2004, when it sought to merge with Bank One. But in July of that year federal authorities approved the merger, despite the objections of consumer groups and the reduction in competition which the merger would inevitably cause. The newly created banking giant now has, for example, a nearly 50% market share in key areas of Texas, including Houston. It is remarkable that the Department of Justice did not challenge this merger on antitrust grounds. Merger guidelines established in 1982 under the Reagan administration were designed to prevent such a high local concentration level. They also were supposed to block proposed horizontal mergers (i.e., mergers of firms that were previously direct competitors in the same industry) between firms with individually large *national* market shares in an industry that is already highly concentrated. Banking clearly fits this category. The only plausible explanation is that it never hurts to have friends in high places. The Bush administration has routinely pursued policies favorable to corporate interests, even if those policies include lax enforcement of federal merger guidelines and antitrust laws.

Ironically, despite the wide regulatory latitude given to Chase in recent years, the banking giant has largely been a bottom-line basket case. In 2001, returns on its $800 billion asset base were barely positive and only one-sixth the industry average, and the bank's stock lost a third of its value. In the third quarter of 2002, profits fell 91% to one cent per share—a drop far exceeding those of other major banks. Then-CEO William B. Harrison admitted that Chase had made loans to some of the biggest business failures in history, including Enron, Kmart, and telecom carrier Global Crossing. (This undistinguished record did not stop the company from lavishing Harrison with multimillion dollar pay packages, however.)

Hard times have continued to plague Chase since the Bank One merger as well. For instance, the company experienced a 30% fall in profit during the second quarter of 2005—and that was before the Enron settlement was charged to the books in the third quarter.

THE FUTURE OF BANKING?

Is corporate chicanery an inevitable result of mega mergers like the ones that have made Chase into a financial services colossus? Big is not necessarily supposed to mean bad; in theory, ethical behavior may find a way to exist in a world of giant firms. In reality, however, *mergers confer power*, especially when two mammoth firms are involved. The substantial caches of funds which flow to such firms enable relatively easy payment of fines and out-of-court settlements that are often structured so as to minimize adverse publicity. These war chests also make possible advertising counteroffensives aimed at influencing broader public opinion. Chase has already undertaken a huge public relations blitz, with full-page ads in several large newspapers that offer statements from prominent corporate executives supporting Chase despite its many legal fiascos. It is possible, therefore, for a company like Chase to maintain a generally positive public image by paying handsome sums which smaller firms with more ethical management do not possess.

Behind the PR façade, however, the financial and political power of a megabank like Chase facilitates a culture of corporate greed—with a whole range of negative consequences for consumers and communities—that is far less likely to exist among smaller, more competitive firms.

Resources: Inner City Press, "J.P. Morgan Chase Watch," 2001-07, www.innercitypress.org/jpmchase.html; H. Timmons, "The Besieged Banker," *Business Week*, 4/22/02; E. Sanders, "Bankers Under Fire," *Austin Am. Statesman*, 7/24/02; ongoing *New York Times* coverage; numerous online company press releases.

ARTICLE 5.9 *November 1992*

TRANSFORMING THE FED

BY ROBERT POLLIN

The U.S. financial system faces deep structural problems. Households, businesses, and the federal government are burdened by excessive debts. The economy favors short-term speculation over long-term investment. An unrepresentative and unresponsive elite has extensive control over the financial system. Moreover, the federal government is incapable of reversing these patterns through its existing tools, including fiscal, monetary, and financial regulatory policies.

I propose a dramatically different approach: transforming the Federal Reserve System (the "Fed") into a public investment bank. Such a bank would have substantial power to channel credit in ways that counter financial instability and support productive investment by private businesses. The Fed would use its powers to influence how and for what purposes banks, insurance companies, brokers, and other lenders loan money.

The U.S. government has used credit allocation policies, such as low-cost loans, loan guarantees, and home mortgage interest deductions, extensively and with success. Its primary accomplishment has been to create a home mortgage market that, for much of the period since World War II, provided non-wealthy households with unprecedented access to home ownership.

I propose increasing democratic control over the Federal Reserve's activities by decentralizing power to the 12 district Fed banks and instituting popular election of their boards of directors. This would create a mechanism for extending democracy throughout the financial system.

My proposal also offers a vehicle for progressives to address two separate but equally serious questions facing the U.S. economy:

- how to convert our industrial base out of military production and toward the development and adoption of environmentally benign production techniques; and
- how to increase opportunities for high wage, high productivity jobs in the United States. The U.S. needs such jobs to counteract the squeeze on wages from increasingly globalized labor and financial markets.

Transforming the Federal Reserve system into a public investment bank will help define an economic path toward democratic socialism in the United States.

My proposal has several strengths as a transitional program. It offers a mechanism for establishing democratic control over finance and investment—the area where capital's near-dictatorial power is most decisive. The program will also work within the United States' existing legal and institutional framework. We could implement parts of it immediately using existing federal agencies and with minimal demands on the federal budget.

At the same time, if an ascendant progressive movement put most of the program in place, this would represent a dramatic step toward creating a new economic system. Such a system would still give space to market interactions and the pursuit of greed, but would nevertheless strongly promote

The U.S. financial system faces deep structural problems. Households, businesses, and the federal government are burdened by excessive debts. The economy favors short-term speculation over long-term investment. An unrepresentative and unresponsive elite has extensive control over the financial system. Moreover, the federal government is incapable of reversing these patterns through its existing tools, including fiscal, monetary, and financial regulatory policies.

I propose a dramatically different approach: transforming the Federal Reserve System (the "Fed") into a public investment bank. Such a bank would have substantial power to channel credit in ways that counter financial instability and support productive investment by private businesses. The Fed would use its powers to influence how and for what purposes banks, insurance companies, brokers, and other lenders loan money.

The U.S. government has used credit allocation policies, such as low-cost loans, loan guarantees, and home mortgage interest deductions, extensively and with success. Its primary accomplishment has been to create a home mortgage market that, for much of the period since World War II, provided non-wealthy households with unprecedented access to home ownership.

I propose increasing democratic control over the Federal Reserve's activities by decentralizing power to the 12 district Fed banks and instituting popular election of their boards of directors. This would create a mechanism for extending democracy throughout the financial system.

My proposal also offers a vehicle for progressives to address two separate but equally serious questions facing the U.S. economy:

- how to convert our industrial base out of military production and toward the development and adoption of environmentally benign production techniques; and
- how to increase opportunities for high wage, high productivity jobs in the United States. The U.S. needs such jobs to counteract the squeeze on wages from increasingly globalized labor and financial markets.

Transforming the Federal Reserve system into a public investment bank will help define an economic path toward democratic socialism in the United States.

My proposal has several strengths as a transitional program. It offers a mechanism for establishing democratic control over finance and investment—the area where capital's near-dictatorial power is most decisive. The program will also work within the United States' existing legal and institutional framework. We could implement parts of it immediately using existing federal agencies and with minimal demands on the federal budget.

At the same time, if an ascendant progressive movement put most of the program in place, this would represent a dramatic step toward creating a new economic system. Such a system would still give space to market interactions and the pursuit of greed, but would nevertheless strongly promote general well-being over business profits.

HOW THE FED FAILS

At present the Federal Reserve focuses its efforts on managing short-term fluctuations of the economy, primarily by influencing interest rates. When it reduces rates, it seeks to increase borrowing and spending, and thereby stimulate economic growth and job opportunities. When the Fed perceives that wages and prices are rising too fast (a view not necessarily shared by working people), it tries to slow down borrowing and spending by raising interest rates.

This approach has clearly failed to address the structural problems plaguing the financial system. The Fed did nothing, for example, to prevent the collapse of the savings and loan industry. It stood by while highly speculative mergers, buyouts, and takeovers overwhelmed financial markets in the 1980s. It has failed to address the unprecedented levels of indebtedness and credit defaults of private corporations and households.

NEW ROLES FOR THE FED

Under my proposal, the Federal Reserve would shift its focus from the short to the long term. It would provide more and cheaper credit to banks and other financiers who loan money to create productive assets and infrastructure—which promote high wage, high productivity jobs. The Fed would make credit more expensive for lenders that finance speculative activities such as the mergers, buyouts, and takeovers that dominated the 1980s.

The Fed would also give favorable credit terms to banks that finance decent affordable housing rather than luxury housing and speculative office buildings. It would make low-cost credit available for environmental research and development so the economy can begin the overdue transition to environmentally benign production. Cuts in military spending have idled many workers and productive resources, both of which could be put to work in such transformed industries.

Finally, the Fed would give preferential treatment to loans that finance investment in the United States rather than in foreign countries. This would help counter the trend of U.S. corporations to abandon the domestic economy in search of lower wages and taxes.

The first step in developing the Fed's new role would be for the public to determine which sectors of the economy should get preferential access to credit. One example, suggested above, is industrial conversion from military production to investment in renewable energy and conservation.

Once the public establishes its investment goals, the Fed will have to develop new policy tools and use its existing tools in new ways to accomplish them. I propose that a transformed Federal Reserve use two major methods:

- set variable cash ("asset reserve") requirements for all lenders, based on the social value of the activities the lenders are financing; and
- increase discretionary lending activity by the 12 district Federal Reserve banks.

VARYING BANKS' CASH REQUIREMENTS

The Fed currently requires that banks and other financial institutions keep a certain amount of their assets available in cash reserves. Banks, for example, must carry three cents in cash for every dollar they hold in checking accounts. A bank cannot make interest-bearing loans on such "reserves." I propose that the Fed make this percent significantly lower for loans that finance preferred activities than for less desirable investment areas. Let's say the public decides that banks should allocate 10% of all credit to research and development of new environmental technologies, such as non-polluting autos and organic farming. Then financial institutions that have made 10% of their loans in environmental technologies would not have to hold any cash reserves against these loans. But if a bank made no loans in the environmental area, then it would have to hold 10% of its total assets in reserve. The profit motive would force banks to support environmental technologies without any direct expenditure from the federal budget.

All profit-driven firms will naturally want to avoid this reserve requirement. The Fed must therefore apply it uniformly to all businesses that profit through accepting deposits and making loans. These include banks, savings and loans, insurance companies, and investment brokerage houses. If the rules applied only to banks, for example, then banks could circumvent the rules by redefining themselves as another type of lending institution.

LOANS TO BANKS THAT DO THE RIGHT THING

The Federal Reserve has the authority now to favor some banks over others by making loans to them when they are short on cash. For the most part, however, the Fed has chosen not to exercise such discretionary power. Instead it aids all banks equally, through a complex mechanism known as open market operations, which increases total cash reserves in the banking system. The Fed could increase its discretionary lending to favored banks by changing its operating procedures without the federal government creating any new laws or institutions. Such discretionary lending would have several benefits.

First, to a much greater extent than at present, financial institutions would obtain reserves when they are lending for specific purposes. If a bank's priorities should move away from the established social priorities, the Fed could then either refuse to make more cash available to it, or charge a penalty interest rate, thereby discouraging the bank from making additional loans. The Fed, for example, could impose such obstacles on lenders that are financing mergers, takeovers, and buyouts.

In addition, the Fed could use this procedure to more effectively monitor and regulate financial institutions. Banks, in applying for loans, would have to submit to the Fed's scrutiny on a regular basis. The Fed could more closely link its regulation to banks' choices of which investments to finance.

Implementing this procedure will also increase the authority of the 12 district banks within the Federal Reserve system, since these banks approve the Fed's loans. Each district bank will have more authority to set lending rates and monitor bank compliance with regulations.

The district banks could then more effectively enforce measures such as the Community Reinvestment Act, which currently mandates that banks lend in their home communities. Banks that are committed to their communities and regions, such as the South Shore Bank in Chicago, could gain substantial support under this proposed procedure.

OTHER CREDIT ALLOCATION TOOLS

The Fed can use other tools to shift credit to preferred industries, such as loan guarantees, interest rate subsidies, and government loans. In the past the U.S. government has used these techniques with substantial success. They now primarily support credit for housing, agriculture, and education. Indeed, as of 1991, these programs subsidized roughly one-third of all loans in the United States.

Jesse Jackson's 1988 Presidential platform suggested an innovative way of extending such policies. He proposed that public pension funds channel a portion of their money into a loan guarantee program, with the funds used to finance investments in low cost housing, education, and infrastructure.

There are disadvantages, however, to the government using loan guarantee programs and similar approaches rather than the Fed's employing asset reserve requirements and discretionary lending. Most important is that the former are more expensive and more difficult to administer. Both loan guarantees and direct government loans require the government to pay off the loans when borrowers default. Direct loans also mean substantial administrative costs. Interest subsidies on loans are direct costs to government even when the loans are paid back.

In contrast, with variable asset reserve requirements and discretionary lending policies, the Fed lowers the cost of favored activities, and raises the cost of unfavored ones, without imposing any burden on the government's budget.

INCREASING PUBLIC CONTROL

The Federal Reserve acts in relative isolation from the political process at present. The U.S. president appoints seven members of the Fed's Board of Governors for 14 year terms, and they are almost always closely tied to banking and big business. The boards of directors of the 12 district banks appoint their presidents, and these boards are also composed of influential bankers and business people within each of the districts.

The changes I propose will mean a major increase in the central bank's role as an economic planning agency for the nation. Unless we dramatically improve democratic control by the public over the Fed, voters will correctly interpret such efforts as an illegitimate grasp for more power by business interests.

Democratization should proceed through redistributing power downward to the 12 district banks. When the Federal Reserve System was formed in 1913, the principle behind creating district banks along with the headquarters in Washington was to disperse the central bank's authority. This remains a valuable idea, but the U.S. government has never seriously attempted it. Right now the district banks are highly undemocratic and have virtually no power.

One way to increase the district banks' power is to create additional seats for them on the Open Market Committee, which influences short-term interest rates by expanding or contracting the money supply.

A second method is to shift authority from the Washington headquarters to the districts. The Board of Governors would then be responsible for setting general guidelines, while the district banks would implement discretionary lending and enforcement of laws such as the Community Reinvestment Act.

The most direct way of democratizing the district banks would be to choose their boards in regular elections along with other local, regional, and state-wide officials. The boards would then choose the top levels of the banks' professional staffs and oversee the banks' activities.

HISTORICAL PRECEDENTS

Since World War II other capitalist countries have extensively employed the types of credit allocation policies proposed here. Japan, France, and South Korea are the outstanding success stories, though since the early 1980s globalization and deregulation of financial markets have weakened each of their credit policies. When operating at full strength, the Japanese and South Korean programs primarily supported large-scale export industries, such as steel, automobiles, and consumer electronics. France targeted its policies more broadly to coordinate Marshall Plan aid for the development of modern industrial corporations.

We can learn useful lessons from these experiences, not least that credit allocation policies do work when they are implemented well. But substantial differences exist between experiences elsewhere and the need for a public investment bank in the United States.

In these countries a range of other institutions besides the central bank were involved in credit allocation policies. These included their treasury departments and explicit planning agencies, such as the powerful Ministry of International Trade and Industry (MITI) in Japan. In contrast, I propose to centralize the planning effort at the Federal Reserve.

We could create a new planning institution to complement the work of the central bank. But transforming the existing central banking system rather than creating a new institution minimizes both start-up problems and the growth of bureaucracies.

A second and more fundamental difference between my proposal and the experiences in Japan, France, and South Korea is that their public investment institutions were accountable only to a business-oriented elite. This essentially dictatorial approach is antithetical to the goal of increasing democratic control of the financial system.

The challenge, then, is for the United States to implement effective credit allocation policies while broadening, not narrowing, democracy. Our success ultimately will depend on a vigorous political movement that can fuse two equally urgent, but potentially conflicting goals: economic democracy, and equitable and sustainable growth. If we can meet this challenge, it will represent a historic victory toward the construction of a democratic socialist future.

Resources: Robert Pollin, "Transforming the Federal Reserve into a Public Investment Bank: Why it is Necessary; How it Should Be Done," in G. Epstein, G. Dymski and R. Pollin, eds., *Transforming the U.S. Financial System*, M.E. Sharpe, 1993.

CHAPTER 6

UNEMPLOYMENT AND INFLATION

INTRODUCTION

On the day the Bureau of Labor Statistics announced that the April 2003 unemployment rate had jumped to 6%—after the economy had lost a half million jobs over the previous three months—the stock market rallied. The stock market's reaction confused David Johnson, a Dallas stockbroker, business analyst, and commentator on the public radio program "Marketplace."

"A lot of times you look at the market reactions," Johnson confessed to his radio listeners, "and it looks like the market always tries to do whatever it can to confound the greatest number of people."

But it's really no surprise that stock prices should go up as the number of jobs shrinks and unemployment rates rise. The explanation comes down to the trade-off between inflation and unemployment. Standard macroeconomic textbooks depict that tradeoff as a "Phillips curve" in which rising employment (or falling unemployment rates) pushes up prices.

Why does this textbook trade-off affect the stock market? The answer, as economist Robert Pollin points out, is "all about class conflict." Wall Street investors, out to protect the value of their assets and their investment profits, are hyper-concerned with price stability, and this pits them against workers on Main Street, who care about employment and wage growth. Higher unemployment rates and fewer jobs eat away at the bargaining power of workers, keeping wage growth and inflation in check, and corporate profit margins wide.

Pollin captures that dynamic in "The 'Natural Rate' of Unemployment." As he sees it, the unemployment rate consistent with price stability, the so-called "natural rate," declined dramatically in the 1990s because workers' economic power eroded during the decade (Article 6.1). John Miller supplements Pollin's class conflict analysis by showing how deteriorating real wages for workers are what make for the "positive fundamentals," such as declining unit labor costs, so valued by Wall Street insiders (Article 6.3).

Ramaa Vasudevan takes a careful look at the macroeconomics between inflation and unemployment and how that tradeoff changed during the stagflation of the 1970s and productivity boom of the 1990s. Like Pollin, she attributes the sustained low inflation and unemployment during the 1990s to the relatively weak bargaining position of workers (Article 6.7).

Chris Tilly attributes the long-term decline in pay, benefits, and working conditions for U.S. workers to slower economic growth, the business offensive against workers'

protections, such as unions and the minimum wage, and businesses pushing more risks onto workers in the form of temporary work, mass layoffs, and reduced benefits (Article 6.2).

Perhaps no problem haunts the U.S. labor markets more than offshore outsourcing, which began with shipping manufacturing jobs abroad, and has now spread to back office work and a wide swath of service sector jobs. In his second article, John Miller notes that the alarming estimates of the scope of offshore outsourcing have made even given some inveterate free-traders second thoughts (Article 6.4).

William Rodgers looks closely at the gains African Americans made during the 1990s boom that partially narrowed the racial gap in employment and earnings. Unfortunately, most of those gains have been washed away in this decade's economic slowdown (Article 6.5). Attenio Davis laments that young African Americans are leaving the deindustrialized North in search of low-paying service jobs in the South—the mirror image of the choices of her mother's generation (Article 6.6).

DISCUSSION QUESTIONS

1. (Article 6.1) What is the concept of the NAIRU, or natural rate of unemployment? Is there a natural rate? What is it?
2. (Article 6.1) Given the class conflict inherent in the trade-off between inflation and unemployment, what policies might lead to an improved standard of living in today's economy?
3. (Article 6.2) What forces have led to a raw deal for workers over the long run?
4. (Article 6.2) How have the "paradox of corporate thrift," the "neoliberal paradox," and the "Arkansas paradox" complicated the task of winning a fair deal for workers?

KEY TO COLANDER
E = *Economics*   M = *Macroeconomics*

This entire chapter is keyed to chapter E29 or M13. Articles 6.1, 6.2, and 6.7 expose the class conflict that underlies the tradeoff between inflation and unemployment, the topic of chapter E29 or M13. Articles 6.3, 6.4, 6.5, and 6.7 fit squarely with the discussion of inflation and unemployment in chapter E29 or M13 and can also be used with chapter E22 or M6. Article 6.4 also goes with the discussion of outsourcing in E2, E21, or M2.

---

5. (Article 6.3) According to Charles Schwab and the editors of the Wall Street Journal, how do higher wages for workers and rising unit labor costs conflict with the interests of investors?

6. (Article 6.4) Just how big of a problem is offshore outsourcing? For whom?

7. (Article 6.4) What policies would best address the negative impacts of offshore outsourcing?

8. (Article 6.5, 6.6) What forces allowed African American workers to make gains during the 1990s? What forces are undoing those gains in the current decade?

9. (Article 6.7) What are the costs of higher inflation? And according to Vasudevan's evidence, what is the relationship between inflation and growth?

10. (Article 6.1, 6.7) What forces led to the sustained low Inflation and unemployment during the 1990s? How are those conditions changing today?

September/October 1998

THE "NATURAL RATE" OF UNEMPLOYMENT
IT'S ALL ABOUT CLASS CONFLICT

BY ROBERT POLLIN

In 1997, the official U.S. unemployment rate fell to a 27-year low of 4.9%. Most orthodox economists had long predicted that a rate this low would lead to uncontrollable inflation. So they argued that maintaining a higher unemployment rate—perhaps as high as 6%—was crucial for keeping the economy stable. But there is a hitch: last year the inflation rate was 2.3%, the lowest figure in a decade and the second lowest in 32 years. What then are we to make of these economists' theories, much less their policy proposals?

Nobel prize-winning economist Milton Friedman gets credit for originating the argument that low rates of unemployment would lead to accelerating inflation. His 1968 theory of the so-called "natural rate of unemployment" was subsequently developed by many mainstream economists under the term "Non-Accelerating Inflation Rate of Unemployment," or NAIRU, a remarkably clumsy term for expressing the simple concept of a threshold unemployment rate below which inflation begins to rise.

According to both Friedman and expositors of NAIRU, inflation should accelerate at low rates of unemployment because low unemployment gives workers excessive bargaining power. This allows the workers to demand higher wages. Capitalists then try to pass along these increased wage costs by raising prices on the products they sell. An inflationary spiral thus ensues as long as unemployment remains below its "natural rate."

Based on this theory, Friedman and others have long argued that governments should never actively intervene in the economy to promote full employment or better jobs for workers, since it will be a futile exercise, whose end result will only be higher inflation and no improvement in job opportunities. Over the past generation, this conclusion has had far-reaching influence throughout the world. In the United States and Western Europe, it has provided a stamp of scientific respectability to a whole range of policies through which governments abandoned even modest commitments to full employment and workers' rights.

This emerged most sharply through the Reaganite and Thatcherite programs in the United States and United Kingdom in the 1980s. But even into the 1990s, as the Democrats took power in the United States, the Labour Party won office in Britain, and Social Democrats won elections throughout Europe, governments remained committed to stringent fiscal and monetary policies, whose primary goal is to prevent inflation. In Western Europe this produced an average unemployment rate of over 10% from 1990-97. In the United States, unemployment rates have fallen sharply in the 1990s, but as an alternative symptom of stringent fiscal and monetary policies, real wages for U.S. workers also declined dramatically over the past generation. As of 1997, the average real wage for nonsupervisory workers in the United States was 14% below its peak in 1973, even though average worker productivity rose between 1973 and 1997 by 34%.

Why have governments in the United States and Europe remained committed to the idea of fiscal and monetary stringency, if the natural rate theory on which such policies are based is so obviously flawed? The explanation is that the natural rate theory is really not just about predicting a precise unemployment rate figure below which inflation must inexorably accelerate, even though many mainstream economists have presented the natural rate theory in this way. At a deeper level, the natural rate theory is bound up with the inherent conflicts between workers and capitalists over jobs, wages, and working conditions. As such, the natural rate theory actually contains a legitimate foundation in truth amid a welter of sloppy and even silly predictions.

THE "NATURAL RATE" THEORY IS ABOUT CLASS CONFLICT

In his 1967 American Economic Association presidential address in which he introduced the natural rate theory, Milton Friedman made clear that there was really nothing "natural" about the theory. Friedman rather emphasized that: "by using the term 'natural' rate of unemployment, I do not mean to suggest that it is immutable and unchangeable. On the contrary, many of the market characteristics that determine its level are man-made and policy-made. In the United States, for example, legal minimum wage rates ... and the strength of labor unions all make the natural rate of unemployment higher than it would otherwise be."

In other words, according to Friedman, what he terms the "natural rate" is really a social phenomenon measuring the class strength of working people, as indicated by their ability to organize effective unions and establish a livable minimum wage.

Friedman's perspective is supported in a widely-read 1997 paper by Robert Gordon of Northwestern University on what he terms the "time-varying NAIRU." What makes the NAIRU vary over time? Gordon explains that, since the early 1960s, "The two especially large changes in the NAIRU... are the increase between the early and late 1960s and the decrease in the 1990s. The late 1960s were a time of labor militancy, relatively strong unions, a relatively high minimum wage and a marked increase in labor's share in national income. The 1990s have been a time of labor peace, relatively weak unions, a relatively low minimum wage and a slight decline in labor's income share."

In short, class conflict is the spectre haunting the analysis of the natural rate and NAIRU: this is the consistent message stretching from Milton Friedman in the 1960s to Robert Gordon in the 1990s.

Stated in this way, the "Natural Rate" idea does, ironically, bear a close family resemblance to the ideas of two of the greatest economic thinkers of the left, Karl Marx and Michal Kalecki, on a parallel concept—the so-called "Reserve Army of Unemployed." In his justly famous Chapter 25 of Volume I of *Capital*, "The General Law of Capitalist Accumulation," Marx argued forcefully that unemployment serves an important function in capitalist economies. That is, when a capitalist economy is growing rapidly enough so that the reserve army of unemployed is depleted, workers will then utilize their increased bargaining power to raise wages. Profits are correspondingly squeezed as workers get a larger share of the country's total income. As a result, capitalists anticipate further declines in profitability and they therefore reduce their investment spending. This then leads to a fall in job creation, higher unemployment, and a replenishment of the reserve army.

In other words, the reserve army of the unemployed is the instrument capitalists use to prevent significant wage increases and thereby maintain profitability.

Kalecki, a Polish economist of the Great Depression era, makes parallel though distinct arguments in his also justly famous essay, "The Political Aspects of Full Employment." Kalecki wrote in 1943, shortly after the 1930s Depression had ended and governments had begun planning a postwar world in which they would deploy aggressive policies to avoid another calamity of mass unemployment. Kalecki held, contrary to Marx, that full employment can be beneficial to the profitability of businesses. True, capitalists may get a smaller share of the total economic pie as workers gain bargaining power to win higher wages. But capitalists can still benefit because the size of the pie is growing far more rapidly, since more goods and services can be produced when everyone is working, as opposed to some significant share of workers being left idle.

But capitalists still won't support full employment, in Kalecki's view, because it will threaten their control over the workplace, the pace and direction of economic activity, and even political institutions. Kalecki thus concluded that full employment could be sustainable under capitalism, but only if these challenges to capitalists' social and political power could be contained. This is why he held that fascist social and political institutions, such as those that existed in Nazi Germany when he was writing, could well provide one "solution" to capitalism's unemployment problem, precisely because they were so brutal. Workers would have jobs, but they would never be permitted to exercise the political and economic power that would otherwise accrue to them in a full-employment economy.

Broadly speaking, Marx and Kalecki do then share a common conclusion with natural rate proponents, in that they would all agree that positive unemployment rates are the outgrowth of class conflict over the distribution of income and political power. Of course, Friedman and other mainstream economists reach this conclusion via analytic and political perspectives that are diametrically opposite to those of Marx and Kalecki. To put it in a nutshell, in the Friedmanite view mass unemployment results when workers demand more than they deserve, while for Marx and Kalecki, capitalists use the weapon of unemployment to prevent workers from getting their just due.

FROM NATURAL RATE TO EGALITARIAN POLICY

Once the analysis of unemployment in capitalist economies is properly understood within the framework of class conflict, several important issues in our contemporary economic situation become much more clear. Let me raise just a few:

1 Mainstream economists have long studied how workers' wage demands cause inflation as unemployment falls. However, such wage demands never directly cause inflation, since inflation refers to a general rise in prices of goods and

services sold in the market, not a rise in wages. Workers, by definition, do not have the power to raise prices. Capitalists raise prices on the products they sell. At low unemployment, inflation occurs when capitalists respond to workers' increasingly successful wage demands by raising prices so that they can maintain profitability. If workers were simply to receive a higher share of national income, then lower unemployment and higher wages need not cause inflation at all.

2 There is little mystery as to why, at present, the so-called "time-varying" NAIRU has diminished to a near vanishing point, with unemployment at a 25-year low while inflation remains dormant. The main explanation is the one stated by Robert Gordon—that workers' economic power has been eroding dramatically through the 1990s. Workers have been almost completely unable to win wage increases over the course of the economic expansion that by now is seven years old.

3 This experience over the past seven years, with unemployment falling but workers showing almost no income gains, demonstrates dramatically the crucial point that full employment can never stand alone as an adequate measure of workers' well-being. This was conveyed vividly to me when I was working in Bolivia in 1990 as part of an economic advising team led by Keith Griffin of the University of California-Riverside. Professor Griffin asked me to examine employment policies.

I began by paying a visit to the economists at the Ministry of Planning. When I requested that we discuss the country's employment problems, they explained, to my surprise, that the country *had no employment problems.* When I suggested we consider the situation of the people begging, shining shoes, or hawking batteries and Chiclets in the street just below the window where we stood, their response was that these people *were* employed. And of course they were, in that they were actively trying to scratch out a living. It was clear that I had to specify the problem at hand far more precisely. Similarly, in the United States today, we have to be much more specific as to what workers should be getting in a fair economy: jobs, of course, but also living wages, benefits, reasonable job security, and a healthy work environment.

4 In our current low-unemployment economy, should workers, at long last, succeed in winning higher wages and better benefits, some inflationary pressures are likely to emerge. But if inflation does not accelerate after wage increases are won, this would mean that businesses are not able to pass along their higher wage costs to their customers. Profits would therefore be squeezed. In any case, in response to *either* inflationary pressures or a squeeze in profitability, we should expect that many, if not most, segments of the business community will welcome a Federal Reserve policy that would slow the economy and raise the unemployment rate.

Does this mean that, as long as we live in a capitalist society, the control by capitalists over the reserve army of labor must remain the dominant force establishing the limits of workers' strivings for jobs, security, and living wages? The challenge for the progressive movement in the United States today is to think through a set of policy ideas through which full employment at living wages can be achieved and sustained.

Especially given the dismal trajectory of real wage decline over the past generation, workers should of course continue to push for wage increases. But it will also be crucial to advance these demands within a broader framework of proposals. One important component of a broader package would be policies through which labor and capital bargain openly over growth of wages and profits after full employment is achieved. Without such an open bargaining environment, workers, with reason, will push for higher wages once full employment is achieved, but capitalists will then respond by either raising prices or favoring high unemployment. Such open bargaining policies were conducted with considerable success in Sweden and other Nordic countries from the 1950s to the 1980s, and as a result, wages there continued to rise at full employment, while both accelerating inflation and a return to high unemployment were prevented.

Such policies obviously represent a form of class compromise. This is intrinsically neither good nor bad. The question is the terms under which the compromise is achieved. Wages have fallen dramatically over the past generation, so workers deserve substantial raises as a matter of simple fairness. But workers should also be willing to link their wage increases to improvements in productivity growth, i.e., the rate at which workers produce new goods and services. After all, if the average wage had just risen at exactly the rate of productivity growth since 1973 and not a penny more, the average hourly wage today for nonsupervisory workers would be $19.07 rather than $12.24.

But linking wages to improvements in productivity then also raises the question of who controls the decisions that determine the rate of productivity growth. In fact, substantial productivity gains are attainable through operating a less hierarchical workplace and building strong democratic unions through which workers can defend their rights on the job. Less hierarchy and increased workplace democracy creates higher morale on the job, which in turn increases workers' effort and opportunities to be inventive, while decreasing turnover and absenteeism. The late David Gordon of the New School for Social Research was among the leading analysts demonstrating how economies could operate more productively through greater workplace democracy.

But improvements in productivity also result from both the public and private sector investing in new and better machines that workers put to use every day, with the additional benefit that it means more jobs for people who produce those machines. A pro-worker economic policy will therefore also have to be concerned with increasing investments to improve the stock of machines that workers have at their disposal on the job.

In proposing such a policy approach, have I forgotten the lesson that Marx and Kalecki taught us, that unemployment serves a purpose in capitalism? Given that this lesson has become part of the standard mode of thinking among mainstream economists ranging from Milton Friedman to Robert Gordon, I would hope that I haven't let it slip from view. My point nevertheless is that through changing power relationships at the workplace and the decision-making process through which investment decisions get made, labor and the left can then also achieve a more egalitarian economy, one in which capitalists' power to brandish the weapon of unemployment is greatly circumscribed. If the labor movement and the left neglect issues of control over investment and the workplace, we will continue to live amid a Bolivian solution to the unemployment problem, where full employment is the by-product of workers' vulnerability, not their strength.

Resources: A longer version of this article appears as "The 'Reserve Army of Labor' and the 'Natural Rate of Unemployment': Can Marx, Kalecki, Friedman, and Wall Street All Be Wrong?," *Review of Radical Political Economics*, Fall 1998. Both articles derive from a paper originally presented as the David Gordon Memorial Lecture at the 1997 Summer Conference of the Union for Radical Political Economics. See also Robert Pollin and Stephanie Luce, *The Living Wage: Building A Fair Economy*, 1998; David Gordon, *Fat and Mean*, 1997; David Gordon, "Generating Affluence: Productivity Gains Require Worker Support," *Real World Macro*, 15th ed., 1998.

ARTICLE 6.2

July/August 2003

RAW DEAL FOR WORKERS

BY CHRIS TILLY

Few people have seen the inside of a "secondary meat processor"—a factory where large cuts of beef are turned into hamburger patties, roast beef, and other beef products. The workers who process beef do not have it easy. Many stand for long hours on wet floors. They are in constant contact with raw meat. In a typical plant the temperature ranges from 50° down to 3°F. Some workers rake 30-pound beef slabs from a huge bin onto a scale. Others heave giant roasts from one transmission belt to another. The work is repetitive and boring, but at the same time requires extreme attention to detail because of the potential for injury as well as food safety regulations. At one typical plant, entry-level pay is $7.75 an hour, or $16,000 a year—a poverty-level wage. There is no question that meat processors are getting a raw deal.

But the raw deal for workers is not limited to those workers who deal with raw meat. Pay, opportunities, and job quality have gotten worse for most workers in the United States over the past 30 years, across most sectors of the economy.

Obviously, the 2001 recession and the current jobless recovery have meant two-plus years of severe job shortages. But the deterioration of U.S. labor market conditions is a longer-term phenomenon. The spread of second-class jobs in the past three decades relates to fundamental changes in the economy and society, including sluggish productivity growth and employer assaults on workers' rights and protections.

The strongest evidence for the raw deal comes from looking at how workers were doing at the peak of the 1990s boom, three years ago. It was the longest boom in recorded U.S. history (lasting from March 1991 to March 2001).

The expansion drove unemployment down to its lowest level in 30 years and spurred talk about a "new economy" that would turn productivity growth into endless prosperity. It should have been the best of times. But as a glance at the numbers reveals, it was not the best of times for working people.

WHY THE RAW DEAL?

Why are workers getting such a raw deal? First, the economic pie is growing more slowly. Productivity growth during the "new economy" 1990s was only two-thirds as fast as in the "old economy" 1960s. That reflects the fact that companies have not invested as much in upgrading their equipment and training their workers as they once did—although the numbers are up compared to the 1980s, when productivity growth was even slower.

Why are these investments down? Businesses make an investment when they expect a payoff. But total global demand for goods and services grew only about half as fast in the 1980s and 1990s as it did in the 1960s and 1970s, and the increasing globalization of trade and investment meant that businesses were much more likely to face new competitors.

Second, over the last 20 years, businesses have aggressively attacked the protections that workers had built up for themselves. They have busted and blocked unions, shredded the unspoken agreements that governed many non-union workplaces, and lobbied to weaken pro-worker legislation. One consequence of these efforts: private sector workers are now less than one-third as likely to belong to a union now as they were in the mid-1950s. The minimum wage is only worth about two-thirds as much as it was at its high point in the late 1960s (after taking inflation into account). Because the low-wage workforce includes disproportionate numbers of women and people of color, the minimum wage and unions particularly benefit these groups.

Republican presidents have joined in the attacks on these protections. Every Republican administration since Ronald Reagan has doggedly opposed minimum wage increases. When Reagan fired striking air traffic controllers in 1981, he set a precedent for the permanent replacement of strikers. George W. Bush out-did Reagan in 2002 when he demanded that the Department of Homeland Security not have civil service protections and announced plans to privatize half of the federal workforce. Republicans in the White House have also stacked the National Labor Relations Board (NLRB), other federal agencies, and the courts with anti-labor appointees. As a result, these agencies offer at best weak enforcement of labor protections. To provide two recent examples: the NLRB recently ruled that unions have no right to hand out leaflets in company parking lots, and the Supreme Court ruled in 2002 that if a company terminates an undocumented worker, it need not pay the worker his or her back pay. Further, under-funding of the Occupational Safety and Health Administration (OSHA) has reduced inspections in hazardous workplaces—like meat processors. Self-styled New Democrats have backed many of these changes in the name of aiding business.

Of course, at the same time as corporations have attacked rank-and-file workers' protections, they have increased the rewards to top executives and stockholders. CEO pay kept growing through 2001, even while profits and stock values declined.

The third reason for the raw deal is that businesses have pushed more and more risk onto workers. The most extreme example of this is the growth of temporary work, which has expanded more than twenty-fold since the late 1960s. (Temporary work has been shrinking for the last two years—which of course is exactly the point: you hire temporary workers so you can dump them when the economy goes south.) But beyond the temps themselves, the frequency of mass layoffs highlights the fact that really, almost all jobs are temporary today.

Benefits are another area where workers bear more and more risk. Twenty-five years ago, most workers with pensions had "defined benefit" plans which specified the amount they would be paid upon retirement. Today, fewer than half of all workers are covered by any retirement plan, and fewer than one in five has a defined-benefit pension plan. Businesses prefer to offer defined-contribution plans like 401(k)s which require employee contributions and tie retirement income to market returns. In the last two years, we saw the results for those who had invested their 401(k) savings in Wall Street. Similarly, employers who offer health insurance have made workers take on more and more of the cost of health benefits—with the result that a growing number of workers decide they can't afford their health plan and go without coverage.

BECAUSE THEY CAN

Why are businesses attacking worker protections and demanding that workers bear more risk? The first answer that many people give is "globalization"—and the increased competition that comes with it. Globalization has certainly had an important impact, but it does not offer an adequate explanation for business's newly combative stance. After all, it is the National Restaurant Association—representing an industry that experiences absolutely no global competition—that has fought hardest to keep the minimum wage low. To a large extent, businesses have gone on the offensive not because they *must*, but because they *can*.

Of course, businesses have always had the ability to lobby against the minimum wage, to cut health benefits, and to run anti-union campaigns. What has changed is the social acceptability of such actions. Princeton economist Paul Krugman recently argued that this is what accounts for the stratospheric rise of CEO pay: businesses have torn up the old social contract that placed important restraints on corporate self-seeking. Once a few large companies did this, the pressure mounted for other companies to go along or else face a competitive disadvantage, both in the stock market and in the market for goods and services. And as the social contract got rewritten, the government stopped enforcing the old rules. Cases in point are recent changes by the Supreme Court, the NLRB, and OSHA, mentioned earlier.

What can be done about this raw deal? It's tempting to think about the Arnold Schwarzenegger solution. In the 1986 movie *Raw Deal* ("They gave him a raw deal. *Nobody* gives him a raw deal."), Schwarzenegger used fists, guns, and explosives to wipe out the Chicago mob. But leveling the playing field for workers is no Hollywood action film. Complicating the task of winning a fairer share are three paradoxes.

THREE PARADOXES

The first is the *paradox of corporate thrift*. Again, businesses are spending less on investments in equipment and training, and are also doing their best to keep wages and benefits low, all because the demand for the goods and services they sell is not growing very fast. For any business individually, this kind of thrift makes sense. But the paradox is that for businesses taken as a whole, it's counterproductive. Because if businesses are keeping down their own spending, and giving workers as little as possible, the overall result is to keep down the demand for goods and services. It's a vicious circle.

Handing another million dollars to a CEO is not a good way to stimulate the economy. True, some CEOs, like Tyco's Dennis Kozlowski, found creative ways to spend the money—on art, furniture, boats, and travel. But in general, rich people save most of their income. If you took a million dollars of executive pay and divided it among 1,000 poor families, you would get a lot more economic impact.

The second paradox is what University of Massachusetts economist James Crotty calls the *neoliberal paradox*. With slow global growth and increased global competition, it's become harder for most businesses to keep profits up. But at the same time, changes in the stock market mean that investors now demand consistently high profits. The growth of large institutional investors and the invention of the hostile takeover have made it possible for investors to threaten companies with takeover or destruction unless they generate high returns. Crotty points out that profit for nonfinancial corporations actually peaked in 1997. But corporations knew what would happen if they told their shareholders this bad news. In this context, the pressures for accounting games and even fraud became irresistible.

These first two paradoxes point out that the economy is far too important to let businesses run it. But when we think about how to take more control away from businesses, we run into the third paradox, the *Arkansas Traveler paradox*, named for an old song in which a traveler comes upon a man whose roof is leaking in a rainstorm. When the traveler asks him why he doesn't fix the roof, he says, "I can't fix it when it's raining." Asked why he doesn't then repair the roof when it's sunny, he replies, "When it's sunny, there's no need to fix it."

Similarly, when the economy is booming, workers have more economic leverage. Businesses run up against labor shortages, so they're more willing to make concessions to in order to ensure they can get the workers they need. It's a good time to organize a union, push for a higher minimum wage, or demand that employers provide a training program. Governments have the money to enforce regulations or to help pay for training.

But when the economy is booming, many workers don't see as much need to band together to defend their interests. Why form a union or lobby for a higher minimum wage when you can hop to a better paying job? Why push for a training program when even unskilled workers are getting jobs? The 1990s may not have amounted to a workers' paradise, but employment rates and wages were relatively edenic compared to the two decades that came before.

On the other hand, when the economy crashes, all of a sudden even the corporate media and mainstream politicians begin to focus on all the ways that business falls short. But when businesses are struggling for survival, they will fight desperately against any attempt to give workers a bigger share. The large numbers of unemployed job seekers put a damper on any attempts to organize unions or boost minimum wages. Governments face budget shortfalls, so they are not inclined to take on new activities.

The only way out of this box is not economic, but political. We have to build a movement that sees beyond the current situation in any given year. In the boom years, we have to remember all the problems of a business-dominated economy and use our economic leverage to strengthen institutions and business practices that help workers. In the bust years, like now, we have to keep in mind that economic resources will soon enough be growing again, and put in place rules that will more equitably distribute and effectively use them. We know what rules make a difference: the most important are strong wage floors and collective bargaining protections. By making businesses work under a better set of rules, we can actually help grow those resources by steering the economy out of the paradox of thrift and the neoliberal paradox.

If the problem is a raw deal, the solution is a new New Deal. The New Deal of the 1930s and 1940s saved U.S. capitalism from itself. It looks like we're going to have to do it again.

COMING CLEAN ON CLASS CONFLICT

BY JOHN MILLER

New evidence that American companies are having a hard time keeping labor costs under control raised worries about a pickup in inflation, sending stocks tumbling.

The Labor Department reported that the sum nonfarm businesses pay their workers for each unit of production rose at an annualized rate of 1.8% in the first quarter, sharply exceeding its initial estimate of 0.6%.

The jump in so-called unit labor costs stemmed from a combination of factors: sharper compensation growth, which was revised upward to 2.8% from 2.3%, and lower growth in productivity—or output per hour—which was revised down to 1% from 1.7%.

While strong growth in jobs and wages is good for workers, it raises the possibility that companies, unable to offset higher labor costs by increasing productivity, will try to pass those costs along to consumers, a trend that could fuel inflation and prompt the Federal Reserve to raise interest rates in response.

Concerns that the Fed might ride harder on the economic brakes contributed to yesterday's decline in stocks, market participants said.

The U.S. economy is coming off a decade-long boom in productivity growth. In 2002 and 2003, labor productivity surged at an average annual rate of almost 4%, then slowed to about 2.5% growth in 2004 and 2005. Since then, it has grown at an annualized rate of about 1.5%. Much of that decline is the natural result of the economy's slowdown: When economic growth slows faster than companies cut back on hiring and shifts, output per hour also slows.

—*Wall Street Journal*, June 7, 2007

The degree to which a unit labor costs index meets expectations is typically one of the most influential aspects of the [Bureau of Labor Statistics quarterly] report. ... Bond prices typically fall (yields rise) in reaction to higher-than-expected unit labor costs ... . Stock prices may also fall. ... Alternatively, if unit labor costs become subdued, this can give a boost to stock and bond prices. Low growth rates of unit labor costs help reduce inflation pressure while potentially increasing corporate profits, thereby supporting stocks.

—Charles Schwab & Co., "*Guide to Economic Indicators*," Sept. 28, 2006

Ever had any doubts that class conflict is what drives the economy? Check out the story the *Wall Street Journal* ran this June about how wage gains for workers will puncture the ebullience of the markets.

The *Journal* article describes explicitly how class conflict is driving the reaction of U.S. investors to gains made by ordinary workers:

> While strong growth in jobs and wages is good for workers, it raises the possibility that companies, unable to offset higher labor costs by increasing productivity, will try to pass those costs along to consumers, a trend that could fuel inflation and prompt the Federal Reserve to raise interest rates in response. ... Concerns that the Fed might ride harder on the economic brakes contributed to yesterday's decline in stocks.

This explanation departs entirely from the story found in most mainstream economics reporting: that we are all—workers and investors alike—on the same elevator, moving up or down in concert. Makes you wonder if reporters at the *Journal* have been sneaking off to read Marx's *Capital* on their lunch break.

Or take the Guide to Economic Indicators put out by Charles Schwab, one of the largest U.S. financial services corporations, to educate its investor clients. Schwab's document is even more explicit about the fact that deteriorating real wages for workers are what make for the positive fundamentals—rising productivity and declining unit labor costs, improved competitiveness, and low inflation—so prized by the markets. This is a reality that financial industry analysts, unlike many economists, have never felt the need to mask.

The Schwab guide explains the importance of "unit labor costs," the actual dollar costs firms pay for employees to make a unit of output, as follows: "Low growth rates of unit labor costs help reduce inflation pressure while potentially increasing corporate profits, thereby supporting stocks." Schwab's simple chart, reproduced above, could not make the point more clearly: rising wages *bad*; falling wages *good*.

THE REAL STORY

Bare bones, here is the class conflict that drives the story. Economic growth creates jobs, lowering unemployment.

Low unemployment gives workers greater bargaining power to press for higher wages and benefits. Businesses can either absorb these higher labor costs by cutting profits, or pass them along by raising prices.

Either way, investors lose out. If their profits decline, corporations may pay their stockholders less in dividends and/or see their share prices fall. If prices rise, that inflation cuts into the real value of investor assets and may provoke the Federal Reserve to hike interest rates, dampening economic growth.

When the Labor Department published its revised first-quarter unit labor cost numbers on June 6, a larger than expected 1.8% jump in the unit labor costs of U.S. nonfarm businesses is what set off the financial alarm bells reported in the *Journal*. That day, the Dow Jones Industrial Average lost 129.7 points, or 1% of its value.

But were investors' fears justified? To the extent their concern was focused on the risk of higher inflation, perhaps not. Labor compensation does make up the largest chunk of business costs. Nonetheless, in recent years unit labor costs have ceased to correlate with inflation. When Jared Bernstein, labor economist at the Washington, D.C.-based Economic Policy Institute, tracked changes in unit labor costs and core inflation (price growth with volatile food and energy prices removed) from 1995 to 2006, he found the two to be "essentially unrelated."

Ironically, the new disconnect between unit labor costs and inflation may itself have something to do with class conflict. More than in the past, recent rises in unit labor costs reflect high-end compensation—those million-dollar bonuses paid out by investment banking firms, for instance. As Bernstein notes, businesses appear to be less likely to pass these bonuses through to consumers in the form of higher prices than they are the costs of wage increases for low- and mid-level workers. Why? No one is sure, but some economists speculate that executives may view oversize compensation packages for themselves and their friends as a kind of profit sharing rather than a wage cost.

LESS THAN MEETS THE EYE

Even with the recent gains in compensation that have rendered investment types apoplectic, most workers are hardly getting rich. Labor's share of national income (64.3%) remains at its lowest level in nearly a decade and well below its level at the start of the expansion in 2001. At the same time, corporate profits as a share of national income are at record levels. (See "Bumpy Landing," page X.)

These compensation gains have done little to improve the purchasing power of most workers. Hourly compensation in nonfarm businesses (the compensation measure that the Bureau of Labor Statistics uses to calculate unit labor costs) is up 8.9% after correcting for inflation since the current expansion began in 2001, which may sound impressive. But that measure includes bonuses, stock options, and the value of employee benefits, including health insurance and even employer 401(k) contributions. The Employment Cost Index for private industry, a similar measure that excludes the salaries of self-employed business owners and stock options, is up just 3.3% over the same period after correcting for inflation. And when benefits are excluded, wages and salaries are just a scant 0.6% higher today in real terms than when the expansion began six years ago, according to the Employment Cost Index.

In other words, most of the rise in the wage numbers that so worries Wall Street stems from outsize stock options and from higher health insurance costs—not from genuine wage gains for ordinary Americans.

These numbers not only unmask the class oppression that undergirds financial accumulation. They also reveal the utter unwillingness of the financial powers to share with workers any of the gains of economic growth that come from higher productivity, a mean-spiritedness disturbing even by capitalist standards.

But none of this should really be surprising. For Wall Street remains, as Woody Guthrie once put it, "the street that keeps the rest of us off Easy Street."

OUTSIZED OFFSHORE OUTSOURCING

THE SCOPE OF OFFSHORE OUTSOURCING GIVES SOME ECONOMISTS AND THE BUSINESS PRESS THE HEEBIE-JEEBIES.

BY JOHN MILLER

At a press conference introducing the 2004 *Economic Report of the President*, N. Gregory Mankiw, then head of President Bush's Council of Economic Advisors, assured the press that "Outsourcing is probably a plus for the economy in the long run [and] just a new way of doing international trade."

Mankiw's comments were nothing other than mainstream economics, as even Democratic Party-linked economists confirmed. For instance Janet Yellen, President Clinton's chief economist, told the *Wall Street Journal*, "In the long run, outsourcing is another form of trade that benefits the U.S. economy by giving us cheaper ways to do things." Nonetheless, Mankiw's assurances were met with derision from those uninitiated in the economics profession's free-market ideology. Sen. John Edwards (D-N.C.) asked, "What planet do they live on?" Even Republican House Speaker Dennis Hastert (Ill.) said that Mankiw's theory "fails a basic test of real economics."

Mankiw now jokes that "if the American Economic Association were to give an award for the Most Politically Inept Paraphrasing of Adam Smith, I would be a leading candidate." But he quickly adds, "the recent furor about outsourcing, and my injudiciously worded comments about the benefits of international trade, should not eclipse the basic lessons that economists have understood for more than two centuries."

In fact Adam Smith never said any such thing about international trade. In response to the way Mankiw and other economists distort Smith's writings, economist Michael Meeropol took a close look at what Smith actually said; he found that Smith used his invisible hand argument to favor domestic investment over far-flung, hard-to-supervise foreign investments. Here are Smith's words in his 1776 masterpiece, *The Wealth of Nations*:

> By preferring the support of domestic to that of foreign industry, he [the investor] intends only his own security; and by directing that industry in such a manner as its produce may be of the greatest value, he intends only his

own gain, and he is in this, as in many other cases, led by an invisible hand to promote an end, which was no part of his intention.

Outsized offshore outsourcing, the shipping of jobs overseas to take advantage of low wages, has forced some mainstream economists and some elements of the business press to have second thoughts about "free trade." Many are convinced that the painful transition costs that hit before outsourcing produces any ultimate benefits may be the biggest political issue in economics for a generation. And some recognize, as Smith did, that there is no guarantee unfettered international trade will leave the participants better off even in the long run.

KEYNES'S REVENGE

Writing during the Great Depression of the 1930s, John Maynard Keynes, the pre-eminent economist of the twentieth century, prescribed government spending as a means of compensating for the instability of private investment. The notion of a mixed private/government economy, Keynes's prosthesis for the invisible hand of the market, guided U.S. economic policy from the 1940s through the 1970s.

It is only fitting that Paul Samuelson, the first Nobel Laureate in economics, and whose textbook introduced U.S. readers to Keynes, would be among the first mainstream economist to question whether unfettered international trade, in the context of massive outsourcing, would necessarily leave a developed economy such as that of the United States better off—even in the long run. In an influential 2004 article, Samuelson characterized the common economics wisdom about outsourcing and international trade this way:

> Yes, good jobs may be lost here in the short run. But ...the gains of the winners from free trade, properly measured, work out to exceed the losses of the losers. ... Never forget to tally the real gains of consumers alongside admit-

ted possible losses of some producers. … The gains of the American winners are big enough to more than compensate the losers.

Samuelson took on this view, arguing that this common wisdom is "dead wrong about [the] *necessary* surplus of winning over losing" [emphasis in the original]. In a rather technical paper, he demonstrated that free trade globalization can sometimes give rise to a situation in which "a productivity gain in one country can benefit that country alone, while permanently hurting the other country by reducing the gains from trade that are possible between the two countries."

Many in the economics profession do admit that it is hard to gauge whether intensified offshoring of U.S. jobs in the context of free-trade globalization will give more in winnings to the winners than it takes in losses from the losers. "Nobody has a clue about what the numbers are," as Robert C. Feenstra, a prominent trade economist, told *Business Week* at the time.

The empirical issues that will determine whether offshore outsourcing ultimately delivers, on balance, more benefits than costs, and to whom those benefits and costs will accrue, are myriad. First, how wide a swath of white-collar workers will see their wages reduced by competition from the cheap, highly skilled workers who are now becoming available around the world? Second, by how much will their wages drop? Third, will the U.S. workers thrown into the global labor pool end up losing more in lower wages than they gain in lower consumer prices? In that case, the benefits of increased trade would go overwhelmingly to employers. But even employers might lose out depending on the answer to a fourth question: Will cheap labor from abroad allow foreign employers to out-compete U.S. employers, driving down the prices of their products and lowering U.S. export earnings? In that case, not only workers, but the corporations that employ them as well, could end up worse off.

BIGGER THAN A BOX

Another mainstream Keynesian economist, Alan Blinder, former Clinton economic advisor and vice-chair of the Federal Reserve Board, doubts that outsourcing will be "immiserating" in the long run and still calls himself "a free-trader down to his toes." But Blinder is convinced that the transition costs will be large, lengthy, and painful before the United States experiences a net gain from outsourcing. Here is why.

First, rapid improvements in information and communications technology have rendered obsolete the traditional notion that manufactured goods, which can generally be boxed and shipped, are tradable, while services, which cannot be boxed, are not. And the workers who perform the services that computers and satellites have now rendered tradable will increasingly be found offshore, especially when they are skilled and will work for lower wages.

Second, another 1.5 billion or so workers—many in China, India, and the former Soviet bloc—are now part of the world

---

OFFSHORED? OUTSOURCED? CONFUSED?

The terms "offshoring" and "outsourcing" are often used interchangeably, but they refer to distinct processes:

Outsourcing—When a company hires another company to carry out a business function that it no longer wants to carry on in-house. The company that is hired may be in the same city or across the globe; it may be a historically independent firm or a spinoff of the first company created specifically to outsource a particular function.

Offshoring or *Offshore Outsourcing*—When a company shifts a portion of its business operation abroad. An offshore operation may be carried out by the same company or, more typically, outsourced to a different one.

---

economy. While most are low-skilled workers, some are not; and as Blinder says, a small percentage of 1.5 billion is nonetheless "a lot of willing and able people available to do the jobs that technology will move offshore." And as China and India educate more workers, offshoring of high-skill work will accelerate.

Third, the transition will be particularly painful in the United States because the U.S. unemployment insurance program is stingy, at least by first-world standards, and because U.S. workers who lose their jobs often lose their health insurance and pension rights as well.

How large will the transition cost be? "Thirty million to 40 million U.S. jobs are potentially offshorable," according to Blinder's latest estimates. "These include scientists, mathematicians and editors on the high end and telephone operators, clerks and typists on the low end."

Blinder arrived at these figures by creating an index that identifies how easy or hard it will be for a job to be physically or electronically "offshored." He then used the index to assess the Bureau of Labor Statistics' 817 U.S. occupational categories. Not surprisingly, Blinder classifies almost all of the 14.3 million U.S. manufacturing jobs as offshorable. But he also classifies more than twice that many U.S. service sector jobs as offshorable, including most computer industry jobs as well as many others, for instance, the 12,470 U.S. economists and the 23,790 U.S. multimedia artists and animators.

In total, Blinder's analysis suggests that 22% to 29% of the jobs held by U.S. workers in 2004 will be potentially offshorable within a decade or two, with nearly 8.2 million jobs in 59 occupations "highly offshorable." Table 1 provides a list of the broad occupational categories with 300,000 or more workers that Blinder considers potentially offshorable.

Mankiw dismissed Blinder's estimates of the number of jobs at risk to offshoring as "out of the mainstream." Indeed, Blinder's estimates are considerably larger than earlier ones. But these earlier studies either aim to measure the number of U.S. jobs that will be outsourced (as opposed to the number at risk of being outsourced), look at a shorter period of time, or have shortcomings that suggest they underestimate the number of U.S. jobs threatened by outsourcing. (See "Studying the Studies," below.)

GLOBAL ARBITRAGE

Low wages are the reason U.S. corporations outsource labor. Table 2 shows just how large the international wage differentials were for computer programmers in 2002. Programmers in the United States make wages nearly *ten times* those of their counterparts in India and the Philippines, for example.

Today, more and more white-collar workers in the United States are finding themselves in direct competition with the low-cost, well-trained, highly educated workers in Bangalore, Shanghai, and Eastern and Central Europe. These workers often use the same capital and technology and are no less productive than the U.S. workers they replace. They just get paid less.

This global labor arbitrage, as Morgan Stanley's chief economist Stephen Roach calls it, has narrowed international wage disparities in manufacturing, and now in services too, by unrelentingly pushing U.S. wages down toward international norms. ("Arbitrage" refers to transactions that yield a profit by taking advantage of a price differential for the same asset in different locations. Here, of course, the "asset" is wage labor of a certain skill level.) A sign of that pressure: about 70% of laid-off workers in the United States earn less three years later than they did at the time of the layoff; on average, those reemployed earn 10% less than they did before.

And it's not only laid-off workers who are hurt. A study conducted by Harvard labor economists Lawrence F. Katz, Richard B. Freeman, and George J. Borjas finds that every other worker with skills similar to those who were displaced also loses out. Every 1% drop in employment due to imports or factories gone abroad shaves 0.5% off the wages of the remaining workers in that occupation, they conclude.

Global labor arbitrage also goes a long way toward explaining the poor quality and low pay of the jobs the U.S. economy has created this decade, according to Roach. By dampening wage increases for an ever wider swath of the U.S. workforce, he argues, outsourcing has helped to drive a wedge between productivity gains and wage gains and to widen inequality in the United States. In the first four years of this decade, nonfarm productivity in the United States has recorded a cumulative increase of 13.3%—more than double the 5.9% rise in real compensation per hour over the same period. ("Compensation" includes wages, which have been stagnant for the average worker, plus employer spending on fringe benefits such as health insurance, which has risen even as, in many instances, the actual benefits have been cut back.) Roach reports that the disconnect between pay and productivity growth during the current economic expansion has been much greater in services than in manufacturing, as that sector weathers the powerful forces of

TABLE 1: MAJOR OCCUPATIONS RANKED BY OFFSHORABILITY			
Occupation	Category	Index Number	Number of Workers
Computer programmers	I	100	389,090
Telemarketers	I	95	400,860
Computer systems analysts	I	93	492,120
Billing and posting clerks and machine operators	I	90	513,020
Bookkeeping, accounting, and auditing clerks	I	84	1,815,340
Computer support specialists	I and II	92/68	499,860
Computer software engineers: Applications	II	74	455,980
Computer software engineers: Systems software	II	74	320,720
Accountants	II	72	591,311
Welders, cutters, solderers, and brazers	II	70	358,050
Helpers—production workers	II	70	528,610
First-line supervisors/managers of production and operating workers	II	68	679,930
Packaging and filling machine operators and tenders	II	68	396,270
Team assemblers	II	65	1,242,370
Bill and account collectors	II	65	431,280
Machinists	II	61	368,380
Inspectors, testers, sorters, samplers, and weighers	II	60	506,160
General and operations managers	III	55	1,663,810
Stock clerks and order fillers	III	34	1,625,430
Shipping, receiving, and traffic clerks	III	29	759,910
Sales managers	III	26	317,970
Business operations specialists, all other	IV	25	916,290

Source: Alan S. Blinder, "How Many U.S. Jobs Might Be Offshorable?" CEPS Working Paper #142, March 2007, figures from Bureau of Labor Statistics and author's judgments.

global labor arbitrage for the first time.

DOUBTS IN THE BUSINESS PRESS?!

Even in the business press, doubts that offshore outsourcing willy-nilly leads to economic improvement have become more acute. Earlier this summer, a *Business Week* cover story, "The Real Cost of Offshoring," reported that government statistics have underestimated the damage to the U.S. economy from offshore outsourcing. The problem is that since offshoring took off, *import* growth, adjusted for inflation, has been faster than the official numbers show. That means improvements in living standards, as well as corporate profits, depend more on cheap imports, and less on improving domestic productivity, than analysts thought.

Growing angst about outsourcing's costs has also prompted the business press to report favorably on remedies for the dislocation brought on by offshoring that deviate substantially from the non-interventionist, free-market playbook. Even the most unfazed pro-globalization types want to beef up trade adjustment assistance for displaced workers and strengthen the U.S. educational system. But both proposals are inadequate.

More education, the usual U.S. prescription for any economic problem, is off the mark here. Cheaper labor is available abroad up and down the job-skill ladder, so even the most rigorous education is no inoculation against the threat of offshore outsourcing. As Blinder emphasizes, it is the need for face-to-face contact that stops jobs from being shipped overseas, not the level of education necessary to perform them. Twenty years from now, home health aide positions will no doubt be plentiful in the United States; jobs for highly trained IT professionals may be scarce.

Trade adjustment assistance has until now been narrowly targeted at workers hurt by imports. Most new proposals would replace traditional trade adjustment assistance and unemployment insurance with a program for displaced workers that offers wage insurance to ease the pain of taking a lower-paying job and provides for portable health insurance and retraining. The pro-globalization research group McKinsey Global Institute (MGI), for example, claims that for as little as 4% to 5% of the amount they've saved in lower wages, companies could cover the wage losses of all laid-off workers once they are reemployed, paying them 70% of the wage differential between their old and new jobs (in addition to health care subsidies) for up to two years.

While MGI confidently concludes that this proposal

ATTRIBUTES OF JOBS OUTSOURCED

- No Face-to-Face Customer Servicing Requirement
- High Information Content
- Work Process is Telecommutable and Internet Enabled
- High Wage Differential with Similar Occupation in Destination Country
- Low Setup Barriers
- Low Social Networking Requirement

The McKinsey Global Institute (MGI), a research group known for its unabashedly favorable view of globalization, has done its best to put a positive spin on offshore outsourcing. Its 2003 study, which relied on the Forrester offshoring estimates, concluded that offshoring is already benefiting the U.S. economy. For instance, MGI calculates that for every dollar spent on a business process outsourced to India, the U.S. economy gains at least $1.12. The largest chunk—58 cents—goes back to the original employer in the form of cost savings, almost exclusively in the form of lower wages. In addition, 30% of Indian offshoring is actually performed by U.S. companies, so the wage savings translate into higher earnings for those companies. The study also argues that offshore outsourcing frees up U.S. workers to do other tasks.

A second MGI study, in 2005, surveyed dozens of companies in eight sectors, from pharmaceutical companies to insurers. The study predicted that multinational companies in the entire developed world will have located only 4.1 million service jobs in low-wage countries by 2008—a figure equal to only 1% of the total number of service jobs in developed countries.

But the MGI outsourcing studies have serious limitations. For instance, Blinder points out that MGI's analysis looks at a very short time frame, and that the potential for outsourcing in English-speaking countries such as the United States is higher than elsewhere, a fact lost in the MGI studies' global averages.

In their 2005 book *Outsourcing America*, published by the American Management Association, public policy professors Ron Hira and Anil Hira argue that MGI's 2003 report "should be viewed as a self-interested lobbying document that presents an unrealistically optimistic estimate of the impact of offshore outsourcing." For instance, most of the data for the report came from case studies conducted by MGI that are unavailable to the public and unsupported by any model. Moreover, the MGI analysis assumes that the U.S. economy will follow its long-term trend and create 3.5 million jobs a year, enough to quickly reemploy U.S. workers displaced by offshoring. But current U.S. job creation falls far short of that trend. A recent White House fact sheet brags that the U.S. economy has created 8.3 million jobs since August 2003. Still, that is less than 2.1 million jobs a year, and only 1.8 million jobs over the last 12 months.

MGI's Farrell is right about one thing. "If the economy were stronger," she says, "there wouldn't be such a negative feeling" about work getting offshored. But merely assuming high job growth doesn't make it so.

STUDYING THE STUDIES

When economist Alan Blinder raised alarm bells in 2006 about the potentially large-scale offshoring of U.S. jobs, his results were inevitably compared to earlier research on offshore outsourcing. Three studies have been especially influential. The 2002 study (revised in 2004) by Forrester Research, a private, for-profit market research firm, which estimated that 3.3 million U.S. service sector jobs would move offshore by 2015, caused perhaps the biggest media stir. It was picked up by *Business Week* and the *Wall Street Journal*, and hyped by Lou Dobbs, the CNN business-news anchor and outspoken critic of offshoring.

Forrester researcher John McCarthy developed his estimate by poring over newspaper clippings and Labor Department statistics on 505 white-collar occupations and then making an educated guess about how many jobs would be shipped offshore by 2015.

The Forrester study projects actual offshoring, not the number of jobs at risk of offshoring, so its estimate is rightfully lower than Blinder's. But the ample possibilities for technological change between now and 2015 convince Blinder that the Forrester estimate is nonetheless too low.

A 2003 study by University of California economists Ashok Bardhan and Cynthia Kroll estimated that about 11% of all U.S. jobs in 2001 were vulnerable to offshoring. Bradhan and Kroll applied the "outsourceability attributes" listed in Figure 1 to occupations where at least some outsourcing either has already taken place or is being planned.

Blinder considers the Bardhan and Kroll estimate for 2001 to be comparable to his estimate that 20% to 30% of the employed labor force will be at risk of offshore outsourcing within the next ten to twenty years, especially considering that Bardhan and Kroll do not allow for outsourcing to spread beyond the occupations it is currently affecting. This is like "looking only slightly beyond the currently-visible tip of the iceberg," according to Blinder.

TABLE 2: AVERAGE SALARIES OF PROGRAMMERS

Country	Salary Range
Poland and Hungary	$4,800 to $8,000
India	$5,880 to $11,000
Philippines	$6,564
Malaysia	$7,200
Russian Federation	$5,000 to $7,500
China	$8,952
Canada	$28,174
Ireland	$23,000 to $34,000
Israel	$15,000 to $38,000
USA	$60,000 to $80,000

Source: CIO magazine, November 2002, from Merrill Lynch Smart Access Survey.

borders [for trade] requres making a radical change in fiscal policy." He proposes eliminating the Social Security-Medicare payroll tax on the bottom half of workers—roughly, those earning less than $33,000 a year—and making up the lost revenue by raising the payroll tax on higher earners.

The goal of these economists is to thwart a crippling political backlash against trade. As they see it, "using the tax code to slice the apple more evenly is far more palatable than trying to hold back globalization with policies that risk shrinking the economic apple."

Some even call for extending global labor arbitrage to CEOs. In a June 2006 *New York Times* op-ed, equity analyst Lawrence Orlowski and NYU assistant research director Florian Lengyel argued that offshoring the jobs of U.S. chief executives would reduce costs and release value to shareholders by bringing the compensation of U.S. CEOs (on average 170 times greater than the compensation of average U.S. workers in 2004) in line with CEO compensation in Britain (22 times greater) and in Japan (11 times greater).

Yet others focus on the stunning lack of labor mobility that distinguishes the current era of globalization from earlier ones. Labor markets are becoming increasingly free and flexible under globalization, but labor enjoys no similar freedom of movement. In a completely free market, the foreign workers would come here to do the work that is currently being outsourced. Why aren't more of those workers coming to the United States? Traditional economists Gary Becker and Richard Posner argue the answer is clear: an excessively restrictive immigration policy.

ONSHORE AND OFFSHORE SOLIDARITY

Offshoring is one of the last steps in capitalism's conversion

will "go a long way toward relieving the current anxieties," other globalization advocates are not so sure. They recognize that economic anxiety is pervasive and that millions of white-collar workers now fear losing their jobs. Moreover, even if fears of actual job loss are overblown, wage insurance schemes do little to compensate for the downward pressure offshoring is putting on the wages of workers who have not been laid off.

Other mainstream economists and business writers go even further, calling for not only wage insurance but also taxes on the winners from globalization. And globalization has produced big winners: on Wall Street, in the corporate boardroom, and among those workers in high demand in the global economy.

Economist Matthew Slaughter, who recently left President Bush's Council of Economic Advisers, told the *Wall Street Journal*, "Expanding the political support for open of the "physician, the lawyer, the priest, the poet, the man of science, into its paid wage laborers," as Marx and Engels put it in the *Communist Manifesto* 160 years ago. It has already done much to increase economic insecurity in the workaday world and has become, Blinder suggests, the number one economic issue of our generation.

Offshoring has also underlined the interdependence of workers across the globe. To the extent that corporations now organize their business operations on a global scale, shifting work around the world in search of low wages, labor organizing must also be global in scope if it is to have any hope of building workers' negotiating strength.

Yet today's global labor arbitrage pits workers from different countries against each other as competitors, not allies. Writing about how to improve labor standards, economists Ajit Singh and Ann Zammit of the South Centre, an Indian nongovernmental organization, ask the question, "On what could workers of the world unite" today? Their answer is that faster economic growth could indeed be a positive-sum game from which both the global North and the global South could gain. A pick-up in the long-term rate of growth of the world economy would generate higher employment, increasing wages and otherwise improving labor standards in both regions. It should also make offshoring less profitable and less painful.

The concerns of workers across the globe would also be served by curtailing the ability of multinational corporations to move their investment anywhere, which weakens the bargaining power of labor both in advanced countries and in the global South. Workers globally would also benefit if their own ability to move between countries was enhanced. The combination of a new set of rules to limit international capital movements and to expand labor mobility across borders, together with measures to ratchet up economic growth and thus increase worldwide demand for labor, would alter the current process of globalization and harness it to the needs of working people worldwide.

Resources: Alan S. Blinder, "Fear of Offshoring," CEPS Working Paper #119, Dec. 2005; Alan S. Blinder, "How Many U.S. Jobs Might Be Offshorable?" CEPS Working Paper #142, March 2007; N. Gregory Mankiw and P. Swagel, "The Politics and Economics of Offshore Outsourcing," Am. Enterprise Inst. Working Paper #122, 12/7/05; "Offshoring: Is It a Win-Win Game?" McKinsey Global Institute, August 2003; Diane Farrell et al., "The Emerging Global Labor Market, Part 1: The Demand for Talent in Services," McKinsey Global Institute, June 2005; Ashok Bardhan and Cynthia Kroll, "The New Wave of Outsourcing," Research Report #113, Fisher Center for Real Estate and Urban Economics, Univ. of Calif., Berkeley, Fall 2003; Paul A. Samuelson, "Where Ricardo and Mill Rebut and Confirm Arguments of Mainstream Economists Supporting Globalization," J Econ Perspectives 18:3, Summer 2004; Alan S. Blinder, "Free Trade's Great, but Offshoring Rattles Me," *Washington Post,* 5/6/07; Michael Mandel, "The Real Cost of Offshoring," *BusinessWeek,* 6/18/07; Aaron Bernstein, "Shaking Up Trade Theory," *BusinessWeek,* 12/6/04; David Wessel, "The Case for Taxing Globalization's Big Winners," *Wall Street Journal,* 6/14/07; Bob Davis, "Some Democratic Economists Echo Mankiw on Outsourcing," *WSJ;* N. Gregory Mankiw, "Outsourcing Redux," gregmankiw.blogspot.com/2006/05/outsourcing-redux; David Wessel and Bob Davis, "Pain From Free Trade Spurs Second Thoughts," *WSJ,* 3/30/07; Ajit Singh and Ann Zammit, "On What Could Workers of the World Unite? Economic Growth and a New Global Economic Order," from *The Global Labour Standards Controversy: Critical Issues For Developing Countries,* South Centre, 2000; Michael Meeropol, "Distorting Adam Smith on Trade," *Challenge,* July/Aug 2004.

BLACK WORKERS NEED MORE THAN AN ECONOMIC BOOM

BY WILLIAM M. RODGERS III

At the end of the 1990s economic boom, Hugh Price, the former president of the Urban League, reflected, "The truth is that for black Americans the 'glass'–their overall situation– is both half-empty and half-full." That glass is even less full today, as many of the gains African Americans made during the boom decade have melted away.

During the 1990s economic expansion, the longest on record, the U.S. unemployment rate fell from 6.8% in March 1991 to 4.3% in March 2001. Over those 10 years, the economy created almost 24 million jobs, an average of 200,000 jobs a month. That was enough to more than comfortably absorb the 150,000 new entrants into the labor force each month, pushing the jobless rate to 4.5% or below for 34 months.

Many hoped that the sustained economic boom would make a significant dent in the nation's persistent racial inequality. From the end of World War II to the 1990s, the unemployment rate for blacks had typically been twice that of whites, and black earnings had been 25% less than white earnings. The 1990s boom did substantially improve the absolute and relative economic positions of African Americans, although not as much as some had hoped. By the end of the boom, the ratio of black to white unemployment rates had fallen below the two-to-one ratio, and the black unemployment rate fell below 10% for a sustained period. The earnings of African Americans, particularly of young African Americans, increased. But during the short economic recession that began in March 2001, and the jobless recovery that has followed, much of the hard-fought progress made by blacks has eroded.

Below, we look at why the absolute and relative gains that African Americans made were less than hoped for during the 1990s boom and especially fragile in the period of economic decline that followed. Given that the economic boom of the 1990s by itself was not sufficient to put African Americans on an equal footing with white workers over the long term, we also look at the public policies that would be necessary to sustain the gains that blacks are likely to make during the next economic expansion.

A BOOM FOR SOME

African Americans, particularly those who are young and low skilled, typically make the greatest advances during boom years, when labor markets tighten. However, a closer look at the numbers calls into question whether the boom years were as good for African Americans as they should have been. In 2000, 63.6% of the 16-and-over African-American male civilian population were employed, up slightly from 63.4% in 1979. For young African Americans, the data provide an even bleaker picture. In 2000, only 52% of young African-American men with no more than a high school education were employed, compared to 62% in 1979. Studies have shown that the decline in the level of employment for inner-city black youth could not be explained by demographic shifts (like the growth of the suburbs) and labor market trends (such as the decline in manufacturing jobs) alone. A study by the Urban Institute suggests that the growing incarceration rate of young black men is undermining their labor market position. Young black men with histories of incarceration are more likely targets of workplace discrimination. Furthermore, more stringent enforcement of child support orders may have created the unintended side effect of reducing incentives for young African-American men to enter the formal economy.

A lesson of the boom is that sustained economic growth is one condition for lessening racial inequality, but is not by itself sufficient to erase it. Economic growth must be supplemented with public policies that attack the discrimination and structural impediments that make minorities second-class labor.

THEN COMES THE BUST

Many economists predicted that the boom would break down discrimination and other structural barriers to success. They hoped that young workers would gain enough experience to reduce the adverse effects of a future recession on their earnings and employment rates. The hope was that instead of taking two steps back during a recession, young African-American workers might only take one step back.

The first few months of the 2001 recession seemed to fulfill this hope. As the economic slowdown took hold, the employment-population ratio for whites fell by 0.7%, while the African-American ratio declined by only 0.3%. (The employment-population ratio measures the share of the civilian population that is employed. It has an advantage over the unemployment rate because it captures people who have given up their search for employment.) But the greater hit that white workers took was likely due to their overrepresentation in the manufacturing and information technology (IT) sectors where in the latter, jobs melted away with the dot-com bust. But as the downturn worsened, the African-American employment ratio began to fall faster. By the recession's end in November 2001, their employment-population ratio had fallen by almost 2%, compared to a 1.2% decline in the white ratio. This return to the "typical" pattern of recessions, where the least skilled are the first fired, continued during the jobless recovery. Today, the African-American unemployment rate has been above 10% for 23 of the past 24 months. The jobless rate of African-American teenagers, which reached a still-too-high historical low of 20% in April 2000 and averaged 29% during the recession, is 30.8% today, almost twice the white teenage unemployment rate.

Most discouragingly, education no longer provides African Americans a strong protection during periods of economic downturn and stagnation. In December 2000 the unemployment rates of white and African-American college graduates were virtually indistinguishable, both below 2.0%. A year later, when the recession officially ended, jobless rates for both groups had risen to 2.7%. By 2004, however, the white college-graduate unemployment rate had fallen to 2.0%, while the African-American rate jumped to 5.0%.

Why do minorities have such fragile and persistently low employment rates? Although racial differences in educational attainment have narrowed over the past few decades, the remaining differences in the years and quality of education remain major contributors to racial differences in labor market outcomes. In its 1999 report "Futurework: Trends and Challenges for the 21st Century," the U.S. Department of Labor identified several additional factors. Employer perceptions, racial discrimination, limited early work experience, spatial mismatch between where jobs are and where minority workers live, and involvement with crime all contribute to racial inequality in the labor market, according to the report. These are all factors that even the best economy in decades cannot undo.

LOOKING TO THE FUTURE

If even the best economy in 30 years did little to correct persistent racial unemployment and earnings gaps, and what gains did come were fragile, will strong economic growth in the future do any better? If we can't rely on future growth alone, how can we make any positive changes that do stick? Economists are deeply split on this issue. Some argue that improving the education system is key. Others would strengthen the government's ability to protect workers from discrimination, bad working conditions, and inappropriate workplace policies. Still others continue to believe that economic growth alone is the key to eliminating racial differences in the labor market. This debate should not be cast as a zero-sum game. None of these policies alone are likely to be effective.

A number of economists have analyzed data from the National Longitudinal Survey of Youth, which has been following a cohort of young men and women since 1979, and concluded that the wage gap between African Americans and whites is fully explained by racial differences in test scores. Wage differences are due solely to pre-market factors such as racial differences in school quality, and parent's education and occupation, these economists contend—not to discrimination and other problems in labor markets.

Continued discrimination in the labor market, however, is well documented, for example, by Phillip Moss and Chris Tilly's research on employer preferences. Research on housing and credit markets also finds evidence of discrimination—and if there is wide consensus on the presence of racial discrimination in these other markets, it is hard to believe that the labor market is immune.

SUMMING UP

To generate a boom that lessens racial inequality, government must adopt a range of policies that have disproportionately positive impacts on African Americans even if they are race-neutral. This includes not only improving education and training opportunities, but also implementing the appropriate monetary and fiscal policies. For example, the dollar value of the 2001 and 2003 tax cuts should have been tilted more toward lower and middle-income households. These are the families that ultimately bore the brunt of the recession and the weak recovery as well as of rising energy and health care costs. They are more likely to spend a tax cut than to save it, which would have provided the economy with more stimulus.

But even during a vigorous 1990s-style boom, there remains ample room for race-specific approaches to addressing inequality. Even in a robust economy, vigorous enforcement of affirmative action, anti-discrimination laws, and support of minority and women-owned business creation are necessary.

"We know," Hugh Price has noted, "that there are many ways government at the national, state, and local levels can assist individuals and the private sector in reducing the 'empty' portion of the 'glass' black America holds, and making it more and more full. That is the task ahead."

Resources: Harry J. Holzer and Paul Offner, *Left Behind in the Labor Market: Recent Employment Trends Among Young Black Men*, 2002; Phillip Moss and Chris Tilly, *Stories Employers Tell: Race, Skill, and Hiring in America*, 2000; William M. Rodgers III, "Male Sub-Metropolitan Black-White Wage Gaps: New Evidence for the 1980s," *Urban* Studies, 34, (8): 1201-1213, 1997; U.S. Department of Labor, "Futurework: Trends and Challenges for the 21st Century," 1999.

WHERE IS THE NORTH OF TODAY?

BY ATTIENO DAVIS

Ellen Williams was 16 years old when she left Butler County, Georgia, one of the innumerable backwoods Georgia counties with Jim Crow and "Negroes Need Not Apply," no indoor plumbing and one-room schoolhouses. When she arrived in Boston in 1946, she thought she'd died and gone to heaven. Though she'd left her family behind, her dream of accessing just a bit of the pie seemed realizable at last.

Momma never quite achieved her dream, but she did have a job for 41 years, a job that helped stabilize our lives. When she retired in the early 1990s, that job provided her a pension she lives on today, back in her beloved Georgia. My mother worked for Raytheon and was a member of the International Brotherhood of Electrical Workers. She never had a car until the early '70s, but she said she never thought of herself as poor because she had a good job, which gave her a sense of hope.

I understood as a girl that the job was the key to my family's security. Momma could pay our rent, buy groceries, pay the insurance man, and take my sister and me to the doctor. Raytheon was a cornerstone in my family's life.

Momma made sure that her family members in the South did okay, regularly sending money home to help out. Our three-bedroom apartment was a temporary home to at least three other extended family members who fled the economically depressed South in the 1960s. Two of them also managed to get jobs at Raytheon.

It was a struggle for women working in the plants. Promotions weren't as forthcoming, especially if you were Black. Momma said the combined issue of race and gender was a problem even in the union. But she was a card-carrying member of IBEW, and she supported the union for the job security it gave her. She said, "The union was my key. We had health care, vacation, pension, and the union protected my rights." With the union's support, she took community college courses and broke ground to become one of Raytheon's first women inspectors.

None of my daughters or nieces have worked in manufacturing jobs, and none of them have been union members. They've worked at hotels and in stores. One niece went to community college in a certified nursing assistant program, and got a job at a unionized hospital—but it was a temporary contract job for six months, not a permanent union job. Now she works in a nursing home.

Many younger members of my family have moved south again because that's where the jobs are. But companies have a "let me hold my nose, I think I smell a union" attitude. Some of these young people have gone to college and found better-paying jobs—but not everyone can go to college, and the jobs for those without college now have no benefits and no union. Unlike their parents, they can't have a car or purchase a home. No matter what they do, a stable life seems to always be just beyond.

Today as I watch young people of color enter the workforce, it's almost as if we've come full circle, back to that same place my mother started out. She left a state with no opportunity for her and moved to a state with abundant good jobs. The young Black adults coming up today all live in states with a shrinking base of options for those without college educations—but there is now nowhere to move to find abundant good jobs. Where's their boost up the ladder?

THE RELATIONSHIP OF UNEMPLOYMENT AND INFLATION

BY RAMAA VASUDEVAN

Dear Dr. Dollar:
Back in first-year economics we learned that there is a tradeoff between unemployment and inflation, so you can't really have both low inflation and low unemployment at the same time. Do economists still consider that to be true?
—*Edith Bross, Cambridge, Mass.*

The trade-off between inflation and unemployment was first reported by A. W. Phillips in 1958—and so has been christened the Phillips curve. The simple intuition behind this trade-off is that as unemployment falls, workers are empowered to push for higher wages. Firms try to pass these higher wage costs on to consumers, resulting in higher prices and an inflationary buildup in the economy. The trade-off suggested by the Phillips curve implies that policymakers can target low inflation rates or low unemployment, but not both. During the 1960s, monetarists emphasized price stability (low inflation), while Keynesians more often emphasized job creation.

The experience of so-called stagflation in the 1970s, with simultaneously high rates of both inflation and unemployment, began to discredit the idea of a stable trade-off between the two. In place of the Phillips curve, many economists began to posit a "natural rate of unemployment." If unemployment were to fall below this "natural" rate, however slightly, inflation would begin to accelerate. Under the "natural rate of unemployment" theory (also called the Non-Accelerating Inflation Rate of Unemployment, or NAIRU), instead of choosing between higher unemployment and higher inflation, policymakers were told to focus on ensuring that the economy remained at its "natural" rate: the challenge was to accurately estimate its level and to steer the economy toward growth rates that maintain price stability, no matter what the corresponding level of unemployment.

The NAIRU has been extremely difficult to pin down in practice. Not only are estimates of it notoriously imprecise, the rate itself evidently changes over time. In the United States, estimates of the NAIRU rose from about 4.4% in the 1960s, to 6.2% in the 1970s, and further to 7.2% in the 1980s. This trend reversed itself in the 1990s, as officially reported unemployment fell. In the latter half of the 1990s, U.S. inflation remained nearly dormant at around 3%, while unemployment fell to around 4.6%. In the later Clinton years many economists warned that if unemployment was

brought any lower, inflationary pressures might spin out of control. But growth in these years did not spill over into accelerating inflation. The United States, apparently, had achieved the Goldilocks state—everything just right!

What sustained this combination of low inflation and low unemployment? Explanations abound: a productivity boom, the high rates of incarceration of those who would otherwise fall within the ranks of the unemployed, the openness of the U.S. economy to world trade and competition, among others.

The full story, however, has to do with class conflict and the relatively weak position of workers in the 1990s. Both the breakdown of the Phillips curve in the 1970s and the recent "disappearance" of the natural rate of unemployment are in essence a reflection of institutional and political changes that affect the bargaining strength of working people—in other words, their ability to organize effective unions and establish a decent living wage.

Following the Reagan offensive against trade unions, workers' power fell dramatically. Consequently, unionization rates and the real value of the minimum wage each fell precipitously between the late 1970s and the 1990s. The period of stagflation, in contrast, had been one of labor militancy and rising wages. (Although "stagflation" has a negative ring, by many measures nonsupervisory workers—i.e., the vast majority of the U.S. labor force—fared better in the economy of the early- to mid-1970s than they do today, even after the long 1990s economic expansion.) Labor's weaker position in the 1990s meant that despite low unemployment, workers were not able to win higher wages that would have spurred inflation.

The long period of stable prices and low interest rates in the United States now seems to be coming to a close. The cost of the Iraq War and rising oil prices, among other factors, have fueled expectations of a resurgence of inflation. At the same time, the near jobless recovery from the last recession might suggest that the "natural rate" of unemployment is on the rise again—and that we are witnessing yet another twist in the strange history of the Phillips curve!

With inflation rising (albeit slowly, and still relatively mild at around 4.2%), some business sectors will no doubt begin clamoring for tighter monetary policies that sacrifice job-creation and wage growth by slowing the economy growth. But these fears of inflation are probably misplaced.

A moderate rate of inflation is conducive to the growth of real investment, and in the context of a decades-long squeeze on workers' wage share, there is room to expand employment without setting off a wage-price spiral. What workers need is not greater fiscal and monetary austerity, but rather a revival of a Keynesian program of "employment targeting" that would sustain full employment and empower workers to push for higher wages. It's not likely, however, that the owners of capital and their political allies would sit idly by were such a program to be enacted.

CHAPTER 7

PERSPECTIVES ON MACROECONOMIC POLICY

INTRODUCTION

A few years back, political economist Bob Sutcliffe developed a sure-fire economic indicator that he called the Marx/Keynes ratio—the ratio of references to Karl Marx to references to John Maynard Keynes in Paul Samuelson's *Economics*, the best-selling introductory economics textbook during the decades following World War II. In a recession or a period of sluggish economic growth, the Marx/Keynes ratio would climb, as social commentators and even economists fretted over the future of capitalism. In economic booms, however, Marx's predictions of the collapse of capitalism disappeared from the pages of Samuelson's textbook, while the paeans to Keynesian demand-management policies multiplied.

Today Sutcliffe's ratio wouldn't work very well. Marx has been pushed off the pages of most introductory macroeconomics textbooks altogether, and even Keynes has been given only a minor role. Mainstream textbooks now favor the "New Classical" economics, which depicts the private economy as inherently stable and self-regulating, and dismiss Keynesian demand-management policies as ineffectual or counterproductive. Our authors disagree. In this chapter, they reintroduce schools of thought that have been removed from economics textbooks in recent decades and critically assess New Classical economics.

John Miller and Gina Neff start with a down-to-earth account of New Classical "rational expectations" models, in which markets clear instantaneously and bungling government bureaucrats always make a mess of things. Drawing on the writings of Keynesian and New Keynesian economists, Miller and Neff argue that rational expectations models are contradicted by the historical record, which shows that bigger government has brought milder, not more severe, business cycle fluctuations (Article 7.1).

Robert Pollin (Article 7.2) attacks the underpinnings of the neoliberal policy prescription for the global economy. As he sees it, the unfettered globalization of free markets will be unable to resolve three basic problems: an ever-larger reserve army of the unemployed that reduces the bargaining power of workers in all countries (the Marx problem); the inherent instability and volatility of investment and financial markets (the Keynes problem); and the erosion of the protections of the welfare state (the Polanyi problem).

Ellen Frank explains the development of Keynesian economic institutions in the United States and their subsequent dismantling under the Clinton administration. She also introduces the radical insight of Keynes—"that real wealth lies in the people, resources, and productive apparatus of a society and that citizens can, through the collective power of government, harness those resources for internal development." (Article 7.3)

Alejandro Reuss provides a primer on Marxist economics. Marx rejected the idea of a self-equilibrating economy, and argued that capitalism was inherently dynamic and unstable. Reuss describes some of Marx's key ideas, including the nature of capitalist exploitation, and what Marx saw as two ingredients of an eventual crisis of capitalism: overproduction and the falling rate of profit (Article 7.4). Rick Wolff explains why Marxian class analysis remains relevant today (Article 7.6).

Randy Albelda offers a feminist analysis of poverty and gender. Feminist economists have illuminated the ways in which having and caring for children alters the economic status of women—including those who are not mothers but are still relegated to poorly-paid care-giving jobs. Feminist economists, argues Albelda, provide the best understanding of the obstacles low-income families face and the options that might improve their position in today's economy (Article 7.5).

KEY TO COLANDER
E = *Economics*   M = *Macroeconomics*

These articles fit with chapters E25-E26 and E22, or M9-M10 and M6.

Article 7.1 complements chapter E25 or M9, especially its presentation of the classical range of the aggregate supply/aggregate demand model.

Article 7.2 works well with any of these chapters.

Article 7.3 works with chapters E25-E26 or M9-M10, or the discussion of debt and deficits in E31 or M15.

Articles 7.4, 7.5, and 7.6 can be introduced with the Appendix to chapter E22 or M6, "Nonmainstream Approaches of Macroeconomics." They can also go with any discussion of the instabilities and inequalities of the modern macroeconomy.

Article 7.6 also fits well with any discussion of the philosophical foundations of capitalism in the early chapters, as well as with the Appendix to chapter E22 or M6.

DISCUSSION QUESTIONS

1. (Article 7.1) How do classical economists argue that macroeconomies are inherently stable, and that government intervention is ineffective or counterproductive? Are their arguments convincing?

2. (Article 7.1) Why are Keynesians convinced that markets don't clear instantaneously, and that government intervention can and must stabilize market economies? Evaluate the evidence for their position.

3. (Article 7.2) Summarize the Marx, Keynes, and Polanyi problems. Why does Pollin think that neoliberal globalization policies will be unable to resolve them?

4. (Article 7.3) What do the terms "fiscal policy," "automatic stabilizer," "cyclical deficit," and "federal deficit" mean? How do they relate to Keynesian policy-making?

5. (Article 7.3) How did the Democrats bring down Keynes?

6. (Article 7.3) What would a macroeconomic policy that captured Keynes's radical insights look like?

7. (Article 7.4) In Marxist theory, how is a dynamic capitalist economy felled by instability? What roles do a "falling rate of profit," a "reserve army of the unemployed," and "overproduction" play in Marx's theory of how capitalism will fall into a crisis? Do you think today's macroeconomy displays any of those tendencies?

8. (Article 7.5) How does feminist economics' focus on gender challenge other theories of poverty? How are feminist theories of poverty different from Keynesian, Marxist, Institutionalist, and neoclassical analyses?

9. (Article 7.6) How does Wolff's class analysis of today's economy differ from the one presented in your textbook?

ARTICLE 7.1

May/June 1996, revised April 2002

THE REVENGE OF THE CLASSICS

BY JOHN MILLER AND GINA NEFF

Nineteen ninety-five was not a good year for the welfare state. A Gingrich-led Congress attempted to pull the plug on universal entitlements for the poor, from welfare to Medicaid. And the Royal Swedish Academy of Science awarded the Nobel Prize in economics to Robert Lucas, a 58-year-old University of Chicago economist, for his "insights into the difficulties of using economic policy to control the economy."

Using sophisticated mathematics and economic models, Lucas has persuaded much of the economics profession that the economic policies John Maynard Keynes developed to combat the Great Depression—the economic underpinnings of the welfare state and the mixed economy—are ineffective.

What would Lucas do instead? Forsake those policies, dismantle the welfare state, and embrace the market. That was a job that, back in the mid-1990s, Gingrich and his crowd seemed only too happy to take up. They were glad to join forces with a Federal Reserve Board (the "Fed") already under the influence of the conservative counterrevolution in macroeconomics, led initially by Milton Friedman, another University of Chicago monetary theorist, and then by Lucas.

The Fed has accepted the futility of using monetary policy to promote long-run employment, leaving inflation alone as the ultimate target of its policies. In addition, the Fed's practice of making early announcements of changes in monetary policy, which is probably a good thing, can be directly attributed to Lucas. He has argued that unannounced changes provoke instability in the private sector instead of muting it.

Lucas and his school of followers call themselves New Classical economists. Like the classical economists who predated Keynes, these modern conservatives believe the economy possesses powerful self-correcting forces that guarantee full employment. Their vision of a stable market economy rests on three building blocks: rational expectations, market clearing, and imperfect information.

Let's look first at rational expectations, a notion which does seem rational enough. After all, every one of our economic actions is directed toward the future. Using whatever economic information we can get our hands on about prices, growth, and other economic activity, we predict our economic future. And usually we are good at it. When fellow workers are getting laid off at the company we are employed in, for instance, chances are that buying an expensive house is not at the top of our to-do list.

When we do get things wrong, we reevaluate our predictions. And, says Lucas, we keep up this process of prediction and evaluation until there is no way to improve those predictions, ensuring that we won't consistently make the same forecasting mistakes. In that way we form what Lucas calls "rational expectations." As he sees it, people act much like experienced bettors at the track. They get good at picking horses, but are never able to pick the winning horse every time.

Lucas has made a career out of expressing these ideas in mathematical terms. He argues that predictions about the rates of interest, unemployment, and inflation shape how consumers, workers, and business people decide their economic future. From consumers buying a new home to workers looking for a new job to bosses hiring or laying off employees, rational expectations theory seeks to describe what motivates economic actors.

ADAM SMITH RETURNS

But Lucas does not stop there—with merely a theory of how people make economic decisions. New Classical economic theory also assumes that markets "clear" instantaneously. In the bat of an eye, prices adjust so that how much sellers bring to market just matches whatever buyers take away. For instance, in a labor market, wages (the price of labor) fall quickly enough to guarantee that every worker willing to work (or sell their labor) at the going wage finds a job with an employer (or buyer of labor). For New Classical economists that constitutes full employment. Only workers unwilling to work at the market clearing wage are out of a job. Those workers are voluntarily unemployed—they chose not to work and brought unemployment upon themselves.

WHILE KEYNESIANS MAY ACCEPT THE IDEA OF RATIONALLY FORMED EXPECTATIONS, THEY FIND THE IDEAS OF FLEXIBLE PRICES AND CLEARING MARKETS PREPOSTEROUS.

The point here is simple: Market capitalism is stable. "Price flexibility" and "market clearing" guarantee a booming full-employment economy—one that does not need economic policymaking to stabilize it. In fact, in Lucas's framework, government attempts to fine tune the economy actually backfire.

Here's why. If people expect the government to change economic policy, they too change their economic actions. That is rational expectations at work. And when prices and wages adjust instantaneously as people scramble to match their economic actions to their new expectations, those adjustments nullify the government's actions.

For instance, suppose the Fed tries to reduce unemployment by increasing the money supply, in the hope of raising spending and putting people to work. Lucas's rational workers anticipate that more spending and hiring will bring not only higher wages but also instantaneously higher prices, leaving their purchasing power unchanged. In this world people are not forced to work to avoid starving, but rather choose to offer their services only when their inflation-adjusted wages are sufficiently high. So no rational worker is lured into the market. The Fed's actions fail to lower unemployment, and succeed only in driving up prices.

As far-fetched as this theory might seem, the stagflation (simultaneous stagnation and inflation) of the 1970s lent these ideas plausibility. New Classical economics gathered adherents as Keynesian policies seemed increasingly ineffectual.

In New Classical economics, meddlesome government is not only ineffective, it is the enemy. Why does Lucas's inherently stable capitalism suffer through the ups and downs of the business cycle? His answer: Washington types trying to fine tune the economy. This is where imperfect information, the third building block of Lucas' theory, enters the model. Even Lucas's rational actors in this market-clearing world possess only limited information and can be fooled by bungling bureaucrats and re-election minded politicians who launch surprise (unannounced) changes in government policy.

People know the economy around them—their own wages or profits, the prices of the products they sell and those that they buy—better than what is going on across the economy. So if the Federal Reserve, without announcing it, increases the money supply in order to beef up spending and lower unemployment, even people with rational expectations can be confounded. They see their prices or wages go up, but don't anticipate prices going up elsewhere in the economy.

And that causes a problem. Corporate managers, for instance, hike up production, thinking that a higher price must signal a soaring demand for their products. Output rises across the economy. But soon inventories pile up, because the price increases were due to general inflation rather than greater demand. Corporate managers realize that the higher production levels were unwarranted, and they order a cutback—below even the initial output. The economy contracts, causing a recession.

What can return stability to the economy? Forsaking government intervention into the economy. In Lucas's world, unannounced changes in government policy cause the ups and downs of the business cycle. And announced changes in government policies are fully anticipated and therefore ineffective. For Lucas, the only rational course of action is to turn our backs on active government attempts to soften the blows of the market economy.

KEYNESIAN CRITICS

Not all economists are convinced by Lucas's arguments or support the draconian policy implications of New Classical economics. The proponents of Keynesian economic policy have been among the most vocal critics. While Keynesians may accept the idea of rationally formed expectations, they find the ideas of flexible prices and clearing markets preposterous. One Nobel laureate, James Tobin, called these ideas a "great myth"—powerful in its effect on how we see the economy, but nonetheless a myth.

Another Keynesian Nobel winner, Franco Modigliani, railed that it is as if "what happened in the United States in the 1930s was a severe attack of contagious laziness." For these dyed-in-the-wool Keynesians, the private economy will not necessarily be driven toward full employment even in the long run and Keynes's fundamental message still holds: "a modern monetized economy needs to be stabilized, can be stabilized, and should be stabilized" by government intervention.

More recently, "New Keynesian" economists have fashioned a different critique of New Classical economics. These modern Keynesians accept not only the idea that people form rational expectations about what will happen in the economy, but also the idea that in the long run the private economy tends toward full employment. Still, they argue that for good economic reasons, wages and prices are "sticky" and much slower to adjust than Lucas suggests. For instance, given the high cost of negotiating a wage settlement, most labor contracts are long term. In the United States, nearly 80% of union contracts are for three years and only about two-fifths of them contain cost-of-living adjustments. Corporations also often rely on long-term pricing agreements to afford them the price stability necessary to bid on contracts.

Thus, while the economy might eventually reach the full employment outcome Lucas's model predicts, the wait is likely to be intolerably long. What's needed is active government intervention designed for the workable policy time frame of three to five years, for as Keynes once wrote, "in the long run we are all dead."

More fundamentally, Lucas's way of thinking exaggerates the amount of power people really have over their economic lives. Economist E. Ray Canterbery writes mockingly that in the New Classical school, "The marginal blue collar worker on his way to the factory anticipates an increase in the money supply then fully anticipates the inflation within his monetarist model ... and a fall in the real interest rates and a fall in real wages. The worker does a U-turn, drives home,

and voluntarily disemploys himself." In New Classical economics bosses raise their workers' wages when the economy is doing well rather than pocketing the extra profits. And workers have the power to choose whether or not to work, to ask for higher wages when they expect inflation to go up, or to move into a different industry when they fear the worst for their own job. This is indeed a great myth.

Perhaps the most mythical aspect of New Classical economics is its claim that capitalism is stable—that if only policy makers would cease their interventions, economic stability would be assured and full employment guaranteed. But the instability of capitalism has been with us since long before Keynesian economic policy, which after all was a response to the Great Depression of the 1930s.

And that instability will worsen if New Classical economics is able to undo what Keynesian policy makers have done to mitigate the instability of capitalism since World War II. Current economic anxiety will heighten as workers struggle with real-life adjustments like stagnant wages and rising layoffs. At the same time, Lucas and his New Classical followers will continue to construct mathematical paeans to the rationality of these adjustments and the inherent stability of capitalism, even if that stability is evident only in their seminar rooms and the the Royal Swedish Academy of Science.

Resources: Robert J. Gordon, *Macroeconomics*, 6th ed., 1994; Robert Lucas, *Studies in Business Cycle Theory*, 1989; N. Gregory Mankiw, "A Quick Refresher Course in Macroeconomics," *Journal of Economic Literature*, December 1990; James Tobin, *Asset Accumulation and Economic Activity*, 1980; *The End of Economic Man*, reviewed by E. Ray Canterbery in *Challenge*, Nov./Dec. 1995.

WHAT'S WRONG WITH NEOLIBERALISM?

THE MARX, KEYNES, AND POLANYI PROBLEMS

BY ROBERT POLLIN

During the years of the Clinton administration, the term "Washington Consensus" began circulating to designate the common policy positions of the U.S. administration along with the International Monetary Fund (IMF) and World Bank. These positions, implemented in the United States and abroad, included free trade, a smaller government share of the economy, and the deregulation of financial markets. This policy approach has also become widely known as *neoliberalism*, a term which draws upon the classical meaning of the word *liberalism*.

Classical liberalism is the political philosophy that embraces the virtues of free-market capitalism and the corresponding minimal role for government interventions, especially as regards measures to promote economic equality within capitalist societies. Thus, a classical liberal would favor minimal levels of government spending and taxation, and minimal levels of government regulation over the economy, including financial and labor markets. According to the classical liberal view, businesses should be free to operate as they wish, and to succeed or fail as such in a competitive marketplace. Meanwhile, consumers rather than government should be responsible for deciding which businesses produce goods and services that are of sufficient quality as well as reasonably priced. Businesses that provide overexpensive or low-quality products will then be out-competed in the marketplace regardless of the regulatory standards established by governments. Similarly, if businesses offer workers a wage below what the worker is worth, then a competitor firm will offer this worker a higher wage. The firm unwilling to offer fair wages would not survive over time in the competitive marketplace.

This same reasoning also carries over to the international level. Classical liberals favor free trade between countries rather than countries operating with tariffs or other barriers to the free flow of goods and services between countries. They argue that restrictions on the free movement of products and money between countries only protects uncompetitive firms from market competition, and thus holds back the economic development of countries that choose to erect such barriers.

Neoliberalism and the Washington Consensus are contemporary variants of this longstanding political and economic philosophy. The major difference between classical liberalism as a philosophy and contemporary neoliberalism as a set of policy measures is with implementation. Washington Consensus policy makers are committed to free-market policies when they support the interests of big business, as, for example, with lowering regulations at the workplace. But these same policy makers become far less insistent on free-market principles when invoking such principles might damage big business interests. Federal Reserve and IMF interventions to bail out wealthy asset holders during the frequent global financial crises in the 1990s are obvious violations of free-market precepts.

Broadly speaking, the effects of neoliberalism in the less developed countries over the 1990s reflected the experience of the Clinton years in the United States. A high proportion of less developed countries were successful, just in the manner of the United States under Clinton, in reducing inflation and government budget deficits, and creating a more welcoming climate for foreign trade, multinational corporations, and financial market investors. At the same time, most of Latin America, Africa, and Asia—with China being the one major exception—experienced deepening problems of poverty and inequality in the 1990s, along with slower growth and frequent financial market crises, which in turn produced still more poverty and inequality.

If free-market capitalism is a powerful mechanism for creating wealth, why does a neoliberal policy approach, whether pursued by Clinton, Bush, or the IMF, produce severe difficulties in terms of inequality and financial instability, which in turn diminish the market mechanism's ability to even promote economic growth? It will be helpful to consider this in terms of three fundamental problems that result from a free-market system, which I term "the Marx Problem," "the Keynes problem," and "the Polanyi problem." Let us take these up in turn.

THE MARX PROBLEM

Does someone in your family have a job and, if so, how much does it pay? For the majority of the world's population, how one answers these two questions determines, more than anything else, what one's standard of living will be. But how is it decided whether a person has a job and what their pay will be? Getting down to the most immediate level of decision-making, this occurs through various types of bargaining in labor markets between workers and employers. Karl Marx argued that, in a free-market economy generally, workers have less power than employers in this bargaining process because workers cannot fall back on other means of staying alive if they fail to get hired into a job. Capitalists gain higher profits through having this relatively stronger bargaining position. But Marx also stressed that workers' bargaining power diminishes further when unemployment and underemployment are high, since that means that employed workers can be more readily replaced by what Marx called "the reserve army" of the unemployed outside the office, mine, or factory gates.

Neoliberalism has brought increasing integration of the world's labor markets through reducing barriers to international trade and investment by multinationals. For workers in high-wage countries such as the United States, this effectively means that the reserve army of workers willing to accept jobs at lower pay than U.S. workers expands to include workers in less developed countries. It isn't the case that businesses will always move to less developed countries or that domestically produced goods will necessarily be supplanted by imports from low-wage countries. The point is that U.S. workers face an increased *credible* threat that they can be supplanted. If everything else were to remain the same in the U.S. labor market, this would then mean that global integration would erode the bargaining power of U.S. workers and thus tend to bring lower wages.

But even if this is true for workers in the United States and other rich countries, shouldn't it also mean that workers in poor countries have greater job opportunities and better bargaining positions? In fact, there are areas where workers in poor countries are gaining enhanced job opportunities through international trade and multinational investments. But these gains are generally quite limited. This is because a long-term transition out of agriculture in poor countries continues to expand the reserve army of unemployed and underemployed workers in these countries as well. Moreover, when neoliberal governments in poor countries reduce their support for agriculture—through cuts in both tariffs on imported food products and subsidies for domestic farmers—this makes it more difficult for poor farmers to compete with multinational agribusiness firms. This is especially so when the rich countries maintain or increase their own agricultural supports, as has been done in the United States under Bush. In addition, much of the growth in the recently developed export-oriented manufacturing sectors of poor countries has failed to significantly increase jobs even in this sector. This is because the new export-oriented production sites frequently do not represent net additions to the country's total supply of manufacturing firms. They rather replace older firms that were focused on supplying goods to domestic markets. The net result is that the number of people looking for jobs in the developing countries grows faster than the employers seeking new workers. Here again, workers' bargaining power diminishes.

This does not mean that global integration of labor markets must necessarily bring weakened bargaining power

and lower wages for workers. But it does mean that unless some non-market forces in the economy, such as government regulations or effective labor unions, are able to counteract these market processes, workers will indeed continue to experience weakened bargaining strength and eroding living standards.

THE KEYNES PROBLEM

In a free-market economy, investment spending by businesses is the main driving force that produces economic growth, innovation, and jobs. But as John Maynard Keynes stressed, private investment decisions are also unavoidably risky ventures. Businesses have to put up money without knowing whether they will produce any profits in the future. As such, investment spending by business is likely to fluctuate far more than, say, decisions by households as to how much they will spend per week on groceries.

But investment fluctuations will also affect overall spending in the economy, including that of households. When investment spending declines, this means that businesses will hire fewer workers. Unemployment rises as a result, and this in turn will lead to cuts in household spending. Declines in business investment spending can therefore set off a vicious cycle: the investment decline leads to employment declines, then to cuts in household spending and corresponding increases in household financial problems, which then brings still more cuts in business investment and financial difficulties for the business sector. This is how capitalist economies produce mass unemployment, financial crises, and recessions.

Keynes also described a second major source of instability associated with private investment activity. Precisely because private investments are highly risky propositions, financial markets have evolved to make this risk more manageable for any given investor. Through financial markets, investors can sell off their investments if they need or want to, converting their office buildings, factories, and stock of machinery into cash much more readily than they could if they always had to find buyers on their own. But Keynes warned that when financial markets convert long-term assets into short-term commitments for investors, this also fosters a speculative mentality in the markets. What becomes central for investors is not whether a company's products will produce profits over a long term, but rather whether the short-term financial market investors *think* a company's fortunes will be strong enough in the present and immediate future to drive the stock price up. Or, to be more precise, what really matters for a speculative investor is not what they think about a given company's prospects per se, but rather what they think *other investors are thinking*, since that will be what determines where the stock price goes in the short term.

Because of this, the financial markets are highly susceptible to rumors, fads, and all sorts of deceptive accounting practices, since all of these can help drive the stock price up in the present, regardless of what they accomplish in the longer term. Thus, if U.S. stock traders are convinced that Alan Greenspan is a *maestro*, and if there is news that he is about to intervene with some kind of policy shift, then the rumor of Greenspan's policy shift can itself drive prices up, as the more nimble speculators try to keep one step ahead of the herd of Greenspan-philes.

Still, as with the Marx problem, it does not follow that the inherent instability of private investment and speculation in financial markets are uncontrollable, leading inevitably to persistent problems of mass unemployment and recession. But these social pathologies will become increasingly common through a neoliberal policy approach committed to minimizing government interventions to stabilize investment.

THE POLANYI PROBLEM

Karl Polanyi wrote his classic book *The Great Transformation* in the context of the 1930s depression, World War II, and the developing worldwide competition with Communist governments. He was also reflecting on the 1920s, dominated, as with our current epoch, by a free-market ethos. Polanyi wrote of the 1920s that "economic liberalism made a supreme bid to restore the self-regulation of the system by eliminating all interventionist policies which interfered with the freedom of markets."

Considering all of these experiences, Polanyi argued that for market economies to function with some modicum of fairness, they must be embedded in social norms and institutions that effectively promote broadly accepted notions of the common good. Otherwise, acquisitiveness and competition—the two driving forces of market economies—achieve overwhelming dominance as cultural forces, rendering life under capitalism a Hobbesian "war of all against all." This same idea is also central for Adam Smith. Smith showed how the invisible hand of self-interest and competition will yield higher levels of individual effort that increases the wealth of nations, but that it will also produce the corruption of our moral sentiments unless the market is itself governed at a fundamental level by norms of solidarity.

In the post-World War II period, various social democratic movements within the advanced capitalist economies adapted the Polanyi perspective. They argued in favor of government interventions to achieve three basic ends: stabilizing overall demand in the economy at a level that will provide for full employment; creating a financial market environment that is stable and conducive to the effective allocation of investment funds; and distributing equitably the rewards from high employment and a stable investment process. There were two basic means of achieving equitable distribution: relatively rapid wage growth, promoted by labor laws that were supportive of unions, minimum wage standards, and similar interventions in labor markets; and welfare state policies, including progressive taxation and redistributive programs such as Social Security. The political ascendancy of these ideas was the basis for a dramatic increase in the role of government in the post-World War II capitalist economies.

As one indicator of this, total government expenditures in the United States rose from 8% of GDP in 1913, to 21% in 1950, then to 38% by 1992. The International Monetary Fund and World Bank were also formed in the mid-1940s to advance such policy ideas throughout the world—that is, to implement policies virtually the opposite of those they presently favor. John Maynard Keynes himself was a leading intellectual force contributing to the initial design of the International Monetary Fund and World Bank.

FROM SOCIAL DEMOCRACY TO NEOLIBERALISM

But the implementation of a social democratic capitalism, guided by a commitment to full employment and the welfare state, did also face serious and persistent difficulties, and we need to recognize them as part of a consideration of the Marx, Keynes, and Polanyi problems. In particular, many sectors of business opposed efforts to sustain full employment because, following the logic of the Marx problem, full employment provides greater bargaining power for workers in labor markets, even if it also increases the economy's total production of goods and services. Greater worker bargaining power can also create inflationary pressures because businesses will try to absorb their higher wage costs by raising prices. In addition, market-inhibiting financial regulations limit the capacity of financial market players to diversify their risk and speculate.

Corporations in the United States and Western Europe were experiencing some combination of these problems associated with social democratic capitalism. In particular, they were faced with rising labor costs associated with low unemployment rates, which then led to either inflation, when corporations had the ability to pass on their higher labor costs to consumers, or to a squeeze on profits, when competitive pressures prevented corporations from raising their prices in response to the rising labor costs. These pressures were compounded by the two oil price "shocks" initiated by the Oil Producing Exporting Countries (OPEC)—an initial fourfold increase in the world price of oil in 1973, then a second four-fold price spike in 1979.

These were the conditions that by the end of the 1970s led to the decline of social democratic approaches to policy-making and the ascendancy of neoliberalism. The two leading signposts of this historic transition were the election in 1979 of Margaret Thatcher as Prime Minister of the United Kingdom and in 1980 of Ronald Reagan as the President of the United States. Indeed, it was at this point that Mrs. Thatcher made her famous pronouncement that "there is no alternative" to neoliberalism.

This brings us to the contemporary era of smaller government, fiscal stringency and deregulation, i.e., to neoliberalism under Clinton, Bush, and throughout the less-developed world. The issue is not a simple juxtaposition between either regulating or deregulating markets. Rather it is that markets have become deregulated to support the interests of business and financial markets, even as these same groups still benefit greatly from many forms of government support, including investment subsidies, tax concessions, and rescue operations when financial crises get out of hand. At the same time, the deregulation of markets that favors business and finance is correspondingly the most powerful regulatory mechanism limiting the demands of workers, in that deregulation has been congruent with the worldwide expansion of the reserve army of labor and the declining capacity of national governments to implement full-employment and macroeconomic policies. In other words, deregulation has exacerbated both the Marx and Keynes problems.

Given the ways in which neoliberalism worsens the Marx, Keynes, and Polanyi problems, we should not be surprised by the wreckage that it has wrought since the late 1970s, when it became the ascendant policy model. Over the past generation, with neoliberals in the saddle almost everywhere in the world, the results have been straightforward: worsening inequality and poverty, along with slower economic growth and far more unstable financial markets. While Margaret Thatcher famously declared that "there is no alternative" to neoliberalism, there are in fact alternatives. The experience over the past generation demonstrates how important it is to develop them in the most workable and coherent ways possible.

ARTICLE 7.3

February 2000, revised May 2001

LIFE AFTER KEYNES

BY ELLEN FRANK

Current conventional wisdom has it that business cycles are obsolete; promarket policies have swept recessions into history's proverbial dustbin. The generation of policymakers nurtured on notions of government economic management after World War II is retiring or dying off, replaced by "new economy" enthusiasts like Bill Clinton, who famously declared in 1996 that "the age of big government is over."

But what happens if the economy slips?

The old-fashioned big-government programs that pulled the United States through many an economic downturn have, in the last decade, been mostly dismantled. Many presume that the government will pick its recession-fighting tactics up again, should the economy falter—priming the economic pump by cutting taxes and raising spending, as Reagan did in the 1980s and Bush in the 1991 recession. Indeed, Treasury Secretary Larry Summers defended the Clinton administration's plan to pay off the federal debt by contending that Clinton was merely "reloading the fiscal cannon": saving against the bad times when heavy federal spending and borrowing might really be needed.

But the tools of macroeconomic management are not so easily discarded and taken up again; not, at least, in the U.S. political environment. From the 1930s, efforts to push through programs to ameliorate recessions and relieve unemployment in this country have been fraught with controversy and fiercely contested.

During the 1930s President Franklin Roosevelt's "New Deal" attempted to implement the "Keynesian Revolution"—the programs proposed by British economist John Maynard Keynes to end depressions, such as public works programs financed through deficit spending. Roosevelt, to

be sure, pressed throughout the 1930s to expand federal jobs programs, but did not actually succeed until the Second World War. After the war, it took years of careful and deliberate effort to craft the political and intellectual infrastructure for continued Keynesian policy in the United States. That infrastructure is now largely gone. Putting it back together again will not be easy.

THE KEYNESIAN CONSENSUS

When Richard Nixon declared in 1972 that "we are all Keynesians now," it seemed that the consensus for active, government management of the economy in the manner of Keynes was unshakable. Just a few years after Nixon's speech, Congress passed the Humphrey-Hawkins Act which committed the federal government to use its virtually unlimited taxing and spending powers to avert economic downturns and promote full employment.

In fact, though, the Keynesian consensus was already shattering. In 1967, the influential American Economic Association elected arch-conservative and Keynesian nemesis Milton Friedman as its president. In 1969, the prestigious *American Economic Review* published a paper by Robert Lucas outlining the new theory of rational expectations which purported to "prove" that government macroeconomic policy was useless.

Keynes had taught that the cycle of economic boom and bust could be eliminated with judicious government spending to create demand for goods and workers. By running deficits, governments could fuel economic growth, borrowing idle funds (or printing new money) to pay the employees that private businesses put to work. Known as fiscal stabilization policy or expansionary macroeconomic policy, these tools proved highly effective in combating business cycles. Even those initially hostile to Keynesian ideas in the 1930s could not deny the evidence of World War II when, thanks to massive government spending, the U.S. economy went from deep depression to rapid boom virtually overnight.

But support forged during the war for federal involvement in taming the business cycle and creating full employment proved hard to sustain once the war ended. The American version of Keynesianism, though tepid and watered-down compared to European programs or to Keynes' own proposals, was sufficiently left-wing to galvanize unending hostility in the deeply conservative pro-business arena of U.S. politics. Continued government spending after the war faced determined opposition from businesses who decried swollen government budgets as "creeping socialism" and complained that government programs amounted to "unfair competition" with the private sector. In 1954, one radical economist pronounced Keynesianism in the United States "deader than the dodo."

> THE CENTRAL INSIGHT OF KEYNESIAN THOUGHT WAS THAT REAL WEALTH LIES IN THE PEOPLE, RESOURCES, AND PRODUCTIVE APPARATUS OF A SOCIETY.

To be sure, business leaders supported the federal highway program, cold war military build-up of weapons, and the Korean and Vietnam wars. But they did not support the deficit financing of these ventures, nor did they back using federal programs as tools of macroeconomic management. By the early 1960s, even moderate gestures toward fiscal stabilization had become a hard sell in Congress. Keynesian economists worried openly about "implementation lags"—the yawning gap between the onset of a recession and the time it might take Congress to do something.

FULL-EMPLOYMENT BUDGETING

Throughout the 1960s and 1970s, coalitions of liberals and moderates tried to stem the backlash, quietly constructing a macroeconomic policy infrastructure that would weave some basic fiscal stabilization into the fabric of federal law. Under the Johnson and Nixon administrations, federal entitlement programs—Social Security, Medicaid, Medicare, Food Stamps, and the plethora of welfare programs—were enacted or vastly expanded. Economists called these automatic stabilizers, because, as enacted, eligible applicants could not be denied benefits for lack of funding. Thus government's mandated spending levels would rise and fall predictably with the unemployment rate. Entitlements legally committed the government to increase spending during economic downturns, regardless of, or despite, sentiment in Congress for Keynesian fiscal policies. Thus the government would automatically send money into the economy via these social programs during downturns.

These programs were neither massive nor generous—especially compared with their European counterparts—but taken together they provided a bedrock level of federal spending in lean years as well as a minimal guaranteed income to prevent wages from plummeting in a recession.

With the sole exception of Reagan's tax cut and military build-up in the early 1980s, automatic increases in entitlement spending have been the only significant source of fiscal stimulus in the United States since 1973. During the recession of 1991, for example, virtually all of the $47 billion increase in the federal deficit came about because of increased welfare and Social Security spending.

Furthermore, Keynesian-trained economists insisted that the budget deficits that resulted when recessions suddenly swelled welfare and Social Security rolls should not really count as deficits at all. In annual economic reports, the president's economic advisors carefully distinguished between a structural deficit—in which the government's budget was out of balance even with a booming economy—and a cyclical deficit—where the deficit soared unavoidably due to rising entitlements and falling tax collections. Full-employment budgeting—the position that balancing the federal budget should take a back seat to expanded financing of entitlements during a recession—sustained Keynesian fiscal policy even during the Reagan-Bush years.

THE END OF MACROECONOMIC POLICY

Though Reagan is credited with killing Keynesian economics, neither the Bush nor Reagan administrations were able to dismantle the policy apparatus inherited from the 1970s. Despite substantial cuts in the average benefit for many welfare programs, for example, total spending on entitlement programs rose throughout the 1980s, contributing (along with tax cuts and a military build-up) to the largest peacetime deficits ever run by the U.S. government. AFDC, Food Stamps, WIC and other programs, though perhaps stingier than before, enlarged their spending with each downward shift in the economy during the 1980s. Deficits ballooned and a Democratic House resisted major changes in entitlements.

Reagan's budget director, David Stockman, contended in 1984 that Reagan's huge deficits were a deliberate strategy to discredit Keynesian policy and part of a larger plan to undermine Congressional support for further expansions of federal spending. While this may well have been Reagan's intention, Keynesian economics was not finished, politically, until Bill Clinton's watch.

Upon attaining a legislative majority in 1994, conservatives in Congress singlemindedly set about dismantling the key legislative vestiges of Keynesian economic policy in the United States. Welfare reform, their most important victory, is instructive. When the Personal Responsibility Act passed in 1996, much was made of the five-year lifetime limit on welfare benefits, the work requirements, and so forth. Rarely noted was the fact that the legislation transformed the fiscal nature of most federal welfare programs. Welfare benefits are no longer an entitlement. Annual spending levels are now capped and will not rise with the unemployment rate unless Congress specifically allocates new funds. It was this provision of the legislation that led official Peter Edelman to resign from the Department of Health and Human Services in protest when Clinton signed the legislation.

The Food Stamp and Medicaid programs remain entitlements in theory, still available to all comers. But in enacting the 1996 reforms, Congress turned responsibility for managing these programs over to local officials who have been known to turn away applicants not already receiving welfare. Meanwhile, conservatives lobby intensely to privatize and effectively dismantle Social Security—the largest of all federal entitlement programs—though so far without success.

Republican leadership had hoped to bury Keynesian stabilization policy altogether by passing a constitutional amendment requiring an annually balanced federal budget, which would put an end once and for all to full-employment budgeting. The amendment failed by one vote to pass the Senate, but conservatives scored a partial victory with the Balanced Budget Agreement of 1997, committing Congress and the administration to balance the budget each year for the next decade, regardless of the state of the economy. Whether the agreement survives an economic downturn remains to be seen, but the strident antideficit rhetoric of the last decade will certainly make stabilization policies a tough, if not an impossible, sell.

Under Clinton, the outlook for macroeconomic policy grew bleak indeed. Clinton attributed the economic boom to tough spending caps and fiscal restraint and made a fetish of further fiscal austerity. White House press releases conceived the future exclusively in terms, not simply of budgetary balance, but of burgeoning surpluses and massive debt repayment. Rather than fight recessions or expand jobs programs, $3.5 trillion of tax revenue would buy back federal bonds from financial institutions. Clinton's millennial State of the Union address laid out the goal of Clintonomics: "Make America debt-free for the first time since 1835." Candidate Al Gore assured voters that he planned to reduce the debt "even if the economy slows." Sounding uncannily like the ghost of Herbert Hoover or Calvin Coolidge, Gore maintained that a recession would provide "an opportunity" to cut government spending "just like a corporation has to cut expenses if revenues fall." When Bill Bradley floated a modest proposal to use surplus funds for health care, Gore attacked the idea as "fiscally irresponsible," and warned it might plunge the U.S. economy in recession. Hillary Clinton, running for the Senate from New York, declared that most problems facing the country "cannot be solved by government" and staunchly supported running budget surpluses to pay off the national debt. When Democrats are hawking debt reduction and warning that deficits cause recessions, Keynesian policy has truly drawn its last gasp.

It is no good thinking these statements can be unsaid, conveniently forgotten when the next recession revives talk of an active, proemployment government. The political programs that buttressed American Keynesianism are gone. The intellectual backing and public rhetoric that sustained Keynesian ideas no longer exist or are dwarfed by the editorial pages of the *Wall Street Journal*. College economics textbooks, through which hundreds of thousands of voters and policymakers learn the rudiments of macroeconomics, barely bother with Keynes these days—or with recessions for that matter. The hottest new text by Gregory Mankiw (for which Prentice-Hall paid an unprecedented $1.4 million advance) does not even mention economic downturns until a few pages at the very end.

LIFE AFTER KEYNES

So what if the "new economy" turns out to be the same old economy? The last U.S. recession officially ended in 1991. In the eight years since, GDP has grown steadily and unemployment rates have fallen. If this is just the start of an endless millennial boom, there is no reason to worry. But what if the United States is on the brink of a Y2K recession? This is not the first time in history that Americans have lived through a prolonged boom—the economy grew for eight years straight in the 1960s—but it is the first time since the Depression that politicians and policymakers have rested their hopes so utterly on the boom's continuing.

Many on the left, of course, do not mourn Keynes' passing. Keynes, after all, despised the British Labor party and proudly proclaimed his allegiance to "the educated bourgeoisie." Socialists have long argued that Keynesian programs were meant not to help workers or humanize the economy, but to placate and defuse a potentially powerful workers' movements awakened by the Depression. Environmentalists too criticize Keynesian thinking for its mindless worship of economic growth, its predilection to solve all economic problems with more production, more work, more growth, more stuff.

But Keynes' understanding of capitalist economies was, nevertheless, profoundly radical. Any effort to construct a new kind of economic policy in the future will need to build on and attend to his fundamental insights. Keynes understood that the matters of debt and budget deficits, of interest payments and paper wealth that so obsess private business people and financial interests are, ultimately, irrelevant to all but the wealthy elite. The central insight of Keynesian thought was that real wealth lies in the people, resources, and productive apparatus of a society and that citizens can, through the collective power of government, harness those resources for internal development.

In the early years of the New Deal, government jobs programs funded public art works, community theaters, oral history projects, and the creation of hiking trails in national forests—programs that would warm the hearts of environmentalists and radicals alike. The government disbanded the efforts in the face of business opposition. In the end, Americans got a timid version of Keynesianism, complete with probusiness tilt and antigovernment bias, that flexed the collective muscle of government weakly indeed and only at the federal level. The most U.S. Keynesians managed to accomplish was to secure a minimal living standard for the very poor and very old, and to provide a fair number of make-shift defense jobs for the otherwise unemployed.

Should the boom prove not to be eternal, it is inevitable that many voices will call to reestablish the dismantled and discredited programs of postwar American Keynesianism. It will be wasted breath. The real challenge for the new millennium will be to forge a post-Keynesian economic policy. This will entail thinking about how citizens can harness their collective power to produce more leisure rather than more jobs, more equity rather than more income, more conservation rather than more production, more satisfaction rather than more consumption, more quality rather than more quantity.

ARTICLE 7.4

February 2000

OPENING PANDORA'S BOX
THE BASICS OF MARXIST ECONOMICS

BY ALEJANDRO REUSS

In most universities, what is taught as "economics" is a particular brand of orthodox economic theory. The hallmark of this school is a belief in the optimal efficiency (and, it goes without saying, the equity) of "free markets."

The orthodox macroeconomists—who had denied the possibility of general economic slumps—were thrown for a loop by the Great Depression of the 1930s, and by the challenge to their system of thought by John Maynard Keynes and others. Even so, the orthodox system retains at its heart a view of capitalist society in which individuals, each equal to all others, undertake mutually beneficial transactions tending to a socially optimal equilibrium. There is no power and no conflict. The model is a perfectly bloodless abstraction, without all the clash and clamor of real life.

KARL MARX AND THE CRITIQUE OF CAPITALIST SOCIETY

One way to pry open and criticize the orthodox model of economics is by returning to the idiosyncracies of the real world. That's the approach of most of the articles in this book, which describe real-world phenomena that the orthodox model ignores or excludes. These efforts may explain particular facts better than the orthodoxy, while not necessarily offering an alternative general system of analysis. They punch holes in the orthodox lines but, ultimately, leave the orthodox model in possession of the field.

This suggests the need for a different conceptual system that can supplant orthodox economics as a whole. Starting in the 1850s and continuing until his death in 1883, the German philosopher and revolutionary Karl Marx dedicated himself to developing a conceptual system for explaining the workings of capitalism. The system which Marx developed and which bears his name emerged from his criticism of the classical political economy developed by Adam Smith and David Ricardo. While Marx admired Smith and Ricardo, and borrowed many of their concepts, he approached economics (or "political economy") from a very different standpoint. He had developed a powerful criticism of capitalist society before undertaking his study of the economy. This criticism was inspired by French socialist ideas and focused on the oppression of the working class. Marx argued that wage workers—those working for a paycheck—were "free" only in the sense that they were not beholden to a single lord or master, as serfs had been under feudalism. But they did not own property, nor were they craftspeople working for themselves, so they were compelled to sell themselves for a wage to one capitalist or another. Having surrendered their freedom to the employer's authority, they were forced to work in the way the employer told them while the latter pocketed the profit produced by their labor.

Marx believed, however, that by creating this oppressed and exploited class of workers, capitalism was creating the seeds of its own destruction. Conflict between the workers and the owners was an essential part of capitalism. But in Marx's view of history, the workers could eventually overthrow the capitalist class, just as the capitalist class, or "bourgeoisie," had grown strong under feudalism, only to supplant the feudal aristocracy. The workers, however, would not simply substitute a new form of private property and class exploitation, as the bourgeoisie had done. Rather, they would bring about the organization of production on a cooperative basis, and an end to the domination of one class over another.

This line of thinking was strongly influenced by the ideas of the day in German philosophy, which held that any new order grows in the womb of the old, and eventually bursts forth to replace it. Marx believed that the creation of the working class, or proletariat, in the heart of capitalism was one of the system's main contradictions. Marx studied capitalist economics in order to explain the conditions under which it would be possible for the proletariat to overthrow capitalism and create a classless society. The orthodox view depicts capitalism as tending towards equilibrium (without dynamism or crises), serving everyone's best interests, and lasting forever. Marx saw capitalism as crisis-ridden, full of conflict, operating to the advantage of some but not others, and far from eternal.

CLASS AND EXPLOITATION

Marx studied history closely. Looked at historically, he saw capitalism as only the latest in a succession of societies based on exploitation. When people are only able to produce the bare minimum needed to live, he wrote, there is no room for a class of people to take a portion of society's production without contributing to it. But as soon as productivity exceeds this subsistence level, it becomes possible for a class of people who do not contribute to production to live by appropriating the surplus for themselves. These are the masters in slave societies, the lords in feudal societies, and the property owners in capitalist society.

Marx believed that the owners of businesses and property—the capitalists—take part of the wealth produced by the workers, but that this appropriation is hidden by the appearance of an equal exchange, or "a fair day's work for a fair day's pay."

Those who live from the ownership of property—businesses, stocks, land, etc—were then a small minority and now are less than 5% of the population in countries like the United States (Marx wrote before the rise of massive corporations and bureaucracies, and did not classify managers and administrators who don't own their own businesses as part of the bourgeoisie.) The exploited class, meanwhile, is the vast majority who lived by earning a wage or salary—not just the "blue collar" or industrial workers but other workers as well.

Marx's view of how exploitation happened in capitalist society depended on an idea, which he borrowed from Smith and Ricardo, called the Labor Theory of Value. The premise of this theory, which is neither easily proved nor easily rejected, is that labor alone creates the value which is embodied in commodities and which creates profit for owners who sell the goods. The workers do not receive the full value created by their labor and so they are exploited.

Students are likely to hear in economics classes that profits are a reward for the "abstinence" or "risk" of a business-person—implying that profits are their just desserts. Marx would argue that profits are a reward obtained through the exercise of power—the power owners have over those who own little but their ability to work and so must sell this ability for a wage. That power, and the tribute it allows owners of capital to extract from workers, is no more legitimate in Marx's analysis than the power of a slaveowner over a slave.

A slaveowner may exhibit thrift and take risks, after all, but is the wealth of the slaveowner the just reward for these virtues, or a pure and simple theft from the slave?

As Joan Robinson, an important 20th-century critic and admirer of Marx, argues, "What is important is that owning capital is not a productive activity. The academic economists, by treating capital as productive, used to insinuate the suggestion that capitalists deserve well by society and are fully justified in drawing income from their property."

THE FALLING RATE OF PROFIT

Marx believed that his theory had major implications for the crises that engulf capitalist economies. In Marx's system, the value of the raw materials and machinery used in the manufacture of a product does not create the extra value that allows the businessman to profit from its production. That additional value is created by labor alone.

Marx recognized that owners could directly extract more value out of workers in three ways: cutting their wages, lengthening their working day, or increasing the intensity of their labor. This need not be done by a direct assault on the workers. Capitalists can achieve the same goal by employing more easily exploited groups or by moving their operations where labor is not as powerful. Both of these trends can be seen in capitalism today, and can be understood as part of capital's intrinsic thirst for more value and increased exploitation.

With the mechanization of large-scale production under capitalism, machines and other inanimate elements of production form a larger and larger share of the inputs to production. Marx believed this would result in a long-term trend of the rate of profit to fall as less of production depended on the enriching contribution of human labor. This, he believed, would make capitalism increasingly vulnerable to economic crises.

MARX'S DISCUSSIONS OF CAPITALISM'S IRRESISTIBLE EXPANSIVE IMPULSE SEEM AS APT TODAY AS THEY DID 150 YEARS AGO.

This chain of reasoning, of course, depends on the Labor Theory of Value (seeing workers as the source of the surplus value created in the production process) and can be avoided by rejecting this theory outright. Orthodox economics has not only rejected the Labor Theory of Value, but abandoned the issue of "value" altogether. After lying fallow for many years, value analysis was revived during the 1960s by a number of unorthodox economists including the Italian economist Piero Sraffa. Marx was not the last word on the subject.

UNEMPLOYMENT, PART I:
THE "RESERVE ARMY OF THE UNEMPLOYED"

Marx is often raked over the coals for arguing that workers, under capitalism, were destined to be ground into ever more desperate poverty. That living standards improved in rich capitalist countries is offered as proof that his system is fatally flawed. While Marx was not optimistic about the prospect of workers raising their standard of living very far under capitalism, he was critical of proponents of the "iron law of wages," such as Malthus, who held that any increase in wages above the minimum necessary for survival would simply provoke population growth and a decline in wages back to subsistence level.

> AS AESTHETICALLY APPEALING AS THE CLOCKWORK HARMONY OF THE ORTHODOX MODEL MAY BE, THIS IS PRECISELY ITS FAILING.

Marx emphasized that political and historical factors influencing the relative power of the major social classes, rather than simple demographics, determined the distribution of income.

One economic factor to which Marx attributed great importance in the class struggle was the size of the "reserve army of the unemployed." Marx identified unemployment as the major factor pushing wages down—the larger the "reserve" of unemployed workers clamoring for jobs, the greater the downward pressure on wages. This was an influence, Marx believed, that the workers would never be able to fully escape under capitalism. If the workers' bargaining power rose enough to raise wages and eat into profits, he argued, capitalists would merely substitute labor-saving technology for living labor, recreating the "reserve army" and reasserting the downward pressure on wages.

Though this has not, perhaps, retarded long-term wage growth to the degree that Marx expected, his basic analysis was visionary at a time when the Malthusian (population) theory of wages was the prevailing view. Anyone reading the business press these days—which is constantly worrying that workers might gain some bargaining power in a "tight" (low unemployment) labor market, and that their wage demands will provoke inflation—will recognize its basic insight.

UNEMPLOYMENT, PART II:
THE CRISIS OF OVERPRODUCTION

Marx never developed one definitive version of his theory of economic crises (recessions) under capitalism. Nonetheless, his thinking on this issue is some of his most visionary. Marx was the first major economic thinker to break with the orthodoxy of "Say's Law." Named after the French philosopher Jean-Baptiste Say, this theory held that each industry generated income equal to the output it created. In other words, "supply creates its own demand." Say's conclusion, in which he was followed by Smith, Ricardo, and orthodox economists up through the Great Depression, was that while a particular industry such as the car industry could overproduce, no generalized overproduction was possible. In this respect,

orthodox economics flew in the face of all the evidence. In his analysis of overproduction, Marx focused on what he considered the basic contradiction of capitalism—and, in microcosm, of the commodity itself—the contradiction between "use value" and "exchange value." The idea is that a commodity both satisfies a specific need (it has "use value") and can be exchanged for other articles (it has "exchange value"). This distinction was not invented by Marx; it can be found in the work of Smith. Unlike Smith, however, Marx emphasized the way exchange value—what something is worth in the market—overwhelms the use value of a commodity. Unless a commodity can be sold, the portion of society's useful labor embodied in it is wasted (and the product is useless to those in need). Vast real needs remain unsatisfied for the majority of people, doubly so when—during crises of overproduction—vast quantities of goods remain unsold because there is not enough "effective demand."

It is during these crises that capitalism's unlimited drive to develop society's productive capacity clashes most sharply with the constraints it places on the real incomes of the majority to buy the goods they need. Marx developed this notion of a demand crisis over 75 years before the so-called "Keynesian revolution" in economic thought (whose key insights were actually developed before Keynes by the Polish economist Michal Kalecki on the foundations of Marx's analysis).

Marx expected that these crises of overproduction and demand would worsen as capitalism developed, and that the crises would slow down more and more the development of society's productive capacities (what Marx called the "forces of production"). Ultimately, he believed, these crises would be capitalism's undoing. He also pointed to them as evidence of the basic depravity of capitalism. "In these crises," Marx writes in the *Communist Manifesto*,

> there breaks out an epidemic that, in all earlier epochs would have seemed an absurdity, the epidemic of overproduction. Society suddenly finds itself put back into a state of momentary barbarism; it appears as if a famine, a universal war of devastation had cut off the supply of every means of subsistence; industry and commerce seem to be destroyed; and why? Because there is too much civilization, too much means of subsistence, too much industry, too much commerce …
>
> And how does the bourgeoisie get over these crises? On the one hand by enforced destruction of productive force; on the other hand, by the conquest of new markets, and by the more thorough exploitation of old ones.

This kind of crisis came so close to bringing down capitalism during the Great Depression that preventing them became a central aim of government policy. While government intervention has managed to smooth out the business cycle, especially in the wealthiest countries, capitalism has hardly become crisis-free.

While the reigning complacency about a new, crisis-free

capitalism is much easier to sustain here than in, say, East Asia, capitalism clearly has not yet run up against any absolute barrier to its development. In fact, Marx's discussions (in the *Communist Manifesto* and elsewhere) of capitalism's irresistible expansive impulse—capital breaking down all barriers, expanding into every crevice, always "thirsting for surplus value" and new fields of exploitation—seem as apt today as they did 150 years ago.

MARX AS PROPHET

Marx got a great deal about capitalism just right—its incessant, shark-like forward movement; its internal chaos, bursting forth periodically in crisis; its concentration of economic power in ever fewer hands. Judged on these core insights, the Marxist system can easily stand toe-to-toe with the orthodox model. Which comes closer to reality? The capitalism that incessantly bursts forth over new horizons, or the one that constantly gravitates towards comfortable equilibrium? The one where crisis is impossible, or the one that lurches from boom to bust to boom again? The one where perfect competition reigns, or the one where a handful of giants towers over every industry?

In all these respects, Marx's system captures the thundering dynamics of capitalism much better than the orthodox system does. As aesthetically appealing as the clockwork harmony of the orthodox model may be, this is precisely its failing. Capitalism is anything but harmonious.

There was also a lot that Marx, like any other complex thinker, predicted incorrectly, or did not foresee. In this respect, he was not a prophet. His work should be read critically, and not, as it has been by some, as divine revelation. Marx, rather, was the prophet of a radical approach to reality. In an age when the "free market" rides high, and its apologists claim smugly that "there is no alternative," Joan Robinson's praise of Marx is apt: "[T]he nightmare quality of Marx's thought gives it … an air of greater reality than the gentle complacency of the orthodox academics. Yet he, at the same time, is more encouraging than they, for he releases hope as well as terror from Pandora's box, while they preach only the gloomy doctrine that all is for the best in the best of all *possible* worlds."

Resources: Joan Robinson, *An Essay on Marxian Economics* (Macmillan, 1952); "Manifesto of the Community Party," and "Crisis Theory (from Theories of Surplus Value)," in Robert C. Tucker, ed., *The Marx-Engels Reader* (W.W. Norton, 1978); Roman Rosdolsky, *The Making of Marx's 'Capital'* (Pluto Press, 1989); Ernest Mandel, "Karl Heinrich Marx"; Luigi L. Pasinetti, "Joan Violet Robinson"; and John Eatwell and Carlo Panico, "Piero Sraffa"; in John Eatwell, Murray Milgate, and Peter Newman, eds., *The New Palgrave: A Dictionary of Economics* (Macmillan, 1987).

ARTICLE 7.5

September/October 2002

UNDER THE MARGINS

FEMINIST ECONOMISTS LOOK AT GENDER AND POVERTY

BY RANDY ALBELDA

For all the hype about welfare-to-work, most former welfare recipients are still living in poverty. It is true that, since the advent of 1990s-style "welfare reform," families no longer on welfare are earning more, on average, than those still on welfare. But more often than not, the jobs that former welfare mothers find don't provide employer-sponsored health insurance, vacation time, sick leave, or wages sufficient to support their families. In fact, the percentage of families who are "desperately" poor (with incomes at or below 50% of the official poverty line) has gone up since the mid-1990s, and so has the percentage of former welfare recipients who report hardships such as difficulty feeding their families or paying bills. And remember: All of this occurred during a so-called economic boom.

So why does the emphasis on work (and now marriage) continue to dominate the welfare debate? In large part, this is because the poverty "story" of the last 20 years—created and perpetuated by conservative ideologues and politicians—blames poor people for their own poverty. Women supposedly have too many children without husbands, poor black urban dwellers exhibit pathological behaviors, and liberal welfare policies—by expanding government spending and providing an attractive alternative to jobs and marriage—have made matters worse.

At least one group of theorists—feminist economists—says it isn't so. It is women's particular economic role in capitalism—as caregiver—that shapes their relationship to the labor market, men, and the state. Feminist economists have shown how having and caring for children affects the economic status of women—including women who are not mothers but are still relegated to poorly paid care-giving jobs. While their voices are largely ignored in research and policy circles, feminist economists' analyses provide the best understanding of the obstacles low-income families face and the range of policy options that might work.

WOMEN AND POVERTY

Almost everywhere, women are the majority of poor adults. Recently, a group of sociologists from several U.S. universities looked at poverty in eight industrialized nations. Using a relative poverty measure (half of median family income), they found that, in the 1990s, women's poverty rates exceeded men's in all countries but Sweden. Further, they found that single-mother poverty rates—even in countries with deep social welfare systems—are exceptionally high. (See Figure 1.)

In the United States in 2000, women comprised just over half of the adult population but constituted 61% of all poor adults. (The U.S. poverty income threshold is based on an absolute dollar figure determined in the 1960s and since indexed for inflation.) Toss in children, and the data are even grimmer; 16.2% of all children were poor, while over one-third of all single-mother families were poor. Together, women and children comprised 76% of the poor in the United States, far surpassing their 62% representation in the population as a whole.

Since the late 1950s (when the data were first collected), single-mother families in the United States have never constituted more than 13% of all families; however, they form just under half of all poor families. Figure 2 depicts the proportion of all families—and all poor families—that are single-mother families. The steepest increase occurred in the late 1960s on the heels of the War on Poverty, as poverty rates for everyone were falling.

ECONOMIC THEORY AND POVERTY

From Adam Smith onward, most economists have understood poverty by looking at labor markets, labor-market inequality, and economic growth. According to this approach, it is underemployment or the lack of employment—and the resulting lack of income—that causes poverty. A brief summary of the dominant economic theories in the last half of the 20th century illustrates the point.

Keynesian economic theory argues that the lack of demand in the economy as a whole leads to unemployment. When investors and consumers can't jumpstart the economy, we need fiscal or monetary economic stimuli to induce demand. It was this wisdom that has guided economists to promote economic growth as a way to reduce poverty, arguing that "a rising tide lifts all boats"—as, for example, during the Kennedy and Johnson administrations.

Marxian theorists say that, under capitalism, unemployment cannot be totally eliminated because it is a necessary component of capitalist production that serves to "discipline" workers. Unless we make radical changes to the economic system, there will always be families that are without employment and therefore poor.

Like Marxian economists, *institutional* economists also believe that economic outcomes aren't simply the result of pure market forces; cultural, social, and political forces also come into play. In the 1970s, economists Peter Doeringer and Michael Piore identified distinct labor-market segments. Younger workers, workers of color, and women tend to end up in what they call the "secondary labor market"—characterized by low wages, few promotional opportunities, and easy-to-acquire skills—more than other workers. These workers are particularly vulnerable to unemployment and hence more likely to be poor. The way to relieve poverty is to help these workers move into better jobs, or to create policies that make their jobs better.

These understandings of poverty offer little or no gender analysis—presumably what ails men is equally applicable to women. Analyses of insufficient (aggregate) demand, unemployment, and labor-market inequality rarely mention women or discuss how and why gender matters—unless feminist scholars provide them.

Neoclassical (mainstream) economists also argue that poverty is caused by lack of employment and low wages—but they consider workers responsible for their own wage levels. Workers who choose not to pursue edu-

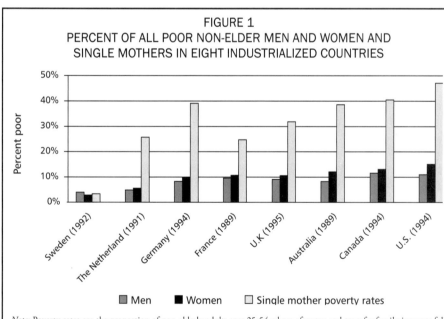

FIGURE 1
PERCENT OF ALL POOR NON-ELDER MEN AND WOMEN AND
SINGLE MOTHERS IN EIGHT INDUSTRIALIZED COUNTRIES

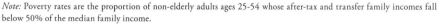

Note: Poverty rates are the proportion of non-elderly adults ages 25-54 whose after-tax and transfer family incomes fall below 50% of the median family income.

Source: Table 1, in Karen Christopher et al., "Gender Inequality in Poverty in Affluent Nations: The Role of Single Motherhood and the State," in Karen Vleminckx and Timothy Smeeding, eds., *Child Well-Being, Child Poverty and Child Policy in Modern Nations* (London: Policy Press, 2001).

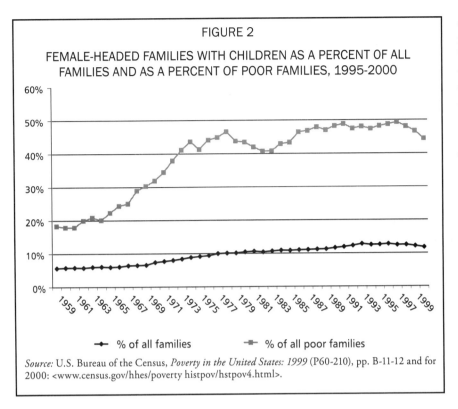

FIGURE 2

FEMALE-HEADED FAMILIES WITH CHILDREN AS A PERCENT OF ALL
FAMILIES AND AS A PERCENT OF POOR FAMILIES, 1995-2000

→ % of all families   ■ % of all poor families

Source: U.S. Bureau of the Census, *Poverty in the United States: 1999* (P60-210), pp. B-11-12 and for 2000: <www.census.gov/hhes/poverty histpov/hstpov4.html>.

cation, training, or on-the-job experience will participate in the labor force less often than more highly trained and skilled workers, be less productive, and receive lower wages. Unlike the political economy theorists just discussed, many non-feminist economists—the most well known being Nobel Prize winner Gary Becker—have tackled the topic of women's lower wages. But they consistently conclude that women's lack of employment, or employment at low wages, results from rational individual choice. Only policies that boost incentives for individuals to invest in themselves (like tax credits for education) will alleviate poverty.

GENDER MATTERS

It is true that one reason women are poor is that they are not in the labor force or are underemployed. But while employment is an important underpinning to understanding poverty, it is not the same for women as for men.

Most economists who study labor markets assume that workers in capitalist economies are "unencumbered"—that they don't have significant constraints on their time outside of paid work. Encumbered workers are treated as a "special case"—worthy of examination, but understood and analyzed as an exception rather than the rule.

Since the beginnings of capitalism, however, female workers have almost always been "encumbered." And women's role as caregivers—their main encumbrance—has shaped their participation in the economy, as feminist historians and economic historians have shown. Historically, women's economic opportunities have been severely constricted, with race, age, and marital status sending important market "signals" about where women could or should be employed. For

example, until the 1960s, many professional and some clerical jobs had "marriage bars," i.e., employers refused to hire married women on the assumption that they did not need the salaries these jobs paid, and would not stick around once they had children. Similarly, before anti-discrimination laws were enacted, many workers of color could not get jobs as managers in many professions, or even as sales clerks if the business catered to a white clientele.

For more than a century, this labor market "ordering" has given rise to employment, income, and wage policies that reinforce and reproduce women's political and economic dependence on men (and non-whites' inferior status in relation to whites). These policies assume that the standard family is a heterosexual married couple with a lone male breadwinner employed in industrial production. For example, in order to collect unemployment insurance benefits, workers must work a minimum number of hours and receive a minimum amount of earnings. Because many women work part-time and earn low wages, they are much less likely to qualify for benefits than men. Similarly, Social Security benefits are based on previous earnings over a sustained period of employment. Women who have spent most of their adult lives as caregivers are thus ineligible for benefits on their own, and must rely on their husbands' contributions instead.

Men's and women's employment patterns are very different. Women's labor force participation rates are lower than men's, and women's employment experiences in economic downturns often differ from men's. Women's job options and choices are also highly influenced by care-giving responsibilities; mothers are more likely than fathers to trade higher-paying jobs for jobs that are closer to childcare, have more flexible schedules, or require fewer hours.

In addition to shaping women's paid labor-market activities, care work has been economically, socially, and politically undervalued, as feminist economists point out. This is true both when that work is done in the home for free and when others do it for low pay. Among the few jobs immigrant women and women of color can almost always find are low-paying care-work jobs, and they are disproportionately represented in those jobs. For example, in 2001, women were 47% of all workers but 97% of child care workers, 93% of registered nurses, 90% of health aides, and 72% of social workers. Black workers comprised 11% of the workforce but were 33% of health aides, 23% of licensed practical nurses, and 20% of cleaning service workers. This type of occupational "stereotyping" reinforces the care-giving roles that women and people of color fill, and the low pay (relative to jobs with similar skill requirements) reinforces women's dependence on men and racial inequality. Economist Nancy Folbre, in her 2001 book *The Invisible Heart: Economics and Family Values*, calls this the "care penalty."

It is because of their low-paid and unpaid care work, then, that women are particularly economically vulnerable and much more likely to be poor than are men. The role of care giving—as distinct from other factors like employment, economic growth, and labor-market inequality—helps to explain not only women's employment patterns but also women's poverty. So theories of poverty that rely on analyses of employment that assume all people are men—or that women are a special case of men—are not only incomplete, they are wrong.

FEMINIST ANALYSES OF POVERTY

It is no coincidence that, when there has been a viable women's movement—in the early part of the 20th century and in the late 1960s—feminists and women researchers have paid particular attention to poor women.

Documenting poor families: early efforts

In the early 20th century, there was a good deal of concern about how women fit into the capitalist economy. Social scientists living in or near poor communities—often in settlement houses established by women reformers—conducted surveys of women workers, mostly through government-sponsored research. Many of the surveys found that the biggest problems faced by two-parent families were a lack of employment and insufficient wages. Researchers readily recognized that families headed by women were constrained by women's role as caregiver and women's low wages. Instead of advocating more employment for women, they promoted relatively meager levels of public assistance.

In the 1910s and 1920s, women reformers were key players not only in doing research but also in creating policies directed toward poor women and children. These women imposed white middle-class values about child-rearing, hygiene, and education; their construction of "deservingness" replicated and reinforced the ways in which women and men, immigrants and non-immigrants, were supposed to act. At the same time, they successfully implemented income supplement programs for single-mother families at the state level, and they were instrumental in incorporating AFDC (Aid to Families with Dependent Children) into the Social Security Act of 1935. Feminist poverty researchers and reformers did not emerge again until the late 1960s.

Sisterhood may be powerful, but motherhood is not: recent efforts

The women's movement of the late 1960s and 1970s laid some important foundations for understanding women's poverty, even though its main economic strategies were aimed at improving the wages of women who were employed. Feminists fought for affirmative action, which was most successful in creating opportunities for college-educated women. Today, women hold 46% of executive and professional jobs—exactly their representation in all jobs—and comprise just under 30% of all doctors and lawyers. Feminists also organized for comparable worth, which was intended to lift wages for low-income women by recognizing and rewarding the skill level and effort needed to perform low-paying women's jobs (including care-giving ones).

At the same time, feminist scholars called attention to women's "double day" (now called "work/family conflict") and theorized about the role of care work and reproduction in capitalist economies. From the outset, feminist analysts understood that "housework" was work and a vital component of capitalist production. This intellectual work paralleled "wages for housework" campaigns that were launched in Italy, Canada, Great Britain, and the United States.

Using these tools to reinterpret poverty was not hard. Among the first to apply a feminist analysis to women's poverty was sociologist Diana Pearce, in an 1978 article entitled "The Feminization of Poverty: Women, Work, and Welfare." Pearce called attention to the fact that women were disproportionately represented among the poor. Her phrase—"the feminization of poverty"—became very popular in feminist circles as well as in the mainstream press.

Economist Nancy Folbre followed up with a theoretical framework directly linking women's care work as mothers to their poverty. In her 1985 article, "The Pauperization of Motherhood: Patriarchy and Social Policy in the U.S.," she argued that, when the costs of raising children are shifted onto women, women (and children) become dependent on men. Then, when fathers abandon their families, women and children are consigned to poverty. Folbre also argues that public policies around divorce, child support, unemployment insurance, and welfare reinforce this relationship. For example, welfare policies—even before the 1990s reforms—never provided enough income for women to support their families without working "under the table" or getting unreported income, paying a big price for not being married.

Single mothers especially bear the burden of these policies in the form of incredibly high poverty rates. But, Folbre points out, the benefits of care labor—healthy, productive children who become tax-paying adults—are enjoyed by all of society, not merely the mothers who provided the care. If society recognized the value of women's care work and compensated them for it, then fewer women would be poor.

Current trends

Currently, some feminist scholars are addressing the ways that gender influences government allocation of income supports (like pensions, unemployment insurance, and welfare) and non-cash assistance (e.g., education and child care). Sociologist Ann Orloff and political scientists Diane Sainsbury and Jane Lewis argue that state welfare policies (construed broadly) embody deeply gendered notions of citizenship and need. Much of this work is theoretical and does not explicitly address poverty. However, it helps to explain the lack of policies that would correct women's poverty.

Other researchers are focusing on how people's capacity—access to health and education, living conditions, how they are treated in a society—affects their potential to generate income and causes poverty. Building on the work of economist Amartya Sen, feminist economists in the United States have shown that it is unreasonable and unlikely to expect single mothers to "work" their way out of poverty—because women earn lower wages than men, because they have care-giving responsibilities, and because the additional costs associated with caring for children restrict their capacity to be employed even while family needs remain high. For example, Barbara Bergmann and Trudi Renwick developed budgets for low-income families in the 1990s. Chris Tilly and I have demonstrated that the income needs of single-mother families far exceed their earnings possibilities—even with full-time employment. This work refutes the claims of liberals who supported welfare reform in the naïve belief that welfare recipients could easily substitute earnings for public assistance.

Finally, feminist economists are documenting how low-income women—especially single-mother families in which the same adult is both caregiver and breadwinner—relate to the labor market, fathers, and the state. Using longitudinal data, feminist social scientists Roberta Spalter-Roth and Heidi Hartmann found that many poor single-mother families either combine government assistance with wages (under or above the table) or cycle between the two. This research is confirmed and extended by feminist sociologists like Kathryn Edin and Laura Lein, who, through extensive interviews with poor single mothers, documented the particular ways and times that poorly paying jobs as well as men and their incomes drift in and out of women's lives. These studies make it clear that women's employment is not family-sustaining, and that, to survive, single-mother families need a sane combination of earnings, child support, *and* government assistance. In contrast to the narrowly focused, incentive-based literature that characterizes poor women's behavior as pathological, these approaches demonstrate that poor women's lives are dynamic yet fragile, and that the decisions they make are creative, adaptive, and almost always child-centered.

WHO CARES?

Despite their efforts, feminist scholars have not had much impact on the poverty literature—at least not in economics—nor have they influenced policies intended to alleviate poverty. Much (though not all) poverty research is grant-funded, and it tends to focus narrowly on evaluating the individual impact of welfare reform, mostly by looking at welfare "leavers." These factors discourage the use of feminist analysis, since most funding goes either to conservative think tanks with a specific ideological aversion to feminism or to "liberal" think tanks that have made their fortunes in mainstream analysis fitted to their main consumer—the federal government.

Further, these conventional studies often preclude the larger political economy approach taken by feminists. Welfare reform is a mechanism of social control over poor single women—especially women of color—that is part of a larger conservative agenda to justify if not exacerbate economic inequality, assure a large pool of low-wage labor, and silence important political movements. Feminist analysis suggests the need for policies that would not only reduce poverty but also change women's (and people of color's) relationship to the labor market, (white) men, and the state, thus loosening the grip of economic dependence. This isn't in line with the right-wing agenda at all.

However, feminist economic analysis has been very useful to activists who are trying to help poor women. For example, in the mid-1990s, Wider Opportunity for Women (WOW), a feminist group based in Washington, D.C., started conducting family economic self-sufficiency standard projects. Currently, WOW operates projects in 40 states and D.C. The studies demonstrate how much income a single-mother family needs to survive, and are being used as organizing tools in the states.

During the mid-1990s welfare reform debates and now in discussions about reauthorization of Temporary Assistance for Needy Families (TANF), feminist scholars—connected informally through the "Women's Committee of 100"—have argued that raising children is work and that responsible legislation should recognize unpaid work as work. The Committee has called for a caregiver's allowances (see "Wages for Housework," article 1.5, and <www.welfare2002.org>). And while Congress has not embraced these ideas, a TANF reauthorization bill sponsored by Representative Patsy Mink (D-Hawaii) in the spring of 2002 garnered support from close to 90 members of the House.

Feminist economists argue that the role of economists is to understand how societies do or do not provide for people's needs. Through their research and skills, they provide the tools for activists to argue that women's employment status and care-giving responsibilities place many at the bottom of the economic pecking order. At the same time, feminist economists are connecting their work directly to social movements, lending their expertise—and their own voices—to living wage campaigns, efforts to improve compensation for child care workers and home health aides, and efforts to eliminate poverty, not welfare.

Resources: Kathryn Edin and Laura Lein, *Making Ends Meet: How Single Mothers Survive Welfare and LowWage Work* (Russell Sage Foundation, 1997); Nancy Folbre, "The Pauperization of Motherhood: Patriarchy and Social Policy in the U.S.," *Review of Radical Political Economics*, vol. 16, no. 4 (1984): 72-88; Nancy Folbre, *The Invisible Heart: Economics and Family Values* (New York: The New Press, 2001); Jane Lewis, "Gender and the Development of Welfare Regimes," *Journal of European Social Policy* 3 (1992): 159-73; Alice

O'Connor, *Poverty Knowledge: Social Science, Social Policy, and the Poor in Twentieth Century U.S. History* (Princeton, N.J.: Princeton University Press, 2001); Ann Orloff, "Gender and the Social Rights of Citizenship: The Comparative Analysis of Gender Relations and Welfare States," *American Sociological Review* 58 (1993): 303-28; Diana Pearce, "The Feminization of Poverty: Women, Work, and Welfare," *Urban and Social Change Review* (February 1978); Trudi Renwick and Barbara Bergmann, "A Budget-based Definition of Poverty with an Application to Single-parent Families," *Journal of Human Resources* 28, no. 1 (1993): 1-24; Diane Sainsbury, *Gender, Equality, and Welfare States* (Cambridge: Cambridge University Press, 1996); Amartya K. Sen, *Development as Freedom* (New York: Alfred A. Knopf, 1999); Roberta SpalterRoth et al., *Welfare That Works: The Working Lives of AFDC Recipients* (Washington, D.C.: Institute for Women's Policy Research, 1995); Chris Tilly and Randy Albelda, "Family Structure and Family Earnings: The Determinants of Earnings Differences among Family Types," *Industrial Relations* 33, no. 2 (1994): 151-167; U.S. Census, *Current Population Surveys* <www.census. gov/hhes/income/histinc/histpovtb.html>; Bureau of Labor Statistics, *Employment and Earnings*, Table 11 <*www.bls.gov/ cps/home.htm#charemp.§§*>

March/April 2005

MARXIAN CLASS ANALYSIS AND ECONOMICS

BY RICHARD WOLFF

Class analysis predates economics. Long before modern economics emerged, ancient Greek thinkers, for example, analyzed their society by *classifying* people into groups by wealth. They viewed understanding the relationships between classes as crucial to improving their society and debated whether wealth should be distributed equally. While class analysis has a long history, no single definition of class has prevailed. Alongside *property* definitions (rich and poor), social theorists have used definitions based on the *power* that various groups wielded and have debated whether power is or should be distributed unequally (to elites, to kings, and so on) or equally (in various versions of democracy).

For Adam Smith and David Ricardo, originators of modern economics, class analysis was central. Here is how Ricardo opened his *Principles of Political Economy and Taxation* (1817): "The produce of the earth ... is divided among three classes of the community ...". He defined these classes as owners of the land, owners of capital (machines, tools, etc.), and owners of labor power who do the work. He continued, "To determine the laws which regulate this distribution is the principal problem in Political Economy." Like many thinkers before and since, Ricardo believed that understanding a society required identifying its main classes and recognizing the nature of their interdependence and conflicts. Class and class differences were the core concerns of economics at the discipline's founding.

Why then do today's dominant economic theories—the neoclassical and Keynesian economics traditions—ignore class analysis? They do that in reaction to what Marx did with class analysis after Ricardo. Building on but also differing from Smith and Ricardo, Marx took class analysis in

new directions. He also linked his new class analysis to a fundamental critique of capitalism; Smith and Ricardo had used their class analyses to celebrate capitalism.

Marx was a radical who criticized his society's unequal distributions of property and power. Like other social critics, he favored collective ownership of property, egalitarian income distribution, and democracy as basic component of social justice. Marx inherited the ancient concept of classes based on property. He made use of Smith's and Ricardo's economics because he valued their class analyses. He also appreciated the power definition of class. But Marx believed that the received definitions of class were inadequate. He developed a new class analysis to equip mass movements for social justice with new insights and strategies for constructing just, egalitarian and democratic societies.

In his new class analysis, Marx defined class not in terms of wealth, income, or power, but rather in terms of the *surplus*. He argued that in all societies, a portion of the people applied brain and muscle to produce a quantity of goods that *exceeded* what they themselves consumed plus what went to replenish the raw materials and equipment used up in the production process. That excess he called a surplus. Societies differed in how they organized this surplus: who produced it, who got it, and what they did with it.

By focusing on the surplus, Marx had changed the very meaning of class. In his work, it referred less and less to groups of *people* (the rich, the poor, labor, management, the rulers, the powerless, and so on). Instead, it increasingly referred to the economic *processes* of producing, appropriating, and distributing the surplus that occur in every society. A "class structure" came to mean a particular set of these processes. Because the dominant class structure in Marx's time was capitalist, it was the particular capitalist processes of surplus production, appropriation, and distribution that he analyzed.

Capitalism is still dominant, and Marx's analysis still applies. Here is a capsule summary. Capitalists promise workers wages in return for producing an output which the capitalists own, immediately and entirely. The capitalists sell the output in markets and pocket the revenues. One portion of capitalists' revenues provides workers their promised wages, which workers then use to buy back *from* the capitalists a portion of what they had produced *for* the capitalists. After paying wages and replenishing materials used up in production, the remaining revenues comprise the capitalists' surplus. The workers produce the surplus; the capitalists appropriate it.

As Marx stressed, capitalism resembles feudalism and slavery in this organization of the surplus. Slaves produced more than they got back from their slave masters; feudal serfs kept part of their product for themselves and delivered the rest—the surplus—as rents to feudal lords. Whenever workers produce a surplus *that other people get,* Marx labeled that "exploitation." Thus, in his scheme, the transitions from slavery and feudalism that established capitalism had not freed workers from exploitation.

Marx's surplus-based concept of class turned out to be a powerful analytical tool that those in the Marxist tradition have used to make sense of a wide range of political and economic questions. One fruitful area of research has focused on how changes in economic, political, and cultural conditions affect the size of the surplus pumped out of the workers, how workers and capitalists struggle over that size, and how the supplies, demands, and prices of goods and services in the market reflect and affect those class struggles. For example, falling food and clothing prices make it easier for capitalists to lower the money wages they pay and thereby extract more surplus from workers. To take another example, if political and cultural developments encourage workers' class consciousness to grow—if they come to understand surplus and exploitation—they may reduce the surplus they deliver to capitalists or even demand the right to appropriate the surplus themselves.

Marxian analysis also follows the surplus after the capitalists appropriate it. Competition among capitalists and their struggles with workers impose demands on the surplus. Thus, for example, capitalists distribute some of the surplus to pay supervisors to squeeze more surplus from workers. Capitalists distribute another portion of the surplus to attorneys to fend off lawsuits, another portion to pay managers who buy new machines to overcome competitors, and so on.

Class-analytical economics distinguishes workers who *produce* the surplus ("productive workers") from those who *provide the conditions* that capitalists need to keep appropriating it ("unproductive workers" such as supervisors, lawyers, and managers). Since productive workers create the surplus that capitalists then distribute to unproductive workers, these two groups relate differently to class processes even though members of both are wage-earners. Thus, Marxian economists can ask and answer questions about class differences among different groups of workers that other economists, lacking an analysis of class in surplus terms, cannot ask let alone answer.

Marxian economics also explores interactions among class processes. How surpluses get produced and appropriated shapes how those surpluses are then distributed and vice versa. For example, intensified exploitation (e.g., speed-ups, closer supervision, or cuts in paid time off) produces stress that often requires capitalists to devote more of the surplus for programs like counseling that help workers cope with alcoholism, absenteeism, and so on. Similarly, when capitalists distribute more of the surplus to buy new machines, that usually changes the number of workers hired, the intensity of their labor, and the resulting rate of their exploitation. Class analysis further shows how commodity prices, enterprise profits, and individual incomes depend on and influence class processes. For example, when workers succeed in raising their wages at the expense of capitalists' surpluses, capitalists often respond by automation, outsourcing to cheaper workers abroad, layoffs, or still other strategies that change individual incomes, corporate profits, prices, and government tax revenues both at home and abroad.

Those in the Marxist tradition also study the interactions among politics, culture, and capitalist class processes. For example, capitalists spend part of their surpluses on campaign contributions and lobbyists to shape government policies in the interests of exploiting more surplus from their workers, of beating out their capitalist competitors, and so on. Needless to say, such distributions out of the surplus have a heavy impact on politics in capitalist societies. Another example: When Wal-Mart recently found its surpluses hurt by employees' class action suits over discrimination and unfair labor practices, it decided to distribute more of its huge surpluses to "media expenditures." In plain English, this money aims to influence what TV programs we see, how newspapers shape stories, what messages films emphasize, and so forth. Beyond Wal-Mart's image, these distributions of the surplus help to shape the larger culture and thereby the development of the societies whose media Wal-Mart intends to "engage."

Marxian economists recognize that capitalism often yields rising output and consumption levels. But their analyses typically underscore the contradictions and injustices of capitalism's uneven distributions of its costs and benefits and demonstrate how the economic problems of capitalism, including unemployment, waste of natural and human resources, and cyclical instability, emerge in part from the system's particular class structure.

An analysis of class in terms of surplus has also allowed thinkers in the Marxian tradition to develop an economics of post-capitalism. A post-capitalist economy begins when revolutionary economic change brings about an end to exploitation, not merely changes in its form. Then, the workers who produce the surplus will also be the people who appropriate and distribute that surplus. In a sense, productive workers become their own board of directors; they collectively appropriate their own surpluses within enterprises. Imagine that Monday through Thursday, the workers produce output. Fridays they perform three very different activities collectively: return a portion of their output to themselves as individual wages, replenish the used-up means of production, and devote what remains—the surplus—to maintain this new class structure. Such a nonexploitative class structure is what Marxian class analysis means by *communism*. Of course, a nonexploitative class structure is no automatic utopia; it will have its distinctive economic, political, and cultural problems, but they will differ from those of capitalism.

Marxian economists argue about how class processes interact with other economic, political, and cultural processes to shape the evolution of capitalist societies. They differ as well in their analyses of nonexploitative class structures—past, present, and future. Generations of these debates have yielded a complex, sophisticated, and diverse Marxian class analytical economics that offers distinctive understandings of capitalism and the communist alternative.

Yet Marxian class analysis is now largely excluded from books, newspapers, classrooms, and most people's consciousness by the neoclassical and Keynesian economics orthodoxies. Instead of welcoming debate among alternative kinds of economics, most orthodox economists endorse the silencing of alternatives generally and Marxian class analysis in particular. Neither neoclassical nor Keynesian economics argues about the production, appropriation, and distribution of surpluses. They simply deny that surpluses or class processes exist. Students mostly study neoclassical or Keynesian models of how economies work. Practical economists apply the models to statistics and statistics to the models. The public hears their conclusions not as results of one kind of (class-blind) economics but rather as *the* truth of economic science, applicable always and everywhere.

Nonetheless, Marxian class analyses thrive despite their exclusion from the mainstream. Capitalism's problems plus the struggles and oppositions they provoke continue to generate critics. Many find capitalism's inequalities of wealth, income, and power unacceptable. Some find their way to Marxian class analyses focused on the social organization of the surplus as a key to the insights and strategies needed to take societies beyond capitalism.

CHAPTER 8

INTERNATIONAL TRADE AND FINANCE

INTRODUCTION

When it comes to the global economy, most textbooks line up behind the "Washington Consensus"—a package of free trade and financial liberalization policies that the U.S. Treasury Department, the International Monetary Fund (IMF), and the World Bank have spun into the prevailing prescriptions for the world's developing economies. Mainstream textbook discussions of exchange rates, international trade, and economic development policies almost always promote a market-dictated integration into the world economy. Outside the classroom, however, popular discontent with the Washington Consensus has spawned a worldwide movement calling into question the myth of self-regulating markets on which these policies rest.

While the doctrines of free trade and financial liberalization are seldom questioned in mainstream economics textbooks, both are scrutinized here. Arthur MacEwan gives an overview of the process of globalization today, what is new and what continues long-established patterns, and the difficulties opposition groups face coming to grips with the power and the complexity of these forces (Article 8.1). MacEwan's second article shows how industrialized economies developed by protecting their own manufacturing sectors—never preaching the "gospel of free trade" until they were highly developed. Today, he argues, these countries prescribe free trade not because it's the best way for others to develop, but because it gives U.S. corporations free access to the world's markets and resources, which in turn strengthens the power of business against workers (Article 8.2). Economist Ramaa Vasudevan takes a critical look at the doctrine of comparative advantage, the backbone of free trade theory, and shows that it comes up short as a guide for economic development (Article 8.3). John Miller replies to *New York Times* columnist Nicholas Kristof, who steadfastly maintains that more sweatshops, not fewer, is the key to lifting young men and women in Sub-Saharan Africa out of poverty. Miller then offers an alternative set of policies to bring development to the region (Article 8.10). Economist Thomas Palley argues that even China, with the fastest growing economy in the world and one of the chief beneficiaries of the expiration of the Multifiber Agreement, will eventually have to turn away from a policy of export-led growth to one led by meeting domestic demand (Article 8.9). Sociologist Stephen Philion interviews economist Han Deqiang, one of China's leading critics of that country's

neoliberal development strategy. Deqiang totes up the devastating social costs of this strategy, including its toll on China's workers and farmers (Article 8.7).

John Miller debunks the *Wall Street Journal*'s editors' claim that policies that promote equality stand in the way of rapid economic growth. Miller argues that, contrary to the claims of the editors, the experience of the East Asian economies shows that poverty reduction depends on both raising a nation's income and reducing its inequality (Article 8.5). Miller then follows up with an analysis of the imperial financial policies that lie behind the unprecedented current account deficit and the decline of the dollar, and examines the worries that both pose for the U.S. and global economies (Article 8.6). In another article, MacEwan explains the ins and outs of the trade deficit and the threat it poses for the U.S. economy (Article 8.4).

Other articles look at the institutions of the global economy. Larry Peterson argues that Paul Wolfowitz's departure from the World Bank, no matter how welcome, has not put an end to World Bank practices of pushing developing countries into building up their currency reserves at the cost of failing to invest in developing their own countries (Article 8.8). Nafta From Below, an excerpt from the outstanding collection of essays with the same title, paints a devastating picture of the effects of the North American Free Trade Agreement (NAFTA) on workers in maquiladoras, or border factories, over the

---

KEY TO COLANDER
E = *Economics*   M = *Macroeconomics*

The articles in this chapter are linked to chapters E32, E34, and E21, or M16, M17, and M19 which take up macroeconomic policies in developing countries and international policy issues.

Articles 8.7-8.12 fit with chapters E32, E34, and E21, or M16, M17, and M19. They take a critical look at the most powerful institutions of the global economy, such as the World Trade Organization, the World Bank, and the International Monetary Fund, the devastating impact their policies have had on the developing world, and what would constitute genuine reform of the global economy.

Articles 8.1, 8.2, 8.3, and 8.5 take on the advocacy of trade liberalization found in most economics textbooks, and should be read with E21 and E34, or M16-M19.

Articles 8.4 and 8.6 delve into the U.S. trade deficit and its impact on the global economy. They go with E32 and E33 or M17 and M18.

last twenty years. The excerpt here recounts how women played a central role in the struggle for workers to establish a democratic union at a Sony plant in Nuevo Laredo, a Mexican border town (Article 8.9).

We close the chapter with a debate about fair trade and farm subsidies (Article 8.12). Gawain Kripke, a senior policy analyst at Oxfam America, argues that fairer trade rules would provide enormous benefits to the world's poorest people. Dean Baker and Mark Weisbrot, co-directors of the Center for Economic and Policy Research, maintain that while ending agricultural subsidies for wealthy nations would make them less hypocritical, it wouldn't do much to help the developing world.

DISCUSSION QUESTIONS

1. (Article 8.1) According to MacEwan, what aspects of today's globalization are new and what continues earlier trends? How might opposition forces best push for a more democratic and equitable globalization process?

2. (Article 8.2) MacEwan claims that the "infant industry" argument for trade protection is much more widely applicable than standard theory suggests. To what countries and industries might it apply in today's world economy? Explain your answer.

3. (Article 8.2) Free trade, MacEwan argues, gives business greater power relative to labor. Why is this so? Is it a good reason to oppose free trade?

4. (Article 8.3) What is the doctrine of comparative advantage? And why, according to Vasudevan, is it not a good guide to successful economic development?

5. (Article 8.4) What is a current account deficit and what causes it? When does a current account deficit become a problem?

6. (Article 8.5) What does the experiencee of the East Asian economies suggest about the relationship between equity, economic growth, and poverty alleviation? Give specific examples from the 22 developing countries studied by the Asian Development Bank.

7. (Article 8.6) What economic and political forces enable the United States to run an unprecedented current account deficit that is now the equivalent of 1% of the world's GDP? Which of the three prospects for the U.S. economy that Miller outlines at the close of his article— a dollar crisis, a long slow decline in the value of the dollar, or a dollar propped up through repeated interest rate hikes—do you think is most likely (or do you think a different scenario is more likely)?

8. (Article 8.7) According to Philion and Deqiang, what has been the impact of China's neoliberal development policies on Chinese workers in the export factories, in state-owned enterprises, in small shops, and on farms?

9. (Article 8.8) According to Peterson, how have World Bank policies compromised the economic prospects of developing countries?

10. (Article 8.9) What was the role of women workers in organizing the Sony maquiladora factory? How has NAFTA impacted the rights of Mexican workers in the maquiladora plants?

11. (Article 8.10) What is the basis of journalist Nicholas Kristof's claim that what young men on the streets of Namibia's capital city need is the opportunity to work in sweatshops? Why does Miller find Kristof's claim unconvincing? Who do you think is right? Why?

12. (Article 8.12) Who do you find more convincing in the debate about fair trade, Kripke or Baker and Weisbrot? Do you think fairer trade rules pay off for poor countries? If not, what policies would do a better job of improving the lot of poor people in the developing world?

WHAT IS GLOBALIZATION?

BY ARTHUR MacEWAN

Ever since Adam and Eve left the garden, people have been expanding the geographic realm of their economic, political, social and cultural contacts. In this sense of extending connections to other peoples around the world, globalization is nothing new. Also, as a process of change that can embody both great opportunities for wealth and progress and great trauma and suffering, globalization at the beginning of the 21st century is following a well established historical path. Yet the current period of change in the international system does have its own distinctive features, not the least important of which is the particular sort of political conflict it is generating.[1]

"GREATEST EVENTS" AND "DREADFUL MISFORTUNES"

We are fond of viewing our own period as one in which great transformations are taking place, and it is easy to recite a list of technological and social changes that have dramatically altered the way we live and the way we connect to peoples elsewhere in the world. Yet, other surges of globalization in the modern era have been similarly disruptive to established practices. The first surge by which we might mark the beginning of modern globalization came with the invasion of the Western Hemisphere by European powers and with their extension of ocean trade around Africa to Asia. Adam Smith, writing *The Wealth of Nations* in 1776, did not miss the significance of these developments:

The discovery of America, and that of a passage to the East Indies by the Cape of Good Hope, are the two greatest and most important events recorded in the history of mankind... By uniting, in some measure, the most distant parts of the world, by enabling them to relieve one another's wants, to increase one another's enjoyments, and to encourage one another's industry, their general tendency would seem to be beneficial.

Alongside of what Adam Smith saw as the great gains of globalization (not his term!), were the slaughter, by battle and disease, of millions of Native Americans, the enslave-

ment and associated deaths of millions of Africans, and the subjugation of peoples in Asia. Smith did recognize the "dreadful misfortunes" that fell upon the peoples of the East and West Indies as a result of these "greatest events" (though he does not mention Africans in this expression of concern). He saw these misfortunes, however, as arising "rather from accident than from any thing in the nature of the events themselves."

The first stage of modern globalization illustrates not only the combined great gains and "dreadful misfortunes" that have characterized globalization but also the vast scope of the process. The political and economic changes that followed from the European conquest of the Americas and forays into Asia are relatively well known. Equally momentous were the huge cultural transformations that were tied to the great expansion of economic contacts among the continents. Peoples moved, or they were moved by force. As they came to new locations and in contact with other peoples, almost every aspect of their lives was altered—from what people eat ("Italian" spaghetti with tomato sauce comes from Asia, the spaghetti, and America, the tomatoes) to their music (jazz is now the best known example, blending the backgrounds of different continents to emerge in America) to religion (the cross accompanied the sword in the era of colonial conquest).

The second great surge of modern globalization came in the 19th century, both as product and cause of the Industrial Revolution. On the one hand, the expansion of industry generated large reductions in transport costs that brought huge increases in international commerce. On the other hand, for the emerging commercial centers of Europe and North America, the opening of foreign markets and access to foreign sources of raw materials fueled (sometimes literally) the expansion of industry. Great Britain, as the "workshop of the world," was at the center of these changes and over the course of the century saw its foreign trade increase three times as rapidly as national income.

Britain during the 19th century provided a foreshadowing of current-day globalization as it officially touted "free

---

[1] We usually measure "the extent of economic connections" by levels of imports and exports relative to total production or by the level of international investment relative to total production. For example, in 1913, US exports were 6% as large as Gross Domestic Product (GDP); the figure had fallen to 4.6% in 1950, but was up to 7.1% in 1973 and 10.6% in 1999. For Europe, the figures are: 22% in 1913, 16.7% in 1950, 21.8% in 1973, and 32.1% in 1999. Interestingly, Japan, for which exports were 20% of GDP in 1913, saw this figure remain relatively stable at around 10% of GDP in the latter half of the 20th century. Figures on foreign investment are harder to come by for the early part of the 20th century, but they seem to show a similar pattern. In recent years, the foreign investment figures show strong increases of economic connections. In the 1985-90 period, for the world as a whole, foreign direct investment (i.e., not including financial investments) were 5.4% of the level of GDP in the countries making the investments and 6.0% of GDP in the countries receiving the investments; in the 1996-98 period, the figures had risen to 8.2% and 8.4%, respectively.

trade" as the proper mode of organization for commerce—not just for itself, but for the entire world. The gospel of "free trade" was then carried around the globe by the British navy, and heroic ideological gymnastics allowed a growing colonial empire to be included under this same rubric. As the British historian E. J. Hobsbawm has commented, "British industry could grow up, by and large, in a protected home market until strong enough to demand free entry into other people's markets, that is 'Free Trade'." In today's globalization it is the United States, a country that also attained its economic power on the foundation of protectionism, that preaches the gospel of "free trade" to the rest of the world.

Current day globalization is, by and large, a continuation of the process that began in the 19th century (which in turn had its roots in the great transformation that began along with the 16th century). Two world wars and the Great Depression disrupted the progress of globalization for some sixty years and shifted its center from Britain to the United States, but it is now back on track. By the 1980s, the extent of economic connections that had been established among the world's national economies by 1913 had been reattained, and in subsequent years international trade and investment have continued to expand their roles in the economies of most nations.

HOMOGENIZATION AND COMPETITION

Change in the world economy today, however, is not simply an extension of what went on in earlier periods, not simply a quantitative extension of well established trends. What distinguishes the current era from earlier phases of globalization is that now capitalism is ubiquitous. Virtually everywhere, production takes place for profit and is based on wage labor. In the 19th century, capitalism may have provided the leading dynamic of the international economy, but in many parts of the world—most everywhere outside of Europe and North America—a great deal of economic activity was organized through families (peasant farms or shops), under semi-feudal conditions, or through slavery. These activities were all connected to markets and to a world capitalist system, but they were not capitalist in themselves. Certainly there are important aspects of life and work today which take place outside of markets and are not directly capitalist—for example, work in the home, interactions within governments, volunteer activity, and some other forms of production. Yet capitalism holds sway, dominating and defining economic relationships in almost all parts of the world.

The ubiquity of capitalism gives a new character to the economic connections among peoples in distant parts of the world. There has, in particular, been a grand homogenization, both of consumer markets and of production activity. Wal-Mart and McDonald's establish themselves in Mexico to sell the same sorts of products in the same way as in the United States. At the same time, Mexican workers at the Ford plant in Hermosillo produce the same cars that are produced in US factories and they do so with equipment and procedures that are among the most "modern" in the world. Also on the production side, plants in Mexico and the United States are sometimes integrated with one another in a "global assembly line," with Mexican workers engaged in the labor intensive aspects of the operation and US workers engaged in the more highly skilled activities; for example, in clothing production, design and cutting is done in the United States while the pieces are stitched together on the Mexican side of the border.

Mexico, because of its proximity to the United States and the reduction of trade restrictions between the two countries, presents an extreme example of the cross-border integration of production. Yet in broad terms, we are presented today with a new international organization of production, as people on different corners of the globe produce the same sorts of products with the same technologies and often for the same employers—though the ultimate employers often operate through local subcontractors.

The homogenization of the world economy creates a new set of relationships, a direct competition, among workers in different parts of the world. Although such competition always existed, it is much more extensive and intense than in the past and, most important, it takes place between workers whose wages are dramatically different from each other. It is one thing when US and Canadian workers, who have very similar wages and standards of living, are in competition with each other. It is quite another thing when the US and Canadian workers are in competition with Mexican workers.

This new relationship among workers in different countries presents obvious problems for the workers in the rich countries: they simply cannot compete with workers who, using the same equipment and methods of production (i.e., the same technology), are paid far, far lower wages. Yet similar, though perhaps less obvious, problems exist for the low-wage workers as well. With wage labor markets existing throughout most of the world, virtually all workers are placed in competition with one another. While workers in Bangladesh may be willing to accept very low wages to assemble clothing for the European market, they are always faced with the prospect that Vietnamese workers may accept even lower wages. Or Indonesian workers, who assemble sports shoes for the US market, may face the prospect of production innovations that will substitute machinery and skilled workers for unskilled workers on an assembly line, making it profitable for the firms to move their production back to the United States.

In a capitalist world, where many different sites around the world provide firms with the labor markets they need, those firms can have a great advantage over workers. That advantage, however, depends upon "free trade," the elimination of government barriers to the movement of goods and funds across national boundaries. Free trade has given firms the option of either moving themselves or moving their sources of supply in response to cost differences (wage differences, but also other cost differences). Free trade, however, does not include the reduction—let alone the elimination—of barriers to the movement of workers. So labor does not enjoy the same freedom in the globalized economy as does capital. Since "freedom" means having alternatives, and having alternatives means having power, a system that enhances the freedom of firms relative to the freedom of labor means giving businesses more power relative to labor. (Even were barriers to migration to be reduced, there are still substantial costs to labor movement compared to capital movement; and capital's advantage, while reduced, would not be eliminated.)

The drive for free trade existed, as pointed out above, in the British-led globalization of the 19th century, but the United States has been able to push the concept to a whole new level. In part, free trade is important for the power it confers on business, but it is also important as ideology. The ideology of free trade has provided the defining rationale for the North American Free Trade Agreement (NAFTA), the Free Trade Agreement of the Americas (FTAA), the World Trade Organization (WTO), and the programs pushed on low income countries by the International Monetary Fund (IMF) and the World Bank. The opening of markets, the opening of sources of supply, the spread of private economic activity—all of this is supposed to provide a new era of rapid economic growth for the world and serve the needs of the poor as well as the rich.

NOT SO FAST

The concept of free trade has a certain intuitive appeal. After all, if the firms and people of a nation are free to buy their supplies from the lowest-cost source of supply, then they will be able to buy more and satisfy their needs more thoroughly than if their government limits the sources from which they can buy those supplies (bans imports) or imposes extra costs (tariffs) on supplies from abroad. For low income countries, desperate for economic growth, it would seem absurd for their governments to place restrictions on imports, forcing firms and people to waste resources on expensive domestic goods. Moreover, it only takes a moment's reflection to note the huge gains we attain from international commerce: not only the banana I eat for breakfast and a good portion of the oil that fuels my car and heats my home, but also the ideas and culture from elsewhere in the world—to say nothing of the competitive pressures from abroad that help drive economic advances in my own country. For a small country, the gains from foreign commerce are a virtual necessity.

Another moment's reflection, however, reveals that things are not so simple. Free trade is not the only way to engage extensively in international commerce. In fact, none of the countries we now denote as "developed" attained their development through free trade, though all engaged extensively in international commerce. There are, it seems, some substantial advantages to having the production of certain kinds of goods take place within a country, as compared to obtaining those same goods from abroad. The US textile industry in the 19th century, the US auto industry through most of the 20th

century, the Japanese computer industry in the mid-20th century, the South Korean steel and ship building industries later in the 20th century—all generated broad economic gains in terms of the transformation of technology and the formation of a skilled work force that far surpassed the costs that arose from the government protection they received in their early stages of expansion. None of this provides a justification for protectionism in general; continuing protection of sugar and steel production in the United States imposes costs with no off-setting benefits (except to those directly engaged in the industries). Yet the experience of two centuries of capitalist development does demonstrate the fallacy of the free trade argument. Efforts by the US government to push free trade on low income countries today may make sense from the perspective of the interests of US firms, but it is hardly a prescription for economic advancement in low income countries.

But there is more. Globalization as it is being organized under the banner of free trade is doing nothing to reduce the "development gap," the huge difference in material well-being between the peoples of the rich nations and the peoples of most of the rest of the world. In fact, there is some evidence that under the regime of increasingly open world markets, the "development gap" is increasing. Worse yet: there is a good deal of evidence that free trade globalization is contributing to increasing inequality within nations, not only within the low income countries of the "South" but also within the United States and the other high income countries of the "North."

As the international economy is increasingly organized in a way that enhances the power of firms and tends to undermine the power of labor, it is certainly likely that greater inequality would be the outcome. Unfortunately, available data do not allow us to draw strong conclusions about what has been happening to world income inequality in recent decades. What we do know is that income distribution in today's world is already grossly unequal, with hundreds of millions of people living at the edge of subsistence, while the elites in all countries live in obscene luxury. We also know that, although some low income countries have made substantial gains (South Korea and some other countries of East Asia), the current surge of globalization has provided no general relief for the world's poor. Furthermore, we know that globalization—new patterns of international trade and investment—has disrupted people's lives, pushed people out of their traditional lines of work, shifted the location of economic activity, and forced people to adopt new patterns of consumption. All of this makes many people's lives very unpleasant, regardless of what can be uncovered with the aggregate statistics regarding income distribution and economic growth.

WHAT ELSE IS NEW?

One might well absorb this summary of change in the world economy and respond with the comment: So, what else is new? It does seem that periods of great change in the world economy, whatever immediate benefits they may generate for the elite and whatever their long run benefits for society in general, are accompanied by severe disruptions, hardships and inequalities. Current day experience seems to fit well with the pattern established in the 16th and 19th centuries, to say nothing of earlier eras of imperial expansion. (Many commentators quite reasonably reject the term "globalization" in favor of "imperialism" precisely because the latter term underscores the great inequalities of power and income that are always so important in international affairs.)

Yet perhaps there is something new in the current era in the particular type of political response to globalization that has been generated in recent years. The "dreadful misfortunes" of earlier eras have also generated political responses—sometimes in the form of spontaneous rebellion, sometimes as more organized resistance and revolution, and sometimes as waves of new oppositional organizations and alliances. The political response to globalization at the beginning of the 21st century, however, has some distinguishing characteristics that are worth emphasizing.

Most important, parts of the response to globalization are themselves global. The coming out "party" for the anti-globalization movement in Seattle in the fall of 1999 involved people and organizations from all over the world. As a coordinated effort by groups from many rich countries and many poor countries, the action in Seattle—and the ones that have followed in Washington, Quebec, Prague, Puerto Allegre, and elsewhere—suggest something is different about the nature of political action. Many times, opposition movements based on national identities have, at least implicitly, been in conflict with one another; at other times, organizations in rich countries have opted to "support" groups in poor countries, but not as a joint and coordinated effort. While progressive movements have always talked about their internationalism, this time around the talk may translate more effectively into practice.

Also, the globalization of political opposition to globalization has included steps by labor unions, which have long adhered to highly nationalist positions. So far, more of the new internationalism of the US labor movement has been in the realm of rhetoric rather than practice, but US unions have made some important efforts at cross border organizing—in the form, for example, of supporting efforts of Mexican workers to organize firms in their country that supply the US market. (NAFTA, while allowing corporations, the organizations of capital, to operate in both the United States and Mexico, as well as Canada, makes no parallel provision for unions, the organizations of labor.) The rhetoric of internationalism, too, is important, especially because it marks such a departure from the past practices of the US labor movement. Some critics complain that the new-found interest of the US labor movement in conditions abroad arises from its own immediate concerns, the competition from low-cost imports, instead from a concern for workers elsewhere in the world. But that is just the point. If global-

ization forces US unions to secure the interests of their own members by pursuing a new internationalism, then that is certainly a change of significance.

The organized opposition to globalization goes far beyond the labor movement, however, involving a wide spectrum of social movements. Environmental and women's organizations, peasant groupings, student-based action committees, and others have all been a part of the actions. In addition, well established non-governmental organizations such as Oxfam, while not engaged in the protest actions in Seattle and elsewhere, have been a part of the general opposition to globalization. Not only is this opposition based on a wide range of social movements, but these different movements have at least begun to work in alliance with one another. Some aspects of this alliance, particularly that between environmental groups and labor unions, suggest a major shift from past conflicts.

Opposition actions have taken place in a wide spectrum of countries. On the one hand, there have been the much publicized actions led by young, often middle-class activists in the United States, focused on meetings of the principal international economic agencies such as the IMF, World Bank, and WTO. On the other hand, there have been actions in India, where peasant organizations have demonstrated against the international pharmaceutical and seed companies that are trying to use the internationalization of patent regulations to secure their control of world markets. While these geographically disparate actions are not coordinated through any cohesive international organization, they are part of an interconnected movement.

The opposition that has developed to globalization is not a cohesive movement, and it is not so well developed that we can have confidence in its lasting impact. Furthermore, it has many problems. Opposition to globalization sometimes is expressed as an opposition to connections with other peoples rather than as an opposition to the way those connections are exacerbating inequalities of power and income. Thus xenophobic protectionism is sometimes just below the surface of protest actions. By and large, however, the opposition to globalization appears to be based on an internationalism that may provide a basis for a progressive, and perhaps lasting, movement.

The more serious problems of this opposition arise from the difficulties in coming to grips with the power and complexity of the globalization process itself. A small example is provided by efforts in the rich countries to respond to the proliferation of imports of goods produced in "sweat shop" conditions in low income countries. Protests against the companies that utilize these shops—firms such as Nike and Gap—are met with the response that workers in these "sweat shops" are eager to obtain their jobs because these jobs are significantly better in terms of pay and working conditions than other available jobs. What's more, the response is often true. A sophisticated movement can come to terms with this reality by emphasizing the need to alter the context that impoverishes workers in low income countries and by stressing that such a context is most effectively transformed through political struggle. Also, by focusing on workers' right to political freedom—in particular, the right to organize unions—rather than on particular aspects of workers' conditions, anti-sweat shop activists can have a positive impact.

The "sweat shop" example helps clarify that globalization is not simply a collection of practices, not simply a peculiar set of connections among peoples around the globe. It is part of the long historical development and spread of capitalism. Within the framework of capitalism, it is difficult to solve problems that are based on the inequality of income and power, because those problems are generated by the system itself. Nonetheless, capitalism is not an immutable system, and it is probably not a permanent system. The oppositional struggles are not only responses to globalization, but they are part of the process of globalization itself. They will play a role in shaping events and in shaping the entire nature of the process. And they will contribute to answering the question: What is globalization?

Reprinted with permission from *Radical Teacher*, Issue 61, 2001.

ARTICLE 8.2

November/December 1991, updated July/August 2002

THE GOSPEL OF FREE TRADE
THE NEW EVANGELISTS

BY ARTHUR MacEWAN

In the early 1990s, the passage of the North American Free Trade Agreement marked a new epoch of U.S. economic expansion into the Americas. Today, the chimes of "free trade" are ringing out even more loudly in corporate America, as neoliberal economic policies—such as the Free Trade Area of the Americas—continue to make their way around the world.

With his article, "The Gospel of Free Trade," published in November 1991, Arthur MacEwan helped Dollars & Sense *readers to demystify the role of trade in the development of domestic economies. Drawing on the lessons of economic history, MacEwan shows that "free trade" is not the best route to economic prosperity for nations.*

Just as British corporations cheered in favor of free trade in the 19th century, the largest U.S. corporations today are pushing to reduce restraints on trade and investment. The result: downward pressure on wages and social welfare programs in both rich and poor countries, and a reduced capacity of citizens across the globe to control their own economic conditions. —Darius Mehri

Free trade! It's the cure-all for the 1990s. With all the zeal of Christian missionaries, the U.S. government has been preaching, advocating, pushing, and coercing around the globe for "free trade."

While a Mexico-U.S.-Canada free trade pact is the immediate aim of U.S. policy, George Bush has heralded a future free trade zone from the northern coast of Canada to the southern tip of Chile. For Eastern Europe, U.S. advisers prescribe unfettered capitalism and ridicule as unworkable any move toward a "third way." Wherever any modicum of economic success appears in the Third World, free traders extol it as one more example of their program's wonders.

Free traders also praise their gospel as the proper policy at home. The path to true salvation—or economic expansion, which, in this day and age, seems to be the same thing—lies in opening our markets to foreign goods. Get rid of trade barriers, allow business to go where it wants and do what it wants. We will all get rich.

Yet the history of the United States and other advanced capitalist countries teaches us that virtually all advanced capitalist countries found economic success in protectionism, not in free trade. Likewise, heavy government intervention has characterized those cases of rapid and sustained economic growth in the Third World.

Free trade, does, however, have its uses. Highly developed nations can use free trade to extend their power and their control of the world's wealth, and business can use it as a weapon against labor. Most important, free trade can limit efforts to redistribute income more equally, undermine progressive social programs, and keep people from democratically controlling their economic lives.

A DAY IN THE PARK

At the beginning of the 19th century, Lowell, Massachusetts, became the premier site of the country's textile industry. Today, thanks to the Lowell National Historical Park, you can tour the huge mills, ride through thee canals that redirected the Merrimack River's power to the mills, and learn the story of the textile workers, from the Yankee "mill girls" of the 1820s through the various waves of immigrant laborers who poured into the city over the next century.

During a day in the park, visitors get a graphic picture of the importance of 19th-century industry to the economic growth and prosperity of the United States. Lowell and the other mill towns of the era were centers of growth. They not only created a demand for Southern cotton, they also created a demand for new machinery, maintenance of old machinery, parts, dyes, skills, construction materials, construction machinery, more skills, equipment to move the raw materials and products, parts maintenance for that equipment, and still more skills. The mill towns also created markets—concentrated groups of wage earners who needed to buy products to sustain themselves. As centers of economic activity, Lowell and similar mill towns contributed to U.S. economic growth far beyond the value of the textiles they produced.

The U.S. textile industry emerged decades after the industrial revolution had spawned Britain's powerful textile industry. Nonetheless, it survived and prospered. British linens inundated markets throughout the world in the early 19th century, as the British navy nurtured free trade and kept ports open for commerce. In the United States, however, hostilities leading up to the War of 1812 and then a substantial tariff made British textiles relatively expensive. These limitations on trade allowed the Lowell mills to prosper, acting as a catalyst for other industries and helping to create the skilled work force at the center of U.S. economic expansion.

FREE TRADE FORCES DOWN THE GENERAL LEVEL OF WAGES ACROSS THE BOARD, EVEN OF THOSE WORKERS NOT DIRECTLY AFFECTED BY IMPORTS.

Beyond textiles, however, tariffs did not play a great role in the United States during the early 19th century. Southern planters had considerable power, and while they were willing to make some compromises, they opposed protecting manufacturing in general because that protection forced up the price of the goods they purchased with their cotton revenues. The Civil War wiped out Southern opposition to protectionism, and from the 1860s through World War I, U.S. industry prospered behind considerable tariff barriers.

DIFFERENT COUNTRIES, SIMILAR STORIES

The story of the importance of protectionism in bringing economic growth has been repeated, with local variations, in almost all other advanced capitalist countries. During the late 19th century, Germany entered the major league of international economic powers with substantial protection and government support for its industries. Likewise, in 19th-century France and Italy, national consolidation behind protectionist barriers was a key to economic development.

Only Britain—which entered the industrial era first—might be touted as an example of successful development without tariff protection. Yet, in addition to starting first, Britain built its industry through the expansion of its empire and the British navy, hardly prime ingredients in any recipe for free trade.

Japan provides a particularly important case of successful government protection and support for industrial development. In the post-World War II era, when the Japanese established the foundations for the modern "miracle," the government rejected free trade and extensive foreign investment and instead promoted its national firms.

In the 1950s, for example, the government protected the country's fledgling auto firms from foreign competition. At first, quotas limited imports to $500,000 (in current dollars) each year; in the 1960s, prohibitively high tariffs replaced the quotas. Furthermore, the Japanese allowed foreign investment only insofar as it contributed to developing domestic industry. The government encouraged Japanese companies to import foreign technology, but required them to produce 90% of parts domestically within five years.

The Japanese also protected their computer industry. In the early 1970s, as the industry was developing, companies and individuals could only purchase a foreign machine if a suitable Japanese model was not available. IBM was allowed to produce within the country, but only when it licensed basic patents to Japanese firms. And IBM computers produced in Japan were treated as foreign-made machines.

Today, while Japan towers as the world's most dynamic industrial and financial power, one looks in vain for the role free trade played in its success. The Japanese government provided an effective framework, support, and protection for the country's capitalist development.

Likewise, in the Third World, capitalism has generated high rates of economic growth where government involvement, and not free trade, played the central role. South Korea is the most striking case. "Korea is an example of a country that grew very fast and yet violated the canons of conventional economic wisdom," writes Alice Amsden in *Asia's Next Giant: South Korea and Late Industrialization,* widely acclaimed as the most important recent book on the Korean economy. "In Korea, instead of the market mechanism allocating resources and guiding private entrepreneurship, the government made most of the pivotal investment decisions. Instead of firms operating in a competitive market structure, they each operated with an extraordinary degree of market control, protected from foreign competition."

With Mexico, three recent years of relatively moderate growth, about 3-4% per year, have led the purveyors of free trade to claim it as one of their success stories. Yet Mexico has been opening its economy increasingly since the early 1980s, and most of the decade was an utter disaster. Even if the 1980s are written off as the cost of transition, the recent success does not compare well with what Mexico achieved in the era when its government intervened heavily in the economy and protected national industry. From 1940 to 1980, with policies of state-led economic development and extensive limits on imports, Mexican national output grew at the high rate of about 6% per year.

The recent Mexican experience does put to rest any ideas that free market policies will improve the living conditions for the masses of the people in the Third World. The Mexican government has paved the road for free trade policies by reducing or eliminating social welfare programs. In addition, between 1976 and 1990, the real minimum wage declined by 60%. Mexico's increasing orientation toward foreign trade has also destroyed the country's self-sufficiency in food, and the influx of foreign food grains has forced small farmers off the land and into the ranks of the urban unemployed.

THE USES OF FREE TRADE

While free trade is not the best economic growth or development policy, the largest and most powerful firms in many countries find it highly profitable. As Britain led the cheers for free trade in the early 19th century, when its own industry was already firmly established, so the United States—or at least many firms based in the United States—finds it a profitable policy in the late 20th century.

For U.S. firms, access to foreign markets is a high priority. Mexico may be relatively poor, but with a population of 85 million it provides a substantial market. Furthermore, Mexican labor is cheap; using modern production techniques, Mexican workers can be as productive as workers in the United States. For U.S. firms to obtain full access to the Mexican market, the United States must open its borders to Mexican goods. Also, if U.S. firms are to take full advantage of cheap foreign labor and sell the goods produced abroad to U.S. consumers, the United States must be open to imports.

On the other side of the border, wealthy Mexicans face a choice between advancing their interests through national development or advancing their interests through ties to U.S. firms and access to U.S. markets. For many years, they chose the former route. This led to some development of the Mexican economy but also—due to corruption and the massive power of the ruling party—created huge concentrations of wealth in the hands of a few small groups of firms and individuals. Eventually, these groups came into conflict with their own government over regulation and taxation. Having benefited from government largesse, they now see their fortunes in greater freedom from government control and, particularly, in greater access to foreign markets and partnerships with large foreign companies. National development is a secondary concern when more involvement with international commerce will produce greater riches quicker.

In addition, the old program of state-led development in Mexico ran into severe problems. These problems came to the surface in the 1980s with the international debt crisis. Owing huge amounts of money to foreign banks, the Mexican government was forced to respond to pressure from the International Monetary Fund, the U.S. government, and large international banks. That pressure meshed with the pressure coming from Mexico's own richest elites, and the result has been the move toward free trade and a greater opening of the Mexican economy to foreign investment.

Of course, in the United States, Mexico, and elsewhere, advocates of free trade claim that their policies are in everyone's interest. Free trade, they point out, will mean cheaper products for all. Consumers in the United States, who are mostly workers, will be richer because their wages will buy more. In both Mexico and the United States, they argue, rising trade will create more jobs. If some workers lose their jobs because cheaper imported goods are available, export industries will produce new ones.

Such arguments obscure many of the most important issues in the free trade debate. Stated, as they usually are, as universal truths, these arguments are plain silly. No one, for example, touring the Lowell National Historical Park could seriously argue that people in the United States would have been better off had there been no tariff on textiles. Yes, in 1820, they could have purchased textile goods more cheaply, but the cost would have been an industrially backward, impoverished nation. One could make the same point with the Japanese auto and computer industries, or indeed with numerous other examples from the last two centuries of capitalist development.

In the modern era, even though the United States already has a relatively developed economy with highly skilled workers, a freely open international economy does not serve the interests of U.S. workers, though it will benefit large firms. U.S. workers today are in competition with workers around the globe. Many different workers in many different places can produce the same goods and services. Thus, an international economy governed by the free trade agenda will bring down wages for U.S. workers.

The problem is not simply that of workers in a few industries—such as auto and steel—where import competition is the most obvious and immediate problem. A country's openness to the international economy affects the entire structure of earnings in that country. Free trade forces down the general level of wages across the board, even of those workers not directly affected by imports. The simple fact is that when companies can produce the same products in several different places, it is owners who gain because they can move their factories and funds around much more easily than workers can move themselves around. Capital is mobile, labor is much less mobile. Businesses, not workers, gain from having a larger territory in which to roam.

CONTROL OVER OUR ECONOMIC LIVES

But the difficulties with free trade do not end with wages. Free trade is a weapon in the hands of business when it opposes any progressive social programs. Efforts to place environmental restrictions on firms are met with the threat of moving production abroad. Higher taxes to improve the schools? Business threatens to go elsewhere. Better health and safety regulations? The same response.

Some might argue that the losses from free trade for people in the United States will be balanced by gains for most people in poor countries—lower wages in the United States, but higher wages in Mexico. Free trade, then, would bring about international equality. Not likely. In fact, as pointed out above, free trade reforms in Mexico have helped force down wages and reduce social welfare programs, processes rationalized by efforts to make Mexican goods competitive on international markets.

Gains for Mexican workers, like those for U.S. workers, depend on their power in relation to business. Free trade and the imperative of international "competitiveness" are just as much weapons in the hands of firms operating in Mexico as they are for firms operating in the United States. The great mobility of capital is business' best trump card in dealing with labor and popular demands for social change—in the United States, Mexico, and elsewhere.

None of this means that people should demand that their economies operate as fortresses, protected from all foreign economic incursions. There are great gains that can be obtained from international economic relations—when a nation manages those relations in the interests of the great majority of the people. Protectionism often simply supports narrow vested interests, corrupt officials, and wealthy industrialists. In rejecting free trade, we should move beyond traditional protectionism.

Yet, at this time, rejecting free trade is an essential first step. Free trade places all the cards in the hands of business. More than ever, free trade would subject us to the "bottom line," or at least the bottom line as calculated by those who own and run large companies.

For any economy to operate in the interest of the great majority, people's conscious choices—about the environment, income distribution, safety, and health—must command the economy. The politics of democratic decision-making must control business. In today's world, politics operates primarily on a national level. To give up control over our national economy—as does any people that accepts free trade—is to give up control over our economic lives.

Resources: The New Gospel: North American Free Trade," *NACLA's Report on the Americas* 24(6), May 1991; Robert Pollin and Alexander Cockburn, "Capitalism and its Specters: The World, the Free Market and the Left," *The Nation*, 25 February 1991; P. Armstrong, A. Glyn, and J. Harrison, *Capitalism Since World War II*, 1984.

ARTICLE 8.3

July/August 2007

COMPARATIVE ADVANTAGE

BY RAMAA VASUDEVAN

Dear Dr. Dollar:
When economists argue that the outsourcing of jobs might be a plus for the U.S. economy, they often mention the idea of comparative advantage. So free trade would allow the United States to specialize in higher-end service-sector businesses, creating higher-paying jobs than the ones that would be outsourced. But is it really true that free trade leads to universal benefits?
—*David Goodman, Boston, Mass.*

You're right: The purveyors of the free trade gospel do invoke the doctrine of comparative advantage to dismiss widespread concerns about the export of jobs. Attributed to 19th-century British political-economist David Ricardo, the doctrine says that a nation always stands to gain if it exports the goods it produces *relatively* more cheaply in exchange for goods that it can get *comparatively* more cheaply from abroad. Free trade would lead to each country specializing in the products it can produce at *relatively* lower costs. Such specialization allows both trading partners to gain from trade, the theory goes, even if in one of the countries production of *both* goods costs more in absolute terms.

For instance, suppose that in the United States the cost to produce one car equals the cost to produce 10 bags of cotton, while in the Philippines the cost to produce one car equals the cost to produce 100 bags of cotton. The Philippines would then have a comparative advantage in the production of cotton, producing one bag at a cost equal to the production cost of 1/100 of a car, versus 1/10 of a car in the United States; likewise, the United States would hold a comparative advantage in the production of cars. Whatever the prices of cars and cotton in the global market, the theory goes, the Philippines would be better off producing only cotton and importing all its cars from the United States, and the United States would be better off producing only cars and importing all of its cotton from the Philippines. If the international terms of trade—the relative price—is one car for 50 bags, then the United States will take in 50 bags of cotton for each car it exports, 40 more than the 10 bags it forgoes by putting its productive resources into making the car rather than growing cotton. The Philippines is also better off: it can import a car in exchange for the export of 50 bags of cotton, whereas it would have had to forgo the production of 100 bags of cotton in order to produce that car domestically. If the price of cars goes up in the global marketplace, the Philippines will lose out in relative terms—but will still be better off than if it tried to produce its own cars.

The real world, unfortunately, does not always conform to the assumptions underlying comparative-advantage theory. One assumption is that trade is balanced. But many countries are running persistent deficits, notably the United States, whose trade deficit is now at nearly 7% of its GDP. A second premise, that there is full employment within the trading nations, is also patently unrealistic. As global trade intensifies, jobs created in the export sector do not necessarily compensate for the jobs lost in the sectors wiped out by foreign competition.

The comparative advantage story faces more direct empirical challenges as well. Nearly 70% of U.S. trade is trade in similar goods, known as *intra-industry trade*: for example, exporting Fords and importing BMWs. And about one third of U.S. trade as of the late 1990s was trade between branches of a single corporation located in different countries (*intra-firm trade*). Comparative advantage cannot explain these patterns.

Comparative advantage is a static concept that identifies immediate gains from trade but is a poor guide to economic development, a process of structural change over time which is by definition dynamic. Thus the comparative advantage tale is particularly pernicious when preached to developing countries, consigning many to "specialize" in agricultural goods or be forced into a race to the bottom where cheap sweatshop labor is their sole source of competitiveness.

The irony, of course, is that none of the rich countries got that way by following the maxim that they now preach.

These countries historically relied on tariff walls and other forms of protectionism to build their industrial base. And even now, they continue to protect sectors like agriculture with subsidies. The countries now touted as new models of the benefits of free trade—South Korea and the other "Asian tigers," for instance—actually flouted this economic wisdom, nurturing their technological capabilities in specific manufacturing sectors and taking advantage of their lower wage costs to *gradually* become effective competitors of the United States and Europe in manufacturing.

The fundamental point is this: contrary to the comparative-advantage claim that trade is universally beneficial, nations as a whole do not prosper from free trade. Free trade creates winners and losers, both within and between countries. In today's context it is the global corporate giants that are propelling and profiting from "free trade": not only outsourcing white-collar jobs, but creating global commodity chains linking sweatshop labor in the developing countries of Latin America and Asia (Africa being largely left out of the game aside from the export of natural resources such as oil) with ever-more insecure consumers in the developed world. Promoting "free trade" as a political cause enables this process to continue.

It is a process with real human costs in terms of both wages and work. People in developing countries across the globe continue to face these costs as trade liberalization measures are enforced; and the working class in the United States is also being forced to bear the brunt of the relentless logic of competition.

Resources: Arthur MacEwan, "The Gospel of Free Trade: The New Evangelists," *Dollars & Sense*, July/August 2002; Ha-Joon Chang, *Kicking away the Ladder: The Real History of Fair* Trade, Foreign Policy in Focus, 2003; Anwar Shaikh, "Globalization and the Myths of Free Trade," in *Globalization and the Myths of Free Trade: History, Theory, and Empirical Evidence*, ed. Anwar Shaikh, Routledge 2007.

UNDERSTANDING THE TRADE DEFICIT

BY ARTHUR MacEWAN

Dear Dr. Dollar

Can you explain what trade deficits are? Who owes what to whom or is it just an accounting device?

—*Jack Miller, Indianapolis, Ind.*

I see that the United States has had a negative international trade balance for years. What happens to those dollars we've sent overseas?

—*Bill Clark, Chillicothe, Ohio*

Americans collectively import more goods and services from foreigners than we export, we are said to have a *trade deficit*. Paying for the things we import accounts for most of the flow of dollars out of the United States. However, money flows out of the country for other reasons as well. The U.S. government provides foreign aid and supports overseas military bases; immigrants to the United States send dollars back to their families; foreigners who own U.S. businesses or financial assets take income out of the country.

When these factors are added to the trade deficit, the net outflow of dollars is called the *current account deficit*. In 2002, the U.S. trade deficit amounted to $418 billion, and the current account deficit totaled $480 billion. Data for 2003 is not yet available, but preliminary reports indicate the current account deficit will be at least $550 billion.

Once the dollars leave the country, three things can happen.

First, foreigners can use dollars to purchase U.S. assets: stocks, bonds, bank deposits, government debt, real estate, businesses. When Toyota buys land and equipment for a factory in the United States, when a British investment fund buys stock in a U.S. corporation, when a German bank purchases U.S. Treasury bonds, then the United States is said to be

"financing" its current account deficit by selling assets. In 2002, foreigners acquired $612 billion in U.S. assets.

The United States has run persistent and increasing current account deficits since the 1980s, and foreigners have used the dollars to stake significant claims on U.S. assets. At the end of 2002, the value of U.S. assets owned by foreigners exceeded the value of foreign assets owned by U.S. residents by $2.4 trillion. This is the reason the United States is often said to be a debtor nation, with a net debt to the rest of the world of $2.4 trillion. But this "debt" is denominated in our own currency. For that reason, it does not pose the same risks for the United States as developing countries with large debts—which must be repaid in dollars or euro—face.

Foreign central banks provide a second outlet for dollars that leave the United States. The dollar is the most widely used international currency, and many less-developed countries have sizable dollar-denominated debts. Governments sometimes hang on to whatever dollars fall into their hands, parking them in liquid assets like U.S. bank accounts or U.S. government bonds to earn interest. In 2002, foreign governments held almost $95 billion in dollar reserves, which they will use to cover future deficits, repay debts, intervene in financial markets, or simply to exert influence in negotiations with the United States.

If you've followed the arithmetic so far, you will have figured out that in 2002, on balance, more dollars flowed back into the United States to purchase assets then flowed out. This allowed U.S. companies to buy assets overseas, almost $200 billion worth.

As long as the country's large current account deficit is financed by these capital inflows, it is not necessarily a prob-

lem. But a third possible consequence of the massive U.S. current account deficit is that foreigners will lose confidence in the U.S. economy and stop purchasing U.S. assets. If this happens, the supply of dollars in the global banking system will exceed demand and the exchange value of the dollar will fall.

Some people believe this is already happening. Over the past few years, the dollar lost about one-third of its value relative to the euro. This could signify that foreigners are shifting from U.S. to euro-based assets. If the era of dollar supremacy is indeed coming to a close, the value of the dollar will continue to fall. What this would mean for the U.S. and world economies is difficult to predict. A sustained loss of confidence in the dollar could have many potentially serious ramifications.

Imports would grow more expensive, infuriating our trading partners, who depend on the U.S. market for their goods. With less foreign demand for U.S. assets, stock prices might tumble and interest rates rise. United States-based banks and corporations would find it harder to buy foreign assets and expand overseas. The dollar has been in trouble before and, in the past, the U.S. government pressured other countries to buy or hold dollars and prop up its value. Whether other countries agree to this will depend, ultimately, on whether the United States and other major economic powers are still talking to one another.

INEQUALITY WORSENS ACROSS ASIA

BY JOHN MILLER

A report from the Asian Development Bank, comparing more than a decade's worth of data from 22 developing countries, found significant increases in inequality across the region [Asia].

But, as the ADB notes, this doesn't mean the rich are taking food from the mouths of the poor. Rather, the rich are getting richer faster than the poor are. In all but one developing country, per capita incomes for the bottom fifth of the work force increased at least slightly; Pakistan was the only exception.

Poverty remains a serious problem throughout Asia—the ADB estimates 600 million people still live below the $1-a-day line, to use one popular measure. But "fixing" inequality won't fix poverty. As even the ADB recognizes, inequality can be a symptom of economic growth.

While inequality of outcome can be a good thing, inequality of opportunity is another matter.

The ADB worries that too much of the good inequality can lead to the bad variety by entrenching a new set of self-interested elites.

The danger is that all this talk of "inequality" will lead to policies that, in the name of redistributing income, reduce economic growth and thus make it harder for Asia's poor to join the middle class. The Asian "pie" is growing for everyone. The challenge is to keep it that way, instead of quarreling over the relative size of the pieces.

—*Wall Street Journal* editorial, 8/21/07

When ideologues of global capitalism step out of line, who better to let them know about it than the editors of the *Wall Street Journal*, the keepers of the free-market flame?

Just ask the economists and policy wonks at the Asian Development Bank (ADB), financial capital's Manila-based outpost in East Asia, who had the temerity to report in August that increasing inequality was a serious problem for Asia's economies. The *Journal's* editors let them hear about it. "The danger," scolded the editors, "is that all this talk of 'inequality' will lead to policies that, in the name of redistributing income, reduce economic growth and thus make it harder for Asia's poor to join the middle class."

But the warning issued by the *Journal* editors is not just misleading, it is wrong. The evidence shows that countries that enjoy rapid economic growth are not more unequal than countries that grow slowly. In fact, a more equal distribution of income is not merely *compatible* with rapid growth; there are a number of avenues by which greater equality can actually *promote* growth. Finally, and most important for millions of people across Asia: poverty reduction depends on both raising a nation's income *and* reducing its inequality.

It is not that the ADB's bean counters got the numbers wrong. Of the 22 developing Asian economies in the ADB study, 15 saw inequality worsen since the early 1990s. That includes economic powerhouse China, where inequality worsened more rapidly and to higher levels than in any other country in the study other than Nepal. Even South Korea and Taiwan, once paragons of rapid *and* equitable growth, have seen inequality rise since 1993 .

Economists at the ADB tracked changes in the levels of inequality using Gini coefficients, economists' standard measure of economic inequality, in the 22 developing Asian countries for which there are sufficient data. The Gini coefficient ranges from zero to one: zero corresponds to perfect equality (every household has the same income), and one corresponds to maximal inequality (one household gets the entire national income). In the real world, Gini coefficients range from around 0.25 (Sweden, Denmark, Hungary) to nearly 0.60 (South Africa, Brazil, Haiti).

The ADB report found Gini coefficients rising across Asia. China's, for instance, rose from 0.41 in 1993 to 0.47 in 2004; it is now higher than that of the United States, 0.46 in 2004. (See Figure 1, which shows inequality levels by country, and Figure 2, which reports on changes in inequality levels.)

The trend toward a widening gap between the rich and poor in Asia is actually more alarming than even the ADB tables suggest. For one thing, the Asian financial crisis of the late 1990s sucked millions of dollars out of the caches of the continent's economic elites. Had it not been for this hit, Malaysia, Indonesia, and probably Thailand as well would have joined the worsening inequality column of the ADB report. Plus, the ADB tables rely on household expenditure data as opposed to the more difficult-to-obtain income data used in some countries to measure inequality. Inequality levels calculated from expenditure data are normally lower than those calculated from income data for the same population. In the Philippines, for example, where inequality data are available on both measures, the expenditure-based Gini coefficient is 0.40 for 2003, while the income-based figure is about 20% higher at 0.48.

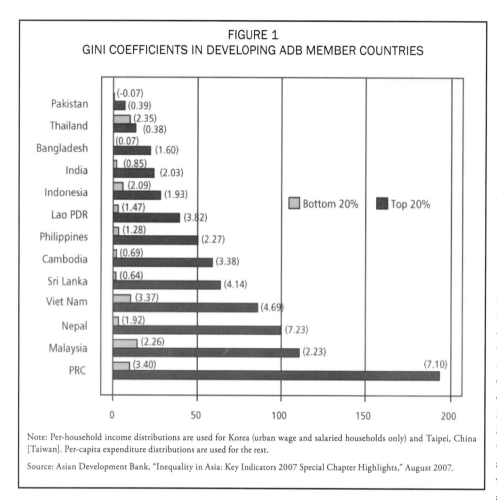

FIGURE 1
GINI COEFFICIENTS IN DEVELOPING ADB MEMBER COUNTRIES

Bottom 20%   Top 20%

Country	Bottom 20%	Top 20%
Pakistan	(-0.07)	(0.39)
Thailand	(2.35)	(0.38)
Bangladesh	(0.07)	(1.60)
India	(0.85)	(2.03)
Indonesia	(2.09)	(1.93)
Lao PDR	(1.47)	(3.82)
Philippines	(1.28)	(2.27)
Cambodia	(0.69)	(3.38)
Sri Lanka	(0.64)	(4.14)
Viet Nam	(3.37)	(4.69)
Nepal	(1.92)	(7.23)
Malaysia	(2.26)	(2.23)
PRC	(3.40)	(7.10)

Note: Per-household income distributions are used for Korea (urban wage and salaried households only) and Taipei, China [Taiwan]. Per-capita expenditure distributions are used for the rest.

Source: Asian Development Bank, "Inequality in Asia: Key Indicators 2007 Special Chapter Highlights," August 2007.

THE EAST ASIAN MIRACLE UNDER THE GUN

While inequality can be a symptom of economic growth in capitalist economies, as the editors argue, what is remarkable about many East Asian economies is that prior to the 1990s they grew rapidly with far lower levels of inequality than elsewhere in the developing world. In some cases they saw inequality decline rather than worsen. For instance, in South Korea inequality declined from 1976 to 1993 even as the country's economy grew rapidly, posting average growth rates of 7.5% a year. Compared to Brazil, Latin America's fastest growing economy of the period, South Korea grew twice as quickly—with about half of Brazil's level of inequality.

The World Bank's famous 1993 "East Asian Miracle" study celebrated East Asia's "remarkable record of high growth *and* declining inequality." (Emphasis in the original.) From 1965 to 1990 the 23 economies of East Asia grew faster than all other regions of the world, three times as fast as the economies of Latin America and the Caribbean. Rapid growth in the region was spearheaded by the miraculous growth of eight high-performance economies—Japan; the "Four Tigers," Hong Kong, South Korea, Singapore, and Taiwan; and the three newly industrializing economies of southeast Asia, Indonesia, Malaysia, and Thailand—in which inequality remained low or improved over the same period. Because they were "unusually successful at shar-

ing the fruits of growth," as the World Bank report put it, poverty declined rapidly and living conditions, from life expectancy to access to clean water and adequate shelter, improved dramatically in these high performance economies. A 1997 World Bank report went so far as to call rapid growth in East Asia "Everyone's Miracle."

"Everyone's" was surely an exaggeration even then. The editors of the *Wall Street Journal* nonetheless contend that today's much more unequal economic growth in Asia should still be considered everyone's miracle. As they read the ADB report, despite widening inequality, at least some of the benefits of the economic growth have trickled down to the poorest 20% of households in these economies. Since 1993 the expenditures of the bottom quintile increased in all of these 22 Asian economies with the exception of Pakistan, albeit by far less than the expenditures of the richest 20%. (See Figure 3.) "These increases in inequality are not a story of the 'rich getting richer and the poor getting poorer'," confirms the ADB report. "Rather it is the rich getting richer faster than the poor."

That is enough to qualify as "pro-poor growth," according to the editors' absolute definition of the term: economic growth that does anything at all to alleviate poverty, no matter now lopsidedly it benefits the well-to-do.

WHAT IS PRO-POOR GROWTH?

It is true that rapid economic growth usually does more to alleviate poverty than slower economic growth. But if inequality grows at the same time, then much of the poverty-fighting potential of rapid economic growth is being lost. In some sense it may be accurate to say that the rich are not taking food from the mouths of the poor—but it's just as accurate to say that the benefits of economic growth that might otherwise have ended up on the tables of the poor have instead gone to the rich.

The evidence is clear. Had levels of inequality only remained unchanged over the last decade in the 15 countries that suffered worsening inequality, they would have seen a dramatic difference in the numbers of their citizens lifted from poverty. The ADB report documents the large reductions in the percentage of the population living on less than $1 a day (a standard U.N. measure of poverty) that

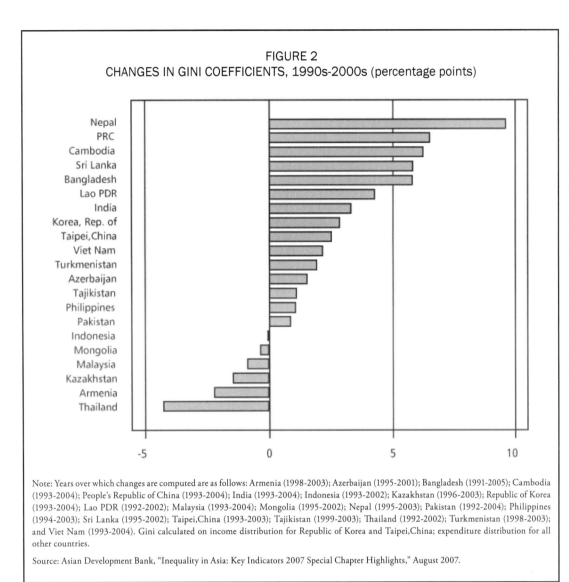

FIGURE 2
CHANGES IN GINI COEFFICIENTS, 1990s-2000s (percentage points)

Nepal
PRC
Cambodia
Sri Lanka
Bangladesh
Lao PDR
India
Korea, Rep. of
Taipei,China
Viet Nam
Turkmenistan
Azerbaijan
Tajikistan
Philippines
Pakistan
Indonesia
Mongolia
Malaysia
Kazakhstan
Armenia
Thailand

-5   0   5   10

Note: Years over which changes are computed are as follows: Armenia (1998-2003); Azerbaijan (1995-2001); Bangladesh (1991-2005); Cambodia (1993-2004); People's Republic of China (1993-2004); India (1993-2004); Indonesia (1993-2002); Kazakhstan (1996-2003); Republic of Korea (1993-2004); Lao PDR (1992-2002); Malaysia (1993-2004); Mongolia (1995-2002); Nepal (1995-2004); Pakistan (1992-2004); Philippines (1994-2003); Sri Lanka (1995-2002); Taipei,China (1993-2003); Tajikistan (1999-2003); Thailand (1992-2002); Turkmenistan (1998-2003); and Viet Nam (1993-2004). Gini calculated on income distribution for Republic of Korea and Taipei,China; expenditure distribution for all other countries.

Source: Asian Development Bank, "Inequality in Asia: Key Indicators 2007 Special Chapter Highlights," August 2007.

Chinese suffered worsening poverty as prices for farm products fell and rural output stagnated—even as the national economy was growing at double-digit rates.

While China's agricultural output subsequently picked up and poverty alleviation resumed, the widening gap between the economic standing of rural and urban Chinese continues to sap Chinese growth of its potential to ease poverty. Neglect of agriculture and of rural areas is a common feature that has contributed to rising inequality in many Asian economies; to improve the lot of the poor, the ADB recommends switching some public expenditures from urban to rural areas and from post-secondary education, which favors urban dwellers, to basic education, which is still not available to all, particularly in rural areas.

would have occurred had economic inequality not worsened. In China, the number would have been just about halved. (See Figure 4.)

By that standard, economic growth in most of these countries can hardly be considered pro-poor. Each percentage point of economic growth now does less to alleviate poverty than in the past. For instance, economists Hafiz Pasha and T. Palanivel found that national poverty in China fell 9.8% during both the 1980s and 1990s. But the economy needed a 9.0% per capita growth rate in the later decade, as opposed to a 7.8% rate in the earlier one, to effect the same reduction in poverty rates.

And contrary to the claims of the *Journal* editors, a widening difference between rich and poor can be, and at times has been, so great as to bring poverty alleviation to a halt altogether. In Thailand, for instance, the same 1993 World Bank study found that despite growth rates averaging 6.4% a year from 1975 to 1986, poverty rates *increased* over the same period. Rural Thais were hard hit by the falling prices of farm products, and economic differences between urban and rural dwellers widened. Similarly, between 1984 and 1991, rural

TACKLING POVERTY AND INEQUALITY

Neglecting to address inequality surely can compromise even the most dynamic economy's ability to fix poverty. That is not to say that fixing inequality alone will fix poverty. But there is now plenty of reason to believe that fixing inequality can enhance economic growth at the same time that it fights poverty. And contrary to the editors' admonishment, the ADB's talk about inequality might help lift the 600 million Asians who still live on less than a dollar a day out of poverty.

Today, even some mainstream economists are moving beyond the notion that rising inequality is necessary during developing countries' initial periods of rapid growth to establish the incentives to work, save, and invest. The record of the East Asian miracle economies provided an important

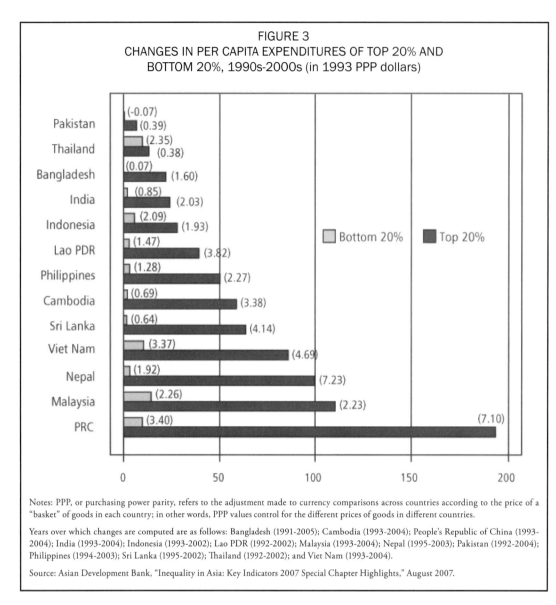

FIGURE 3
CHANGES IN PER CAPITA EXPENDITURES OF TOP 20% AND BOTTOM 20%, 1990s-2000s (in 1993 PPP dollars)

Notes: PPP, or purchasing power parity, refers to the adjustment made to currency comparisons across countries according to the price of a "basket" of goods in each country; in other words, PPP values control for the different prices of goods in different countries.

Years over which changes are computed are as follows: Bangladesh (1991-2005); Cambodia (1993-2004); People's Republic of China (1993-2004); India (1993-2004); Indonesia (1993-2002); Lao PDR (1992-2002); Malaysia (1993-2004); Nepal (1995-2003); Pakistan (1992-2004); Philippines (1994-2003); Sri Lanka (1995-2002); Thailand (1992-2002); and Viet Nam (1993-2004).

Source: Asian Development Bank, "Inequality in Asia: Key Indicators 2007 Special Chapter Highlights," August 2007.

land more intensively than large landholders.

The ADB acknowledges several of these arguments. For instance, in the Beijing news conference launching the report, Ifzal Ali, the ADB's chief economist, called the rise in inequality in Asia today "a clear and present danger to the sustained growth," and warned that growing inequality could in some countries lead to "greater social conflict, from street demonstrations to violent civil wars."

Nonetheless, the ADB was not about to embrace massive redistribution policies that would dull market incentives. They do, however, endorse redistributive policies targeted at promoting "equality of opportunity" and "funded through mechanisms that do not detract from economic growth." Chief among their recommended polices are putting more public moneys into rural infrastructure including irrigation, electricity, transportation, and agricultural extension services, as well as expanding access to basic health care and primary education.

These measures are generally uncontroversial—although that does not mean they will be adopted any time soon. They would surely help. But they would be unlikely to arrest the widening inequality of the current period. To do that, public policy must also address the big picture: the decline in labor's share of the economic pie that corporate-led globalization has brought about.

Greater openness to trade, as economist Dani Rodrik has argued, erodes the bargaining power of labor by exposing workers, especially unskilled workers, to the competition of having their services replaced by imports from abroad.

Beyond that, export-led growth in many developing economies has failed to bring on the expected boom in

exemplar of simultaneous rapid growth *and* low or declining inequality.

In recent years, economists and other social scientists have developed several explanations of how greater equality can in fact promote economic growth. More equal economies have more political stability, grant greater access to credit, spend more on education, and have more widespread land ownership than economies racked by inequality—each a factor that contributes to economic growth. Relative equality eases the social discontents and political conflicts that would otherwise discourage foreign investment and hamper economic growth. A more equal distribution of income allows the poor, who pay much higher interest rates than the rich in many developing countries, greater access to credit, adding to their personal investments and promoting economic growth. In relatively equal societies, more families have the savings necessary to send their children to school—obviously a spur to growth. And land reform, a key policy for reducing inequality in South Korea and Taiwan, raises agricultural productivity because small farmers cultivate their

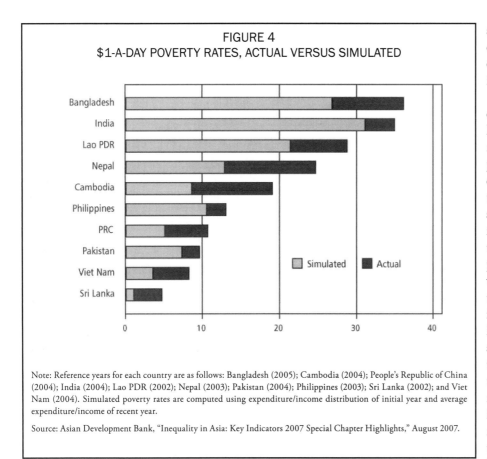

FIGURE 4
$1-A-DAY POVERTY RATES, ACTUAL VERSUS SIMULATED

Bangladesh
India
Lao PDR
Nepal
Cambodia
Philippines
PRC
Pakistan
Viet Nam
Sri Lanka

☐ Simulated   ■ Actual

0   10   20   30   40

Note: Reference years for each country are as follows: Bangladesh (2005); Cambodia (2004); People's Republic of China (2004); India (2004); Lao PDR (2002); Nepal (2003); Pakistan (2004); Philippines (2003); Sri Lanka (2002); and Viet Nam (2004). Simulated poverty rates are computed using expenditure/income distribution of initial year and average expenditure/income of recent year.

Source: Asian Development Bank, "Inequality in Asia: Key Indicators 2007 Special Chapter Highlights," August 2007.

manufacturing employment. As manufacturing exports from these countries increased with greater openness, so too did the quantity of manufactured goods imported into their domestic markets. So while export expansion was adding jobs, other jobs were being lost because of import penetration. Moreover, the new export industries are typically less labor-intensive than the older industries they replace. In China, for instance, relatively labor-saving joint ventures and foreign-owned firms in the country's new export zones have taken the place of relatively more labor-intensive state-owned manufacturing firms.

As a result, export promotion has done little to tighten labor markets and thereby improve labor's bargaining power. In the most detailed study to date, economists J. Felipe and G. Sipin found that in the Philippines, labor's share of national income fell by 6 percentage points from 1980 to 2002 as its economy globalized.

The case of China is also instructive, as economic sociologists Peter Evans and Sarah Staveteig point out. According to official statistics, manufacturing employment in China, the world's workshop, increased steadily from 1978 to 1995, nearly doubling from 53 million to 98 million jobs. But since then Chinese employment in manufacturing has fallen off. Manufacturing's share of Chinese employment has actually declined for nearly two decades now, even as China's share of world manufactured exports has increased more than fivefold.

With the manufacturing share of Chinese employment stagnant, hundreds of millions of people currently dependent on agricultural production for their incomes must either stay in that sector or move to the service sector. Both options suggest increased inequality and a more precarious quality of life for the vast majority of the Chinese population, argue Evans and Staveteig. If they stay in agriculture, the Chinese peasantry are likely to face stagnating incomes. A move into the service sector would allow a few new entrants to gain access to the more lucrative service jobs, but the vast majority will find poorly remunerated, insecure jobs offering personal services as the nannies, maids, drivers, and gardeners that their luckier compatriots will be able to hire.

While this widening inequality in the very countries that not long ago served as exemplars of growth with equality might not present a problem to the editors of the Wall Street Journal, it surely is a serious problem, as even the ADB acknowledges. But genuinely pro-poor economic growth will only come about when public policy confronts the current rules of the global economy— rules that the editors are so dedicated to defending, and that the ADB itself is reluctant to challenge.

Resources: Asian Development Bank, *Key Indicators 2007, Part 1: Inequality in Asia,* August 2007; "Inequality Check," *Wall Street Journal* editorial, 8/21/07; Richard McGregor, "ADB warns on rising inequality in China," *Financial Times,* 8/08/07; Alan Wheatley, "Rising inequality danger for Asia, says ADB," Reuters, 08/08/07; "For whosoever hath, to him shall be given, and he shall have more: Income inequality in emerging Asia is heading towards Latin American levels," *The Economist,* 8/09/07; World Bank, "The East Asian Miracle: Economic Growth and Public Policy," 1993; Vinod Ahuja et al., "Everyone's Miracle," World Bank, 1997; Peter Evans and Sarah Staveteig, "Late 20th Century Industrialization and Changing Employment Structures in the Global South," Univ. of Calif. Berkeley, 8/22/07; Hafiz A. Pasha and T. Palanivel, "Pro-Poor Growth and Policies: The Asian Experience," U.N. Development Programme, 2004; Judith Banister, "Manufacturing Employment in China," *Monthly Labor Review,* July 2005.

DOLLAR ANXIETY

BY JOHN MILLER

The value of the dollar is falling. Does that mean that our economic sky is falling as well? Not to sound like Chicken Little, but the answer may well be yes. If an economic collapse is not in our future, then at least economic storm clouds are gathering on the horizon.

It's what lies behind the slide of the dollar that has even many mainstream economists spooked: an unprecedented current account deficit—the difference between the country's income and its consumption and investment spending. The current account deficit, which primarily reflects the huge gap between the amount the United States imports and the amount it exports, is the best indicator of where the country stands in its financial relationship with the rest of the world.

At an estimated $670 billion, or 5.7% of gross domestic product (GDP), the 2004 current account deficit is the largest ever. An already huge trade deficit (the amount exports fall short of imports) made worse by high oil prices, along with rock bottom private savings and a gaping federal budget deficit, have helped push the U.S. current account deficit into uncharted territory. The last time it was above 4% of GDP was in 1816, and no other country has ever run a current account deficit that equals nearly 1% of the world's GDP. If current trends continue, the gap could reach 7.8% of U.S. GDP by 2008, according to Nouriel Roubini of New York University and Brad Setser of University College, Oxford, two well-known finance economists.

Most of the current account deficit stems from the U.S. trade deficit (about $610 billion). The rest reflects the remittances immigrants send home to their families plus U.S. foreign aid (together another $80 billion) less net investment income (a positive $20 billion because the United States still earns more from investments abroad than it pays out in interest on its borrowing from abroad).

The current account deficit represents the amount of money the United States must attract from abroad each year. Money comes from overseas in two ways: foreign investors can buy stock in U.S. corporations, or they can lend money to corporations or to the government by buying bonds. Currently, almost all of the money must come from loans because European and Japanese investors are no longer buying U.S. stocks. U.S. equity returns have been trivial since 2000 in dollar terms and actually negative in euro terms since the dollar has lost ground against the euro.

In essence, the U.S. economy racks up record current account deficits by spending more than its national income to feed its appetite for imports that are now half again exports.

That increases the supply of dollars in foreign hands.

At the same time, the demand for dollars has diminished. Foreign investors are less interested in purchasing dollar-dominated assets as they hold more of them (and as the self-fulfilling expectation that the value of the dollar is likely to fall sets in). In October 2004 (the most recent data available), net foreign purchases of U.S. securities—stocks and bonds—dipped to their lowest level in a year and below what was necessary to offset the current account deficit. In addition, global investors' stock and bond portfolios are now overloaded with dollar-denominated assets, up to 50% from 30% in the early '90s.

Under the weight of the massive current account deficit, the dollar has already begun to give way. Since January 2002, the value of the dollar has fallen more than 20%, with much of that dropoff happening since August 2004. The greenback now stands at multiyear lows against the euro, the yen, and an index of major currencies.

Should foreign investors stop buying U.S. securities, then the dollar will crash, stock values plummet, and an economic downturn surely follow. But even if foreigners continue to purchase U.S. bonds—and they already hold 47% of U.S Treasury bonds—a current account deficit of this magnitude will be a costly drag on the economy. The Fed will have to boost interest rates, which determine the rate of return on U.S. bonds, to compensate for their lost value as the dollar slips in value and to keep foreigners coming back for more. In addition, a falling dollar makes imports cost more, pushing up U.S inflation rates. The Fed will either tolerate the uptick in inflation or attempt to counteract it by raising interest rates yet higher. Even in this more orderly scenario of decline, the current expansion will slow or perhaps come to a halt.

IMPERIAL FINANCE

You can still find those who claim none of this is a problem. Recently, for example, the editors of the *Wall Street Journal* offered worried readers the following relaxation technique—a version of what former Treasury Secretary Larry Summers says is the sharpest argument you typically hear from a finance minister whose country is saddled with a large current account deficit.

First, recall that a large trade deficit requires a large surplus of capital flowing into your country to cover it. Then ask yourself, would you rather live in a country that continues to attract investment, or one that capital is trying to get out of? Finally, remind yourself that the monetary authorities control the value of currencies and are fully capable of halting the decline.

Feel better? You shouldn't. Arguments like these are unconvincing, a bravado borne not of postmodern cool so much as the old-fashioned, unilateral financial imperialism that underlies the muscular U.S. foreign policy we see today.

True, so far foreigners have been happy to purchase the gobs of debt issued by the U.S. Treasury and corporate America to cover the current account deficit. And that has kept U.S. interest rates low. If not for the flood of foreign money, Morgan Stanley economist Stephen Roach figures, U.S. long-term interest rates would be between one and 1.5 percentage points higher today.

The ability to borrow without pushing up interest rates has paid off handsomely for the Bush administration. Now when the government spends more than it takes in to prosecute the war in Iraq and bestow tax cuts on the rich, savers from foreign shores finance those deficits at reduced rates. And cash-strapped U.S. consumers are more ready to swallow an upside-down economic recovery that has pushed up profit but neither created jobs nor lifted wages when they can borrow at low interest rates.

How can the United States get away with running up debt at low rates? Are other countries' central banks and private savers really the co-dependent "global enablers" Roach and others call them, who happily hold loads of low-yielding U.S. assets? The truth is, the United States has taken advantage of the status of the dollar as the currency of the global economy to make others adjust to its spending patterns. Foreign central banks hold their reserves in dollars, and countries are billed in dollars for their oil imports, which requires them to buy dollars. That sustains the demand for the dollar and protects its value even as the current account imbalance widens.

The U.S. strong dollar policy in the face of its yawning current account deficit imposes a "shadow tax" on the rest of the world, at least in part to pay for its cost of empire. "But payment," as Robert Skidelsky, the British biographer of Keynes, reminds us, "is voluntary and depends at minimum on acquiescence in U.S. foreign policy." The geopolitical reason for the rest of the capitalist world to accept the "seigniorage of the dollar"—in other words, the advantage the United States enjoys by virtue of minting the reserve currency of the international economy—became less compelling when the United States substituted a "puny war on terrorism" for the Cold War, Skidelsky adds.

The tax does not fall only on other industrialized countries. The U.S. economy has not just become a giant vacuum cleaner that sucks up "all the world's spare investible cash," in the words of University of California, Berkeley economist Brad DeLong, but about one-third of that money comes from the developing world. To put this contribution in perspective: DeLong calculates that $90 billion a year, or one-third of the average U.S. current account deficit over the last two decades, is equal to the income of the poorest 500 million people in India.

The rest of the world ought not to complain about these global imbalances, insist the strong dollar types. That the

IF THE UNITED STATES WAS AN EMERGING MARKET

If the United States was a small or less-developed country, financial alarm bells would already be ringing. The U.S. current account deficit is well above the 5%-of-GDP standard the IMF and others use to pronounce economies in the developing world vulnerable to financial crisis.

Just how crisis-prone depends on how the current account deficit affects the economy's spending. If the foreign funds flowing into the country are being invested in export-producing sectors of the economy, or the tradable goods sectors, such as manufacturing and some services, they are likely over time to generate revenues necessary to pay back the rest of the world. In that case, the shortfall is less of a problem. If those monies go to consumption or speculative investment in non-tradable (i.e., non-export producing) sectors such as a real estate, then they surely will be a problem.

By that standard, the U.S. current account deficit is highly problematic. Economists assess the impact of a current account deficit by comparing it to the difference between net national investment and net national savings. (Net here means less the money set aside to cover depreciation.) In the U.S. case, that difference has widened because saving has plummeted, not because investment has picked up. Last year, the United States registered its lowest net national savings rate ever, 1.5%, due to the return of large federal budget deficits and anemic personal savings. In addition, U.S. investment has shifted substantially away from tradable goods as manufacturing has come under heavy foreign competition toward the non-traded goods sector, such as residential real estate whose prices have soared in and around most major American cities.

Capital inflows that cover a decline in savings instead of a surge in investment are not a sign of economic health nor cause to stop worrying about the current account deficit.

United States racks up debt while other countries rack up savings is not profligacy but a virtue. The United States, they argue, is the global economy's "consumer of last resort." Others, especially in Europe, according to U.S. policymakers, are guilty of "insufficient consumption": they hold back their economies and dampen the demand for U.S. exports, exacerbating the U.S. current account deficit. Last year U.S. consumers increased their spending three times as quickly as European consumers (excluding Britain), and the U.S. economy grew about two and half times as quickly.

GLOBAL UPRISING

Not surprisingly, old Europe and newly industrializing Asia don't see it that way. They have grown weary from all their heavy lifting of U.S. securities. And while they have yet to throw them overboard, a revolt is brewing.

Those cranky French are especially indignant about the unfairness of it all. The editors of Le Monde, the French daily, complain that "The United States considers itself innocent: it refuses to admit that it lives beyond its means through weak savings and excessive consumption." On top of that, the drop of the dollar has led to a brutal rise in the value of the euro that is wiping out the demand for euro-zone exports and slowing their already sluggish economic recoveries.

Even in Blair's Britain the Economist, the newsweekly, ran an unusually tough-minded editorial warning: "The dollar's role as the leading international currency can no longer be taken for granted. ... Imagine if you could write checks that were accepted as payment but never cashed. That is what [the privileged position of the dollar] amounts to. If you had been granted that ability, you might take care to hang to it. America is taking no such care. And may come to regret it."

But the real threat comes from Asia, especially Japan and China, the two largest holders of U.S. Treasury bonds. Asian central banks already hold most of their reserves in dollar-denominated assets, an enormous financial risk given that the value of the dollar will likely continue to fall at current low interest rates.

In late November, just the rumor that China's Central Bank threatened to reduce its purchases of U.S. Treasury bonds was enough to send the dollar tumbling.

No less than Alan Greenspan, chair of the Fed, seems to have come down with a case of dollar anxiety. In his November remarks to the European Banking Community, Greenspan warned of a "diminished appetite for adding to dollar balances" even if the current account deficit stops increasing. Greenspan believes that foreign investors are likely to realize they have put too many of their eggs in the dollar basket and will either unload their dollar-denominated investments or demand higher interest rates. After Greenspan spoke, the dollar fell to its lowest level against the Japanese yen in more than four years.

A ROUGH RIDE FROM HERE

The question that divides economists at this point is not whether the dollar will decline more, but whether the descent will be slow and orderly or quick and panicky. Either way, there is real reason to believe it will be a rough ride.

First, a controlled devaluation of the dollar won't be easy to accomplish. Several major Asian currencies are formally or informally pegged to the dollar, including the Chinese yuan. The United States faces a $160 billion trade deficit with China alone. U.S. financial authorities have exerted tremendous pressure on the Chinese to raise the value of their currency, in the hope of slowing the tide of Chinese imports into the United States and making U.S. exports more competitive. But the Chinese have yet to budge.

Beyond that, a fall in the dollar sufficient to close the current account deficit will slaughter large amounts of capital. The Economist warns that "[i]f the dollar falls by another 30%, as some predict, it would amount to the biggest default in history: not a conventional default on debt service, but default by stealth, wiping trillions off the value of foreigners' dollar assets."

Even a gradual decline in the value of dollar will bring tough economic consequences. Inflation will pick up, as imports cost more in this bid to make U.S. exports cheaper. The Fed will surely raise interest rates to counteract that inflationary pressure, slowing consumer borrowing and investment. Also, closing the current account deficit would require smaller government deficits. (Although not politically likely, repealing Bush's pro-rich tax cuts would help.)

What will happen is anyone's guess given the unprecedented size of the U.S. current account deficit. But there is a real possibility that the dollar's slide will be anything but slow or orderly. Should Asian central banks stop intervening on the scale needed to finance the U.S. deficit, then a crisis surely would follow. The dollar would drop through the floor; U.S. interest rates would skyrocket (on everything from Treasury bonds to mortgages to credit cards); the stock market and home values would collapse; consumer and investment spending would plunge; and a sharp recession would take hold here and abroad.

The Bush administration seems determined to make things worse. Should the Bush crew push through their plan to privatize Social Security and pay the trillion-dollar transition cost with massive borrowing, the consequences could be disastrous. The example of Argentina is instructive. Privatizing the country's retirement program, as economist Paul Krugman has pointed out, was a major source of the debt that brought on Argentina's crisis in 2001. Dismantling the U.S. welfare state's most successful program just might push the dollar-based financial system over the edge.

The U.S. economy is in a precarious situation held together so far by imperial privilege. Its prospects appear to fall into one of three categories: a dollar crisis; a long, slow, excruciating decline in value of the dollar; or a dollar propped up through repeated interest rates hikes. That's real reason to worry.

Resources: "Dollar Anxiety," editorial, *Wall Street Journal*, 11/11/04; D. Wessel, "Behind Big Drop in Currency: U.S. Soaks Up Asia's Output," *WSJ*, 12/2/04; J. B. DeLong, "Should We Still Support Untrammeled International Capital Mobility? Or are Capital Controls Less Evil than We Once Believed," *Economists' Voice*, 2004; R. Skidelsky, "U.S. Current Account Deficit and Future of the World Monetary System" and N. Roubini and B. Setser "The U.S. as A Net Debtor: The Sustainability of the U.S. External Imbalances," 11/04, Nouriel Roubini's Global Macroeconomic and Financial Policy site <www.stern.nyu.edu/globalmacro>; Rich Miller, "Why the Dollar is Giving Way," *Business Week*, 12/6/04; Robert Barro, "Mysteries of the Gaping Current-Account Gap," *Business Week*, 12/13/04; D. Streitford and J. Fleishman, "Greenspan Issues Warning on Dollar," *L.A. Times*, 11/20/04; S. Roach, "Global: What Happens If the Dollar Does Not Fall?" Global Economic Forum, Morgan Stanley, 11/22/04; L. Summers, "The U.S. Current Account Deficit and the Global Economy," The 2004 Per Jacobsson Lecture, 10/3/04; "The Dollar," editorial, *The Economist*, 12/3/04; "Mr. Gaymard and the Dollar," editorial, *Le Monde*, 11/30/04.

THE SOCIAL COST OF NEOLIBERALISM IN CHINA
INTERVIEW WITH ECONOMIST HAN DEQIANG

BY STEPHEN PHILION

Han Deqiang is a prolific economist at the Economics and Management School, Beijing University of Aeronautics and Astronautics, and one of a growing number of Chinese scholars critical of the country's neoliberal development strategy. Han, however, did not just arrive at this stance. He has been critical of neoliberal ideology in China for almost two decades and has written many books and articles on the social crises that rural and urban workers have faced under China's new economic regime.

When I first met Han, in 2000, he was making his way around the country delivering sharp and eloquent lectures to university students refuting the then-dominant faith. At the time, I was conducting research on workers' protests against privatization in Zhengzhou, and most of the labor activists and workers' leaders I met were familiar with Han's devastating critiques of the privatization craze that swept China in the late 1990s and early 2000s. It would not be wrong to characterize him as a Chinese Noam Chomsky, albeit with his own oratorical flair!

In September 2005, I interviewed Han for about three hours. Our discussion focused on the impact of China's 2001 entry into the World Trade Organization and on the social costs, both in and outside of China, of the accelerated neoliberal development that followed that milestone. In January 2007, I followed up with a second interview. What follows is a translated and edited version of both interviews.

STEPHEN PHILION: The last time I met with you was during the height of the East Asian financial crisis. At that time, we discussed the consequences you foresaw for China of entering the World Trade Organization (WTO). Five years later, which of those consequences have come about?

HAN DEQIANG: At the time, I argued the greatest damage would be to China's capacity to control its industrial and technological development autonomously. I think it's safe to say these last five years have more than proven that true. In China, any industry that wants to develop its own technology or markets has encountered increasingly great barriers.

Second, I predicted that unemployment would rise dramatically; this has also shown itself to be a reality. Of course, some say that there has been a shortage of migrant workers from the countryside recently, which allegedly proves that the WTO has not produced greater unemployment. But this requires a more careful analysis. In the late 1990s, agricultural commodity prices fell, and taxes became heavier. Hence the large mass of migrant workers and the ensuing rise in urban unemployment we saw then. However, starting around 2002-2003, the government implemented new tax cuts for farmers and increased education subsidies in poor rural districts. As a result of these new policies, the contradictions in the countryside were mollified some. Also, when the price of rice plummeted, large numbers of farmers stopped producing it. As a result, the price rebounded, improving the livelihood of farmers in 2003 and 2004. So rural dwellers now had less motivation to accept the kind of exploitation that exists in the for-export sector of urban industry, much less migrate to the cities in search of it! However, this doesn't nullify our argument that when foreign companies conquer national industries, greater unemployment results. The opposite actually. When Wal-Mart goes to Gweiyang or Beijing, say, they knock out, in an instant, four or five department stores.[1]

PHILION: And smaller shops?

HAN: Hah! Don't even go there! Medium-size department stores, neighborhood sellers, ones that were supposed to be able to dominate local markets by virtue of their size—they saw those advantages disappear.

Third, I have always acknowledged that WTO entry would provide China certain short-term gains. For example, increases in investment and exports undoubtedly occurred. But I argued that WTO entry was the equivalent of drinking moonshine to deal with thirst. This has two outcomes. One, of course, is the removal of thirst. After all, if there are no other liquids around, I have no choice but to turn to moonshine. But the other result, of course, is your death!

---

1   *By 2006, there were already more than 50 Wal-Mart stores in China.*

So Chinese industry has resolved its investment problem, but that has been accompanied by its death knell.

From what I see, the social crisis facing China will continue to intensify, as will the neglect of China's economic autonomy, in addition to the eventual breakdown of the country's financial system. This is entirely foreseeable; it's only a matter of time before China faces something along the lines of the 1997 East Asian financial crisis. We cannot predict exactly when it will occur, but I suspect it isn't that far off in the future.

PHILION: How has the WTO affected large state-owned enterprises?

HAN: State-owned enterprises (SOEs) fall into two categories. The first are SOEs, like Shenyang Machine Factory or Luoyang Tractor Company, that are subject to competition with private companies. These quickly went bankrupt. Monopoly-sector SOEs, such as petroleum producers, are less directly affected by China's membership in the WTO.

PHILION: The Chinese leadership seems to be working under the assumption that as long as the SOEs that produce the greatest revenues remain vital, Chinese socialism can be sustained.

HAN: First of all, China's not socialist now.

PHILION: Yes, right. I mean in their sense of the phrase, so-called "socialism with Chinese characteristics."

HAN: Not likely either. It is true that in terms of tax contributions and profits, the small and medium-size SOEs are not great, but in the absolute numbers they employ, they are considerable. Their influence on local employment and finances is pretty substantial. So, in the aftermath of the near complete collapse of these small and medium-size SOEs, for the central state to rely on large enterprises alone for maintaining the subsistence of China's population of 1.3 billion becomes extremely difficult.

PHILION: It seems as though the leadership's hope is for local and foreign private capital to replace these small and medium-size companies as the source of investment and to resolve the unemployment problem in the process.

HAN: What I would contend is that for every one job saved by foreign capitalist investment, three to four will be lost unless the foreign investment produces for foreign export alone. This situation does exist, assuredly. Right now 60% of our export is fueled by foreign companies' investment. However, the potential for foreign investment to instigate future Chinese economic growth is weak. It can only largely resolve a segment of the unemployment problem. It can't do much in terms of advancing the upgrading or expansion of China's industrial system.

And its use to resolve the fiscal crisis facing China is even more problematic. From '49 on, we built our nation by using state enterprise to supplement or replace foreign enterprise's contribution to the economy. The idea of doing the opposite is a fantasy.

PHILION: China's leaders also seem to believe that as long as the monopoly-based state-owned enterprises are run well, their ability to determine the direction of the economic development will be strong.

HAN: This is a twofold issue. First, whether or not it's possible for the political leadership of a country with no state-owned enterprise to control the direction of the national economy. I think it might be possible. It's the European model, after all, and even in a certain way the American model. In these economies, by and large, control of enterprises is in the hands of private parties. But this doesn't have that much impact on the state's tax receipts and its role in regulating the economy. If the state is powerful, it can play a crucial role in the management of the economy even if it doesn't control much enterprise.

On the other hand, where the state controls a major portion of enterprises but is weak, it has a difficult time managing the economy. And if the collaboration between that weak state and private interests is deep, the result is distortion of policy by capitalists to the point that the state loses more and more capacity to control the economy and the direction of economic development. The key factor here is the strength of the government, not how many companies it controls.

PHILION: Then what is the likelihood of China going in the direction of Japan developmentally?

HAN: I don't think it's possible for China to go that route. The leadership doesn't even have that as a working concept. The Japanese experience is one that greatly emphasizes the role of state planning.

PHILION: Interesting, because the U.S. government complains that China still places too much emphasis on central planning in the economy.

HAN: America likewise is dissatisfied with Japan's level of state planning. America is also dissatisfied with France in this respect. [Laughs.] Is there any country that America is satisfied with? Seriously, today the role of the state and of monopoly SOEs is far greater in Japan than in China. Also, from what I understand of Japanese history, Japan has an elite that has a strong sense of responsibility for the nation's future. But I can't find any such elite in China today. If Japan's leaders lose a war, they feel great shame. They don't send their children off to America.

PHILION: What is your assessment of how different classes view the WTO and liberalization in China?

HAN: Chinese workers and farmers are in a pickle. But is it the damage caused by political power elites or that caused by markets that is greatest? Right now, in their view the pain caused by entry into the WTO is not as great as that caused by the power of government cadres. For example, state workers view layoffs as only indirectly caused by markets; the abuse of power by the Party is viewed as their direct cause.

PHILION: Of course they're interconnected.

HAN: That's right. Domestically it's a matter of a corrupt officialdom; internationally it's a matter of submitting to the will of international capital. The WTO represents international capital's control over China. But of course it is Chinese government policies that make this control possible. So what the masses experience is a problem created by their government, not by the WTO or global monopoly capital.

For example, state workers have to pay income tax once their wages exceed 800 yuan a month. But a worker in a foreign-owned enterprise does not have to pay the tax until after 2,000 or 3,000 yuan a month. This government tax policy results in a positive feeling toward foreign-owned companies on the part of the average Chinese worker. They don't see that the better wages and better profits in the private sector are a product of the government support that sector enjoys. Not to mention many other kinds of special benefits that foreign capitalists enjoy thanks to government policies that simultaneously disadvantage domestic state companies. The ironic result is that many state companies go to Hong Kong and falsely register as foreign companies in order to enjoy these advantageous policies—the so-called fake foreign devil problem.

PHILION: In the past few years, have these views changed at all?

HAN: There has been some change in attitude, yes—especially in terms of recognizing the threat that WTO entry poses to China's future. So the push for economic autonomy is a theme that you now see cropping up in every Chinese web discussion board, far more than five years ago.

PHILION: You've spoken about the kinds of losses that have befallen China upon entering the WTO. In the United States we hear the same concerns, only it's America that is considered to be the victim of China's entry into the WTO! This is so especially in terms of unemployment: it is frequently said that China should be held responsible for America's unemployment problems.

HAN: To be accurate, we should say that America's bosses need to take responsibility for America's unemployment problems. Why? Because since China entered the WTO, both China's workers and America's workers have been hurt. However, in fact, many bosses in China have also suffered losses due to the WTO. The operation of the WTO causes great losses to both workers *and* bosses in developing countries as well as to workers in developed countries. Broadly speaking, only one group doesn't suffer losses, namely, bosses in developed countries. So to get to the source of the United States' unemployment problem, Americans need to analyze the responsibility of the Bush administration, the bosses at GM and Microsoft, etc.

PHILION: Not to mention the Democratic Party!

HAN: Indeed. Whoever is promoting the WTO is promoting the interests of transnational corporations and doing harm to American and Chinese workers. It's not only developing countries' workers who are hurt by globalization; it's really the world. Globalization gives rise to global recession, not prosperity. Consider a number of indicators that demonstrate this. Globally, debt levels have increased since the 1980s, in terms of both national debt and average citizens' credit overload. Second, the whole world exists in a state of high unemployment. The U.S. unemployment rate is much higher than it was in the 1950s and 1960s. Ditto Europe, whose unemployment rate is even higher! Japan likewise. Third, growth rates have fallen globally compared to those in the 1950s and 1960s. This, of course, is hidden by large rates of credit-fuelled debt, without which growth rates would be even lower. All of this indicates global recession, not global prosperity.

PHILION: What about China's economy? Its promoters argue that liberalization has generated constant growth.

HAN: In the 1990s, China and the United States both grew. However, look at the overall global economic picture. Latin America has seen great declines in growth and serious crises; Africa even worse. The Middle East is in a state of chaos and misfortune, Russia's GDP is only half of what it was in the 1980s, and the East Asian "tigers" have been in a state of recession since the region's financial crisis. Japan's debt in proportion to GDP is the highest in the world, roughly 130%, and its rate of growth has been somewhere near zero. If the government hadn't invested so much in the economy, it's possible Japan's rate of growth would be negative, -4% or -5%! If this isn't depression, what is?

Thus, my definition of globalization is global depression. This departs, of course, from mainstream propaganda. Even many of the anti-globalization movements are fond of arguing that globalization still has its positive points, that it just needs to take into account and protect the interests of developing countries and of workers in developed countries. It's as though if we just removed some of the shortcomings of the process, all would be well. My view is that globalization is nothing short of a massive mistake.

PHILION: In the United States, especially but not solely in the Democratic Party, there's a common notion that the U.S. government must implement economic sanctions against China and pursue higher tariffs in order to protect American jobs. So, for example, Rep. Charles Schumer (D-N.Y.) recently asserted that the conditions China sets for foreign investors aren't as good as those the United States provides for Chinese importers.

HAN: That's quite the exaggeration, eh? Laughable! It's actually the exact opposite. American corporations have enjoyed such high profits in China. Which is in the better position to buy up a company abroad, China or the United States? The benefits China gives to U.S. investments in terms of tax breaks, reductions in land prices, and the like are the kinds of things a Chinese investor in the United States can only dream about. And in terms of volume, Chinese investment in the United States is small in comparison to what it's imagined to be by Schumer types. His words are typical politician rhetoric.

In any event, I welcome America protecting its own markets. Likewise, I can declare American commodities unwelcome in China, along with American investment. If the countries of the world stopped welcoming U.S. investment, watch and see how long America could stand it! Its empire would erode quickly! Its existence is dependent on foreign investment and foreign consumption of its exports in order to maintain a higher standard of living.

PHILION: How much influence will a recession or a worse crisis in the United States have on China? It seems as if China is more and more able to withstand the impact.

HAN: Well, I would say rather that if America catches a cold, China will catch a very serious cold or flu. The United States is still the main market for China's exports. An economic crisis in the United States would definitely result in large numbers of bankruptcies throughout China's coastal regions. And if a U.S. crisis caused the value of the dollar to drop, that would also have a huge impact on the Chinese economy because the real size of the U.S. debt would decrease, as would China's foreign exchange holdings. It would basically mean all our hard work in the service of American profits was a waste.

PHILION: How do you regard the possibility of revaluing the renminbi [the official name of China's currency, abbreviated RMB]?

HAN: To date we haven't seen a real revaluation, only a very small one. The pressure in China against revaluation is huge. Why? If we revalue the RMB upwards, China's exports will be less competitively priced, and the strategy of relying on foreign exports for development will fall apart. I suspect

America's leadership wants us to devalue the currency by 20% or 30%. Or at the very least 10%. But even at 10%, the export companies in the coastal provinces would face a crisis of survival.

Of course, U.S. pressure on China to revalue is great. If the U.S. government is not willing to compromise on this issue, Chinese leaders will have a hard time dealing with the political discontent that would result. And if Chinese exports can't go to America, but American imports continue apace, the cycle of trade that makes China's development possible will not last. The United States simultaneously wants to reduce imports in order to protect its markets *and* open up more markets in China that it can export to. Short-term, that's possible; long-term, forget it.

PHILION: But in any case the reliance is mutual, no? The United States is quite reliant on cheap Chinese imports.

HAN: Yes, but American reliance on China is not as great as Chinese reliance on America's economy. Why is that? China's exports are low relative to overall U.S. imports, whereas China's exports to the United States are high in relation to total Chinese exports. Furthermore, American exports to China tend to be those that are less replicable. But what China produces can be produced in almost any country. Thus, when China negotiates, it's from a weaker position.

American politicians are shortsighted. Too much power is concentrated in U.S. hands now, and they don't wish to let other hands in on that control. They don't even take into consideration the needs of foreign leaders who collaborate on behalf of U.S. interests abroad. If American politicians continue like this, they won't have any collaborators left—they'll all be overthrown! What good is that in the eyes of the American ruling class, eh? [Laughs.] So if U.S. leaders really want to extend America's capacity to exploit the world's resources, they're going to have to learn to compromise more.

PHILION: Perhaps from their vantage point there is no alternative. Under this current stage of intensified global competition for profits, perhaps they have little choice but to enforce U.S. hegemony more forcefully and totally.

HAN: But if they really want to reorganize this world economy, they're going to have to increase demand for goods and services in developing countries. That would save the world economy, no? But U.S. politicians and elites won't do this.

PHILION: Has the pace of privatization since WTO entry been faster or slower than you anticipated?

HAN: Privatization has been the basic thrust of China's economic reform policies for the last 20 years. While privatization was already moving along quite rapidly, entering the WTO only added to that.

PHILION: What about privatization of large state-owned companies in China?

HAN: That's underway, but its form differs from other sectors of the state enterprise economy. Small enterprises are subjected to buy-outs or else bankruptcy. Larger companies typically don't need to declare bankruptcy—their profits are still guaranteed because of their monopoly position. And if they were sold off, too much "face" would be lost. However, there are still ways to move in that direction.

One way is to convert state enterprises into stock-holding companies and allow foreign purchase of the stock, thus handing part of the management power over to foreign investors. This mechanism presents an increased threat to the autonomy of the Chinese state—which wouldn't be the case if we were talking about Chinese investors buying up these shares, even though we'd still be talking about privatization. This kind, however, is not only a sell-off of companies, but in effect the sell-off of the country—a re-colonization! A foreign company doesn't even have to buy up an entire state enterprise; a proportion of shares that enables it to dominate production decisions and priorities will do the trick. It's a classic form of imperial control in the economic realm.

PHILION: In 2000, there was a widespread concern in the Chinese media, in academic and business circles, about the problem of insufficient domestic demand—consumers not buying goods, investors not investing, instead waiting to see if prices would go lower. The Chinese government made large investments in public projects to stimulate demand. Have the government's efforts to address the demand problem had any results?

HAN: There are two policies that could be used: expand national demand by reducing the income gap and getting more money into the hands of the masses; or create a bubble. What we're doing is the second one: creating a bubble to cover up the problems spawned by inadequate national demand. Primarily this is seen in real estate bubbles: real estate markets experienced great investment after portions of real estate were subjected to market reforms. Meanwhile, the first strategy has not been employed. In fact, the gap between the incomes of the rich and the poor has grown to a shocking degree, far faster than the growth in GDP.

PHILION: Can you talk about the economic policies of the current government?

HAN: In 2002, with the nomination of Hu Jintao as Party secretary, his apparent commitment to protecting China's national interests, unlike the previous leadership, gave those like myself some hope. He also expresses more concern about the gap between rich and poor, as well as the rights of urban and rural laborers. Our optimism has not been entirely mistaken. But we still feel that his responses to these problems have been inadequate.

The policy of eliminating rural taxes was well received; plainly, taxing the wealthy should come before taxing farmers! Also, the recent arrest of Go Cujun, who represents the pro-privatization wing of the Party, would not likely have taken place without Hu Jintao's support. These actions have contributed to a certain comfort level among critics of privatization in China, as have other developments. For example, recently the National Research Institute published a white paper on the failure of health care reform. This is the first time an official institution has publicly repudiated a particular aspect of economic reform. Also, the Technology Ministry recently took issue publicly with the view of China's head WTO negotiating representative Long Yuantu that China doesn't need its own technology, that we can purchase it all from foreign companies investing in China. This we consider an important event as well.

Naturally, the things that I see as positive, the neoliberal rightwingers in China see as a disaster.

PHILION: There is a neoliberal economist at Peking University who has come under considerable public criticism recently, and you've been a party to that. Five years ago, it would have been hard to imagine so many intellectuals and other comrades in such an open struggle with neoliberal economists in China.

HAN: You're right—now there are more academics who are critical of neoliberalism's price tag in China. Our numbers are better these days, as is our ability to coordinate with each other.

We are not critical of reform. There is obviously a need for reform and for attracting a certain amount of foreign investment in China. We don't at all advocate the closing off of China's market. Our opponents like to accuse us of being against reform. What we are opposed to is their neoliberalism that sees markets as the be-all and end-all. We support socialist reform that improves the social position of workers and farmers and that strengthens the position of China. We're not against that kind of reform at all!

PHILION: Wal-Mart's agreement to allow unions in its facilities in China has been in the news. Will this have any impact, or is it more appearance than substance?

HAN: As I see it, China's requirement that a union be established at Wal-Mart does not mean the situation of Wal-Mart's workers has improved. Nor does it mean that China's workers will be able to create independent unions, free from the official Party-controlled All China Federation of Trade Unions (ACFTU). Instead, we see Wal-Mart creating a union that will be under the control of the employer in order to erode the pressure from unofficial, underground union movements. This ends up making the ACFTU look good and seem able to accomplish something real. At the same time, it can put a pretty face on foreign investors' role in China as being no different from Chinese companies. Look at it this way: Wal-Mart has established a union, so it's become a Chinese company! This suits ACFTU leaders who are sympathetic with such employer-friendly unions as well as many intellectuals who stand by such unions and look at labor issues from the perspective of employers, whether we're talking about state-owned enterprises or domestic or foreign-owned capitalist companies.

PHILION: The government has recently placed some regulations on multinational corporations investing in China—which, tellingly, the corporations have been resisting. Do you think they are likely to be effective?

HAN: Regulations on foreign investors have existed forever, and when concern is expressed in civil society about investors, new regulations are devised. Nonetheless, whether it's central government ministries, or local governments, or state-owned enterprise administrators, none tend to take these regulations too seriously. Attracting business investment and allowing foreign investors access to China's national resources and control over critical industrial sectors remain the central policy directions—ones that are proceeding at a rapid pace.

PHILION: What are the present prospects for household income distribution in terms of developing a viable domestic consumer market for China's future growth?

HAN: In 2006, across sectors, salaries generally increased, especially among lower-level wage earners. The rate of unpaid back wages has also decreased. These are all favorable phenomena. However, consumer goods have seen rapid price inflation, which has hit low-wage workers especially hard, essentially eliminating what wage gains they've experienced. That's in part why income disparities continue to grow.

PHILION: Have there been any improvements in the conditions for workers in the SOEs? Is the SOE sector likely to continue to be a source of labor protests in the future, or do you see it becoming quieter? Why so?

HAN: The policy of mass layoffs that was so widespread in the state sector until recently has basically ended. Also, state workers who are presently employed have more wage security than private-sector workers, so they are less inclined toward conflict. However, those state workers who have been laid off or reassigned remain dissatisfied with the status quo.

ARTICLE 8.8   *July/August 2007*

WOLFOWITZ AND THE WORLD BANK
A TEMPORARY FARCE, BUT A CONTINUING TRAGEDY.

BY LARRY PETERSON

For many on the left, the departure of Paul Wolfowitz from his position as head of the World Bank was cause for celebration. To see one of the architects of a vicious, illegal war brought down by a conflict-of-interest scandal that would embarrass any ordinary personnel director made for a good laugh. And this despite the fact that the scandal, over Wolfowitz's reassignment of his companion to the State Department (under nepotism rules, she couldn't retain her job at the World Bank) at a salary higher than Secretary Rice's, didn't begin to approach the spectacular levels of conspicuous corruption we've come to expect from Bush & Co. But the Wolfowitz episode, however gossip-worthy, is a distraction from the complex trends that have recently been reshaping the World Bank's role in the global economic development game and that will determine the contours of its role well into the future.

In recent years, the World Bank and its sister organization, the International Monetary Fund (IMF), have adopted a lower profile. Today one rarely reads about the banks imposing structural adjustment programs on countries which have no choice but to comply or risk their continued access to capital (though coerced structural adjustment programs still exist: Naomi Klein notes that Sri Lanka was forced to privatize its water system as a condition of receiving aid in the wake of the 2004 tsunami).

But it was only a decade ago, following the Asian financial meltdown, that such conditions were forced on numerous economies, including ones that the World Bank and IMF themselves had acclaimed as star performers not long before: South Korea, Thailand, and Argentina, to name a few. To qualify for desperately needed loans to repay foreign creditors, with the aim of restoring their currencies to health and staunching capital flight, several of these countries were directed by the World Bank and the IMF to impose the usual austerity measures—cuts in health and education spending, for instance—*and* to privatize state assets. The austerity measures hastened the bankruptcies of many domestic companies, some of which had been quite profitable; and many of these assets were then scooped up by Western firms at fire-sale prices.

Policymakers in these countries not only witnessed the damage that bank-mandated policies did to their economies. They also saw China and Malaysia emerge from the Asian crisis not only intact, but invigorated, thanks to the use of strategies such as capital controls to limit the damage done by global currency speculators—strategies the World Bank prohibited to its protégés. These experiences convinced finance ministries throughout Asia and Latin America that they might be better off accumulating their own reserves than relying on international institutions like the World Bank and the IMF, with their sadistic lending practices.

And lo, as a post-9/11 Federal Reserve pumped money into the staggering U.S. economy, American businesses and consumers bought imported goods by the boatload with those dollars, thus piping them into the coffers of major exporters to the United States. This accumulation of U.S. dollars, in turn, gave many of these economies the means to protect themselves from future financial panics. Moreover, super-low global interest rates and financial liberalization ensured that cheap capital would remain available in global markets, so recourse to the IMF and the World Bank for loans just wouldn't be as necessary as it once was. The global boom in commodities (oil, copper, tin, etc.) has only reinforced this trend, expanding the cash reserves of a number of poor countries unable to export much in the way of manufactured goods but whose minerals or other natural resources are suddenly garnering greater demand and higher prices. In addition, some developing countries, especially China and Venezuela, flush with cash, have become alternative sources of loans and grants to poorer countries.

These developments, taken together, have increased the financial wiggle room of many poor countries considerably; this has allowed them to keep the international financial institutions at bay, at least for now.

Even before Wolfowitz's appointment, but especially under his tenure, the catchwords at the World Bank have been "good governance" and "anti-corruption measures" rather than those old mainstays of fiscal prudence and monetary austerity. This shift reflects the fact that the bank's purview is increasingly limited to some of the most benighted economies on the planet: Congo, Angola, and—God help us (or them)—Iraq. In countries like these, the bank continues to fund infrastructure projects employing expensive foreign consultants from multinational corporations even though these countries can finance such projects only by exposing themselves to dangerous levels of debt. As Mark Weisbrot,

economist and co-director of the Washington, D.C.-based Center for Economic and Policy Research, has written, the bank is still active primarily in places where it can do the most harm.

To be fair, the bank will also still be tapped if important but fragile economies like Turkey find themselves in the midst of a panic. The bank also remains, as attorney and global justice activist Terra Lawson-Remer has noted, a crucial—if not at all adequate—source of funding for things like malaria eradication, subsistence agriculture, and education for young girls. Another possible role for the bank has been mentioned by former U.S. Treasury Secretary Lawrence Summers: as a kind of clearinghouse for climate-change reduction subsidies for the developing world.

So given the complex mixture of trends currently shaping the World Bank's role, how should progressives view the bank today?

First of all, we should be extremely cautious about the anticorruption push. For one thing, the campaign reeks of double standards. As I write, news has emerged from the UK that the attorney general there not only halted an anticorruption investigation into payments of more than one *billion* pounds (about $1.97 billion) to Saudi Arabia's Prince Bandar for his role in setting up Britain's largest-ever arms deal, but misled the Organization for Economic Cooperation and Development's anticorruption watchdog as well. When corruption in some countries is treated as no big deal, other countries can be forgiven for questioning the motivations behind the bank's high-profile focus on *their* corruption.

Here's one step that might begin to reassure the developing world. The United States should relinquish the right to appoint the head of the bank—especially as U.S. contributions to the bank's coffers have lagged behind its agreed-upon obligations. The demand for broader participation in the selection of the bank's head looks all the more salient given that Bush's choice for a successor to Wolfowitz, former U.S. Trade Representative Robert Zoellick, has shown himself to be an economic nationalist of the first order, cajoling desperate economies like Nicaragua into lopsided bilateral trade agreements worse (for them) than even the draft regional or WTO agreements would have been. Even economist Jagdish Bhagwati, an outspoken advocate of free trade and corporate globalization, has characterized Zoellick's appointment as nothing less than "a dagger drawn at the developing countries."

It's ironic: The World Bank and IMF were created to allow countries experiencing difficulties balancing their international books the opportunity to retain access to credit in a manner compatible with steady economic development—and so avoid the downward spiral of capital flight, monetary gyrations, and protectionism that led to the Depression and World War II. Instead, they have ended up prompting their clients to liberate themselves by building up humungous reserves, at some cost to development and with no small distorting effects on the global economy. Far from being aided by the multilateral banks, middle- and even low-income developing economies now go out of their way to amass reserves while skimping on crucial expenditures in such arenas as education and health care for their own people. This is a huge price to pay to keep the World Bank and the IMF at bay, but it's one that many developing countries (or their elites, anyway) consider worth paying.

Resources: Naomi Klein, "The World Bank Has the Perfect Standard Bearer," *Guardian*, 4/27/07; Tessa Lawson-Remer, "Neocons in the Wings," TomPaine.com, 5/23/07; David Leigh & Rob Evans, "Attorney General Knew of BAE and the One Billion Pounds. Then Concealed It," *Guardian*, 6/8/07; Bradford Plumer, "Is Bob Zoellick the Next Paul Wolfowitz?" *New Republic*, 6/8/07; Lawrence Summers, "Practical Steps to Climate Control," *Financial Times*, 5/28/07; Mark Weisbrot, "Wolfowitz and the Bank," *The Nation*, 6/11/07; James Crotty & Gary Dymski, "Can the Global Neoliberal Regime Survive Victory in Asia? The Political Economy of the Asian Crisis," *Int'l Papers in Political Economy* 5(2), 1998.

ARTICLE 8.9   *September/October 2007*

WOMEN OF NAFTA

BY MARTHA OJEDA

The outstanding collection *NAFTA From Below: Maquiladora Workers, Farmers, and Indigenous Communities Speak Out on the Impact of Free Trade in Mexico*, combines worker testimony with analytical and historical essays to provide a devastating picture of the effects of neoliberal international trade policies—culminating in the North American Free Trade Agreement (NAFTA)—on workers throughout Mexico. The book, available in both English and Spanish, also offers inspiring accounts of resistance to those policies.

The book's early chapters focus on *maquiladora* workers in the north of the country, addressing key labor issues such as health and safety, environmental concerns, and freedom of association. Later chapters take up organizing by agricultural workers in the south, especially in the state of Chiapas, in response to neoliberal "reforms." That the Zapatista uprising in Chiapas began on January 1, 1994, the very day that NAFTA went into effect, was no accident.

One of the book's achievements is to show how the struggles of industrial workers in the north of Mexico are related to those of agricultural workers in the south. Knitting these struggles together is one of the central aims of the Coalition for Justice in the Maquiladoras, which produced *NAFTA From Below*. The coalition has helped bring *maquila* workers and organizers from the north together with members of grassroots *campesino* and indigenous groups in the south to help strengthen cooperative projects in both regions and to share information about the history of organized struggle in the workplace. Women's strong leadership roles in workplace struggles in the north have been of particular interest to organizers in the south, especially as former agricultural workers from the south migrate to work in *maquiladoras* near the northern border.

Women played a central role in the struggle of workers at a Sony plant in Nuevo Laredo for a democratic union, described in the selections that follow. The events at Sony vividly illustrate the frequent conflicts between Mexico's corrupt official unions and rival independent unions that Chris Tilly and Marie Kennedy describe (pp. 26-30). The Sony workers' struggle was also a key early test of NAFTA's labor side-agreement, the North American Agreement on Labor Cooperation, and the bodies it established, known as National Administrative Offices (NAOs), to investigate violations.

These excerpts include testimony from Martha Ojeda (co-editor of *NAFTA From Below*, with Rosemary Hennessy), a *maquila* worker from 1973 to 1994 who is now executive director of the Coalition for Justice in the Maquiladoras; from Felicitas (Fela) Contreras, an activist with CETRAC (Center for Workers and Communities) in Nuevo Laredo who worked at the Sony plant from 1985 through 1998; and from Yolanda Treviño, a former Sony worker who testified before the NAO as part of the Sony workers' NAFTA complaint.

To order *NAFTA From Below* or for more information, visit www.coalitionforjustice.net write to The Coalition for Justice in the Maquiladoras, 4207 Willowbrook Dr., San Antonio, TX 78228, or call 210-732-8324.

MARTHA A. OJEDA: Official history is always written so that the reality people were living is hidden. If everyone told the part they lived or knew, the truth would be in their collective word.

* * *

In 1979 Sony arrived in my town [Nuevo Laredo]…. Sony manually assembled audiocassettes and Beta videocassettes. In 1982, after the first devaluation of the peso, there were more than 1,000 workers working three shifts in five plants, and by then the workers were also producing the VHS videocassette and the 3.5 inch diskette.

They began to bring machines for semiautomatic and automatic assembly of the cassettes. The plastic molding injection plant was providing the plastic cases and the components for the audio and video plants. It was the boom of assembly line production.

In this era children with birth defects began to be born, but the company doctor said that this happened because the parents were alcoholics or because they had genetic problems. By 1993 there were 2,000 employees in seven plants in three shifts. There was a lot of overtime, but still it wasn't enough to meet production quotas.

The molding ingestion plants never stopped working; they were going three shifts seven days a week. For the first time the company proposed 12 hour shifts for four and three days a week. This implied that Sony got their production, because the machines were running around the clock, but they avoided paying overtime. This twelve-hour shift was unknown to workers because it didn't exist in the Federal Labor Law.

It was in this labor and political context that in October 1993 we visited Fidel Velázquez, the CTM national leader, in Mexico City and solicited union elections within the framework of the CTM. All of the *maquilas* were affiliated with this union because it was the only one; if you didn't belong to them there was no other alternative for workers anywhere. But the leaders negotiated the contract with the company even before it was established in the locality.

Fidel told us that he agreed with the elections (but he never said when they would be). We trusted his word and began the process that the Federal Labor Law sets down for forming the union sections.

* * *

On January 1, 1994, we were informed of the Zapatista uprising, but equally surprising to us was to find out in the newspaper on January 4 that Chema Morales had declared that on the order of Fidel Velázquez he would be the new Secretary General of the *maquilas*—without sectionals—and, worst of all, he was already named to the Labor Board at the state level because of his position as Secretary General, not only of the Maquila Union but also of the Workers Federation of Nuevo Laredo.

Shocked, we tried to communicate with Fidel Velázquez, but our efforts were in vain. Then we learned that he was coming to Ciudad Victoria, the capital of Tamaulipas, on January 12. We traveled all night. But when we arrived it was obvious that they would not let us enter. We guessed that Fidel would come in by the side door and we waited there until he arrived with the media.

I demanded publicly that he retract his authorization of Chema Morales as Secretary General. Then I asked for a public debate with him and with Chema. I don't know if I was the only woman from the provinces who had publicly challenged him, but what I do know is that so much corruption repulsed me and gave me the courage to make sure that the two of them, both Chema and Fidel, would be exposed even to the President of the Labor Board of the state who was present. He had authorized naming Chema to be Secretary General even though he had never worked in the *maquilas*, and according to the union by-laws that was one of the requirements.

In the face of the media and all of the evidence, Fidel looked ridiculous and he had no alternative but to accept that there would be union elections. So he declared that he would send a national representative to hold them. When I went to say goodbye to him at the podium he told me, "You are going to eat fire." And I told him, "I'm ready." But I never imagined what he was referring to.

FELICITAS ("FELA") CONTRERAS: In 1993 they began to change the delegates in all of the *maquiladoras* who were not agreed with the CTM. I heard that there were going to be elections in all the *maquilas*, not only in Sony, and we were asking when Sony's turn would be. But before the elections they were changing the delegates. They fired the ones we wanted and after work we had meetings to change the delegates so that they would really be for us. We met in one house and another with Martha because we wanted to change the delegates who were imposed by the CTM. I would get home at 4:00 or 5:00 in the morning. We always were hiding here and there, and that is how we put together a slate, even though they fired our candidates.

Those union delegates who were with Chema Morales (of the CTM) developed their slates with the old delegates from Sony… They preferred Chema instead of our democratic union. In April of 1994 the day arrived for the elections, and Chema's representative from the union and a representative of Fidel Velázquez were set up in the parking lot of Plant #7. We had our slate, but they didn't give us a chance to let our other co-workers know that the voting was taking place.

Representatives of Fidel Velázquez and of the company were there. They told the people to go to the parking lot and they arranged to meet the other shift and take them out to vote. They said on this side go all those in favor of the blue slate, on the other side those in favor of the CTM slate. Our slate won because everyone came to our side. But Fidel's representative said that the other delegates from the CTM won. And so we said, "How is that possible if we are all here, voting for our slate? We were the majority. What are we going to do?" We were really mad! Those who were working came out and we took to the streets to protest that they were doing this fraudulent election, and we made signs that said, "We want democratic elections!!"

YOLANDA TREVIÑO: On Saturday April 16, which was my day off, I went to plant #3 to see what resolution Mayor Horacio Garza had been able to make as to when we would have new elections. The *compañeras* who had spoken with him told us that he wasn't going to help us. That's when we started to hold our protest on the sidewalk in front of the plants, showing our frustration, but in a peaceful manner. We didn't stop anyone who wanted to from going into work and we didn't commit any act of violence.

We continued protesting in this way until Horacio Garza and Maricela López arrived. We had a meeting there with Horacio and he told us to stop the protest and that afterwards he would help us. We answered that the only thing we wanted was Señor Avila's word that they would hold new elections. But he said no. So Horacio Garza left and soon afterward the police and the firemen arrived. The girls were afraid when they saw the police and some of them asked if the were going to take us away, but we told them if we didn't act violently then they shouldn't either.

But that wasn't the case. Francisco Xavier Rios [Vice President of Human Resources at Sony] signaled to the police with a motion of his hand to enter through a side door, and they positioned themselves on the inside lot of the company. Then without any warning the police began to push us with their Plexiglas shields and their billy clubs. They beat us badly; they knocked a *compañera* unconscious, a woman named Alicia Soto, and they pushed the rest of us down with their shields, insulting us all the while, calling us names like "goddamn bitches."

I have been told that the company claims that the police didn't commit any acts of violence and that they only person who acted violently was Alicia who attacked the police with a magazine. I ask you: how is it possible that a 24 year old woman can harm a group of 35 well-armed police agents carrying Plexiglas shields and billy clubs? How is it possible to say they didn't commit acts of violence when my friend Alicia was knocked out by a blow to the head and has had problems ever since? I have here the newspaper *El Mañana*, dated 17 April, which shows very clearly a picture of Alicia unconscious. If they don't want to read the newspapers they should just look at their own videos because they were filming the entire attack.

FELICITAS ("FELA") CONTRERAS: They had pressed charges against us—Martha Ojeda and various others—because Sony had lost millions with the work stoppage. They issued a summons for us to appear at the police department and told us that our lives were not even worth enough to pay for the company's losses.

They wanted us to say that Martha was responsible, and they pitted us against each other. They told Lupe that I had confessed that Martha was doing it all, and they told me that Lupe confessed that Martha told us to stop working. But of the 40 they called to testify all of us said, "We are all responsible, and so you will have to arrest all of us not just Martha." All of our *compañeras* were outside the police department yelling that they would have to arrest everyone. But since there were more than a thousand and we didn't all fit in the cells, after hours of interrogations and threats they let us go.

* * *

On the fifth day, in the early morning, around 5:00 am the governor –Manuel Cavazos Lerma- ordered that they state police from Reynosa, Matamoros and Cd. Victoria be brought in. The police arrived and the soldiers with machine guns and rifles. And they said to you, "Get out of here or I'll kill you." According to them they came to restore order, and with blows and kicks. They awakened us and ran after those who were sleeping on the sidewalk. You were waking up with a gun pointing in your face and they were yelling, "Get out or we will kill you."

We withdrew, and we were like this for five days and nights. In those days the trucks tried to mow us down because they wanted to take out the production, but we were all sleeping in the main gate so they couldn't cross and take it out.

Unfortunately, we didn't get it. We didn't get our union, and they fired a lot of people without giving them any severance payment because they said that they were leaders of the movement. We stayed there because we wanted an independent union.

* * *

In 1994 NAFTA was signed, and they said that the rights of workers would not be violated. But they beat us up and violated our rights. With the help of CJM and the lawyers from ANAD a demand was presented to the NAO. In 1995 we had a hearing and we all went to San Antonio to testify. Sony brought lawyers from New York and they said that our testimony was a lie, but we took the newspapers and the evidence, the videos. We won this trial, but we didn't really win anything because they didn't punish or fine Sony and we never had the elections or anything. They just put in these offices [the NAO] just to prop us NAFTA.

* * *

For me NAFTA was no good. The workers are still just as poor. The only difference is that now there are many settlements, *colonias*, many squatters, a lot of insecurity and a contaminated river. Before I used to drink water from the river and now you cant, and you cant go into it either. Our air is contaminated. There is a lot of sickness. There is a lot of illiteracy. The only one NAFTA helped were the businessmen because they are the ones that have gotten rich. And now they say, "I am going to China; I screwed the Mexicans so now I'm going to screw the Chinese." That is what says with me about NAFTA. We are poor and screwed.

MARTHA A. OJEDA: Each one of my *compañeras* risked her life, her children, and her family. They kidnapped Yolanda and threatened her. They persecuted the others, calling them on the phone and intimidating them. Wherever any of them are, because there were many and I will never forget one, to each of them I render homage and a special tribute to their "*coraje*"—their courage and bravery—for trying to reclaim workers' right to freedom of association. For resisting and never giving up.

That is what NAFTA left me after 20 years in the *maquilas*: it gave me the opportunity to denounce at a global level the failure of this agreement and of the side agreements and to share the rebellion and resistance of my *compañeras*. It taught me that there is a world of solidarity. It clarified the horizon we are looking for, and above all the hope to reach it with a team like this team of women, united until the end.

NIKE TO THE RESCUE?

AFRICA NEEDS BETTER JOBS, NOT SWEATSHOPS.

BY JOHN MILLER

IN PRAISE OF THE MALIGNED SWEATSHOP

WINDHOEK, Namibia—*Africa desperately needs Western help in the form of schools, clinics and sweatshops.*

On a street here in the capital of Namibia, in the southwestern corner of Africa, I spoke to a group of young men who were trying to get hired as day laborers on construction sites.

"I come here every day," said Naftal Shaanika, a 20-year-old. "I actually find work only about once a week."

Mr. Shaanika and the other young men noted that the construction jobs were dangerous and arduous, and that they would vastly prefer steady jobs in, yes, sweatshops. Sure, sweatshop work is tedious, grueling and sometimes dangerous. But over all, sewing clothes is considerably less dangerous or arduous—or sweaty—than most alternatives in poor countries.

Well-meaning American university students regularly campaign against sweatshops. But instead, anyone who cares about fighting poverty should campaign in favor of sweatshops, demanding that companies set up factories in Africa.

The problem is that it's still costly to manufacture in Africa. The headaches across much of the continent include red tape, corruption, political instability, unreliable electricity and ports, and an inexperienced labor force that leads to low productivity and quality. The anti-sweatshop movement isn't a prime obstacle, but it's one more reason not to manufacture in Africa.

Imagine that a Nike vice president proposed manufacturing cheap T-shirts in Ethiopia. The boss would reply: "You're crazy! We'd be boycotted on every campus in the country."

Some of those who campaign against sweatshops respond to my arguments by noting that they aren't against factories in Africa, but only demand a "living wage" in them. After all, if labor costs amount to only $1 per shirt, then doubling wages would barely make a difference in the final cost.

One problem ... is that it already isn't profitable to pay respectable salaries, and so any pressure to raise them becomes one more reason to avoid Africa altogether.

One of the best U.S. initiatives in Africa has been the African Growth and Opportunity Act, which allows duty-free imports from Africa—and thus has stimulated manufacturing there.

—Op-ed by Nicholas Kristof, *New York Times*, June 6, 2006

Nicholas Kristof has been beating the pro-sweatshop drum for quite a while. Shortly after the East Asian financial crisis of the late 1990s, Kristof, the Pulitzer Prize-winning journalist and now columnist for the *New York Times*, reported the story of an Indonesian recycler who, picking through the metal scraps of a garbage dump, dreamed that her son would grow up to be a sweatshop worker. Then, in 2000, Kristof and his wife, *Times* reporter Sheryl WuDunn, published "Two Cheers for Sweatshops" in the *Times Magazine*. In 2002, Kristof's column advised G-8 leaders to "start an international campaign to promote imports from sweatshops, perhaps with bold labels depicting an unrecognizable flag and the words 'Proudly Made in a Third World Sweatshop.'"

Now Kristof laments that too few poor, young African men have the opportunity to enter the satanic mill of sweatshop employment. Like his earlier efforts, Kristof's latest pro-sweatshop ditty synthesizes plenty of half-truths. Let's take a closer look and see why there is still no reason to give it up for sweatshops.

A BETTER ALTERNATIVE?

It is hardly surprising that young men on the streets of Namibia's capital might find sweatshop jobs more appealing than irregular work as day laborers on construction sites.

The alternative jobs available to sweatshop workers are often worse and, as Kristof loves to point out, usually involve more sweating than those in world export factories. Most poor people in the developing world eke out their livelihoods from subsistence agriculture or by plying petty trades. Others on the edge of urban centers work as streethawkers or hold other jobs in the informal sector. As economist Arthur MacEwan wrote a few years back in *Dollars & Sense*, in a poor country like Indonesia, where women working in manufacturing earn five times as much as those in agriculture, sweatshops have no trouble finding workers.

But let's be clear about a few things. First, export factory jobs, especially in labor-intensive industries, often are just "a ticket to slightly less impoverishment," as even economist and sweatshop defender Jagdish Bhagwati allows.

Beyond that, these jobs seldom go to those without work or to the poorest of the poor. One study by sociologist Kurt Ver Beek showed that 60% of first-time Honduran maquila workers were previously employed. Typically they were not destitute, and they were better educated than most Hondurans.

Sweatshops don't just fail to rescue people from poverty. Setting up export factories where workers have few job alternatives has actually been a recipe for serious worker abuse. In *Beyond Sweatshops,* a book arguing for the benefits of direct foreign investment in the developing world, Brookings Institution economist Theodore Moran recounts the disastrous decision of the Philippine government to build the Bataan Export Processing Zone in an isolated mountainous area to lure foreign investors with the prospect of cheap labor. With few alternatives, Filipinos took jobs in the garment factories that sprung up in the zone. The manufacturers typically paid less than the minimum wage and forced employees to work overtime in factories filled with dust and fumes. Fed up, the workers eventually mounted a series of crippling strikes. Many factories shut down and occupancy rates in the zone plummeted, as did the value of exports, which declined by more than half between 1980 and 1986.

Kristof's argument is no excuse for sweatshop abuse: that conditions are worse elsewhere does nothing to alleviate the suffering of workers in export factories. They are often denied the right to organize, subjected to unsafe working conditions and to verbal, physical, and sexual abuse, forced to work overtime, coerced into pregnancy tests and even abortions, and paid less than a living wage. It remains useful and important to combat these conditions even if alternative jobs are worse yet.

The fact that young men in Namibia find sweatshop jobs appealing testifies to how harsh conditions are for workers in Africa, not the desirability of export factory employment.

Oddly, Kristof's desire to introduce new sweatshops to sub-Saharan Africa finds no support in the African Growth and Opportunity Act (AGOA) that he praises. The Act grants sub-Saharan apparel manufacturers preferential access to U.S. markets. But shortly after its passage, U.S. Trade Representative Robert Zoellick assured the press that the AGOA would not create sweatshops in Africa because it requires protective standards for workers consistent with those set by the International Labor Organization.

ANTISWEATSHOP ACTIVISM AND JOBS

Kristof is convinced that the antisweatshop movement hurts the very workers it intends to help. His position has a certain seductive logic to it. As anyone who has suffered through introductory economics will tell you, holding everything else the same, a labor standard that forces multinational corporations and their subcontractors to boost wages should result in their hiring fewer workers.

But in practice does it? The only evidence Kristof produces is an imaginary conversation in which a boss incredulously refuses a Nike vice president's proposal to open a factory in Ethiopia paying wages of 25 cents a hour: "You're crazy! We'd be boycotted on every campus in the country."

While Kristof has an active imagination, there are some things wrong with this conversation.

First off, the antisweatshop movement seldom initiates boycotts. An organizer with United Students Against Sweatshops (USAS) responded on Kristof's blog: "We never call for apparel boycotts unless we are explicitly asked to by workers at a particular factory. This is, of course, exceedingly rare, because, as you so persuasively argued, people generally want to be employed." The National Labor Committee, the largest antisweatshop organization in the United States, takes the same position.

Moreover, when economists Ann Harrison and Jason Scorse conducted a systematic study of the effects of the antisweatshop movement on factory employment, they found no negative employment effect. Harrison and Scorse looked at Indonesia, where Nike was one of the targets of an energetic campaign calling for better wages and working conditions among the country's subcontractors. Their statistical analysis found that the antisweatshop campaign was responsible for 20% of the increase in the real wages of unskilled workers in factories exporting textiles, footwear, and apparel from 1991 to 1996. Harrison and Scorse also found that "antisweatshop activism did not have significant adverse effects on employment" in these sectors.

Campaigns for higher wages are unlikely to destroy jobs because, for multinationals and their subcontractors, wages make up a small portion of their overall costs. Even Kristof accepts this point, well documented by economists opposed to sweatshop labor. In Mexico's apparel industry, for instance, economists Robert Pollin, James Heintz, and Justine Burns from the Political Economy Research Institute found that doubling the pay of nonsupervisory workers would add just $1.80 to the production cost of a $100 men's sports jacket. A recent survey by the National Bureau of Economic Research found that U.S. consumers would be willing to pay $115 for the same jacket if they knew that it had not been made under sweatshop conditions.

GLOBALIZATION IN SUB-SAHARAN AFRICA

Kristof is right that Africa, especially sub-Saharan Africa, has lost out in the globalization process. Sub-Saharan Africa suffers from slower growth, less direct foreign investment, lower education levels, and higher poverty rates than most every other part of the world. A stunning 37 of the region's 47 countries are classified as "low-income" by the World Bank, each with a gross national income less than $825 per person. Many countries in the region bear the burdens of high external debt and a crippling HIV crisis that Kristof has made heroic efforts to bring to the world's attention.

But have multinational corporations avoided investing in sub-Saharan Africa because labor costs are too high? While labor costs in South Africa and Mauritius are high, those in the other countries of the region are modest by international standards, and quite low in some cases. Take Lesotho, the largest exporter of apparel from sub-Saharan Africa to the

United States. In the country's factories that subcontract with Wal-Mart, the predominantly female workforce earns an average of just $54 a month. That's below the United Nations poverty line of $2 per day, and it includes regular forced overtime. In Madagascar, the region's third largest exporter of clothes to the United States, wages in the apparel industry are just 33 cents per hour, lower than those in China and among the lowest in the world. And at Ramatex Textile, the large Malaysian-owned textile factory in Namibia, workers only earn about $100 per month according to the Labour Resource and Research Institute in Windhoek. Most workers share their limited incomes with extended families and children, and they walk long distances to work because they can't afford better transportation.

On the other hand, recent experience shows that sub-Saharan countries with decent labor standards *can* develop strong manufacturing export sectors. In the late 1990s, Francis Teal of Oxford's Centre for the Study of African Economies compared Mauritius's successful export industries with Ghana's unsuccessful ones. Teal found that workers in Mauritius earned ten times as much as those in Ghana—$384 a month in Mauritius as opposed to $36 in Ghana. Mauritius's textile and garment industry remained competitive because its workforce was better educated and far more productive than Ghana's. Despite paying poverty wages, the Ghanaian factories floundered.

Kristof knows full well the real reason garment factories in the region are shutting down: the expiration of the Multifiber Agreement last January. The agreement, which set national export quotas for clothing and textiles, protected the garment industries in smaller countries around the world from direct competition with China. Now China and, to a lesser degree, India, are increasingly displacing other garment producers. In this new context, lower wages alone are unlikely to sustain the sub-Saharan garment industry. Industry sources report that sub-Saharan Africa suffers from several other drawbacks as an apparel producer, including relatively high utility and transportation costs and long shipping times to the United States. The region also has lower productivity and less skilled labor than Asia, and it has fewer sources of cotton yarn and higher-priced fabrics than China and India.

If Kristof is hell-bent on expanding the sub-Saharan apparel industry, he would do better to call for sub-Saharan economies to gain unrestricted access to the Quad markets—the United States, Canada, Japan, and Europe. Economists Stephen N. Karingi, Romain Perez, and Hakim Ben Hammouda estimate that the welfare gains associated with unrestricted market access could amount to $1.2 billion in sub-Saharan Africa, favoring primarily unskilled workers.

But why insist on apparel production in the first place? Namibia has sources of wealth besides a cheap labor pool for Nike's sewing machines. The *Economist* reports that Namibia is a world-class producer of two mineral products: diamonds (the country ranks seventh by value) and uranium

(it ranks fifth by volume). The mining industry is the heart of Namibia's export economy and accounts for about 20% of the country's GDP. But turning the mining sector into a vehicle for national economic development would mean confronting the foreign corporations that control the diamond industry, such as the South African De Beers Corporation. That is a tougher assignment than scapegoating antisweatshop activists.

MORE AND BETTER AFRICAN JOBS

So why have multinational corporations avoided investing in sub-Saharan Africa? The answer, according to international trade economist Dani Rodrik, is "entirely due to the slow growth" of the sub-Saharan economies. Rodrik estimates that the region participates in international trade as much as can be expected given its economies' income levels, country size, and geography.

Rodrik's analysis suggests that the best thing to do for poor workers in Africa would be to lift the debt burdens on their governments and support their efforts to build functional economies. That means investing in human resources and physical infrastructure, and implementing credible macroeconomic policies that put job creation first. But these investments, as Rodrik points out, take time.

In the meantime, international policies establishing a floor for wages and safeguards for workers across the globe would do more for the young men on Windhoek's street corners than subjecting them to sweatshop abuse, because grinding poverty leaves people willing to enter into any number of desperate exchanges. And if Namibia is closing its garment factories because Chinese imports are cheaper, isn't that an argument for trying to improve labor standards in China, not lower them in sub-Saharan Africa? Abusive labor practices are rife in China's export factories, as the National Labor Committee and *Business Week* have documented. Workers put in 13- to 16-hour days, seven days a week. They enjoy little to no health and safety enforcement, and their take-home pay falls below the minimum wage after the fines and deductions their employers sometimes withhold.

Spreading these abuses in sub-Saharan Africa will not empower workers there. Instead it will take advantage of the fact that they are among the most marginalized workers in the world. Debt relief, international labor standards, and public investments in education and infrastructure are surely better ways to fight African poverty than Kristof's sweatshop proposal.r insignia products. They have no system, however, to track apparel production around the world, and often no idea where their production is occurring. Monitoring systems are still in their fledgling stages, so the universities are starting from a difficult position, albeit one they have profited from for years.

What can universities do about this? They should do what they are best at: produce information. They should take the lead in demanding that corporations—beginning with those they do business with—open themselves up to public inspection and evaluation. Universities have done this before, such as during the anti-apartheid campaign for South Africa. By doing this on the sweatshop issue, universities could spur a critical dialogue on labor issues around the world.

To start, the universities could establish a central coordinating office to collect and compare information on factory performance for member universities' licensees. (The WRC has proposed such a model.) This new office would be responsible for keeping records on licensee compliance, for making this information available over the Internet, for registering local NGOs and worker organizations to conduct independent verifications of factory conditions, and for assessing sanctions.

Such a program would allow universities to evaluate different strategies for improving conditions in different parts of the world. This would avoid the danger of locking in one code of conduct or one certification system. In place of sporadic media exposés embarrassing one company at a time, we would have an international system of disclosure and learning—benchmarking good performers, identifying and targeting the worst performers, and motivating improvements.

It is clearly no longer enough to expose one company at a time, or to count on industry-paid consulting firms. The building blocks of a new system depend on information. This fits the mission of universities. Universities should focus on information gathering and dissemination, and most importantly, on learning. If the universities learn nothing else from "Sweatshops 101," they should learn that they still have a lot of homework do to—and that their next test will be coming soon.

Resources: Arthur MacEwan, "Ask Dr. Dollar," *Dollars & Sense*, Sept–Oct 1998; John Miller, "Why Economists Are Wrong About Sweatshops and the Antisweatshop Movement," *Challenge*, Jan–Feb 2003; R. Pollin, J. Burns, and J. Heintz, "Global Apparel Production and Sweatshop Labor: Can Raising Retail Prices Finance Living Wages?" Political Economy Research Institute, Working Paper 19, DATE; N. Kristof, "In Praise of the Maligned Sweatshop,"*New York Times*, June 6, 2006; N. Kristof, "Let Them Sweat," NYT , June 25, 2002; N. Kristof, "Two Cheers for Sweatshops," *NYT* , Sept 24, 2000; N. Kristof, "Asia'[s Crisis Upsets Rising Effort to Confront Blight of Sweatshops," *NYT*, June 15, 1998; A. Harrison and J. Scorse, "Improving the Conditions of Workers? Minimum Wage Legislation and Anti-Sweatshop Activism," Calif. Management Review, Oct 2005; Herbert Jauch, "Africa's Clothing and Textile Industry: The Case of Ramatex in Namibia," in *The Future of the Textile and Clothing Industry in Sub-Saharan Africa*, ed. H. Jauch and R. Traub-Merz (Friedrich-Ebert-Stiftung, 2006); Kurt Alan Ver Beek, "Maquiladoras: Exploitation or Emancipation? An Overview of the Situation of Maquiladora Workers in Honduras," *World Development*, 29(9), 2001; Theodore Moran, *Beyond Sweatshops: Foreign Direct Investment and Globalization in Developing Countries* (Brookings Institution Press, 2002); "Comparative Assessment of the Competitiveness of the Textile and Apparel Sector in Selected Countries," in *Textiles and Apparel: Assessment of the Competitiveness of Certain Foreign Suppliers to the United States Market*, Vol. 1, U.S. International Trade Commission, Jan 2004; S. N. Karingi, R. Perez, and H. Ben Hammouda, "Could Extended Preferences Reward Sub-Saharan Africa's Participation in the Doha Round Negotiations?," World Economy, 2006; Francis Teal, "Why Can Mauritius Export Manufactures and Ghana Can Not?," *The World Economy*, 22 (7), 1999; Dani Rodrik, "Trade Policy and Economic Performance in Sub-Saharan Africa," Paper prepared for the Swedish Ministry for Foreign Affairs, Nov 1997.

IS IT OIL?

BY ARTHUR MacEWAN

Before U.S. forces invaded Iraq, the United Nations inspection team that had been searching the country for weapons of mass destruction was unable to find either such weapons or a capacity to produce them in the near future. As of mid-April, while the U.S. military is apparently wrapping up its invasion, it too has not found the alleged weapons. The U.S. government continues to claim that weapons of mass destruction exist in Iraq but provides scant evidence to substantiate its claim.

While weapons of mass destruction are hard to find in Iraq, there is one thing that is relatively easy to find: oil. Lots of oil. With 112.5 billion barrels of proven reserves, Iraq has greater stores of oil than any country except Saudi Arabia. This combination—lots of oil and no weapons of mass destruction—begs the question: Is it oil and not weapons of mass destruction that motivates the U.S. government's aggressive policy towards Iraq?

THE U.S. "NEED" FOR OIL?

Much of the discussion of the United States, oil, and Iraq focuses on the U.S. economy's overall dependence on oil. We are a country highly dependent on oil, consuming far more than we produce. We have a small share, about 3%, of the world's total proven oil reserves. By depleting our reserves at a much higher rate than most other countries, the United States accounts for about 10% of world production. But, by importing from the rest of the world, we can consume oil at a still higher rate: U.S. oil consumption is over 25% of the world's total. Thus, the United States relies on the rest of the world's oil in order to keep its economy running—or at least running in its present oil-dependent form. Moreover, for the United States to operate as it does and maintain current standards of living, we need access to oil at low prices. Otherwise we would have to turn over a large share of U.S. GDP as payment to those who supply us with oil.

Iraq could present the United States with supply problems. With a hostile government in Baghdad, the likelihood that the United States would be subject to some sort of boycott as in the early 1970s is greater than otherwise. Likewise, a government in Baghdad that does not cooperate with Washington could be a catalyst to a reinvigoration of the Organization of Petroleum Exporting Countries (OPEC) and the result could be higher oil prices.

Such threats, however, while real, are not as great as they might first appear. Boycotts are hard to maintain. The sellers of oil need to sell as much as the buyers need to buy; oil exporters depend on the U.S. market, just as U.S. consumers depend on those exporters. (An illustration of this mutual dependence is provided by the continuing oil trade between Iraq and the United States in recent years. During 2001, while the two countries were in a virtual state of war, the United States bought 284 million barrels of oil from Iraq, about 7% of U.S. imports and almost a third of Iraq's exports.) Also, U.S. oil imports come from diverse sources, with less than half from OPEC countries and less than one-quarter from Persian Gulf nations.

Most important, ever since the initial surge of OPEC in the 1970s, the organization has followed a policy of price restraint. While price restraint may in part be a strategy of political cooperation, resulting from the close U.S.-Saudi relationship in particular, it is also a policy adopted because high prices are counter-productive for OPEC itself; high prices lead consumers to switch sources of supply and conserve energy, undercutting the longer term profits for the oil suppliers. Furthermore, a sudden rise in prices can lead to general economic disruption, which is no more desirable for the oil exporters than for the oil importers. To be sure, the United States would prefer to have cooperative governments in oil producing countries, but the specter of another boycott as in the 1970s or somewhat higher prices for oil hardly provides a rationale, let alone a justification, for war.

THE PROFITS PROBLEM

There is, however, also the importance of oil in the profits of large U.S. firms: the oil companies themselves (with ExxonMobil at the head of the list) but also the numerous drilling, shipping, refining, and marketing firms that make up the rest of the oil industry. Perhaps the most famous of this latter group, because former CEO Dick Cheney is now vice president, is the Halliburton Company, which supplies a wide range of equipment and engineering services to the industry. Even while many governments—Saudi Arabia, Kuwait, and Venezuela, for example—have taken ownership of their countries' oil reserves, these companies have been able to maintain their profits because of their decisive roles at each stage in the long sequence from exploration through drilling to refining and marketing. Ultimately, however, as with any resource-based industry, the monopolistic position—and thus the large profits—of the firms that dominate the oil industry depends on their access to the supply of the resource. Their access, in turn, depends on the relations they are able to establish with the governments of oil-producing countries.

From the perspective of the major U.S. oil companies, a hostile Iraqi government presents a clear set of problems. To begin with, there is the obvious: because Iraq has a lot of oil, access to that oil would represent an important profit-making opportunity. What's more, Iraqi oil can be easily extracted and thus produced at very low cost. With all oil selling at the same price on the world market, Iraqi oil thus presents opportunities for especially large profits per unit of production. According to the *Guardian* newspaper (London), Iraqi oil could cost as little as 97 cents a barrel to produce, compared to the UK's North Sea oil produced at $3 to $4 per barrel. As one oil executive told the *Guardian* last November, "Ninety cents a barrel for oil that sells for $30—that's the kind of business anyone would want to be in. A 97% profit margin—you can live with that." The *Guardian* continues: "The stakes are high. Iraq could be producing 8 million barrels a day within the decade. The math is impressive—8 million times 365 at $30 per barrel or $87.5 billion a year. Any share would be worth fighting for." The question for the oil companies is: what share will they be able to claim and what share will be claimed by the Iraqi government? The split would undoubtedly be more favorable for the oil companies with a compliant U.S.-installed government in Baghdad.

Furthermore, the conflict is not simply one between the private oil companies and the government of Iraq. The U.S.-based firms and their British (and British-Dutch) allies are vying with French, Russian, and Chinese firms for access to Iraqi oil. During recent years, firms from these other nations signed oil exploration and development contracts with the Hussein government in Iraq, and, if there were no "regime change," they would preempt the operations of the U.S. and British firms in that country. If, however, the U.S. government succeeds in replacing the government of Saddam Hussein with its preferred allies in the Iraqi opposition, the outlook will change dramatically. According to Ahmed Chalabi, head of the Iraqi National Congress and a figure in the Iraqi opposition who seems to be currently favored by Washington, "The future democratic government in Iraq will be grateful to the United States for helping the Iraqi people liberate themselves and getting rid of Saddam.... American companies, we expect, will play an important and leading role in the future oil situation." (In recent years, U.S. firms have not been fully frozen out of the oil business in Iraq. For example, according to a June 2001 report in the *Washington Post*, while Vice President Cheney was CEO at Halliburton Company during the late 1990s, the firm operated through subsidiaries to sell some $73 million of oil production equipment and spare parts to Iraq.)

The rivalry with French, Russian and Chinese oil companies is in part driven by the direct prize of the profits to be obtained from Iraqi operations. In addition, in order to maintain their dominant positions in the world oil industry, it is important for the U.S. and British-based firms to deprive their rivals of the growth potential that access to Iraq would afford. In any monopolistic industry, leading firms need to deny their potential competitors market position and control of new sources of supply; otherwise, those competitors will be in a better position to challenge the leaders. The British *Guardian* reports that the Hussein government is "believed to have offered the French company TotalFinaElf exclusive rights to the largest of Iraq's oil fields, the Majoon, which would more than double the company's entire output at a single stroke." Such a development would catapult Total-FinaElf from the second ranks into the first ranks of the major oil firms. The basic structure of the world oil industry would not change, but the sharing of power and profits among the leaders would be altered. Thus for ExxonMobil, Chevron, Shell and the other traditional "majors" in the industry, access to Iraq is a defensive as well as an offensive goal. ("Regime change" in Iraq will not necessarily provide the legal basis for cancellation of contracts signed between the Hussein regime and various oil companies. International law would not allow a new regime simply to turn things over to the U.S. oil companies. "Should 'regime change' happen, one thing is guaranteed," according to the *Guardian*, "shortly afterwards there will be the mother of all legal battles.")

Oil companies are big and powerful. The biggest, Exxon-Mobil, had 2002 profits of $15 billion, more than any other corporation, in the United States or in the world. Chevron-Texaco came in with $3.3 billion in 2002 profits, and Phillips-Tosco garnered $1.7 billion. British Petroleum-Amoco-Arco pulled in $8 billion, while Royal Dutch/Shell Group registered almost $11 billion. Firms of this magnitude have a large role affecting the policies of their governments, and, for that matter, the governments of many other countries.

With the ascendancy of the Bush-Cheney team to the White House in 2000, perhaps the relationship between oil and the government became more personal, but it was not new. Big oil has been important in shaping U.S. foreign policy since the end of the 19th century (to say nothing of its role in shaping other policy realms, particularly environmental regulation). From 1914, when the Marines landed at Mexico's Tampico Bay to protect U.S. oil interests, to the CIA-engineered overthrow of the Mosadegh government in Iran in 1953, to the close relationship with the oppressive Saudi monarchy through the past 70 years, oil and the interests of the oil companies have been central factors in U.S. foreign policy. Iraq today is one more chapter in a long story.

THE LARGER ISSUE

Yet in Iraq today, as in many other instances of the U.S. government's international actions, oil is not the whole story. The international policies of the U.S. government are certainly shaped in significant part by the interests of U.S.-based firms, but not only the oil companies. ExxonMobil may have had the largest 2002 profits, but there are many additional large U.S. firms with international interests: Citibank and the other huge financial firms; IBM, Microsoft, and other information technology companies; General Motors and Ford; Merck, Pfizer and the other pharmaceutical corporations; large retailers like MacDonald's and Wal-Mart (and many more) depend on access to foreign markets and foreign sources of supply for large shares of their sales and profits.

The U.S. government (like other governments) has long defined its role in international affairs as protecting the interests of its nationals, and by far the largest interests of U.S. nationals abroad are the interests of these large U.S. companies. The day-to-day activities of U.S. embassies and consular offices around the world are dominated by efforts to further the interests of particular U.S. firms—for example, helping the firms establish local markets, negotiate a country's regulations, or develop relations with local businesses. When the issue is large, such as when governments in low-income countries have attempted to assure the availability of HIV-AIDS drugs in spite of patents held by U.S. firms, Washington steps directly into the fray. On the broadest level, the U.S. government tries to shape the rules and institutions of the world economy in ways that work well for U.S. firms. These rules are summed up under the heading of "free trade," which in practice means free access of U.S. firms to the markets and resources of the rest of the world.

In normal times, Washington uses diplomacy and institutions like the International Monetary Fund, the World Bank, and the World Trade Organization to shape the rules of the world economy. But times are not always "normal." When governments have attempted to remove their economies from the open system and break with the "rules of the game," the U.S. government has responded with overt or covert military interventions. Latin America has had a long history of such interventions, where Guatemala (1954), Cuba (1961), Chile (1973) and Nicaragua (1980s) provide fairly recent examples. The Middle East also provides several illustrations of this approach to foreign affairs, with U.S. interventions in Iran (1953), Lebanon (1958), Libya (1981), and now Iraq. These interventions are generally presented as efforts to preserve freedom and democracy, but, if freedom and democracy were actually the goals of U.S. interventions the record would be very different; both the Saudi monarchy and the Shah of Iran, in an earlier era, would then have been high on the U.S. hit list. (Also, as with maintaining the source of supply of oil, the U.S. government did not intervene in Guatemala in 1954 to maintain our supply of bananas; the profits of the United Fruit Company, however, did provide a powerful causal factor.)

The rhetorical rationale of U.S. foreign policy has seen many alterations and adjustments over the last century: at the end of the 19th century, U.S. officials spoke of the need to spread Christianity; Woodrow Wilson defined the mission as keeping the world safe for democracy; for most of the latter half of the 20th century, the fight against Communism was the paramount rationale; for a fleeting moment during the Carter administration, the protection of human rights entered the government's vocabulary; in recent years we have seen the war against drugs; and now we have the current administration's war against terrorism.

What distinguishes the current administration in Washington is neither its approach toward foreign affairs and U.S. business interests in general nor its policy in the Middle East and oil interests in particular. Even its rhetoric builds on well established traditions, albeit with new twists. What does distinguish the Bush administration is the clarity and aggressiveness with which it has put forth its goal of maintaining U.S. domination internationally. The "Bush Doctrine" that the administration has articulated claims legitimacy for preemptive action against those who might threaten U.S. interests, and it is clear from the statement of that doctrine in last September's issuance of The National Security Strategy of the United States of America that "U.S. interests" includes economic interests.

The economic story is never the whole story, and oil is never the whole economic story. In the particular application of U.S. power, numerous strategic and political considerations come into play. With the application of the Bush Doctrine in the case of Iraq, the especially heinous character of the Hussein regime is certainly a factor, as is the regime's history of conflict with other nations of the region (at times with U.S. support) and its apparent efforts at developing nuclear, chemical, and biological weapons; certainly the weakness of the Iraqi military also affects the U.S. government's willingness to go to war. Yet, as September's Security Strategy document makes clear, the U.S. government is concerned with domination and a major factor driving that goal of domination is economic. In the Middle East, Iraq and elsewhere, oil—or, more precisely, the profit from oil—looms large in the picture.

FAIR TRADE AND FARM SUBSIDIES: HOW BIG A DEAL?

TWO VIEWS

In September 2003, the global free-trade express was derailed—at least temporarily—when the World Trade Organization talks in Cancún, Mexico, collapsed. At the time, the inconsistency of the United States and other rich countries—pressing poor countries to adopt free trade while continuing to subsidize and protect selected domestic sectors, especially agriculture—received wide attention for the first time. Where does ending agricultural subsidies and trade barriers in the rich countries rank as a strategy for achieving global economic justice? Dollars & Sense *asked progressive researchers on different sides of this question to make their case.*

MAKE TRADE FAIR

BY GAWAIN KRIPKE

Trade can be a powerful engine for economic growth in developing countries and can help pull millions of people out of poverty. Trade also offers an avenue of growth that relies less than other development strategies on the fickle charity of wealthy countries or the self-interest of multinational corporations. However, current trade rules create enormous obstacles that prevent people in developing countries from realizing the benefits of trade. A growing number of advocacy organizations are now tackling this fundamental problem, hoping to open a route out of poverty for tens of millions of people who have few other prospects.

WHY TRADE?

Poor countries have few options for improving the welfare of their people and generating economic growth. Large debt burdens limit the ability of governments in the developing world to make investments and provide education, clean water, and other critical services. Despite some recent progress on the crushing problem of debt, only about 15% of the global South's $300 billion in unpayable debt has been eliminated.

Poor countries have traditionally looked to foreign aid and private investment to drive economic development. Both of these are proving inadequate. To reach the goals of the United Nations' current Millenium Development campaign, including reducing hunger and providing universal primary education, wealthy countries would have to increase their foreign aid from a paltry 0.23% of GDP to 0.7%. Instead, foreign aid flows are stagnant and are losing value against inflation and population growth. In 2001, the United States spent just 0.11% of GDP on foreign aid.

FALSE PROMISES ON TRADE

BY DEAN BAKER AND MARK WEISBROT

Farmers throughout the Third World are suffering not from too much free trade, but from not enough. That's the impression you get from most media coverage of the recent World Trade Organization (WTO) meetings in Cancún. The *New York Times*, *Washington Post*, and other major news outlets devoted huge amounts of space to news pieces and editorials arguing that agricultural subsidies in rich countries are a major cause of poverty in the developing world. If only these subsidies were eliminated, and the doors to imports from developing countries opened, the argument goes, then the playing field would be level and genuinely free trade would work its magic on poverty in the Third World. The media decided that agricultural subsidies were the major theme of the trade talks even if evidence indicated that other issues—for example, patent and copyright protection, rules on investment, or developing countries' right to regulate imports—would have more impact on the well-being of people in those countries.

There is certainly some element of truth in the argument that agricultural subsidies and barriers to imports can hurt farmers in developing countries. There are unquestionably farmers in a number of developing countries who have been undersold and even put out of business by imports whose prices are artificially low thanks to subsidies the rich countries pay their farmers. It is also true that many of these subsidy programs are poorly targeted, benefiting primarily large farmers and often encouraging environmentally harmful farming practices.

However, the media have massively overstated the potential gains that poor countries might get from the elimination of farm subsidies and import barriers. The risk of this exag-

continued on page 204

continued on page 205

MAKE TRADE FAIR
continued from page 203

Likewise, although global foreign direct investment soared to unprecedented levels in the late 1990s, most developing countries are not attractive to foreign investors. The bulk of foreign private investment in the developing world, more than 76%, goes to ten large countries including China, Brazil, and Mexico. For the majority of developing countries, particularly the poorest, foreign investment remains a modest contributor to economic growth, on a par with official foreign aid. Sub-Saharan Africa, with the highest concentration of the world's poor, attracted only $14 billion in 2001.

In this environment, trade offers an important potential source of economic growth for developing countries. Relatively modest gains in their share of global trade could yield large benefits for developing countries. Gaining an additional 1% share of the $8 trillion global export market, for example, would generate more revenue than all current foreign aid spending.

But today, poor countries are bit players in the global trade game. More than 40% of the world's population lives in low-income countries, but these countries generate only 3% of global exports. Despite exhortations from the United States and other wealthy countries to export, many of the poorest countries are actually losing share in export markets. Africa generated a mere 2.4% of world exports of goods in 2001, down from 3.1% in 1990.

Many factors contribute to the poorest countries' inability to gain a foothold in export trade, but the core problem is that the playing field is heavily tilted against them. This is particularly true in the farm sector. The majority of the global South population lives in rural areas and depends on agriculture for survival. Moreover, poverty is concentrated in the countryside: more than three-quarters of the world's poorest people, the 1.1 billion who live on less than one dollar a day, live in rural areas. This means that agriculture must be at the center of trade, development, and poverty-reduction strategies throughout the developing world.

Two examples demonstrate the unfair rules of the global trading system in agriculture.

"IT'S NOT WHITE GOLD ANYMORE"

Cotton is an important crop in Central and West Africa. More than two million households depend directly on the crop for their livelihoods, with millions more indirectly involved. Despite serious social and environmental problems that have accompanied the expansion of cotton cultivation, cotton provides families with desperately needed cash for health care, education, and even food. The cotton crop can make a big difference in reducing poverty. For example, a 2002 World Bank study found a strong link between cotton prices and rural welfare in Benin, a poor West African country.

Cotton is important at a macroeconomic level as well; in 11 African countries, it accounts for more than one-quarter of export revenue. But since the mid-1990s, the cotton market has experienced chronic price depression. Though prices have rebounded in recent months, they remain below the long-term average of $0.72 a pound. Lower prices mean less export revenue for African countries and lower incomes for African cotton farmers.

But not for U.S. cotton farmers. Thanks to farm subsidies, U.S. cotton producers are insulated from the market and have produced bumper crops that depress prices worldwide. The global price of cotton is 20% lower than it would be without U.S. subsidies, according to an analysis by the International Cotton Advisory Committee. Oxfam estimates that in 2001, as a result of U.S. cotton subsidies, eight countries in Africa lost approximately $300 million—about one-quarter of the total amount the U.S. Agency for International Development will spend in Africa next year.

DUMPING ON OUR NEIGHBOR

Mexico has been growing corn (or maize) for 10,000 years. Today, nearly three million Mexican farmers grow corn, but they are facing a crisis due to sharply declining prices. Real prices for corn have fallen 70% since 1994. Poverty is widespread in corn-growing areas like Chiapas, Oaxaca, and Guerrero. Every year, large numbers of rural Mexicans leave the land and migrate to the cities or to the United States to try to earn a living.

The price drops are due to increased U.S. corn exports to Mexico, which have more than tripled since 1994. These exports result in large part from U.S. government policies that encourage overproduction. While Mexican farmers struggle to keep their farms and support their families, the United States pours up to $10 billion annually into subsidies for U.S. corn producers. By comparison, the entire Mexican government budget for agriculture is $1 billion. Between 2000 and 2002, a metric ton of American corn sold on export markets for $20 less than the average cost to produce it. The United States controls nearly 70% of the global corn market, so this dumping has a huge impact on prices and on small-scale corn farmers in Mexico.

To be fair, the Mexican government shares some of the responsibility for the crisis facing corn farmers. Although the North American Free Trade Agreement (NAFTA) opened trade between the United States and Mexico, the Mexican government voluntarily lowered tariffs on corn beyond what was required by NAFTA. As NAFTA is fully phased in, though, Mexico will lose the option of raising tariffs to safeguard poor farmers from a flood of subsidized corn.

WHAT DO POOR COUNTRIES WANT?

Cotton and corn illustrate the problems that current trade regimes pose for developing countries and particularly for the world's poorest people. African countries want to engage in global trade but are crowded out by subsidized cotton from the United States. The livelihood of Mexican corn farmers is undermined by dumped U.S. corn. In both of these cases, and many more, it's all perfectly legal. WTO and NAFTA rules provide near impunity to rich countries that subsidize agriculture, and increasingly restrict developing countries' ability to safeguard their farmers and promote development.

How much do subsidies and trade barriers in the rich countries really cost the developing world? One study estimates that developing countries lose $24 billion annually in agricultural income—not a trivial amount. In today's political climate, it's hard to see where else these countries are going to find $24 billion to promote their economic development.

The benefits of higher prices for farmers in the developing world have to be balanced against the potential cost to consumers, both North and South. However, it's important to remember that many Northern consumers actually pay more for food *because of* subsidies. In fact, they often pay twice: first in higher food costs, and then in taxes to pay for the subsidies. Consumers in poor countries will pay more for food if farm commodity prices rise, but the majority of people who work in agriculture will benefit. Since poverty is concentrated in rural areas, the gains to agricultural producers are particularly important.

However, some low-income countries are net food importers and could face difficulties if prices rise. Assuring affordable food is critical, but this goal can be achieved much more cheaply and efficiently than by spending $100 billion on farm subsidies in the rich countries. The World Bank says that low-income countries that depend on food imports faced a net agricultural trade deficit of $2.8 billion in 2000-2001. The savings realized from reducing agricultural subsidies could easily cover this shortfall.

Each country faces different challenges. Developing countries, in particular, need flexibility to develop appropriate solutions to address their economic, humanitarian, and development situations. Broad-stroke solutions inevitably fail to address specific circumstances. But the complexity of the issues must not be used as an excuse for inaction by policy-makers. Failure to act to lift trade barriers and agricultural subsidies will only mean growing inequity, continuing poverty, and endless injustice.

Resources: Xinshen Diao, Eugenio Diaz-Bonilla, and Sherman Robinson, "How Much Does It Hurt? The Impact of Agricultural Trade Policies on Developing Countries," (International Food Policy Research Institute, Washington, D.C., 2003); "Global Development Finance: Striving for Stability in Development Finance," (World Bank, 2003); Lyuba Zarksy and Kevin Gallagher, "Searching for the Holy Grail? Making FDI Work for Sustainable Development,"(Tufts Global Development and Environment Institute/WWF, March 2003); Oxfam's website on trade issues <www.maketradefair. com>.

FALSE PROMISES ON TRADE
continued from page 203

geration is that it encourages policy-makers and concerned nongovernmental organizations (NGOs) to focus their energies on an issue that is largely peripheral to economic development and to ignore much more important matters.

To put the issue in perspective: the World Bank, one of the most powerful advocates of removing most trade barriers, has estimated the gains from removing all the rich countries' remaining barriers to trade in manufactured and farm products *and* ending agricultural subsidies. The total estimated gain to low- and middle-income countries, when the changes are phased in by 2015, is an extra 0.6% of GDP. In other words, an African country with an annual income of $500 per person would see that figure rise to $503 as a result of removing these barriers and subsidies.

SIMPLISTIC TALK ON SUBSIDIES
The media often claim that the rich countries give $300 billion annually in agricultural subsidies to their farmers. In fact, this is not the amount of money paid by governments to farmers, which is actually less than $100 billion. The $300 billion figure is an estimate of the excess cost to consumers in rich nations that results from all market barriers in agriculture. Most of this cost is attributable to higher food prices that result from planting restrictions, import tariffs, and quotas.

The distinction is important, because not all of the $300 billion ends up in the pockets of farmers in rich nations. Some of it goes to exporters in developing nations, as when sugar producers in Brazil or Nicaragua are able to sell their sugar in the United States for an amount that is close to three times the world price. The higher price that U.S. consumers pay for this sugar is part of the $300 billion that many accounts mistakenly describe as subsidies to farmers in rich countries.

Another significant misrepresentation is the idea that cheap imports from the rich nations are always bad for developing countries. When subsides from rich countries lower the price of agricultural imports to developing countries, consumers in those countries benefit. This is one reason why a recent World Bank study found that the removal of *all* trade barriers and subsidies in the United States would have no net effect on growth in sub-Saharan Africa.

In addition, removing the rich countries' subsidies or barriers will not level the playing field—since there will still often be large differences in productivity—and thus will not save developing countries from the economic and social upheavals that such "free trade" agreements as the WTO have in store for them. These agreements envision a massive displacement of people employed in agriculture, as farmers in developing countries are pushed out by international competition. It took the United States 100 years, from 1870 to 1970, to reduce agricultural employment from 53% to under 5% of the labor force, and the transition nonetheless caused considerable social unrest. To compress such a process into a period of a few years or even a decade, by removing remaining agricultural trade barriers in poor countries, is a recipe for social explosion.

It is important to realize that in terms of the effect on developing countries, low agricultural prices due to subsidies for rich-country farmers have the exact same impact as low agricultural prices that stem from productivity gains. If the opponents of agricultural subsidies consider the former to be harmful to the developing countries, then they should be equally concerned about the impact of productivity gains in the agricultural sectors of rich countries.

Insofar as cheap food imports might have a negative impact on a developing country's economy, the problem can be easily remedied by an import tariff. In this situation, the developing world would gain the most if those countries that benefit from cheap imported food have access to it, while those that are better served by protecting their domestic agricultural sector are allowed to impose tariffs without fear of retaliation from rich nations. This would make much more sense, and cause much less harm, than simply removing all trade barriers and subsidies on both sides of the North-South economic divide. The concept of a "level playing field" is a false one. Mexican corn farmers, for example, are not going to be able to compete with U.S. agribusiness, subsidies or no subsidies, nor should they have to.

It is of course good that such institutions as the *New York Times* are pointing out the hypocrisy of governments in the United States, Europe, and Japan in insisting that developing countries remove trade barriers and subsidies while keeping some of their own. And the subsidy issue was exploited very skillfully by developing-country governments and NGOs at the recent Cancún talks. The end result—the collapse of the talks—was a great thing for the developing world. So were the ties that were forged among countries such as those in the group of 22, enabling them to stand up

to the rich countries. But the WTO remedy of eliminating subsidies and trade barriers across the board will not save developing countries from most of the harm caused by current policies. Just the opposite: the removal of import restrictions in the developing world could wipe out tens of millions of farmers and cause enormous economic damage.

AVOIDING THE KEY ISSUES

While reducing agricultural protection and subsidies just in the rich countries might in general be a good thing for developing countries, the gross exaggeration of its importance has real consequences, because it can divert attention from issues of far more pressing concern. One such issue is the role that the IMF continues to play as enforcer of a creditors' cartel in the developing world, threatening any country that defies its edicts with a cutoff of access to international credit. One of the most devastated recent victims of the IMF's measures has been Argentina, which saw its economy thrown into a depression after the failure of a decade of neoliberal economic policies. The IMF's harsh treatment of Argentina last year, while it was suffering from the worst depression in its history, is widely viewed in the developing world as a warning to other countries that might deviate from the IMF's recommendations. One result is that Brazil's new president, elected with an overwhelming mandate for change, must struggle to promote growth in the face of 22% interest rates demanded by the IMF's monetary experts.

Similarly, most of sub-Saharan Africa is suffering from an unpayable debt burden. While there has been some limited relief offered in recent years, the remaining debt service burden is still more than the debtor countries in that region spend on health care or education. The list of problems that the current world economic order imposes on developing countries is long: bans on the industrial policies that led to successful development in the West, the imposition of patents on drugs and copyrights on computer software and recorded material, inappropriate macroeconomic policies imposed by the IMF and the World Bank. All of these factors are likely to have far more severe consequences for the development prospects of poor countries than the agricultural policies of rich countries.

Resources: Elena Ianchovichina, Aaditya Mattoo, and Marcelo Olareaga, "Unrestricted Market Access for Sub-Saharan Africa: How much is it worth and who pays," (World Bank, April 2001); Mark Weisbrot and Dean Baker, "The Relative Impact of Trade Liberalization on Developing Countries," (Center for Economic and Policy Research, June 2002).

CONTRIBUTORS

Randy Albelda, a *Dollars & Sense* Associate, teaches economics at the University of Massachusetts-Boston.

Sylvia Allegretto is currently an economist at the Institute for Research on Labor and Employment at the University of California, Berkeley.

Dean Baker is co-director of the Center for Economic and Policy Research.

William Black is an associate professor of economics and law at the University of Missouri-Kansas City.

Esther Cervantes is a former *Dollars and Sense* collective member.

Angel Chen is a former *Dollars & Sense* intern.

James M. Cypher is profesor-investigador, Programa de Doctorado en Estudios del Desarrollo, Universidad Autónoma de Zacatecas, Mexico and a *Dollars & Sense* associate.

Attieno Davis is the Racial Wealth Divide Education Coordinator at United for a Fair Economy.

Daniel Fireside is co-editor of *Dollars & Sense.*

Ellen Frank, a *Dollars & Sense* collective member, teaches economics at Emmanuel College in Boston.

James K. Galbraith is professor at the Lyndon B. Johnson School of Public Affairs, University of Texas at Austin, and Senior Scholar of the Levy Economics Institute.

Amy Gluckman is a co-editor of *Dollars & Sense.*

Will Goldberg is a policy analyst at the Prison Policy Initiative.

Elise Gould is a staff economist at the Economic Policy Institute.

Lena Graber is a former *Dollars & Sense* intern.

William Greider has been a political journalist for more than 35 years. He is currently the National Affairs Correspondent for the *Nation* magazine.

Howard Karger is professor of social policy at the University of Houston.

Paul Krugman teaches economics at Princeton and is a columnist for the *New York Times.*

Gawain Kripke is a senior policy advisor at Oxfam America.

Arthur MacEwan, a *Dollars & Sense* Associate, teaches economics at the University of Massachusetts-Boston.

Ann Markusen is a former Senior Fellow at the Council on Foreign Relations and Professor of Public Policy and Planning at the Humphrey Institute of Public Affairs, University of Minnesota.

Gretchen McClain, a former member of the *Dollars & Sense* collective, is an economic consultant.

John Miller, a *Dollars & Sense* collective member, teaches economics at Wheaton College.

Monique Morrissey is a policy analyst at the Economic Policy Institute.

Gina Neff is the associate director of Economists Allied for Arms Reduction.

Martha A. Ojeda is the Executive Director of the Coalition for Justice in the Maquiladoras.

Doug Orr teaches economics at Eastern Washington University.

Thomas I. Palley is an economist who has held positions at the AFL-CIO, Open Society Institute, and the U.S./China Economic and Security Review Commission.

Larry Peterson is a member of the *Dollars & Sense* collective and the Union for Radical Political Economics.

Stephen Philion is an assistant professor of sociology in the Department of Sociology and Anthropology at St. Cloud State University.

Joseph Pluta is a professor and chair of the economics department at St. Edward's University in Austin, Texas.

Robert Pollin teaches economics and is co-director of the Political Economy Research Institute at the University of Massachusetts-Amherst. He is also a *Dollars & Sense* Associate.

Alejandro Reuss is former co-editor of *Dollars & Sense.*

William M. Rodgers III teaches economics at Rutgers University and is the chief economist at the John J. Heldrich Center for Workforce Development. He was the chief economist at the U.S. Department of Labor from 2000-2001.

Jonathan Rowe is a contributing editor at the *Washington Monthly.*

Adria Scharf is former co-editor of *Dollars & Sense.*

Michelle Sheehan is a member of the *Dollars & Sense* collective.

William E. Spriggs is a senior fellow with the Economic Policy Institute and was formerly the executive director of the National Urban League Institute for Opportunity and Equality.

Bob Sutcliffe is an economist at the University of the Basque Country in Bilbao, Spain.

Chris Tilly, a former *Dollars & Sense* collective member, teaches at the University of Massachusetts-Lowell.

Ramaa Vasudevan teaches economics at Barnard University and is a member of the *Dollars & Sense* collective.

Mark Weisbrot is co-director of the Center for Economic and Policy Research in Washington, D.C.

Richard Wolff teaches economics at the University of Massachusetts-Amherst.

James Woolman is a health policy analyst and a member of the *Dollars & Sense* collective.